'This book draws a cultural map of who we are, where we've come from and how we think and feel about our surroundings. Meticulously researched, imaginative in scope and rich in strange stories and rewarding insights. Fascinating reading.'
Malcolm Gaskill, author of *The Ruin of All Witches*

'The best overall view of the subject currently available, written by its most dynamic partnership of scholars. It not only covers the traditional remit of folklore but extends it into many less conventional areas, right up to the present moment.'
Ronald Hutton, author of *The Witch: A History of Fear, from Ancient Times to the Present*

'An inspiring, insightful, authoritative and entertaining survey of folklore and folklorists, covering everything from cryptids to Krampus, fairies to fakelore, beating the bounds to Brexit, urban legends to UFOs: brilliant.'
Marion Gibson, author of *Witchcraft: A History in Thirteen Trials*

'Folklore is a hidden superpower in every part of our land and our culture. The stories we tell let us know who, where and what we are, and here they can be found in their richness and complexity. I learned from every page.'
Diane Purkiss, author of *English Food: A Social History of England Told through the Food on Its Tables*

'An illuminating exploration of folklore's role in shaping national identity. Davies and Houlbrook masterfully untangle how traditions are preserved, reinvented and contested across Britain. Essential reading for understanding our multi-folkloric present.'
Dee Dee Chainey, co-author of the *Treasury of Folklore* series and co-founder of #FolkloreThursday

'A fascinating, insightful, contemporary take on British folklore that bridges past and present. This book reveals how tradition lives on in unexpected places, from ancient customs to internet memes. It offers a nuanced, inclusive view of folklore as dynamic, diverse and deeply embedded in everyday life.'
Ben Edge, author of *Folklore Rising: An Artist's Journey Through the British Ritual Year*

'Ceri Houlbrook and Owen Davies have created a magnificent exploration of why folklore is important to today. It shows us that folklore is not static but something that is living and constantly evolving. Full of surprising and brilliant research, the book is an excellent overview of folklore in the past and present. Essential reading for all budding folklorists.'
Lally MacBeth, author of *The Lost Folk: From the Forgotten Past to the Emerging Future of Folk*

'Respected academic folklorists Owen Davies and Ceri Houlbrook have penned an accessible, meaningful and entertaining look at the state of folklore in the twenty-first century. This vital work paints a picture of modern folklore that shows how it has adapted for modern times, still providing us with our sense of identity and place but now in a global community as well as a local one. Recommended for all folklore scholars and enthusiasts alike.'
Mark Norman, folklorist, author and creator of The Folklore Podcast

'*Folklore* is a timely and rigorous work, confirming both the authors' unparalleled expertise and the ongoing relevance of folklore today. A highly engaging and accessible must-read, this comprehensive exploration of the ever-evolving nature of folklore deserves a place on every bookshelf.'
Willow Winsham, co-author of the *Treasury of Folklore* series and co-founder of #FolkloreThursday

'Not just a fascinating tour of past practice but a compelling argument for the evergreen, sprouting nature of folklore. This book provides a refreshing lens through which to view a fertile, living subject.'
Zoe Gilbert, author of *Folk*

Folklore

Manchester University Press

Folklore

Folklore

A journey through the past and present

Owen Davies and Ceri Houlbrook

MANCHESTER UNIVERSITY PRESS

Copyright © Owen Davies and Ceri Houlbrook 2025

The right of Owen Davies and Ceri Houlbrook to be identified as the authors of this work has been asserted in accordance with the Copyright, Designs and Patents Act 1988.

Published by Manchester University Press
Oxford Road, Manchester, M13 9PL

www.manchesteruniversitypress.co.uk

British Library Cataloguing-in-Publication Data
A catalogue record for this book is available from the British Library

ISBN   978 1 5261 8038 4   hardback

First published 2025

The publisher has no responsibility for the persistence or accuracy of URLs for any external or third-party internet websites referred to in this book, and does not guarantee that any content on such websites is, or will remain, accurate or appropriate.

EU authorised representative for GPSR:
Easy Access System Europe, Mustamäe tee 50, 10621 Tallinn, Estonia
gpsr.requests@easproject.com

Typeset
by New Best-set Typesetters Ltd

Contents

Introduction: a tale of British folklore studies   *page* 1

Part I: Coming together and taking part

1. The ritual year   19
2. Performance   41

Part II: Stories

3. Storytelling   65
4. Legends   77

Part III: Environment

5. Folklore of the natural world   97
6. Folk medicine   116

Part IV: Spiritual life

7. Living with a supernatural world   137
8. Ritual in the landscape   155

Part V: Intimate life

9. Childlore   177
10. Domestic life   194

Part VI: Modern media

11. Broadcasting folklore   217
12. Digital folklore   236

Contents

Part VII: Identity

13 The folklore of nations   255

Figures   272
A note on calendar reform and bank holidays   274
Select bibliography   276
Notes and references   279
Index   320

Introduction: a tale of British folklore studies

Folklore means different things to different people. They might think of Morris dancers or local customs, fairytales or ghostly legends. People read folklore books for pleasure, to be entertained, and to feed the imagination. But folklore is also complex, and challenging. It was, and still is, entangled with religion, culture, class, gender, and politics. There have been many academic attempts to define folklore, and the contents of this book represent what we think are the main, broad themes of British folklore across the last few hundred years, though others will understandably identify absences or place different emphases. We cannot cover everything. Any definition of folklore inevitably also has to be revised as societies and cultures change, which has led, for instance, to a wave of redefinitions in our digital age and the rise of the internet.[1] In its broadest possible sense, then, we use folklore to mean the generation, transmission, and enaction of traditions as a *creative* process, communicated through oral, literary, visual, and digital means.

While this book does explore the dwindling of a folkloric past, it will also demonstrate that folklore is a vibrant and ever-developing facet of British society and culture, forever being invented and reinvigorated through new cultural influences, from pandemic clapping to love-locks and ghost tours to internet memes. This book explores the diversity and richness of British folklore, but not through rose-tinted glasses. We need to move on from popular associations of folklore with the rustic past and see British folklore as contemporary and multicultural. Indeed, folklore has much to tell us about Britain today: about its constituent national, regional, and ethnic identities, and its wider place in the world.

Over the last two centuries folklorists of Britain have usually opted to write books in the form of dictionaries, calendars, compendia, gazetteers, and county surveys; it makes sense to systematise folklore in these well-established formats when the amount of material to synthesise and interpret is huge, diverse, confusing, and challenging, and ranges back to the medieval period. British folklore includes the traditions, beliefs, and languages of three different nations, numerous regional and local cultures, and centuries of influence from overseas. It can be represented by the individual, the family, the community, and the nation. As this book shows, it encompasses the themes of nature, the life cycle, medicine, religion, sport, performance, communication, media, and the creative mind. Above all, we have tried to show how all these manifestations can be understood and how they are still relevant. You may not think you are *doing* folklore in your everyday life, but you probably are, and it all has a heritage.

In the beginning ...

Folklore obviously existed long before the word 'folk-lore' was coined in 1846 by the writer, librarian, and demographer William John Thoms (1803–1885). For Thoms, 'folk-lore' consisted of 'the manners, customs, observances, superstitions, ballads, proverbs, &c., of the olden time'. He wished for it to replace an older, patronising vocabulary regarding beliefs and customs. 'Vulgar errors' was a phrase commonly used in the seventeenth and eighteenth centuries to describe folk explanations of the natural world, while 'popular antiquities' denoted the idea that the customs, traditions, and beliefs of the common people were relics of an ancient past.[2] As the British antiquarian and clergyman John Brand (1744–1806) explained in his *Observations on Popular Antiquities* (1777), one of the earliest published collections of folklore, 'the prime Origin of the superstitious Notions and Ceremonies of the People is absolutely unattainable; we despair of ever being able to reach the Fountain Head of Streams which have been running and increasing from the Beginning of Time'.[3]

'Superstition' was another loaded term, and from the Reformation onwards was used by Protestants as a derogatory label for Catholic rites and liturgy. Early antiquarians also used it in the sense of 'exceedingly credulous' popular beliefs and practices. The English philosopher Francis Bacon (1561–1626) memorably described the root of 'superstition' as 'Namely, that *Men* observe when *Things Hit*, and not when they *Misse*: And commit to Memory the one, And forget and passe over the other.'[4] Despite this historical baggage, folklorists came to embrace the term to describe omens, popular magic, divination rituals, and the like without necessarily casting judgement on them. As one contemporary folklorist has put it, 'superstitions were not simply mistaken beliefs, but indicated an alternative universe of interpretation'. Modern historians, by contrast, tend to place the word in inverted commas these days to denote that it has a problematic usage in the past and needs to be used sensitively.[5]

Brand was inspired in his endeavours by Newcastle clergyman Henry Bourne (1694–1733), and he used Bourne's book *Antiquitates Vulgares* (1725) as the basis for his own. Bourne's aim was to delineate between the harmless and harmful customs and beliefs of the common people, and thereby enable the abolition of those that were 'sinful and wicked': 'I would not be thought a Reviver of old Rites and Ceremonies to the burdening of the People, nor an Abolisher of Innocent Customs, which are their Pleasures and Recreations.' New Year's mumming performance was accordingly a custom 'which ought to be laid aside', and the observation of omens was 'sinful', whereas the making of bonfires on midsummer's eve, 'when they are only kindled as Tokens of Joy, to excite innocent Mirth and Diversion, and promote Peace and good Neighbourhood, they are lawful and innocent, and deserve no Censure'.[6] Bourne's understanding of folklore was rooted deeply in post-Reformation thinking which considered popular customs and rites as relics of either pre-Christian paganism or Catholic 'superstition', or of both. Sixteenth- and seventeenth-century Protestant theologians wasted much energy and ink on attacking these 'pernicious' survivals. But Bourne represented a subtle shift in his time, whereby something of intrinsic value and interest could be found in the right sort of folklore. The Wiltshire antiquarian John Aubrey (1626–1697) adopted a similar position, expressing regret at vanishing traditions and defending the value of collecting them: 'I know that some will nauseate these old Fables: but I do prefer to regard them as the most considerable pieces of Antiquity I collect.' It has been said of Aubrey's writings that they 'could pass for the notebook of a modern folklore collector'.[7]

Brand's motives and interests were more in line with Aubrey's, and for his *Popular Antiquities* he set about tracking down every manuscript and printed record he could find of customs, beliefs, and traditions from around the country. What turned the book from a useful addition to eighteenth-century antiquarianism into a foundation text for British folklore studies was its afterlife following Brand's death. A much-expanded edition by the British Museum librarian Henry Ellis (1777–1869) was published in 1813, based on manuscripts Brand had compiled since 1777. Then, in 1848, Ellis produced a further, much expanded edition that appeared in three volumes, while in 1870 writer and lawyer William Carew Hazlitt (1834–1913) edited another revised edition, and then turned it into a dictionary in 1905. Public interest was growing, meanwhile, and so were the opportunities for publishing items of folklore contributed by the public.

The monthly periodical the *Gentleman's Magazine*, founded in 1731, had long been an important vehicle for reporting titbits of lore from around the country, and then, in the 1820s, the entrepreneurial bookseller and satirist William Hone (1780–1842) created a series of serial weekly miscellanies that invited contributions, including the *Every-Day Book; or Everlasting Calendar of Popular Amusements, Sports, Pastimes, Ceremonies, Manners, Customs, and Events*. At the suggestion of Thoms, *The Athenaeum*, a popular British literary magazine, also published items on folklore between 1846 and 1849, and then Thoms established the weekly periodical *Notes & Queries*, which later inspired several short-lived county *Notes & Queries*.[8] It was in an edition of *Notes & Queries* for 1850 that an advertisement appeared announcing the imminent publication of Thoms's own two-volume book entitled *The Folk-Lore of England*. But this potential landmark in the foundation of British folklore studies never saw the light of day, and folklore publication became focused on regional and county studies rather than national surveys. Still, from the late 1850s the term 'folk-lore' began to gain traction and 'popular antiquities' slowly fell out of use. The adoption of the term by the Scottish publisher and antiquary Robert Chambers (1802–1871) in his successful miscellany, *The Book of Days* (1862–1864), undoubtedly helped. The periodical *The Bookseller* reviewed the first volume, declaring that it superseded Hone's *Every-Day Book* and would be 'one of the most valuable assistants a literary man could desire'.[9]

Thoms was also instrumental in founding the Folk-Lore Society in 1878, the first such learned society in the world, and was its initial director.[10] The ethos and activity of the Society in its early years was very much in the mould of Brand and Thoms – mostly snippet folklore research, trawling through printed literature for items. This fed the Society's early initiatives, including a series of county collections, though, as one eminent folklorist, Sidney Oldall Addy (1848–1933), grumbled in 1907, they were 'a farrago of material from local histories and guide-books, of which not one item in twenty was worth reproducing'.[11] One of the Society's founders, and its fifth president, George Laurence Gomme (1853–1916), beavered away at mining the *Gentleman's Magazine* for relevant information, publishing multiple volumes culled from its contents, including one on *Popular Superstitions* (1884). An index of the folklore columns in *Notes & Queries* was also started but never finished. This was one of a number of ambitious publication plans that fell by the wayside in the early years, including an *Index to the Names of British Spirits, Ghosts, Boggarts, Fairies, &c.*[12]

Introduction

In 1910, the Society also set up a Brand Committee charged with producing a new, supplemented edition of Brand's *Popular Antiquities*, 'utilising the great stores of National Folklore dispersed through the publications of the Society, as well as in the considerable literature on the subject which has grown up since the publication of Brand's work'. Nearly a hundred members volunteered to help, though some experienced difficulties because, in a telling comment, they lived 'out of reach from libraries'.[13] Once again, the proposed edition never appeared, interrupted by the First World War and the sheer effort involved. However, the material collected over the years was eventually turned into a valuable multivolume survey of *British Calendar Customs* in England and Scotland, published between 1936 and 1946.[14]

All this toilsome compiling left a valuable legacy, and the results have been industrially mined ever since by academics and the authors of popular folklore literature, but it was a very library-bound approach to folklore studies, divorced from the 'folk' who were deemed the very source and essence of folklore. In 1892 the Society, along with several other London-based learned organisations, was involved in setting up a United Kingdom Ethnographic Survey led by the British Association for the Advancement of Science, which aimed to record the prehistoric monuments, dialects, 'physical types', beliefs, and traditions in 380 or so villages across the four nations. One of those funded to go into the field was the Scottish folklorist the Revd Walter Gregor (1825–1897), who set off for the district of Galloway on two occasions in 1895 and 1896. He collected head measurements of the locals and folk objects, and recorded children's games and 'curious superstitions'.[15] Several annual reports were published, but after a few years a lack of funds and volunteers meant the Survey floundered.

There were a small army of middle-class amateurs doing fieldwork among the folk, quite a few of them unconnected with the activities of the Folklore Society, and some whose activities pre-dated the Society. These included the young librarian Thomas Sternberg (1831–1880), whose *Dialect and Folk-Lore of Northamptonshire* was published in 1851, and William Henderson, whose important *Notes on the Folk Lore of the Northern Counties of England and the Borders* (1866) the Society reprinted with extra material in 1879. Women were among the early pioneers.[16] In 1876 Thoms, writing in *Notes & Queries*, had suggested with regard to the founding of a Folk-Lore Society that 'Ladies should be specially invited to take part in the work, who, in their kindly ministrations in the cottages of their poorer neighbours, must often come across traces of old world customs and beliefs.'[17] Thoms was replying to a correspondent called 'St Swithin', who had first suggested the setting up of a Folk-Lore Society for the 'collecting, arranging and printing all the scattered bits of folklore which we read of in books and hear of in the flesh.'[18] St Swithin was, in fact, the pseudonym of long-time *Notes & Queries* contributor Eliza Gutch (1840–1931), an active churchwoman, member of the Yorkshire Archaeological Society, and wife of a York solicitor named John James Gutch. She replied enthusiastically to Thoms's response, though she pointed out that she differed regarding the purpose of such a Society. Thoms thought its primary aim should be to continue to gather and reprint literary items of folklore not included in Brand-Ellis's *Popular Antiquities*, whereas Gutch thought it should focus on folklore '*brand*-new to literature' as with her work, and that of numerous others, recording people's language and idioms for the English Dialect Society (founded in 1873).[19]

The first volume of the Society's journal, the *Folk-Lore Record* (later *Folklore*), published in 1878, included a lengthy article by Charlotte Latham (1801–1883) on 'West Sussex Superstitions' which demonstrated the value of the Gutch approach. At this time, Latham was resident in Torquay, Devon, but her article concerned information gathered while living a decade earlier in the Sussex village of Fittleworth, where her second husband, who died in 1866, had been the vicar. 'During the long desultory process of collecting the following instances of our existing superstitions', wrote Latham, 'it has been my practice always to write down at the very earliest opportunity, the scraps of homely conversation in which they were communicated to me by the professed believer.' The first woman president of the Folklore Society, Charlotte Burne (1850–1923), was quite clear that 'the *best* collecting is that which is done by *accident*, by living among the people'. 'You must know what the folk think, and how they act, on subjects such as folk-lore touches, and observe how their minds form the natural background to the superstitions they act on, the customs they practise, the tales they tell.'[20]

Yet a quick search through the early years of the journal of the Folklore Society uncovers a profusion of articles about overseas folklore concerned with Japan, France, the United States, Eastern Europe, China, Madagascar, and Portugal. There is a strong showing from the British African colonies and India. This rather moderates the impression that the Society's members were focused laser-like on the imperative of gathering disappearing British customs, beliefs, and traditions. Colonial administrators were also avid folklore collectors, and their motives and activities were an aspect of empire-building and racist stereotyping – getting to know the 'native'.[21] As a medical superintendent in South Africa wrote:

> Perhaps one of the most difficult investigations possible is the study of the mental characteristics of savage and semi-savage races, and, before formulating any theories regarding their psychic history, it is necessary that a careful study should be made of their mode of life, their normal mental state, and such folk lore as is accessible to us.[22]

There was one section of the British folk – indeed the largest in the country – that hardly any folklorists bothered to engage with: the urban population. By the mid-nineteenth century half of the country's population was designated as urban, and by 1900 over 75 per cent were living in towns and cities. It was assumed that urban life was inimical to the continuance of old traditions and beliefs. Divorced from an agricultural way of life, and enclosed in a built environment, the common folk shed their ancestral cultures, they became knowing, dismissive, and cynical. In short, folklore could not be found there and there was no point in looking for it. Meanwhile, the grinding poverty and insanitary conditions of country life were largely ignored by folklorists, artists, and novelists, who instead constructed a romanticised idyll that was deemed to be fast vanishing due to the encroachment of urbanisation, mechanisation, and universal education. This sense of an ancient rural culture slipping away fuelled the urge to record folklore during the late nineteenth and early twentieth centuries.[23]

This sense of an ancient culture was also expressed in the phrase 'Merrie England', an idealised view of ye olde rustic times when life was simpler, better, and more pure of heart – the world of Shakespeare, Robin Hood, cricket, and maypoles, a rose-tinted view of village life with its quaint customs and traditions, its hearty songs and joyous dances. As the clergyman and historian Peter Hampson Ditchfield (1854–1930) opined in his *Old English Sports* (1891): 'We remember that our land once rejoiced in the name of "Merry England," and perhaps feel some regret that many of the outward signs of happiness have passed away from us, and that in striving to become a great and prosperous nation, we have ceased to be a genial, contented, and happy one.'[24] A Merrie England Society was even founded in the early twentieth century.

But, of course, many aspects of folklore were and are vibrant in Britain's urban industrial centres; it is just that you will not find much mention of them in the standard works of folklore. One exception is the writings of the City of London bank cashier and amateur folklorist, Edward Lovett (1852–1933), who headed to the bustling streets of East London and talked to its residents. As he explained in 1909, 'It is a common idea that few traces of folk belief can be found in great cities, but my own experience is that, at any rate for the seeker of amulets, there is no better hunting ground than the hawkers' handbarrows in the poorest parts or slums of such dense aggregations of people as London.'[25] For the modern folklorist looking for sources on historic urban folklore, then, newspapers and ballads prove valuable, as do asylum casebooks. A survey of the latter for parts of northern England confirms that many urban working-class patients believed in witches, ghosts, fairies, and magic into the early twentieth century.[26]

This yawning urban gap in British folklore studies had another consequence in terms of the under-representation of ethnic or migrant communities. The Romani, who moved between town and country, were an exception and became the focus of a dedicated group of researchers who formed the Gypsy Lore Society in 1888 and published a journal (now called *Romani Studies*). A search through *Folklore* from the beginning to the present reveals only a handful of articles concerning Britain's external migrant ethnic communities, and three of them were published in the 1970s: one on Chinese New Year celebrations in London, and two by Anglo-American folklorist and one-time President of the Society, Venetia Newell (1935–2017), on the Caribbean community in London.[27] As we shall see, this does not mean that no folkloristic research on multicultural Britain has been going on, only that little of it has been done by folklorists rather than sociologists, anthropologists, and healthcare researchers. John Widdowson, who founded the Centre for English Cultural Tradition and Language in 1975, has repeatedly called for a national folklore survey that covers 'all parts of the country, both urban and rural, and from representatives of all ages and social and ethnic groups'.[28]

Survivals and the kitchen sink

At the mention of 'theory' the reader may be tempted to skip ahead, but bear with us, because the old works of the folklorists cannot be understood properly without knowing something of the forces that shaped their thinking and their motivation. Casting a revisionist eye on the development of the discipline of Folklore in 1969, the American folklorist Alan Dundes (1934–2005) asked, 'are folklorists doomed to study only the disappearing, the dying, and the dead?'[29] He was referring to the idea of cultural evolution and devolution and the entwined theory of survivals that dominated early folklore studies and collecting. 'Cultural evolution' was inspired by advances in the understanding of geological time, Darwinism, and human anthropology. Yet it also had roots in the antiquarian notion we heard about earlier, that popular antiquities were remnants of paganism and Catholicism. In essence, it was the idea that as human culture and psychology *evolved* from its primitive origins through to the present – in other words, *advanced* from a lower to a higher state, or from an uncivilised to a civilised stage – original ideas, notions, and practices about the natural and supernatural world lost their meaning, fragmented, decayed, or were discarded. A three-stage model was proposed that posited progression from an age of magic, through an age of religion, to an age of science.

In this framework of thinking folklore was, by definition, of ancient origin. As George Laurence Gomme, one of the leading proponents of the theory, explained: 'in folklore there is no development from one stage of culture to a higher one'.[30] It consisted instead of survivals, the fossils or culture artefacts of primitive religions and peoples that were preserved in the stratum of beliefs and customs of the rural poor of Europe. Those folklorists who subscribed to the theory, therefore, were not just collecting folklore. They were looking for *evidence*, searching for the remains of prehistoric horse cults, sun worshipping, animism, and sacrificial practices in the calendar customs and 'superstitions' of the 'peasantry'. Fairytales were the devolved remnants of prehistoric myths, folk dances the residue of fertility rites, objects concealed in buildings an echo of sacrifices to the gods, and 'superstitions' the relics of ancient religion.[31] This quest for survivals elevated folklore collecting in the villages and hamlets of Britain to the status of a human science.

Gathering the remnants of archaic cultures in folklore was only one half of the equation, though, for the same 'uncivilised' beliefs were thought to be found fully alive in the many cultures encountered across Britain's Empire. In other words, there were many peoples who, according to cultural evolution, had not yet progressed from the primitive stratum, or age of magic. The concept and language were, of course, inherently racist and fuelled by colonial condescension. Survival theory was also made material in this respect in the collections of late nineteenth- and early twentieth-century museums, with amulets and charms collected in Britain placed together with items from indigenous cultures in the colonies. The displays of the Pitt Rivers Museum were a classic example of such a cultural evolutionary approach to the past and present. Founded at Oxford University in 1884 to house some twenty thousand artefacts collected by the archaeologist and ethnologist Augustus

Pitt Rivers (1827–1900), its curators also purchased items of current British folk magic to place alongside ones from the Empire. Their place in a museum was justified because they demonstrated an *archaic* way of thinking. The ethos of the museum was heavily influenced by the leading proponent of survival theory, Edward Burnett Tylor (1832–1917), who was the first professor of anthropology at Oxford University and author of the influential book, *Primitive Culture* (1871).[32]

The comparative method meant that books and articles on British folklore sometimes adopted a kitchen-sink approach. Because everything was deemed related to each other in the same stratum of cultural evolution, there was no need to give serious consideration to the chronological development of lore within any one culture or place, and instead references to folklore from around the globe were liberally thrown into the mix. Just one example is a brief, four-page article on 'Animal Apparitions in Lincolnshire' in *Lincolnshire Notes & Queries* (1896), which managed to include references to Denmark, Sweden, Germany, France, South America, and Africa. Very little of the article actually concerned Lincolnshire, once the author had also made numerous comparisons with other English counties.[33] It was surely fun to research and write such comparative folklore; there was the buzz of collecting, again, and it could uncover some interesting insights, but the approach also had a muddying effect, whereby the original focus got bogged down with all the dizzying examples that often had only a superficial relevance. The Devonshire folklorist the Revd Sabine Baring-Gould was aware of this when writing his *Book of Folklore* (1913), which he described as 'a popular introduction to the study of the science': 'I have confined myself as much as possible to the beliefs of the peoples who occupied the British Isles, and have not gone like other writers to the usages of savages for explanation of customs and traditions, except very occasionally'.[34] That said, he could not resist making use of a profusion of European examples, and only a few pages in he was making references to Ceylon and an Arabian tale.

By no means were all early British folklorists fully paid-up survivalists. As early as 1893, Joseph Jacobs (1854–1916), well known for his work on fairytales, observed that 'survivals are folk-lore, but folk-lore need not be all survivals', and argued that folklorists ought to be 'studying the Folk of to-day'. He gave the example of music halls and the rise of new folk words.[35] Arthur Wright (1862–1932) also declared in his Folklore Society presidential address of 1928:

Introduction

> Folklore is very much a thing of life and growth today, and not a mere 'survival' from the smelly and fear-haunted days of 'primitive' man, no more capable of development or growth than a fossil bone or stone axe.

And he went on to make 'the case for "modern folklore" as a perfectly legitimate and important part of folklore in general'.[36]

Some folklorists were motivated simply to record vanishing traditions without theorising them, and besides, as we shall see later in this book, nineteenth-century revivals and the invention of traditions complicated the simplicity of the cultural evolution model. But survival hunting, whether conducted in the library or out in the field, was seductive and even addictive for both practitioner and the reading public. James Frazer's multivolume *Golden Bough* was a huge, full-blooded demonstration of comparative folklore and survival theory. It has been reprinted many times since the early twentieth century. Frazer (1854–1941) was a Cambridge University academic, and a council member of the Folklore Society. In celebrating the publication of the third volume, the then president of the Folklore Society, Robert Ranulph Marett (1866–1943), declared in his presidential address of 1914: 'There is scarcely a page of his encyclopaedic work that does not bear witness to the activity of our Society. Hence Dr. Frazer's triumph is likewise our triumph.'[37] The book fell out of academic favour fairly quickly, though, along with survival theory, but when published in an abridged single volume in 1922 it proved hugely influential on art, literature, and public understanding of magic, folklore, and religion.[38] It remains a fatally flawed tour de force of armchair endeavour and imagination, weaving together a seductive thesis of universal religion, a means of understanding magic, and a simple roadmap for the development of humanity.

Life or lore?

The folk museum movement in early twentieth-century Britain developed along individual national lines. The establishment of an English national folk museum was discussed repeatedly. In the early 1930s the Office of Works and the Board of Education suggested the founding of such a museum as 'a sort of key to the social history of peasant and middle-class England'.[39] Nothing came of it. Then, in 1948, the Royal Anthropological Institute proposed an English folk museum, but no funding was forthcoming, though a logo was designed showing St George slaying the dragon. In the 1950s the founding of the Museum of English Rural Life finally, sort of, filled the brief. There were other local museums showcasing English rural life, but the only one with 'folk' in the title was the Cambridge and County Folk Museum, now known as the Museum of Cambridge, which opened in 1936. Its first curator was the former schoolteacher and folklorist Enid Porter (1909–1984), author of the much-praised *Cambridgeshire Customs and Folklore* (1969).

Meanwhile, the Welsh Folk Museum, now St Fagans National Museum of History, opened in the village of St Fagans in 1948. Its brainchild, the poet, curator, and folklorist Iorwerth Peate (1901–1982), thought Wales was particularly well suited to having such a museum because of the unifying aspects of the language and 'compact' topography of the country; 'consequently Wales possessed not only an important body of folklore but also a well-defined cultural life, expressed in its domestic customs and agricultural methods'.[40] In Scotland, the Highland Folk Museum opened its doors in 1935 and still retains 'folk' in its title, while others eventually dropped it as being rather quaint and old fashioned. Its driving force was the Scottish historian and ethnographer, Isabel Grant (1887–1983), who had been much impressed with the folk museums she had visited during a cruise around Scandinavia.[41]

Grant and Porter exchanged ideas and experiences about museums. Both were uneasy about the word 'folk' in terms of engaging the public, but could not find a better alternative.[42] Then, from the 1950s, the discipline of 'folklife' studies emerged from the museum sector, influenced by developments in America and Scandinavia, and in 1961 the Society for Folk Life Studies was founded to explore traditional crafts and rural ways of life in Britain and Ireland. For some, 'folklife' became a more respectable replacement for 'folklore'. The oral historian George Ewart Evans (1909–1988), author of a raft of enduringly popular books about traditional rural life in East Anglia, was part of this mid-century zeitgeist troubled by what he called 'the doubtful overtones of the word *folk*'. Yet, he could live with it by adding 'life', whereas 'it must be admitted that folklore has become synonymous not with reasoned and objective inquiry but with a kind of prurient unearthing of the merely curious. It asks no questions.'[43]

'It is said ...'

This is one of the most frequent phrases found in folklore literature when some nugget of folklore is presented. It seems innocent enough, a way of suggesting that a belief, tradition, or legend had some currency or legitimacy, and so, was or is worth noting. But who said it? When was it said? Where was it said? Answers to these questions rarely follow the utterance of the three words. There is usually no identifiable source or fixed point in time to assess the value of the item. The nugget becomes unusable as an analytical tool. It was this sort of concern that led Iona Opie and Moira Tatem, in their *Dictionary of Superstitions* (1989), to introduce quotes for each entry chronologically, in order 'to show the history and development of each belief'. Steve Roud adopted a similar approach, explaining in his *Guide to the Superstitions of Britain and Ireland* (2003) that his book was 'fiercely historical-bound by historical dates and chronologies in a way that some readers may find too rigid'.[44] That rigidity is essential if we are to understand and appreciate fully the folklore we enjoy reading today. Context is crucial. Knowing when and where a legend, belief, story, or custom was first recorded, whether in the medieval period or the twenty-first century, helps us to think about why people created it when they did, and then how and why it declined, continued, or changed over time.

The numerous collections of omens in old county and regional studies are a case in point. Recorded omens were often contradictory even within the same county, let alone nationally. We often do not know if they were held widely or only in a village or even just a family. Were the omens passed down orally? Were they from old almanacs and chapbooks? Or imbibed from newspapers and folklore publications? And then we must consider the degree to which people set store by them and omens influenced everyday behaviour. Life would have been a constant source of anxiety. Take the omens listed over four pages in Jonathan Caredig Davies's *Folk-Lore of West and Mid-Wales* (1911), and imagine an innocent afternoon's walk across the Mid-Wales countryside.

It is a Tuesday, considered a lucky day by some in the region, but unlucky by others. You choose the more positive interpretation. As you put your boots on you feel an itch on the sole of your right foot. This augurs well. The journey will be a pleasant one. It is a fine spring day, but on stepping out of your cottage you see the sheep flocking together. Hmm. A sign of rough weather ahead. But you also see the first lamb of the season staring at you: a fortunate sign for the start of the walk. A few yards later, however, you stumble and drop your walking stick. Ah, that betokens bad luck! Maybe one will cancel out the other, you hope. Stick firmly back in hand, you make progress in good spirits, but then you meet a white horse. Bad omen. But by spitting on your little finger you turn this encounter into a positive omen. Phew! A good half an hour later you spot a coin on the road. Hopefully it is head's side up for good fortune. Damn! The tale's side is showing. No good will come of that. Things get worse. While crossing a field you come across an old knife – a very bad omen, according to Davies. You are tiring a little now, what with the exercise and the anxious changes of fortune, so you rest against a tree and your hat catches in a branch. That means someone has fallen in love with you. Things are getting better! You start off again, but your new-found good spirits disappear as you pass by a young woman. Perhaps she's the one. Oh, but she's whistling – a very unlucky encounter. Finally, as you haul your weary legs along the final stretch you begin to feel the heel of your left foot itching. You know what that means.

'It is said' also invoked a timelessness inherent in another common phrase found in folklore writing: 'time immemorial'. From the folklorist's perspective, referring to some custom or belief as having been held since 'time immemorial' was sometimes merely a facile means to evoke the solidity and unchanging nature of folklore, or it could explicitly reference the concept of survivals and the primitive stratum of unfathomable antiquity.[45] But it was also used in the defence of customary rights by 'the folk'.[46] Customs 'were said' to have been practised 'time out of mind', or 'beyond memory', and therefore above petty rules and regulations imposed by local authority. The appeal to what 'tradition says' or 'asserts' gave communities agency and was most often invoked with regard to maintaining public rights of way, performing calendar rituals on the public highway, or accessing private land for the customary collection of firewood, grazing, or gleaning. When, in 1857, two youths of Milburn, Westmorland, were prosecuted for burning tar barrels on the highway on 5 November, their defence lawyer argued in mitigation that 'it had been the custom of the village to light a fire on the same place from time immemorial'. In 1871, three inhabitants of Tingewick, Buckinghamshire, were summonsed for trespassing in Tingewick Woods, which was owned by New College, Oxford. As a letter to the local press, signed 'FAIR-PLAY', complained, 'From time immemorial the parishioners have gathered nuts, acorns, and rotten wood therein.'[47]

Authenticity

Before we delve at last into Britain's folklore past and present, the issue of authenticity needs to be considered. Is the folklore you see about you, that you watch on the screen, or read in books *genuine*? In other words, is it unchanged from its original form? Has it been made up or deliberately transformed beyond recognition? For decades the quest for authenticity shaped not only the development of folklore as a discipline but also the way in which the public engaged with folklore, the history of Morris dancing in the twentieth century

Introduction

being a classic example.⁴⁸ Then, in the mid-twentieth century, international folklorists came up with several words to describe inauthentic folklore.

The term folklorism (*folklorismus*) was introduced into folklore studies in the early 1960s by the German folklorist Hans Moser as a critique of 'second-hand folk culture'. Moser and others were responding to the post-war folklore revival and the involvement of tourism and commerce at a time when old traditional forms were dying. Although originally formulated to understand the contemporary situation, and the playful and political uses of folklore, examples were then identified of similar processes going back centuries. Moser set out three broad aspects of folklorism. First, there was the adoption of customs in places or countries divorced from the original locality of the tradition. One thinks of Krampus, the horned winter folk figure of the Alpine region, who has been adopted in popular culture around the world. Second was the playful appropriation or mimicking of the folklore of one social class by another, such as the wearing of traditional 'peasant' costumes by the middle and upper classes; and third was the invention of folklore with no direct link to known tradition. The term never really caught on in Britain, but it became an important and much-debated tool in German and East European folklore scholarship.⁴⁹

Another, related term, 'fakelore', was coined in 1950 by Richard Dorson, initially as a critique of recently published popular books of American legends, tales, and ballads that had been turned into debased 'literary confections'. Over the years, the label was applied to a whole range of customs, performances, and music. It caused a considerable debate at a time when folklore studies was being established in American universities, and, years later, Dorson reflected that 'fakelore was intended as a rallying cry against the distortion of a serious subject', a push back against a false presentation of authenticity in the media and through heritage tourism.⁵⁰ The game of 'folklore vs fakelore' has been played numerous times since, such as with Big Foot and the Loch Ness monster. The cry of 'fakelore' was heard in Britain, but only faintly. More influential was an edited collection, *The Invention of Tradition* (1983), in which British historians explored similar themes with regard to the building of national political identities through the creation of Scottish clan tartans, Welsh druidism, traditions surrounding the monarchy, and the manipulation of tradition in colonial contexts as a tool of social control.

You might ask, 'what has all this handwringing over authenticity got to do with me?' Well, the labels of fakelore, folklorism, and invented tradition could be applied to much of the participatory folklore enjoyed in Britain today.

Folklore

People either are not aware of it or are just not bothered. Mainstream thinking in folklore studies these days is that fakelore or folklorism *is* still folklore and not separate from it. It is part of the flux of tradition as societies and cultures change over time. Indeed, in Britain, the study of the contemporary revival, reinvention, migration, and adaptation of folklore has become an integral aspect of folklore studies, rather than an exercise in creating boundaries of authenticity. After all, while tourism and commercial interests have long shaped the expression of folklore, it is often members of the general public, the new 'folk', that resurrect and reinvent traditions. And their sources of inspiration? Why, the work of folklorists of course.

Part I

Coming together and taking part

Part 1

Coming together and taking part

Chapter 1
The ritual year

While current bank holidays and the modern school year have, to some extent, origins in old calendar traditions, the notion of holidays in the past was also very different to our modern experience. The word 'holiday' means 'holy day', and in the Catholic medieval era there were dozens of religious days of celebration and commemoration that punctuated the arduous working year and were often occasions for free drink, food, and entertainment. Most of these religious holidays were done away with following the Protestant Reformation, but over ensuing centuries the ritual calendar developed to become a complex mix of events based around the Christian liturgical year, the agricultural cycle, momentous national events, politics, charity, and commercial interests. But, before you go any further, do read the note on calendar reform and bank holidays at the end of this book, because it is essential to understanding when and why we mark certain days today. There is a long tradition among British folklorists of presenting the ritual year to readers in the form of a calendar, charting customs sequentially from month to month. This is certainly engaging, great for dipping into and seeing what is and was going on from day to day across the country. But this approach can also fragment our understanding of the different origins and forces shaping the development of the ritual year and how they are manifest today.

The religious calendar

Conception and birth. The Christian calendar used to begin on 25 March, which was *old* New Year's Day. It was also known as Lady Day (the Feast of the Annunciation), when the archangel Gabriel informed the Virgin Mary that she had miraculously conceived and would give birth to Christ. Lady Day was not a holiday and did not accrue much ritual activity outside of church services. Protestants played down the worship of Mary. The Assumption of Mary (when she died and her body was taken to heaven) on 15 August is a public holiday in Catholic countries today, but not in Britain. The key thing is that the date of Lady Day was calculated by the tradition that Christ was born on 25 December and so, following the notion of a strict nine-month pregnancy period, he must have been conceived on 25 March. Much has been written about Christmas and its transformation during the nineteenth century, with the advent of the Christmas tree, crackers, cards, Santa Claus, stockings, and manufactured decorations. Prior to this, it was common to deck homes and streets with evergreen boughs. Customary plays, mumming, carolling, and the like took place across Christmastide or the Twelve Days, ending with Epiphany (6 January new calendar), which marked the day when the three magi visited the baby Jesus in his crib. There was also much drinking. The northern wool merchant Joseph Lawson (1821–1890), looking back on growing up in the town of Pudsey, reflected: 'We should not wonder if some heathen visiting Pudsey on Christmas Day had asked if their Christ lived and died a drunkard, that made them honour His birthday in such a way.'[1]

Then we have the periods and days marking the adult life, death, and resurrection of Christ – Lent, Easter, and Whitsun (Pentecost). These are all moveable feasts, calculated according to Easter, which is fixed each year as the first Sunday following the full moon that falls on or after the spring equinox (19, 20, or 21 March). Lent, which begins with Ash Wednesday, commemorates the forty days and nights Christ spent in the desert being tempted by Satan, and was traditionally observed by fasting. Even today there are some British people who are not necessarily religious who use the opportunity to formally 'give something up' for Lent. A national opinion poll in 2023 revealed that 5 per cent of Britons still observed Lent by denying themselves a pleasure, down from 12 per cent in 2012. Of those that did in 2023, 50 per cent gave up chocolates or sweets, 17 per cent alcohol, 8 per cent sex, and 5 per cent meat.[2] Lent was obviously not a time of communal festivity, but, before the period began, there were pre-Lenten customs of relief and entertaining around Shrovetide, which commenced on the seventh Sunday before Easter. Shrove Sunday and Monday accrued their customs, but it was Shrove Tuesday that was an informal 'half-day' holiday for many until the twentieth century and was one of the key customary days in the year when it came to popular feasting and sports. Today it is largely celebrated by the making of pancakes, but in the past it was a day for blood sports, inter-village or street football, and tug of war competitions.

Easter Week or Holy Week venerates the last days of Christ, his death, and resurrection. It starts with Palm Sunday (the Sunday before Easter), commemorating his triumphant entry into Jerusalem, when, according to the New Testament, people laid palm branches in front of him and waved them in the air. This continued to be celebrated in British towns and villages with outings to collect spring leaves and flowers, and parades with bands in some towns. Palm leaves were obviously difficult to find, so people usually collected branches of willow full of catkins to bedeck churches and homes. In nineteenth-century South Wales the day was traditionally marked by visiting the graves of family and loved ones and strewing flowers and willow boughs upon them. However, in 1892, the *Cardiff Times* reported that the tradition had become a competitive and commercial menace. There were 'disorderly and unbecoming scenes' at cemeteries as people tried to outdo their neighbours with the abundance of floral tributes, and the rush at the appearance of flower and branch hawkers led to unseemly stampedes over graves. It got so bad that the Ystradyfodwg and Rhondda Joint Burial Board even temporarily banned wreaths and flowers on Palm Sunday.[3]

Good Friday commemorates the crucifixion of Christ. It was obviously intended to be a solemn holiday, though in parts of nineteenth-century England there are examples of traditional festive skipping. Shops remained shut in bustling nineteenth-century London, but bakers across England and Wales were busy making traditional buns and bread. The rest of Easter was marked by a familiar set of holiday traditions, with customary begging, mumming, games, and fairs. Then followed the feast of Ascension, the day when Christ ascended to Heaven after his miraculous resurrection forty days earlier, on Easter Sunday. The day itself was, by and large, a church ritual affair, but it was associated with the processual tradition of Rogationtide 'beating the bounds', which usually took place from Monday to Wednesday before Ascension Day (which always falls on a Thursday).

Beating the bounds had deep medieval roots in the need for a community to remember the boundary of the parish, which for centuries was essential to both religious and secular administration. The procession around the boundary also originally served as an occasion for the blessing of crops and the spiritual protection of the communities within.[4] Led by the parish clergyman, it did, indeed, consist of physically beating the boundary with sticks at certain points. Ten days after Ascension Day, at some point between mid-May and mid-June, Whitsunday or Pentecost (meaning 'fiftieth'), marked the descent of the Holy Spirit and the inspiration of the Apostles. The Whitsuntide days that followed were, for centuries, an opportunity for spring festivities, with warmer weather and longer days encouraging communal outdoor events such as Whitsun walks, fairs, Morris dancing, races, and more idiosyncratic local contests such as cheese rolling.

The saints were the other key Christian influence on the folkloric ritual year. While Protestantism did away with the official worship of saints, it failed to remove the significance of saints' days in the customary calendar. St Valentine's Day is one example and another is St Mark's Eve (24 April). This was a day associated with divining the future and, in particular, the custom of porch watching in England. Those who stood in the church porch at midnight would see a ghostly procession of all those that would die in the parish over the next year. This became a staple April newspaper story in the nineteenth and early twentieth centuries. In 1931, for instance, the *Yorkshire Post* called it 'a red-letter day in the ghostlover's calendar'.[5] But most reports in papers and folklore archives are of the 'it is said' or legend type, with little evidence of people actually observing the tradition. As we shall see shortly, other saints' days were marked by more charitable customs. Most importantly, despite the Reformation, from one parish to the next, communities continued to celebrate annually their church's patron saint. Rather than being marked by solemn ecclesiastical ritual, most such feast or 'wake' days were actually a much-valued moment in the local calendar for drinking, playing games, blood sports, and generally letting off steam. Such wake days also flourished in the expanding urban-industrial towns of northern England in the nineteenth century.[6]

Then there was the day dedicated to all the saints, All Hallows or All Saints Day (1 November), which was followed by All Souls (2 November), and preceded by Halloween (All Hallows Eve). Unsurprisingly, the Reformation churches abolished the old worship of the day, and until the twentieth century little widespread customary activity marked either All Hallows or Halloween. The day was notable in the calendar as propitious for performing divinatory practices, and in some parts also for the game of apple bobbing. In northern Scotland there was a tradition of 'mischief night', as in Ireland. Otherwise, the period was marked in some areas of England by the custom of 'souling', which consisted of bands of children and poor people going from door to door requesting a biscuit known as a 'soul cake', or simply asking for food and drink.

Since the 1950s, the British religious year has been invigorated by the communal celebration of non-Christian festivities, such as Diwali, which marks the start of the Hindu New Year. The date is determined by the position of the moon, but it usually falls between October and November. It will have been celebrated in Britain as long as there have been immigrant Hindu communities there, but it was in the mid-1900s that large-scale communal celebrations began to take place. In Leicester, home to a significant Hindu population since the 1950s, a Diwali party featuring 'stick dances, songs, speeches and comedy' was held in a boys' school in 1964, attended by about 550 people.[7] By 1976, the first open-air Diwali celebration was held in Leicester, at St Margaret's Pastures, and about five thousand Hindus celebrated in Leicester's Granby Halls. Today, the city of Leicester holds the largest Diwali celebrations outside of India.

With Diwali often falling near Bonfire Night, the two celebrations are usually held in parallel. However, by the 1980s, they began to be combined, fireworks and light shows being appropriate for both.[8] Indeed, by 1990 a Labour councillor was accusing Harrow Council of racism for not including Diwali in their Bonfire Night celebrations, despite the area having a substantial Hindu population. A council spokesperson responded: 'Guy Fawkes night is a traditional, historic event. It would seem inappropriate for a religious festival to be linked directly or indirectly with the burning of an effigy.'[9] An ironic statement, considering that many Diwali celebrations involve the burning of effigies of the demon king Narakasura.

Eid al-Fitr and Eid al-Adha are two other religious holidays that have immigrated to Britain. Eid al-Fitr marks the end of the holy month of Ramadhan, during which Muslims abstain from eating from dawn until sunset. The first identified reference to a community Eid celebration in Britain was in 1896, at the Royal Forest Hotel, Chingford, hosted by the pan-Islamic society Anjuman-i-Islam.[10] As more mosques were established across Britain, more communal Eid celebrations were held. However, it was not until the 1930s that such celebrations took to British streets. In 1937, two hundred people paraded through South Shields in celebration of Eid, singing Alawi *nashids* (praises of God) and holding banners bearing the Arabic words *la ilaha il allah* (There is only one God). A local newspaper noted the festival's 'cosmopolitan flavour rarely found in an English town'.[11]

As the observance of Eid involves communal prayer, preferably in an open space, challenges faced by Muslim communities have included the characteristically inclement British weather and access to large-enough open spaces. In 1915, fifty Muslim soldiers observed Eid al-Fitr by praying on a lawn covered with mats, rugs, and tablecloths in front of the mosque in Woking. On Eid 1968, nine large marquees were erected on the grounds of the London Central Mosque to accommodate ten thousand Muslims, who prayed 'in driving sleet' on prayer mats spread over newspapers to soak up the mud; while in 2022, Blackburn Rovers became the first football club in Britain to host Eid celebrations, inviting three thousand people to pray on the pitch.[12]

The agricultural cycle

The ritual agricultural calendar was based primarily around arable farming. The hay harvest, which provided winter fodder for horses and cattle, accrued less recorded custom in Britain, though the cycle of livestock farming partly dictated the timings of many markets and fairs, and annual tasks like sheep shearing often involved a feast. The arable cycle began with the preparatory ploughing and tilling of the land and then sowing and planting, but these moments did not generate a widespread, unified body of calendar celebrations. This was in large part because there was no single period in the calendar when the land was ploughed and crops were sown. We think of spring as such a time, but that depended on crop types and farming methods, which both changed over the centuries. Winter sowing of wheat was a common practice in recent centuries, as it is today. Ploughing and planting of some root crops was often a late summer or autumn affair.

The first ploughing, whenever it was, was sometimes marked by localised celebrations. In parts of Scotland, for instance, there was the custom of 'streeking the plough', which involved a modest ceremonial meal and drink during which a piece of the food was placed on or tied to the plough. Folklorists inevitably considered this a remnant of an ancient fertility ritual.[13] In the eighteenth century, marlers, who dug up marl, a calcareous clay, and spread it on the fields to improve arable soils before planting, also had their rituals at the end of the marling period. Flowers were left at the marl pit, posies and nosegays decorated the carters' horses, and a fine feast was put on.[14] Orchard wassailing or 'howling' was also a preparatory ritual, usually conducted at Christmastide, to promote a good crop of fruit, and was one of the few customs to have a continuous record of practice back to the medieval period. Participants sang wassailing songs, saluted, and gave a toast to one of the principal trees. Bonfires were sometimes lit, pots and pans banged, and shotguns fired into the air. A piece of toast was also placed at the roots or in the branches of a principal tree.

Harvesting was the principal focus of most agricultural calendar customs. Whether sown during winter or spring, cereal crops were still harvested during the same summer period, in late July or August. The success of the harvest was of national as well as local importance. Bread was life. Hay making, which could be a lengthy process depending on the weather, due to the need to turn and dry the grass before gathering, was also usually done in June or July, creating great demand for scything gangs throughout the summer, and the need for large numbers of women and children for the gathering. Both hay and cereal crop harvests traditionally required a huge communal effort, and it is not surprising that in cultures across the world they have long been marked by festivities that reinforced the bonds of customary obligation. The main themes in arable customs, apart from the obligatory drinking, dancing, and feasting, were ceremonies involving the last sheaf of corn, such as crying the neck in Devon and Cornwall, the making of craft figures from straw, and processions involving the last laden cart to leave the harvest fields. The Harvest Home meal, also known by dialect terms such as a horkey or mell, was an important moment of community bonding whereby the farmer paid for and attended a feast for his workforce. It was an event that was often associated with the singing of popular songs like 'The Farmer's Boy', 'All Jolly Fellows', and tributes to the farmer such as 'Here's a Health unto the Master, The founder of the feast'.[15]

The customary collection of harvest remnants from the fields, known as gleaning, was one of those seasonal rights that was a fundamental part of what historians call the 'makeshift economy'. This is a term little used by folklorists but it is fundamental to understanding the ritual year. It describes the various strategies and opportunities open to the poor in supplementing meagre incomes and the institutional support under the systems of welfare known as the Old and New Poor Laws.[16] Another relevant, related term is that of 'social crime', the idea of activities considered criminal under the law that were viewed as acceptable among sections of the poor as a means of keeping absolute poverty at bay, the most obvious examples being begging, poaching, and smuggling. Customary rights sometimes cut across both factors, such as the picking of firewood from private woods and hedgerows, and more widely the gleaning and theft and trespass laws.[17]

Gleaning days were not usually fixed in the calendar but were determined by the completion of the harvest, which was obviously dictated by the weather. In cereal-growing areas they were generally in late August or September, but there were customary rules about the time of day that gleaning was permitted. Up until the early twentieth century, in many communities the churchwarden or a bell ringer would ring what was known as the 'gleaning bell' to notify the villagers (usually women and children) of the start and finish of the gleaning hours. Each gleaning family paid the ringer one penny. One of the last times the gleaning bell was rung was in the hamlet of Farnham, Essex, in 1919.[18] The start of the gleaning day was usually eight or nine o'clock in the morning to ensure that married women were not disadvantaged by those with no childcare responsibilities or who did not have to prepare breakfast for husbands.

Gleaning was not just about arable crops. In the cider regions of western England there was also the custom of 'griggling'. A correspondent to William Hone's *Every-Day Book*, writing in 1826, fondly remembered the custom from his boyhood days and noted that it was still in practice. Apple growers would leave the deformed or small apples or 'griggles' on the trees after the harvest and allow boys in the community to collect them for their families to eat.[19] While the rituals around cereal-crop gleaning disappeared by the 1930s, in part due to the end of the local milling of grain, the practice of gleaning continued further into the century with regard to potatoes, leading to a number of prosecutions.[20] In 1950 the Uxbridge juvenile court heard the case of a fifteen-year-old boy charged with stealing 4s 6d worth of potatoes from a farmer's field after the harvest. In his defence the boy stated, 'I was gleaning them ... Gleaning potatoes has been done over our way for a long time.'[21]

During the winter months work was scarcer in arable districts, and incomes dropped. There was a significant seasonal increase of labourers in the workhouse between December and March, until ploughing, marling, and seeding picked up again. Pastoral farming also had its seasonal fluctuations, but less extreme. It is no surprise, then, that it is in winter that we find more calendar customs for the purpose of collecting money. Begging was technically illegal under the Poor Laws and Vagrancy Acts but was more culturally accepted if it was expressed in ritual or customary terms. By singing or putting on a show, however limited, at certain times of the year, money or goods given were money or goods earned rather than begged.

Over the centuries a wide range of such regional customs have been recorded, some stretching back to the medieval period and others arising across subsequent centuries.[22] It is possible that the harshness of the New Poor Law of 1834 and the workhouse system reinvigorated the resort to customary means of earning charity. Mumming plays, or performances such as those on Plough Monday, have attracted the most attention. On Plough Monday, the first Monday after Epiphany, young men dressed up in costume and pulled a plough through the community, accompanied by singing and dancing. As well as accruing the inevitable pagan interpretations, it has sometimes been represented as a ritual marking the start of the arable year, but it is more appropriately understood as an aspect of customary charity.[23] This is nicely demonstrated by an instance, in December 1849, when unemployed filesmiths in Sheffield's manufacturing district decided to replicate the Plough Monday tradition on the streets of the city. They dressed in costumes and a sympathetic local gentleman supplied them with a plough, which they painted in red. A local printer provided them with the following sign, which they carried through the streets: 'We are the men who have not been burdensome to the parish, and have saved the ratepayers more than £10,000. God speed the plough. Remember the poor filesmiths, &c.'[24]

There was also 'Clementing' on St Clement's Day (23 November), which seems to have been popular in the West Midlands in the nineteenth century as a vehicle for children to solicit gifts, such as apples. 'Thomasing' or 'gooding' on St Thomas's Day (21 December), when poor people sought charity in kind from their better-off neighbours, was widespread in England (though not Wales or Scotland). Wassailing (distinct from orchard wassailing) consisted of going from door to door with a decorative wassail bowl, cup, or box to collect money at Christmas, New Year, or Twelfth Night – or Candlemas in Wales. The wassailers, mostly women and children, would sing a carol or traditional wassail song that usually hinted at the expectation of a gift or food and drink, such as this from early twentieth-century South Yorkshire:

> We are not daily beggars that beg from door to door
> We are your neighbours' children that you have seen before,
> We've got a little purse made of stretchy leather skin
> We want a little of your money to line it well within.[25]

The Welsh word *calennig* was used for such a New Year's gift.[26] Scottish Hogmanay was likewise a key moment for ritual alms giving. In 1932 the *Aberdeen Press and Journal* printed a big headline, 'Is Hogmanay Dying Out?' and lamented the 'southernisation' of the day. But in some villages, it insisted, one could still hear the children's refrain:

> Get up, guidwife, an' shak' yer feathers
> And dinna think that we are beggars;
> For we are bairnies oot to play,
> Get up an' gie's oor Hogmanay.[27]

Some such customs have been defined by scholars as seasonal 'house entry' or 'house-visiting' traditions, where the right to hospitality and alms included welcoming performers indoors as an act of Christian charity and customary neighbourliness. Crossing the threshold was a ritual social contract allowable only at specific moments of the calendar.[28] The *Mari Lwyd* in South Wales is a classic example. The small party of costumed performers would tour around houses in their community with a striking hobbyhorse consisting of a decorated horse's skull on a pole covered in a white sheet that also concealed the man carrying the *Mari Lwyd*. At the door of each house a competitive song would be sung called the *pwnco*, which consisted of the repeated request to enter and then the rebuttals from inside as to why they could not, until finally the excuses ran out and the party was allowed to enter.

Customary rituals for alms giving were not just an agricultural tradition. Begging on the streets of eighteenth- and early nineteenth-century cities had its own familiar calendar rhythm. Christmas in particular normalised street begging. Apprentices collected money between old and new Christmas Day by asking people to pop a coin in their Christmas boxes. The governors of Christ's Hospital, London, complained in 1727 about children 'going abroad to the houses of the governors and others in and about London especially at this season of year with a money box and the singing of carols in order to beg money'. Old men hung around churches at Christmas time requesting people to 'put a penny in the old man's hat'. On May Day, London milkmaids and chimney sweeps put on a show in the streets and asked for money. It was a time of year when sweeps had less work. Other calendar days that legitimised London begging included the Lord Mayor's Procession, Hocktide (the Monday and Tuesday after Easter), and Guy Fawkes.[29]

Market fairs

As well as the village wakes and fairs mentioned earlier, market fairs were fundamental to the ritual agricultural year. They still shape the calendar of annual fun fairs in our towns and cities today. The story starts in the medieval period. At a time of considerable mercantile growth and the formation and expansion of provincial towns in the later medieval period, the monarchs of Wales, Scotland, and England held control over the creation of annual markets and fairs to facilitate local, national, and international trading of animals and goods, thereby also raising toll revenues from market traders. Around 2,800 royal charters were granted between the years 1199 and 1483 – mostly in the thirteenth century. The days chosen for holding the markets were usually tied to religious calendar feasts and vigil days, often connected to the patron saint of the local church. From early on, these annual charter fairs also became important

The ritual year

Figure 1.1 The Charter Pole Fair held in Corby, Northamptonshire, every twenty years. 1902. *Sir Benjamin Stone's Pictures: Records of National Life and History* (London, 1906), Vol. 1.

days of leisure and entertainment (Figure 1.1). The mercantile importance of the charter fairs began to decline from the sixteenth century onward as the nature of commerce changed. But royal grants and licences for the creation of new market days continued to be issued, usually to private individuals, into the nineteenth century. Yet it was the maintenance of tradition that kept the old fairs alive, along with the ever-increasing emphasis on entertainment.

Mop or hiring fairs were also legislated by statute, and in origin date back to the fourteenth century. The 'mop' likely refers to servants with no particular skills who would hold a mop to advertise themselves to prospective employers. The fairs' primary purpose was for the annual hiring of live-in agricultural labour and farm servants, both men and women.[30] By custom there was usually a 'fastening' payment of a shilling, rather than a written contract, and the term of service was fifty-one weeks, allowing for one week's holiday. Many such fairs, but by no means all, were held on Michaelmas Day (29 September). With hundreds of young men and women, dressed in their finest clothes, lining the streets to be inspected by prospective employers, it is no surprise that hiring fairs became notorious for raucous behaviour. Newspapers and oral histories have captured some of the flavour of the excitement. A journalist attending the mop fair in Monmouth in 1897 wrote that 'the fun was immense, vigorous without being dangerous, and of an innocent, if not universally agreeable character'. There were roundabouts, shooting galleries, coconut shies, animal and human curiosities, waxworks, boxing booths, and even a diving apparatus in a large glass tank.[31]

In 1792 there were some 3,760 fairs held in over 1,700 places in England and Wales. By 1888 both these figures had halved.[32] Fairs came under sustained attack from clergy, social reformers, and urban local authorities concerned about law and order, immoral behaviour, public nuisance, and the disturbance of normal trade. In industrial communities, factory owners considered them as unnecessary distractions for their workforce and a drag on productivity. The original economic importance of the fairs also faded. Canals and railways bypassed the traditional need for local markets, while professional auction marts took over much of the livestock business. A government report on the employment of women and children in 1868 was highly critical of the old way of doing things: 'There is nothing more degrading to the agricultural population than the "statute fair"', it declared. The fairs were characterised by drunkenness, the tradition of hiring led to a 'kind of vagrant population', and there was 'something very degrading also in the fact of young men and women standing in the market place to be looked over like so many cattle'.[33] A few years later, in 1871, the Fairs Act was passed, which set out that:

> Whereas certain of the fairs held in England and Wales are unnecessary, are the cause of grievous immorality, and are very injurious to the inhabitants of the towns in which such fairs are held, and it is therefore expedient to make provision to facilitate the abolition of such fairs.

Landowners, often town and district councils or corporations, who held the land on which fairs had traditionally taken place, could now petition the Home Secretary to have them abolished. Over the next few decades hundreds of traditional fairs across England and Wales were discontinued as a result.

In one fell swoop the Home Secretary agreed to the abolition in 1876 of four old Manchester fairs, namely Knott Mill Fair (Easter week), Whit Monday Fair, Acre's or Aca's Fair (1 October), and Dirt Fair (17 November). In 1900, the minister agreed to abolish all the traditional fairs in the market town of Wigton, namely its Horse Fair in February, Lady Fair in April, and three-day

The ritual year

charter fair in September.[34] And on it went. Some fairs were relocated from the town centres and high streets to private land, rather than abolished completely. With regard to charter fairs, when locals protested, they could resort to the legal challenge that strictly speaking only the king or queen could actually rescind a royal charter, not the government. The consequences of the Fair Act not only impacted on community leisure but also affected the Romani and the traditional travelling fairground community.[35] Since the 1980s, numerous councils have reinstated their statute and charter fairs as cultural and charitable occasions as a mark of local heritage pride. These reinvigorated charter fairs have also provided a lifeline for the country's remaining travelling fun fairs.

Charitable moments

Over the centuries, across the country there accumulated a myriad charitable bequests or doles for the poor that were honoured on specific days and became local calendar customs and part of the makeshift economy.[36] This rich but disparate body of tradition was collated in the voluminous reports of the Commissioners for Enquiry into Charities in England and Wales (Charities Commission) between 1818 and 1837. Scotland had its own laws on charities, and unfortunately no such list was compiled. Many of these customary doles were handed out on the usual days in the religious calendar, such as Christmas, Good Friday, Martinmas, St Thomas's Day, Easter, and Whitsun. While numerous bequests were religious in nature, such as for strewing the church with clean straw, rushes, or hay on parish feast or wake days, the purposes were myriad. Bequests commonly rewarded the poor in one form or another, mostly with cash payments or payments in kind, such as milk, cheese, bread, and meat, but there were also doles for demonstrations of loyalty, patriotism, and piety, and for sickness, schooling, and even to support bull baiting.

Some of those charities registered by the Commission were quite idiosyncratic. At Stockton-on-the Forest, Yorkshire, there was a small piece of ground called Petticoat Hole, the rental from which supplied a new petticoat or, later, a blue serge gown, to a poor woman of the village each year around Christmas time. At Glentham, Lincolnshire, a yearly rental charge of seven shillings provided one shilling to seven old maids each year to wash the tomb of one Molly Grime with water from the nearby Newell Well every Good Friday. At Piddle Hinton, Dorset, on Old Christmas Day the rector handed out a pound of bread, a pint of ale, and a mince pie to every poor person. Upward of three

Figure 1.2 The Biddenden dole in Kent dates back to at least the early seventeenth century, though legend has it that it was created by conjoined twins, the Biddenden Maids, in the medieval period. *Sir Benjamin Stone's Pictures: Records of National Life and History* (London, 1906), Vol. 1.

hundred persons sometimes took advantage. Some doles involved a traditional scramble for bread or coins. In the late nineteenth century, 'scrambling the loaves' was still practised at Wath, Yorkshire, as part of the Christmas Day bequest of Thomas Tuke in 1810. By 1891, though, only half a dozen loaves were customarily thrown from the church roof and the rest were distributed normally.[37] (Figure 1.2)

Few such customary doles survived into the twentieth century. They were rendered defunct as funds ran out and trustees died or lapsed in their duties, while other doles were simply forgotten by the poor. After all, many of them required that a degree of parish knowledge be passed from one generation to the next. In 1890, the author of an article on the folklore of doles in the *Evening Standard* also blamed their demise on the Charity Commissioners, who 'ruthlessly swept away' such traditions 'in favour of methods more agreeable to modern economic science'.[38] Some doles were transformed beyond recognition, such as the Turton Charity, Penistone, which was managed by the vestry and provided a dole of cake and ale for parish children on Maundy Thursdays. In 1905, the vestry overturned two hundred years of custom by converting the funds into a simple dole of flour for the poor. It was no longer considered appropriate to give children alcohol. But a few continued here and there, such as the Troutbeck Dole, bequeathed by the Revd Robert Troutbeck in 1706. On Easter Sunday in 1938, shillings were still being handed out from the Troutbeck family tombstone in Dacre churchyard, as instructed in the bequest.[39]

Monarchy, war, and politics

Elizabeth I's annual 'Crownation Day' or 'Queen's Holy Day' on 17 November, marking her accession to the throne, was a propaganda tool for fostering national unity. The church bells were rung across England and Wales, bonfires were lit, feasting, drinking, sermons, and street entertainments were on offer. It has been described as the first 'annual concert of bells' that was not tied to the church calendar, and it shaped the pattern of future popular celebration of royal accession. The ringing of church bells on 17 November persisted into the reign of Charles I, whose own Crownation Day was 27 March.[40] The one royal occasion that endured to become fully embedded in popular customary culture across the generations concerned the Restoration of the monarchy and the triumphant entry of Charles II into London on 29 May 1660, which also happened to be his birthday. Parliament declared 29 May a public holiday 'for keeping of a perpetual Anniversary, for a Day of Thanksgiving to God, for the great Blessing and Mercy he hath been graciously pleased to vouchsafe to the People of these Kingdoms, after their manifold and grievous Sufferings, in the Restoration of his Majesty'.

Initially known as Restoration Day, it came to be widely called Royal Oak Day or Oak Apple Day, as it became a common custom to wear oak leaves or to deck buildings with oak branches in reference to the fact that Charles had hidden in an old oak tree at Boscobel House, Shropshire, following the Battle of Worcester in 1651. For decades the celebration of the day was characterised by political rivalry between Tory and Whig sentiments on the streets.[41] But the tradition endured in large part because it remained a statutory thanksgiving day for such a long time – the obligatory service, along with that for 5 November, was repealed only in 1859. Restoration Day became part of broader spring celebrations during the month of May. It was also institutionalised as the day that some nineteenth-century clubs and fraternities, such as the Oddfellows, Ancient Order of Foresters, and St Asaph Brotherly Society, held their annual feasts. The wearing of oak in town and country outlived any other forms of festive expression on the day, but toward the end of the nineteenth century its decline was being widely observed. In 1888, the *Sheffield Evening Telegraph* noted:

> The practice of wearing oak has dwindled down to such an extent that very few twigs from the stately tree are to be seen. Some of the bus and cab drivers have decked out their horses with oak leaves, and a few of the carters in the town may be observed with leaves in their hats, but they are decidedly the exception rather than the rule. What was once a general custom appears likely to die completely.[42]

Further east, the *Lincolnshire Echo* commented in 1894 that the old custom of wearing oak 'seems to be dying out'.[43]

First celebrated in 1902 to mark the late Queen Victoria's birthday, Empire Day became an official annual event from 1916 onward and has been described by one historian as 'a significant feature of the national calendar for over half a century'.[44] It was particularly observed with ceremonies and festive activities in schools. It was an amalgam of royal and political hubris, supported by jingoistic newspapers such as the *Daily Express*, and while it initially attracted considerable 'buy-in' from the British public, it also became highly politicised and an occasion for anti-socialist propaganda. With the Empire crumbling after the Second World War, in 1958 the day was re-titled and marketed as British Commonwealth Day.

Battle commemorations concerning long-historic wars between and within the kingdoms of Britain continue to be marked in a variety of ways. The focus here, though, is on national celebrations of victory against overseas foes that led to 'Days' when the bells were rung and bonfires lit in long-established custom. The defeat of the Spanish Armada in the summer of 1588 led to just such celebrations that were timed to coincide with Elizabeth I's thirtieth jubilee 'Crownation Day' on 17 November. Chroniclers recorded that throughout the realm there were joyful singing of psalms, sermons, bell ringing, and bonfires, though local records from around the country suggest a more muted affair. Although the queen decided not to institute an annual Armada Day, some communities took it upon themselves to celebrate it separately for a few years or so.[45] The Norwich authorities continued to put on a show until 1603. Otherwise, the victory was subsumed within Crownation Day celebrations, while anti-Spanish and anti-Catholic sentiment soon found an enduring expression in Guy Fawkes Night. In subsequent centuries, the anniversary of the defeat of the Armada was marked locally on a few occasions. In 1888, the three-hundredth anniversary Armada celebration at the Hill of Beath, Dunfermline, was hijacked by a Presbyterian minister's ranting attack on the current pope, leading the editor of the *Ayrshire Weekly News* to conclude: 'altogether the proceedings were rather odd, and they impress us with the belief that something ought to be done to prevent the celebration of the defeat of the Armada from generating into mere showmen's twaddle.'[46]

In the nineteenth century a new annual battle celebration (though not an enduring public holiday) arose with the community observance of Waterloo Day on 18 June to remember victory over the French in 1815. As well as military processions, gun salutes, and banquets, numerous local civic events up and down the country marked the day with the ringing of church bells, divine services, and then music and festivities.[47] The thirty-seventh anniversary at Loughborough in 1852 began with the peel of bells and the raising of the Union Jack on the church tower. The Plough Inn in the marketplace was bedecked with flags and hosted a banquet for veterans, while the town brass band played outside and then inside to accompany the singing of patriotic songs well into the evening. It is no surprise that Portsmouth put on one of the largest events each year, which ended with soldiers, sailors, and local men entertaining large crowds with barrow races, jumping in sacks, and leaping competitions.[48] But Waterloo Day dwindled in significance as the last veterans died.

Moving on to the Second World War, and millions celebrated Victory in Europe or VE Day on 8 May 1945. Once again, church bells rang out across the land at intervals throughout the day, bonfires blazed, and bunting and coloured lights decked houses and streets as people partied. Unlike other countries in Western Europe, though, the British government never turned VE day into an annual national holiday (apart from in 1995 and 2020, when the May Day Bank Holiday was moved to 8 May in commemoration). The reasons are multiple. For one, unlike France, Italy, and Netherlands, Britain was not occupied (apart from the Channel Islands) and therefore there is not the same sense of national liberation as well as victory. But another key reason is the way in which the national commemoration of conflict had already been reconfigured by the First World War.

The termination of the war in Europe in November 1918 was heralded by national celebrations in keeping with previous 'victorious' conflicts. But two years later, by contrast, the marking of Armistice Day on 11 November (a public holiday in France), was characterised by national mourning and sombre reflection. This set the tone for conflict memorialisation over the ensuing decades. In 1946, Remembrance Sunday was instituted by the government and church to commemorate both world wars, and all subsequent wars involving the British military. Move on seventy years, and in a much-changed Britain, the rituals around Armistice Day and Remembrance Sunday have remained, such as observing the two-minute silence, while the centenary of the First World War in 2014–2018 reinforced media and public adherence to both days of commemoration. A recent research project on contemporary views about Remembrance Sunday revealed that upholding 'tradition' had become a strong theme. As one interviewee put it, 'the tradition going through time, knowing that you are doing pretty much the same thing that my grandfather has done, that his grandfather has done etc. etc., it is a great thing, it is a great thing'.[49]

There is of course another name for 11 November – Poppy Day – which resonates with how plants had long been used to represent calendar customs. As we will see in Chapter 8, the Royal British Legion began selling poppies in 1921, and within a few years 'Poppy Day' had entered common language. Once reserved for lapels and memorials, the poppy has in recent years become something of a seasonal motif, represented incongruously on anything from pizzas to food packaging, and fixed to car radiator grilles and lampposts in early November. Rather unsettling, life-size poppy effigies have also appeared in public spaces – confused relatives of the guys that appear a few days earlier on 5 November.

Unlike monarchs, politicians were not accorded a place in the calendar, with the exception of Benjamin Disraeli, whose death in 1881 was marked by Primrose Day (19 April). The primrose was Disraeli's favourite flower and Queen Victoria would send him bunches from the royal estates each spring. The day was mostly commemorated in large towns and cities and organised by Conservative Associations and the Primrose League, which was founded in 1883 to promote Tory ideas, monarchy, and empire. Like Royal Oak Day and the wearing of oak leaves, it tapped into venerable themes of spring custom. Reports of the anniversary in Edinburgh in 1892 noted that, despite the paucity of primroses that year, the florists drove a thriving trade on the day and had put up prices. The pattern of annual commemoration was obviously mostly, but not entirely, dependent on political affiliation. Conservative Club entrances were obviously well bedecked with primroses, but in 1892 newspapers noted that most people in Edinburgh's main thoroughfare were wearing the flower. In central Glasgow the same year, by contrast, *The Scotsman* reported that 'Primrose Day seemed almost to have been forgotten'.[50] By the 1920s it had, indeed, been neglected everywhere, apart from the annual honouring of Disraeli's monument at the Palace of Westminster.

May Day became the most politicised day of the calendar, its secular nature making it a malleable vehicle for new interests – having been recorded for centuries as a popular celebration of springtime, with people going into the countryside to collect flowers and boughs to make garlands for sale and display, and the erection of maypoles and associated frolics (less so in Calvinist Scotland). May Day celebrations underwent a sanitising makeover in the second half of the nineteenth century, but, more to the point, in 1889, 1 May was chosen by the International Socialist Congress as International Workers' Day or Labour Day, marked in Britain and elsewhere with marches, speeches, and mass demonstrations. It became a key element in Labour ritual and tradition in the interwar years, and in 1978 the Labour government recognised this by creating an early May Monday bank holiday.[51] Over the ensuing years various politicians and right-wing newspapers have called for the scrapping of the May Day bank holiday and its replacement with a Trafalgar Day holiday on 21 October. A Bill was put forward to abolish it in 1982, and ten years later during a debate in the House of Lords, Lord Fanshaw asked for an 'alternative date in the autumn, such as Trafalgar Day, in view of the collapse of communism and socialism'.

Commercialisation

The last of our forces shaping the observance of calendar customs is modern retail and marketing.[52] Calendar customs had often, by their nature, been intertwined with commerce, but in the twentieth century the ever-expanding influence of advertising and mass marketing came to the fore. Christmas is the prime example, of course, but we can also trace the path of commodification in the development of Valentine's Day and Mother's Day.

A saint may have given his name to Valentine's Day, but little religiosity has been on display over the last few centuries. Studies of its development have explored how the day accrued a variety of customary calendar activities – including ritualised begging, pranking, and gift giving – and the influence of literary influences on the shaping and promotion of the tradition have been explored. The roots of its commercialisation lie in the late eighteenth century, when manufactured Valentine's cards began to be sold in shops and booksellers for a few pence. It has been estimated that between 1804 and the 1830s the number of such cards that were sent grew from sixty thousand to two hundred thousand.[53] The buying of chocolates and flowers came later in the century. In 1888, an early enterprising Norwich retailer placed adverts in the regional press promoting 'fancy boxes of chocolate fondants' for Valentine's Day presents, while around this time artificial flowers seem to have become increasingly common as a gift. The *Retailer's Chronicle* told its readers in 1930 that 'St Valentine's Day lends itself to almost every trade'. The growth of 'flowers by wire', ordered by telegram and delivered to the door, and the Post Office's introduction in 1938 of a decorative telegram form for Valentine's Day, heralded today's huge flower-delivery business for such special occasions, which also includes Mother's Day.[54]

Mother's Day, which is celebrated on different days in different countries, has a coincidental association with the old calendar custom of Mothering Sunday, the fourth Sunday during Lent. The latter's origins stretch back to at least the seventeenth century, and the tradition was largely practised in the western half of England. By the nineteenth century, it was most associated with annually hired, live-in agricultural servants, who were given the day off to visit their families and brought cake and flowers as gifts for their mothers. Several folklorists writing in the early twentieth century noted the disappearance of the custom as a consequence of the decline of the traditional hiring system.[55] The new Mother's Day was introduced at a time, then, when the old one was in terminal decline.

Modern Mother's Day was created in the United States in 1908 by Anna Jarvis (1864–1948), an Episcopalian Methodist and social activist, who launched a high-profile campaign to memorialise the anniversary of her deceased mother. As one scholar put it, the fact that the 'crank idea' of one woman became an annual social custom shows, first, the power of grassroots American Protestant movements in shaping American popular culture, and, second, how an essentially faith-backed initiative quickly became secularised.[56] Although reports of its growing American popularity were mentioned in the British press early on, the idea that it should be adopted in Britain was first promoted heavily here in 1916. It took on a special meaning in Britain due to the First World War, serving as a public appreciation of the toll the conflict was having on the mothers of soldiers and sailors. In July 1916, the Lord Mayor of London, Charles Wakefield, agreed to become the Chief Patron of Mother's Day in Britain, with a date originally fixed as 8 August. The campaign's tag line was 'No Flags, no Collections, No Appeal for Money' – instead, a call to the public conscience. The following suggestions were given as to appropriate acts to mark the day:

> Invite one, two, or three mothers to spend the day with you at home.
> Take one or two out in the country.
> Give a small tea-party.
> Pay some back rent, or a tradesman's bill.
> A gift of clothes, or a week's supply of food.
> A kind word.[57]

By the 1920s, the day had snowballed, taken up by churches, schools, and charitable organisations. On 8 August 1920 fetes and special sermons were arranged around the country, and it was not long before the idea became a fund-raising day against the founding principle that money was not to be solicited. Then, on both sides of the Atlantic, card manufacturers and florists also saw the commercial possibilities, and cemented its future as an enduring calendar custom. Jarvis fought hard against this commercialisation of Mother's Day, but the force was too strong.[58] British department stores and high-street retailers like Woolworths also played a crucial role in its popularisation. In 1940, for instance, the Nottingham department store Griffin and Spalding promoted chocolates, cakes, cards, posies, and ribbons for Mother's Day. A 1950s Woolworths advert announced: 'you need a Mother's Day card, too! It's the most important day in the year for Mother – give her the nicest card you can find. The best place to look for the card she'll love? Woolworths! It'll be Easter soon ... It's not too early to choose your Easter cards now.'

The editor of the *Louth Standard* was in a reflective mood about it all in 1953: 'Christmas spending rush over, the January sales a thing of the past, Mothering Sunday comes along and bridges the no-spending gap between January and Easter. ... It will soon be commercialised almost as much as Christmas.'[59] As to whether this was a good or bad thing, the editor was non-committal, but the English folklorist Violet Alford (1881–1972) was more forthright. She criticised the 'objectionable' American import of Mother's Day in a 1961 article entitled 'Folklore Gone Wrong'. She complained that its imposition 'on our quiet domestic celebration is neither inevitable nor acceptable. To folklorists it is irritating to find a family custom commercialised, wrongly named and wrongly carried out.'[60]

It seems that nearly every day now marks some sort of 'Day'. Some are created for charitable purposes, others to raise medical, social, or cultural awareness, while many are purely marketing and public relations initiatives for tourism or the promotion of national industries. National Fish and Chip

Day, for example, was launched in 2015, and by 'tradition' is usually marked on the first Friday of June. The Welsh toasted cheese dish, rarebit, has its own national day on 3 September. It is the supermarkets, though, that have the biggest cultural influence on the ritual year.

In the twenty-first century, supermarkets have become a major driver of calendar custom awareness – and commodification. The seasonal aisle of the British supermarket is in a near constant state of flux, staff often working in the quiet hours of night to remove the unsold products from the last event and restocking the shelves with products for the next. End-of-aisle displays are likewise on annual rotation, and, as one marketing consultant has described these displays, they 'are not just haphazardly stacked shelves; they are meticulously curated showcases designed to captivate and compel … displays serve as seasonal showcases, featuring festive décor and seasonal offerings that tap into the spirit of the moment' – and capitalize on it. Ultimately, these seasonal displays are designed to 'create a sense of urgency and excitement, driving seasonal sales'.[61] No time is wasted, one event often bleeding into the next. Before the pumpkins of Halloween, the *gulab jamun* of Diwali, and the parkin of Bonfire Night have been removed, the Christmas German *Lebkuchen* and advent calendars appear. The Easter eggs, emerging as early as 26 December, share shelf space with heart-shaped Valentine's Day chocolates. Socks and bottles of beer marketed as Father's Day gifts sometimes sit side by side with rainbow merchandise celebrating Pride Month.

Seasonal supermarket displays can reflect the local area's demography. The supermarket in an area with a large South-East Asian population, for example, may move their large bags of rice and packs of ghee to the seasonal aisle in the run-up to Eid. But supermarkets also create awareness of other cultures' seasonal events, encouraging their shoppers to celebrate them (and spend money doing so). We often see a British or more local take on the appropriate way to mark the event. End-of-aisle displays adorned with that year's Chinese zodiac animal push noodles, sachets of stir-fry sauce, and packets of prawn crackers, enticing shoppers to celebrate the Lunar New Year. Tortilla chips and jars of salsa, guacamole, and Ben's Original chilli con carne get their seasonal display for Dia De Los Muertos. And supermarkets in England sell vegan and chocolate-dessert versions of haggis to mark Burns Night. Rabbie Burns may turn in his grave at this take on the 'Great chieftain o' the puddin'-race', but this is how seasonal events survive in Britain: via commodification and adaptation.

Chapter 2
Performance

The meaning of 'performance' has been the subject of vigorous debate among international folklorists over the decades, tied to concepts of agency, identity, cohesion, and communication. In simple terms, performance, as used here, is essentially the collective 'doing' of folklore, and the means by which community traditions were and are upheld, revived, or invented, whether expressed through sport, games, dance, song, processing, protesting, or some other form of customary display. Issues of authenticity have dogged the understanding of traditional performances. Folk song scholars have had their own arguments about the relationship between oral tradition and the influence of printed ballads in popular culture. Folk dance studies has also had its preoccupations, such as the origins and nature of Morris dancing. Much of this discussion has been carried out in the publications of the English Folk Dance and Song Society, formed in 1932 from the union of the English Folk Dance Society and the Folk-Song Society. But it needs to be emphasised that performers, in the broadest sense of the term, have always been inventive, adapting rituals, rites, songs, and dances according to new cultural influences. As the editors of a major survey of *English Folk Performance* put it, over six hundred years of recorded history it has proven 'endlessly creative, generally conservative, frequently mischievous, occasionally resistant, critical and oppositional. It has never stayed the same.'[1] In this chapter we explore how broad cultural and societal transformations in Britain since the eighteenth century have shaped the performance of folklore and its changing constituents.

Dressing up
Personal and collective invention had long been integral to the role of costume in folk performance from place to place. Take Plough Monday performances.

In 1862 the Plough Monday crew in Leicester were described as dressed in the 'most ridiculous costumes imaginable'. A few years earlier, a court case arose from a man who lent a Plough Monday costume of a spotted leopard's suit to one of the participants. At Raunds, in Northamptonshire, the boys both blackened their faces with soot and raddled their faces with red ochre, wore women's gowns decorated with ribbons and rags, and, in 1885, in a nod to new cultural influences, the lead ploughman or 'witch' dressed as an 'Indian' with war paint was accompanied by his 'squaw'.[2]

The uses of costume and adornment in calendar customs were clearly not unchanging fossils of ancient practice, though it can be difficult to chart over time. The best example is the May Day celebration in London, led by milkmaids and chimney sweeps.[3] Sources from the seventeenth century suggest a simple performance of milkmaids (who delivered milk) dancing with pails on their heads and carrying garlands of greenery, which also decorated their pails. Then, by the latter part of the century, the garland became a rather elaborate piece of headwear consisting of pewter tankards and dairy-related silverware borrowed for the occasion, intertwined with flowers and ribbons (Figure 2.1). The aim was to encourage charity from customers. During the mid-eighteenth century the city's chimney sweeps joined the milkmaids' festivities, sometimes together, sometimes on their own, with their dancing and music involving the tools of their trade. Engravings show sweeps in beribboned best clothes, wearing crowns and wigs in imitation of their 'betters'. During the late eighteenth century, the milkmaids and their garlands started to fade from the scene, but the Jack in the Green, a man wearing a wooden framework decorated with boughs and leaves, began to appear with the sweeps and would become a central figure in May Day celebrations. The sweep now played a mock lord or king with his lady or queen, who was sometimes a boy dressed as a girl. Clowns or other fool figures accompanied them.

During the early twentieth century, folklorists speculated wildly, though without any evidence, that the Jack-in-the-Green and other such Green Men – like the Scottish Queensferry Burry Man, which was associated with an old August fair day – were ancient, pre-Christian fertility figures. The whole supposition was largely based on costume design. The Burry Man was, and is, covered in a body stocking stuck with prickly green burdock burrs and flowers, and is paraded around the streets. One of the earliest records of the custom, written by a local antiquarian in 1851, explains how the procession of the Burry Man was essentially another calendar charity exercise. The Burry Man and his guides went from door to door in expectation of small change,

Figure 2.1 An eighteenth-century London scene of milkmaids dancing on May Day, with a man holding their garland of silver plates. William Hone, *The Every-Day Book* (London, 1841), Vol. 2.

with the money raised 'divided and spent at the fair by the youth associated in the exploit'.[4] Like the Jack-in-the-Green, there is no evidence that the custom and costume dated beyond the second half of the eighteenth century. But the survivalists thought otherwise. A 1908 contributor to *Folklore* on the Burry Man was confident that 'the green appearance of the Burryman and the bunches of leaves and flowers he carries are at once recognisable as signs of some nature cult'.[5]

The Plough Monday 'straw bear' in the villages of Whittlesey and Ramsey, Cambridgeshire, is another example. A young man dressed in a full covering of straw was paraded around like an old performing bear. Accounts of the ceremony exist only from the second half of the nineteenth century. The

Figure 2.2 The Whittlesea Straw Bear and 'its' handler. Photograph by Doc Rowe.

Stamford Mercury reported in January 1893, for instance, how, in Whittlesey, on the Monday the plough boys were 'dressed and painted up in the most gorgeous fashion' and then, on the Tuesday, 'the "straw bear" appeared on the scene, enveloped from head to foot in bands of straw (Figure 2.2). An appeal for coppers was in each case the object.' In nearby Ramsey in the 1880s the straw bear was accompanied by a man playing a concertina. The custom in both villages had disappeared by the 1930s.[6] Similar straw costumes were worn in nineteenth-century Shetland mumming performances and in other parts of Europe. The Shetland 'skeklers', who performed at Hallowtide, Martinmas, and Christmas, were first recorded in 1809, 'their bodies covered with dresses made of straw, ornamented with a profusion of ribbands'.[7] This led James Frazer to the dubious conclusion that the bear and the like 'represent the corn-spirit bestowing his blessing on every homestead in the village'. Animalistic costumes and accoutrements, such as the reindeer horns carried by the Abbots Bromley dancers or the various customs that include hobby horses, also obviously attracted notions of ancient pagan cults.[8]

Examples of men dressing as women in folk performance, whether in protests or calendar customs, can be found around the world. The transgression of cross-dressing can be seen in simple terms as a disguise, or symbolically as a carnivalesque inversion of society, but the practice can have different connotations from culture to culture, as well as changing over time. The popular cultural influence of the pantomime dame is just one example in recent British history. The cross-dressing element in Plough Monday Molly dancing (molly was an eighteenth-century term for a loose woman and an effeminate homosexual) was clearly meant to be absurd rather than accurate – a pantomime performance. It had a satisfying, titillating shock value for some spectators and was just a bit of a laugh for others, just as young men cross-dress today in public during stag parties.[9] Mumming plays and the like were also masculine areas of performance by tradition, and so cross-dressing to represent women was also, paradoxically, conformist and conservative in terms of their exclusion.

Male cross-dressing in folk performance can often be found along with face blackening. Both occurred in nineteenth-century popular protests like the Welsh Rebecca Riots of 1838–1843, and also in community shaming rituals known variously as rough music, skimmingtons, riding the stang, tin panning, shallals, and the *cefyl pren* ('wooden horse'), which have been recorded from the medieval period to the early twentieth century. There were different regional permutations of the custom, but all involved the ostracism of moral transgressors, mostly adulterers, hastily remarried widows and widowers, and wife and husband beaters, though a range of other moral offences could also be punished. Effigies of the offenders were paraded around and often burned, accompanied by a cacophonous band beating pots and pans. At Ombersley, Worcestershire, in 1859 a recent widow, Mrs Lane, who shortly after the funeral of her husband took up with a rag-and-bone dealer known as Billy Fairplay, was subjected to rough music. On the first evening, an effigy of Billy was burned, and on the second evening a group of male villagers with blackened faces paraded an effigy of Lane which was set on fire in the street.[10]

The use of blackface in this ritual context was for disguise or concealment in night-time ritual; but the soot blackening, or reddening of the skin with ochre, in non-confrontational customs clearly had other meanings. In Christmas mummers' plays it was to identify stock foreign characters such as the 'Moor' or the 'Turkish knight'.[11] But in other types of folk performance it was clearly a racist, comedic mimicry of black people, no doubt influenced by the popularity of American minstrelsy bands like the Ethiopian Serenaders, who toured

Britain in the mid-nineteenth century, and the home-grown minstrel groups they inspired.[12] We will return to this contentious issue later.

Suppression

The abolition of fairs that we read about in the previous chapter was part of a much wider story of how the authorities attempted to suppress, replace, or reinvent customary performance and leisure. All three processes were interlinked – though not necessarily conspiratorially planned. Historians have explored this as an aspect of, variously, the growing cultural gulf between 'patricians and plebs', industrialisation, the rise of the middle classes, and changing conceptions of law and order. The customs of the poor were considered barbaric, unruly, time wasting, and disruptive. The crowd needed to be civilized and controlled if popular enlightenment was to spread and British society progress.[13] Equally important was the contested control of spaces where people claimed the right to gather, whether in the urban streets or on common land. The clergy, schoolmasters, magistrates, landowners, tradespeople, and town and borough councillors were the key agents in trying to reform popular cultures. The creation of a uniformed, professional police force in the mid-nineteenth century was also crucial to the reformist agenda, particularly in the expanding urban areas. Unlike the old parish constables, the new police were often not of the communities they policed, and so had no social or emotional investment in local traditions.

There were three main types of customary performance that were vigorously suppressed during the late eighteenth and nineteenth centuries: blood sports, urban begging rituals, and 'riotous' urban street customs. Blood sports were sometimes tied to long-standing calendar days in the form of bull running, bull baiting, and throwing at cocks. There was, of course, hypocrisy in the continuing elite support for fox hunting. Bull running was a rare custom in Britain, largely restricted to East Midlands market towns, and consisted of a bull being let lose in the street, where it was goaded into a rampage, as is still practised in Pamplona, Spain. The best recorded was the bull running at Stamford that took place on 13 November. It dated back to at least the early seventeenth century and was finally suppressed in 1839. The bull running at Oundle, Northamptonshire, which took place between Christmas Day and early January, was less ritualised in nature. Its various ups and downs from year to year were recorded by a late eighteenth-century diarist. He noted his disappointment one time as follows: 'To Day we had two Bulls runn'd in the market street, & they might as well have runn'd me, for the poor beasts were no more mad than I am, & I can hardly walk five yards.'[14] Bull baiting, where a tethered bull was tormented by dogs, was a far more widespread 'sport' across Britain. Customary Shrovetide 'throwing at cocks' was a similarly popular 'pastime' where a cockerel was tethered and beaten to death by throwing sticks or stones at it, the winner being the person who dealt the final blow. Cock fighting was more of an organised 'sport' with trained birds, fighting pits, and gambling.

Eighteenth- and early nineteenth-century campaigners and local authorities employed various laws to suppress blood sports, and in 1824 the Society for the Prevention of Cruelty to Animals was founded, and quickly proved influential. Then, in 1835, the government introduced specific legislation in the form of the Cruelty to Animals Act, whereby those involved in running, baiting, or fighting domestic or wild animals were liable to a fine not exceeding five pounds. This effectively put an end to all blood sports as a customary public spectacle (apart from fox hunting); but, obviously, small illicit gatherings for cock and dog fighting, badger baiting, and the like were more difficult to suppress.

Begging customs were a key target for reformist clergy, gentry, and farmers. There was a hope that the introduction of the New Poor Law in 1834 and the threat of the workhouse would help to reduce the number of 'undeserving' poor who resorted to begging. The main legal tool was the wide-ranging 1824 Vagrancy Act, which punished anyone 'placing himself or herself in any public place, street, highway, court, or passage, to beg or gather alms, or causing or procuring or encouraging any child or children so to do'. Thus, in 1865 the Chief Constable of Cambridge warned that Plough Monday revellers would be arrested as vagrants, declaring that the 'importunate begging' and drinking was making it impossible for the honest public to walk the streets.[15]

Guy Fawkes begging was a much more widespread and enduring target for suppression under the Vagrancy Act. In 1906 three unemployed men were charged at the Bow Street police court. They had blackened their faces, wore women's clothing, and had a donkey that pulled a cart with two guys in it. When confronted by a constable, one of them politely replied: 'You cannot say anything to us, as it is the 5th of November.' Such prosecutions occurred periodically, though they increasingly concerned children and could also be pursued under the Children's Act of 1889, which included the offence of causing children to beg in the street or to 'induce the giving of alms, whether under the pretence of singing, playing, performing'. In 1963, magistrates heard the prosecution against the parents of a seven-year-old girl who was found collecting pennies for her guy in Newcastle-under-Lyme town centre. The case was dismissed. The *Manchester Evening News* ran a headline story in 1992 entitled 'Bonfire Beggars' after five children were questioned by police for six hours for asking for a 'penny for the guy' which they were pushing around in a pram. One of the boys' mothers complained, 'It's just ridiculous ... It's been done for years and years.'[16]

The rowdiness of Bonfire Night was the target of a long campaign of suppression, and the rolling of flaming tar barrels through the streets was effectively eradicated. This had been practised in numerous towns across the country. Sometimes it was a major street spectacle, such as at Lewes before it was banned in 1841, or a rather more pedestrian lark. A few days after Guy Fawkes Night in 1854, the Gravesend magistrates dealt with a long list of offenders, mostly fined for letting off squibs in the streets, but also Daniel Murphy, a porter at Tilbury Railway, for lighting a tar barrel and rolling it along the New Road. Murphy pleaded that he merely 'saw the tar barrel rolled up Princess street, and so he gave it a kick or two'.[17]

It was more challenging to suppress public behaviour in southern England, where societies of local young men effectively orchestrated events and were known as Bonfire Boys or some such, like the 'Guys' in the Surrey town of Guildford and the scary-sounding 'Skeleton Army' in Worthing. They were often costumed and masked, and they used to demand money on the night from passers-by. Sometimes the event was also used as a tool of popular justice, in terms not only of the choice of guy to put on the fire, but also of the targeting of people's houses.[18] Riotousness occasionally remained an element of the day into more recent times. In 1954, Oxford magistrates heard eight charges of assaulting the police and ninety-six summonses for throwing fireworks. Ironically, the Chief Constable, ignorant of the history, told the court that, sadly, 'the harmless fun of November 5 was a thing of the past', and the prosecuting Queen's Counsel opined that 'Guy Fawkes might have become a pretext for what was simply hooliganism'.[19]

The performance of 'folk football' or the 'ba game' in Scotland, which took place just once a year, usually at Shrovetide, but occasionally on other traditional ritual calendar days, has attracted considerable attention from folklorists. This was a quite different game to the modern version. It was a rough-and-tumble, factional community competition between two large groups of mostly young men, with the 'goals' sometimes several miles apart and the open rural landscape or urban streets as the pitch. It was more like rugby in practice, with kicking and handling of the ball and injurious scrums. A newspaper report of the ebb and flow of the Shrove Tuesday game in Chester-le-Street in 1878 describes how the game between the 'upstreeters' and 'downstreeters' started at noon and concluded with the downstreeters winning around 6 p.m. The journalist observed approvingly that there was 'utmost good humour, where blows were freely given and received'. The Fastern's Een (Shrove Tuesday) game in Melrose, Scotland, similarly started at 1 p.m. and went on till dusk. All businesses in the town closed and shop windows were boarded up to prevent them being smashed by players.[20] The ball was not always a ball. In the Plough Monday 'Haxey Hood' game in Haxey, Lincolnshire, the 'hood' is a tight bundle of leather, while the Easter Monday 'bottle kicking' at Hallaton, Leicestershire, involves small wooden kegs as balls.

One by one, the folk football games were extinguished by the authorities under various laws and pretexts, particularly the Highways Act of 1835, which specifically criminalised 'play at football or any other game' on any part of the highway. Only a handful of folk football customs continued into the 1920s and 1930s. In Chester-le-Street the game ended for good in the early 1930s with multiple arrests. The authorities issued a ban in 1930, but the townsfolk ignored it and turned up in their thousands. The football began in usual fashion that year, but a large contingent of police confiscated multiple balls and slit them, and then charged into the crowd and arrested six men and one woman, who were charged under the Highways Act and for obstruction and assaulting the police. The district council condemned the heavy-handed response and sent a letter to the Home Secretary, with one of the councillors telling the press: 'I just wondered whether Trotsky had arrived with a regiment of Cossacks, or that some subversive organisation with a view of undermining the law of this kingdom, had arrived in the town.' The following year, hundreds once again defied the ban, with call-and-response cries of 'Are we going to let them stop Shrovetide football?' and 'Are we afraid of the police?'[21] But over the next two years the police finally prevailed.

Replacement: fetes, pageants, and carnivals

As the traditional fairs and wakes were expunged or dwindled, the village fete came to take their place, often unchained from the old ritual calendar. Writing in 1879, the rural life writer Richard Jefferies observed that 'the club and the fete threaten, indeed, to supplant the feast altogether'.[22] The French word '*fête*' was hardly used in a British customary context prior to the 1850s. Then, during the mid-nineteenth century, carefully stage-managed fetes began to appear, organised by local gentry and clergy and usually for a charitable fund-raising purpose.[23] One of the first was the Harrowden Village Fete, instituted in 1862 to mark the end of harvest time. The local vicar had set up a Savings Bank Club among his parishioners the previous year to encourage saving, and also to fund a fete at the end of the harvest. Tickets were also charged, which went towards paying a savings dividend. The day itself consisted of merry-go-rounds, sack races, foot races, games, and dancing.[24] More such events appeared over the next couple of decades, and then, in the mid-1890s, fetes suddenly sprung up all over the country, held mostly in June and July, with some at Whitsun or on the new August Bank Holiday. Vicarage gardens or rectory grounds, and later school playing fields, became new customary spaces where locals were entertained with rummage sales, coconut shies, bazaars, cake-weighing, ice creams, craft displays, children's competitions, cricket matches, three-legged races, and tug of war. There was lots of tea and no alcohol. Indeed, the religious temperance movement appears to have been a key player in promoting the idea of the fete.

'Carnival' was another foreign term and concept that gained momentum during the second half of the nineteenth century. It derives from the Italian '*carnevale*' or 'farewell to flesh' Shrovetide celebration before the Lenten fast. In 1896, the author of an article on the 'Revival of Carnival' in a London periodical observed that 'though we do not keep carnival in England, the revival of the old Opera balls has marked the influence of the continental movement'. But, out in the provinces a novel carnival culture was already forming. Like fetes, some of these British expressions of carnival were detached from the old customary calendar, and performances were defined by colourful processions with people in recognisable costumes that often reflected the latest cultural influences, such as 'cowboys and Indians' seen in early cinema. In June 1887 it was reported that a carnival had been held in Redruth, Cornwall, which involved people dressed as Dick Turpin, Buffalo Bill, and Minstrels. Around the same time in June that year, a 'carnival' and torchlight 'historical' procession took place in Newton Abbot, Devon.[25]

Hybrid events were sometimes created. In Cockermouth, for instance, there was a 'Carnival and May Festival' on May Day 1894, with a May Queen and Morris dances, and a procession of over two hundred 'dressed in character'.[26] In 1889, the students of Aberdeen University planned the first continental-style Shrovetide carnival extravaganza in Britain. While one correspondent hoped that it would 'be a success and prove a treat to the public', other anonymous letters to the Aberdeen press were less enthusiastic: 'every student is called upon to form one of a band of howling maniacs, whose sole mission on that night seems to be to paint the town a brilliant vermillion. And what is it all for?' The students eventually gave up on their ambitious plans.[27]

Today's carnival tradition is primarily associated with the West Country and London. In the former, fancy-dress processions and decorated carts, and then electrically illuminated floats, became a replacement for the old, raucous Guy Fawkes Night celebrations in several towns. The Bridgwater carnival in Somerset is the best known, and was a template for others in the region. From the 1880s it was carefully managed by a committee of local businessmen and the local 'great and the good', who carefully calibrated how to marry old and new expectations, particularly in its defence of 'squibbing'. This was the firing of hand-held fireworks as an integral part of the night-time street festivities – a tradition which endures today, despite early Home Office disapproval in 1913 and later health and safety concerns. Greater London also had a tradition of carnival culture before the famous Notting Hill Carnival began in the 1960s. Between 1905 and 1914, for instance, the suburb of Ilford hosted a major carnival for charitable purposes, with crowds estimated at around 250,000 at its peak. The floats depicted the area's old rural life as well as representations of national historical identity, from the Crusaders to Charles Dickens.[28]

The pageant, which was originally a medieval urban dramatic spectacle organised by churches and guilds, came back into vogue as a secular event in Britain toward the end of the nineteenth century and reached a peak of popularity early in the next – a phenomenon that was satirically described as 'pageantitis' in 1907.[29] While the carnival was open to outside cultural influences, the central feature of the modern pageant was a dramatic, historical re-enactment concerned with national or local identity which has been described as the 'theatricalisation' of traditional processual performance. It was a costly, large-scale outdoor spectacle sometimes involving thousands of people in historic dress performing episodes from key moments in history and legend.

A good example of such a spectacle is the pageant at Taunton in 1928. The original script was written by a local clergyman, and the pageant involved some 1,500 participants. The play began with a scene set just after the death of King Arthur, with Nimue, the Lady of the Lake, appearing to some frightened Britons to announce that she was 'the Spirit of their Countryside'. Arthur's own spirit enters to announce that he will return one day to lead the country. There then follows a chronological progression of vignettes concerning King Alfred, the Civil War, and the Monmouth Rebellion (1685) – which was obviously of local interest. Arthur returns, besides Queen Victoria, Alfred, and Charles

II in the finale.[30] Such spectacles were repeated over several days and they were usually accompanied by more 'traditional' folkloric side events such as Morris and maypole dancing, though these were usually artistic versions of the dance, devised by professional choreographers and schoolteachers.

These new expressions of community performance emerged at a time when the old 'sense of belonging' to the parish was breaking down, due to migration, urbanisation, and new administrative structures.[31] The rise of the working-class seaside holiday also made possible the joy of 'getting away' from the place where one lived and worked. These broad social changes undermined old customs just as much as authoritarian meddling. The pageants and carnivals provided a stage-managed replacement for community spectacle, though now with more possibilities for working-class women to participate in public performance.[32] Some urban pageants and carnivals also helped fill the economic hole left by the demise of market fairs, drawing visitors from far beyond the local community.

Reinvention

The third of our reform strategies was to take an existing, practised tradition and reshape it according to middle- and upper-class sensibilities and imagined notions of the past. It was fuelled by a romantic sentiment that there was something noble and pure in old popular customs which could be restored by stripping away perceived immorality and taming the popular motives for performance and celebration. The transformation of the Up-helly-aa festival in Shetland is a classic example. The original tradition of tar barrelling was suppressed in the 1870s and replaced with a torch-lit procession through the streets. Then, over the ensuing years, the festival was turned into an impressive fire pageant representing the island's Viking past. The Shetland poet, historian, and novelist James John Haldane Burgess (1862–1927) was one of the leading influences.[33]

The infantilising of customs was a key aspect of reinvention, by which roles once taken by young men were now reallocated to school children. When successfully implemented, this inhibited adult drinking and boisterousness in the community, and also turned children away from their customary role in begging traditions. Harvest celebrations are the most pervasive example.[34] The traditional drinking and feasting of Harvest Home was deemed to be problematic, both morally and financially. While clergy frowned on the inevitable drunkenness, farmers increasingly preferred to give an additional end-of-harvest stipend to labourers rather than provide food and alcohol and join their employees in celebration. Slowly, the Harvest Home dwindled during the second half of the nineteenth century; the alcohol flowed less liberally, there were no late nights, and genteel sports were organised instead to occupy the men.

The Anglican Church, and later Nonconformists, also provided a revised alternative in the form of the church-centred Harvest Festival, with school children and women integral to proceedings. Communities were evidently receptive to the change. The churches were bedecked with sheaves of corn, flowers, bread, and vegetables, a thanksgiving service was read, and then there was the usual procession wearing best clothes – not costume – a brass band played, and people tucked into tea and a cold collation. There were sometimes games, dancing, and the singing of patriotic songs. As the author of a study of contemporary harvest festivals in England notes, it is 'dogmatically light' for a church event and 'carries no expectation of regular commitment'. In rural areas Harvest Festival still serves as a community-binding 'moment' that attracts recent incomers and second-homers, as well as long-term residents.[35]

The reinvention of popular custom was not just a top-down, patronising intervention. There was a strong self-improvement ethos among the upwardly mobile, politically conscious working classes who desired to reform their own ancestral cultures. This sentiment for 'progress' over old tradition was well recorded in the numerous working-class autobiographies that were published in the nineteenth century. We can see this playing out in terms of the influence of master craftsmen and tradespeople on their apprentices and employees. When the London philanthropist Jonas Hanway (1712–1786) offered to give a wig 'to wear on May-day' to a young sweep who had cleaned his chimney, the boy replied that 'my master won't let me go out on May-day' because 'he says its low life'.[36] A century later, a Hastings chimney sweep, thirty years a member of the trade, wrote to his local newspaper in 1879 complaining of the 1 May performance in town: 'I have seen that sight known as "Jack in the Green," which, however amusing to the little trots in the nursery, is a disgrace to any honest members of the trade of chimneysweepers (who by the way never have anything to do with it).'[37] Clubs and friendly societies were an influential force. These were grassroots organisations set up by working-class men and women for mutual self-help that involved the creation of collective funds to support members during ill health, periods of penury and unemployment, and to provide burial costs and the like. They acted as a sort of fraternal insurance and savings cooperative prior to the founding of the modern welfare state.

The clubs and societies also developed codes of social behaviour and ritual performative elements that were expressed in the transformation of Whitsun in many communities. This was the day chosen by many clubs and friendly societies to hold their annual celebration, reinvigorating a calendar period that was losing its cultural importance as the traditional provision of Whit ales disappeared and blood sports were suppressed.[38] In 1873, for instance, the *Taunton Courier* could describe the Whitsun-week annual celebration of the Ilminster Female Friendly Society as 'one of the red letter days in the annals of this town'. The church bells pealed as the women members processed through the main streets in white dresses with sashes of blue ribbon, holding bouquets of flowers. A sermon was preached, tea was had, and then there was genteel music and dancing until ten o'clock.[39] Some societies and clubs paraded with willow wands and garlands, and proudly displayed their club or society banner. There was often a hearty meal – and men's clubs were not always teetotal affairs. Associated festivities such as games involved the whole community. Decorous behaviour was paramount, and often written into club rules. The Quaker writer and social observer, William Howitt (1792–1879), waxed lyrical about these new Whitsuntide processions which he had witnessed in the Staffordshire and Nottinghamshire countryside in the 1830s:

> There they go, passing down the shady lane with all the village children at their heels, to the next hamlet half a mile off, which furnishes members to the club, and must therefore witness their glory. Now the banner and gilded tops of their wands are seen glancing between the hedge-row trees; their music comes merrily up the hill; and as it dies away at the next turn, the drumming of distant villages become audible.[40]

The rise of formal team sports was also an aspect of these grassroots negotiations with changing custom.[41] There is rarely evidence that any modern sport was introduced strategically as a direct replacement for its local folk expression. One exception was the 'Olympian Games' founded in the village of Much Wenlock in 1850 by the doctor and local philanthropist, William Penny Brookes (1809–1895). The aim was the 'moral, physical and intellectual improvement' of the locals. As well as track and field events, the games also included football, cricket, and quoits, and in 1858 there was a Merrie England touch with the introduction of the medieval jousting game 'tilting at the ring', accompanied by much pageantry. The relationship was usually more organic, subtle, and untraceable, as is evident from the development of modern football and cricket. The old orthodoxy among sports historians was that folk football had largely died out in popular culture by the mid-nineteenth century, supressed as a public nuisance, and that the modern game derived largely from public school sports tradition, along with rugby. The revisionists countered that folk football was just one of multiple expressions of the game during the nineteenth century, including informal organised matches as part of sports activities for fetes, workers' outings, and feasts, and casual youth play on waste ground, greens, or in the streets. These, it has been argued, all contributed significantly to the development of modern football.[42]

As with folk football, early folklorists gave cricket a dubious ancient heritage. Andrew Lang claimed, for instance, that the game was of Celtic origin, citing mythic Irish and Scottish texts to prove his point. We do know that a game called 'cricket' is first mentioned in seventeenth-century sources as a popular pastime, sometimes censured by Puritans. It was embraced by the eighteenth-century elites, while it also continued to be played at grassroots level on commons and heaths.[43] As a non-contact sport, it lent itself well to social and cultural transition. The Yorkshire cloth merchant Joseph Lawson enthused greatly about the civilising influence of formal cricket in his book *Progress in Pudsey* (1887). He noted the old ad hoc game of his youth played 'in the lanes or small openings in the village – with a tub leg for a bat'. When the 'new style' game came into vogue it was clannish and involved playing for money. But strict rules helped to improve it and new ideas of sporting behaviour won through. 'Cricketing has had a most wonderful influence for good on the young men of Pudsey', he concluded, 'not only the players, but on the spectators as well. By cricket, players are taught patience, endurance, precision, and courage. They are taught self-respect and gentlemanly conduct.'[44]

All hail the queens

A snobbish thought-piece on the May Queen in the *Illustrated Newspaper* for 1871 declared: 'What a pity it is we cannot drag this May-day festival out of the "dust of ages" and get it once more in the calendar. The poor little dirty queens that throng the London streets on May-day are a miserable satire on the past.' The author considered this the next civilising battle after having 'redeemed the Harvest Home'. 'The good old days of the Autumn festival may be said to have come back again', he declared, 'we commend the hint to our country friends, and hope to strengthen our appeal with this seasonable picture of "The May Queen".'[45]

The middle and upper classes took up the challenge by creating a widespread and uniform May Queen festival that often excluded or demoted the Jack-in-the-Green. Some were modest village affairs, while others were pageants attracting thousands. The May Queen Crowning at Rhyl, in Wales, organised by a large committee, was of the latter variety. The young Queen was chosen not only for her beauty and grace but also her ability to perform the song and dance aspects of her role on the day. Her dress was made of white satin and silk, with a train three and half yards long, and her coach was decked with an abundance of evergreen garlands. She had six maids-in-waiting, four pages, and a guard of honour. All the children who made up her court were taught a set of songs, dances, and drills. It was a huge affair for the town, though there were bitter complaints that townsfolk did not contribute to the occasion by decking their homes with flags and banners.[46] In 1906, a Dulwich schoolmaster named Joseph Deedy created a May Queen Register and put out a circular requesting May Queen organisers to provide him with information about their festivals. The returns for the following year reveal eighty-one entries, and this was certainly not a complete list.[47]

A lot of these new-style May Queen festivals disappeared after a few years or a couple of decades, but a small number have endured down to the present. One is the Bromley and Hayes Common May Queen festival, founded in 1906, which originally involved groups of 'Merrie England children'. In 1915, the child Queen was pulled around in a little cart by children dressed as fairies. There was Morris dancing, a maypole, and a display of archery by Robin Hood and his merry men. When folklorist George Long visited a couple of decades later, he described it as a 'truly delightful festival', and observed that the crowning ceremony was performed by the 'Prince of Merrie England', who was actually a pretty girl dressed as a boy, as in pantomime.[48] (Figure 2.3)

In South London during the 1870s and 1880s, the Revd George Nugee (1819–1892), who ran a mission among the poor of Walworth, also organised a grand 'Rose Queen' celebration for a number of years to crown the most industrious young working girl of good character. In 1878 it was held at Alexandra Palace, with a procession of three hundred children and an audience of two thousand.[49] Nugee was inspired by the French custom of 'La Rosière' that originally took place in the hamlet of Salency, in the French *département* of Oise. Here the villagers elected a chaste, marriageable girl every early May. On 8 June there was a procession to the chapel, where she was crowned with a wreath of roses by the parish priest, followed by a banquet. The custom was widely reported in eighteenth-century literature and subsequently adopted by numerous towns and villages across France over the following century. French folklorists speculated it was, in origin, a spring fertility rite.[50] Transposed

Figure 2.3 The May Queen procession at Knutsford, Cheshire. *Sir Benjamin Stone's Pictures: Records of National Life and History* (London, 1906), Vol. 1.

to the streets of Walworth, one local newspaper covering the 1886 event innocently observed, 'the old fashioned custom of crowning the Rose Queen is not quite dead in England yet'.[51]

A few years later, and presumably inspired by Nugee's events, similar large-scale crownings of a 'Rose Queen' spread across the towns of north-west England. One of the first was at Middleton to mark the ceremonial opening of a new park and recreation ground, while in 1899 a 'picturesque' Rose Queen crowning took place in the vicarage garden of the north Wales town of Conwy in aid of parochial schools.[52] In the early 2000s, dozens of young women were still being crowned, but the tradition has declined in recent years. One of the oldest ceremonies, at Lytham, founded in 1894, was back and proud in 2023 after a pandemic hiatus.[53]

During the twentieth century the responsibility for putting on more modest May Queen festivities was increasingly taken up by Sunday schools, primary schools, and the Girl Guides. The idea of a May King also emerged again, to give boys more of a role in the performances – a distant echo of the old London partnership. A 'Survey of May Rites in the Schools of Northamptonshire', conducted in 1958–1959, provides a snapshot of what had become of the May Queen. Thirty-two per cent of the 220 schools that responded said they celebrated May Day. Every one of them focused on the May Queen, and one in ten also elected a May King. A smaller Northamptonshire schools survey in 2000–2001, asking similar questions, found some significant further changes in terms of performance. This revealed a significant decline in the May Queen and the increased role of maypole dancing. A third of schools now had a May King.[54]

Revival

There are a range of defunct customs that have been revived, though often in new performative ways compared to their original recorded form. Since the 1970s we have seen the return of wassailing and the *Mari Lwyd*, for instance, but revivals have a much longer history.[55] An early example is the Dunmow Flitch, which was a curious custom that dated back to the late medieval period. It was basically a dole of a flitch or side of cured bacon, given to a male applicant who could prove that he had been married a year or more without ever regretting it, quarrelling with his wife, or pining for being single again. Before the Reformation the applicant's evidence was originally considered by the monks of Little Dunmow Priory, Essex. The applicant had to kneel on two sharp stones while testifying under oath, and, if he convinced the jury, he not only got the flitch but was carried around triumphantly in a large chair known as the Prior's Chair. The last such award was given in 1751 and the custom lapsed despite the occasional claim.

In mid-July 1851 it was fully revived by Lord and Lady Maynard of Easton Lodge estate, near Dunmow, who gave it the now familiar makeover. In their park, a flitch was ceremonially given to a local married couple, farmer William Hurrell and his wife, of Felstead. Three hundred school children were in attendance and the crowds were entertained with dancing and rural sports.[56] There was then a hiatus, and in spring 1854 a committee was set up to resurrect the custom in Dunmow town, in good part to help the local economy. It was decided to award the flitch to an Essex couple 'in the middle rank of society'. There was a rural fete, a procession through the streets, and a ball at the Town Hall in the evening. The organisers were given a major boost when the popular novelist William Harrison Ainsworth, whose novel *The Flitch of Bacon: Or, The Custom of Dunmow* (London 1854), had recently been published, agreed to appear and hand over the flitch to the winning couple. He also donated five guineas for the entertainments, while the proprietor of Drury Lane Theatre took on the organisation. Arrangements were made with Eastern Counties Railway to lay on extra trains. The event on 19 July 1855 garnered much national press coverage. A grand procession marched through the high street carrying the two successful couples. It stopped at the market cross, where, with drums and heralds, a public proclamation was made as to the jury's decision. The procession and the large crowd then moved on to a large pavilion where the couples swore an oath before receiving their flitches.[57]

A similar ceremony took place again in 1857, despite the opposition of local curmudgeons, but the following year it was taken over by the Dunmow Agricultural and Labourers' Friend Society and downgraded to a much more sober, po-faced event. A flitch was merely presented, among other prizes, to a labourer and his wife who had brought up the most children without having ever relied on parish relief. One newspaper described it sadly as 'the ghost of the Dunmow flitch'. Then, in August 1869, to much fanfare, the grand ceremony was revived once again by commercial stakeholders. Newspapers reported that an immense number of people gathered at Bishopsgate Station in London to take advantage of cheap excursion tickets for the event. The town had created great triumphal arches to welcome visitors, and there was a circus atmosphere with Punch and Judy shows, maypole dancing, military bands, and a fireworks display. Similar repeat events occurred periodically until 1913. The event was revived again in 1930.[58]

The early twentieth century also witnessed a revival of defunct beating the bounds ceremonies in some towns and cities. In Harpenden, Hertfordshire, in 1906, the Urban District Council, along with the fire brigade, organised the first beating for more than fifty years, culminating with a commemorative public dinner. At Ashburton, Devon, the beating of the bounds had not taken place since 1613 but was then revived by the authorities in 1895, and again in 1921. But the attempt to revive it in the Devon town of Bideford in 1921 led grumpy town council members to raise various objections. Alderman Metherell thought 'it seemed a useless trapesing around', while Alderman Pollard reckoned that it would lead to a 'drunken spree' and attract vagabonds.[59] Nevertheless, this wave of beatings, as with pageants, stemmed from attempts to create civic pride and renew community identity at a time of rapid social and physical urban development in provincial towns. And the same motives appear today in the current enthusiasm for beating the bounds in St Albans. It was briefly revived in 1913 with much pomp, and it thrives again in a now multicultural town. As the mayor said in 2024, 'Beating the Bounds is a wonderful, inclusive event, open to all the generations and I would urge people to join us.'[60]

Inclusivity

Participation in modern revivals brings us to issues of inclusivity. As we have seen with the Dunmow Flitch, there is a venerable precedent for encouraging the general public to attend local customs for the income they generate. In general, the impulse to exclude outsiders is rare, though the refrain of 'this is a local custom for local people', to paraphrase the sinister shopkeeper in the BBC comedy *The League of Gentlemen*, can be heard at times. Indeed, numerous revived folk performances owe their existence to people with no long-standing local connection. Some have started largely from scratch. One example is the Hinckley Bullockers, who performed their first Plough Monday play in 1987 after conducting archival research on traditions in the local area.[61]

Such revivals may be motivated by the idea of bringing back some colour and heritage to a place, but because there is often no living link or even memory of the tradition it also invites buy-in from non-locals who feel less like they are trespassing. The majority of members of the Hinckley Bullockers were not born-and-bred locals, and likewise a study of Molly Dance groups in East Anglia in the 1990s showed that members were composed of mostly middle-class people, many from places outside the villages associated with the performances. Around the same time, only one cast member of the Yorkshire Heptonstall Pace-Egg mumming play was born in the village.[62] With people living longer, there has been a growing pool of retirees investing time and energy into community building, whether it be heritage and museum volunteering, local history societies, parish councils, bell ringing, choirs, or reviving, organising, and performing customary traditions.

The issue of gender and traditional folk dance has its own troubled history. The early twentieth-century folk song and dance revival certainly led to a lot of valuable recording of folk performance, but in defining how traditional dance should be performed it hindered the opportunity for traditional grassroots innovation and equality. While country dancing – in other words, social dancing – was promoted as a healthy pursuit for females, the revival movement came to effectively shut out women from performances of official Morris dancing and mumming. This happened at a time when women performers were integral to carnivals, pageants, harvest festivals, Whitsun walks, and May Queen festivities.⁶³ Formal women's Morris groups began to appear only in the 1970s, and a Women's Morris Federation was established, though it dropped 'Women' from its title in 1982. Morris organisations slowly became open to mixed-sex dancing, with the Equality Act (2010) a major driver in changing institutional attitudes.⁶⁴ The resistance to women in Morris was due to concerns about maintaining authenticity, though the prevailing counter argument is that all such folk performances are living traditions that have changed over time, some traceable, others unknowable.

A similar clash between 'authenticity' and 'inclusive living tradition' was bound to occur over blackface performance. Padstow's 'Darkie Day' which, as the name suggests, is a mumming procession through the town at Christmastide in which the performers wear black face paint, was renamed 'Mummers Day' in 2005. The name change caused the usual complaints about 'being told what to do' by outsiders, political correctness gone mad, and attacks on Britishness/Englishness. During the twenty-first century, though, a number of revival Morris and mumming groups which had originally used blackface changed to using blue or green face paint instead. Indeed, the switch from blackface injected new inventiveness, with the likes of the Gog Magog Molly adopting a striking multicolour face decoration.⁶⁵ In 2020, the Joint Morris Organisation issued a press statement recognising that blackface could cause offence and should be phased out: 'Morris is a unique cultural tradition of which we should be rightly proud. We want people from all races and backgrounds to share in this pride and not be made to feel unwelcome or uncomfortable by any element of a performance.'⁶⁶

Religious, social, and ethnic inclusivity are common themes expressed by the organisers of revivals and recently invented folk festivals. It is the taking part or engagement with the event that is paramount. As one orchard wassail organiser explained, 'we try to be inclusive and neutral and draw in the parallels with all sorts of traditions so that we're not saying, "It is this." "It is a pagan ritual," or, "It is a Christian ritual".'⁶⁷ There is a rather liberating knowingness in the contemporary reimagining of custom, freed from expectations of authenticity and exclusivity. Another example is the recent Bradford on Avon Green Man Festival, the website for which in 2024 drew inspiration from the old folklore interpretations and embraced the fantasy: 'Jack has now evolved into a herald of Summer who must be summoned from his Winter slumber and paraded around to announce the onset of Spring before being ritually torn apart to ensure a good Summer. All completely made up but still good fun.'⁶⁸ Even with long-standing customs that have a recorded history, similar

Figure 2.4 Chinese New Year decorations in London's Chinatown. Unsplash.

imaginative inspiration is at play. Creativity and adaptability are the driving forces. The local community can embrace both change and the wider public on its own terms, as the Notting Hill Carnival, Chinatown New Year's celebrations (Figure 2.4), and the Padstow Obby Oss have admirably demonstrated over the years.

Part II

Stories

Chapter 3
Storytelling

What was the first story told in Britain? We cannot know, although we can say with confidence that it was told in some form or other before there was a 'Britain'. In prehistory, stories – as accounts of incidents or series of events – could have been shared as a way of communicating knowledge even before speech was developed, potentially via a form of gestural protolanguage. As human speech developed, so too could oral storytelling, although the jury is still very much out on when, within prehistory, this took place.[1] Potential evidence of visual narratives may be found in the Palaeolithic cave etchings of a deer and stylised human females or birds in Creswell Crags, on the Nottinghamshire and Derbyshire border – although we cannot know what stories were being told by this imagery. It would be millennia before we would reach a period in British history when stories were being recorded for posterity in written form.

Myth making and nation building

The earliest surviving literary legends we have in Britain show much influence from beyond British shores. The Old English epic poem *Beowulf*, potentially dating to the eighth century but certainly by the eleventh, survives in a single copy in a manuscript known as the Nowell Codex. In mostly West Saxon dialect, the poem provides over three thousand lines about the life and adventures of the Germanic hero Beowulf, from the slaying of the monster Grendel, descendant of the biblical Cain, to his final, fatal encounter with a dragon (the dragon who inspired Tolkien's Smaug).[2] The anonymous *Beowulf* poet set this legend in fifth- and sixth-century Scandinavia, but it remains unclear whether the hero Beowulf existed first in oral legendary tradition or whether the poet invented him. Likewise, it is unclear whether the poem was composed for performance or as a piece of literature. Either way, the poet drew on many Germanic motifs and mythical names in their composition of an Old English poem.

It was traditions of the Classical world that were drawn on in another piece of medieval literature: Geoffrey of Monmouth's *Historia Regum Britanniae*. Written by a Christian cleric in Monmouth, Wales, around 1136, this work provides a pseudohistory of the kings of Britain – but it begins in Italy. Aeneas, a mythical Trojan prince and the son of goddess Aphrodite in Homeric tradition, was adopted by the Latin writer Virgil in the first century BC as a founding ancestor of Rome, having come to Italy after the fall of Troy. Over a millennium later, Geoffrey of Monmouth extended this adoption by having Aeneas's descendant Brutus sail to Britain (then known as Albion), having been instructed by the goddess Diana.[3]

According to this pseudohistory, under Brutus's rule the remaining giants of Albion were slain, including Gogmagog; New Troy (Trinovantum) was built on the banks of the River Thames; and 'Brutus called the island after his own name Britain, and his companions Britons'.[4] The stage was set for a long line of heroic rulers, many of whom are detailed in the *Historia Regum Britanniae*. Arthur – 'whose heroic and wonderful actions have justly rendered his name famous to posterity' – is one of these rulers, shifting during this period from a fifth- or sixth-century chieftain of the Britons to a legendary hero.[5] Geoffrey of Monmouth narrates how, succeeding his father, Uther Pendragon, at the age of fifteen, Arthur was both a great king and a formidable warrior, wielding a sword made on the Isle of Avalon to unite the Britons against the Saxons and the Romans.

The *Historia Regum Britanniae* sits within a body of medieval literature associated with the legendary kings and heroes of Britain, known by mythographers as the 'Matter of Britain'. As with *Beowulf*, it remains unclear to what extent these literary sources adapted earlier oral storytelling traditions and to what extent they invented new material. It was likely a combination. Either way, this corpus of literature came at a time when Britain was a young nation of mixed heritage (Celtic, Anglo-Saxon, Roman, Norse) that turned to myth making to establish an ancient lineage, an independent sovereignty, and a sense of national identity.[6] Both Brutus and King Arthur were central to this, featuring in many pieces of medieval literature as the founder and unifier of Britain, respectively.

Arthur also appears in the *Mabinogion*, a collection of eleven Welsh tales compiled in the twelfth to thirteenth centuries and preserved in two manuscripts, the *White Book of Rhydderch* (c. 1350) and the *Red Book of Hergest* (c. 1400), and translated into English and edited in the nineteenth by English aristocrat Lady Charlotte Guest. The title *Mabinogion* is obscure, modern, and almost certainly the result of a scribal error, but it has come to refer to this corpus of Welsh tales. They are not a unified collection, however, varying in date, content, and style, and the jury remains out on the extent to which these stories formed part of an oral storytelling tradition, or whether they drew on various sources but were conceived as new, written compositions.[7] Some of the earliest of the tales are known as *The Four Branches of the Mabinogi*, which feature many narratives identified today as the Welsh myths, such as the story of Blodeuwedd, the woman made from flowers (considered later in this chapter).

Another of the earliest tales in the *Mabinogion*, *Culhwch and Olwen*, dated c. 1100, is also one of the earliest Arthurian prose tales to survive. Featuring many familiar folktale motifs, it is a bridal quest tale which sees the hero, Culhwch, cursed by his stepmother. Forced to find and marry Olwen, a giant's daughter, Culhwch seeks help in Celliwig, Cornwall, where his cousin Arthur holds court (Figure 3.1). Arthur arranges a great retinue of skilled warriors to accompany Culhwch, who must undertake a series of impossible tasks, including the hunting of a supernatural boar, to prove himself worthy of Olwen. It has been argued that the general themes of this corpus of tales would have been highly relevant to the Wales of its time: the Welsh uniting under one leader, the need for protection from outside forces, and the importance of alliances through marriage.

Translated into German (1841) and French (1842) soon after Guest's translation into English, these Welsh myths and tales became internationally known and were being used by Guest to argue that 'the Cymric nation ... has strong claims to be considered the cradle of European Romance'.[8] Guest, having married a Welsh industrialist and relocated to Wales, wrote in the dedicatory letter to *The Mabinogion* of wanting to pass down to her children the stories of their 'national heritage': 'May you become early imbued with the chivalric and exalted sense of honour, and the fervent patriotism for which its sons have ever been celebrated.'[9]

Scotland, too, looked to storytelling to connect with its national heritage. Following the Union with England in 1707 and the last, failed Jacobite rebellion in 1746, the Scottish literati sought to discover some lost corpus of legend which they could claim as their national epic.[10] It was James MacPherson, a Highlander from Inverness-shire, who provided it. In the 1760s, MacPherson claimed to have discovered ancient poems about Scotland's legendary past through interviewing storytellers in the Highlands and Western Isles. The

Figure 3.1 Culhwch entering King Arthur's court. Illustration from *The Boy's Mabinogion*, edited with an introduction by Sidney Lanier (New York, 1881).

poems, combined to make an epic of over nine thousand lines, and translated from Gaelic into English, told of the life, loves, and wars of Fingal, a Scottish hero of the third century AD, and of his son. It was apparently this son, a blind bard by the name of Ossian, who originally composed the epic. The direct parallels between many of the epic's characters and those from Irish mythology – Fingal and mythical Irish warrior Fionn mac Cumhaill, for example, and Ossian and legendary Irish bard Oisín – were, it was believed, a result of the close historical and cultural ties between Scotland and its neighbours across the sea.

Ossian introduces himself at the start of the epic as an old man reaching again for his harp after many years, glorifying the Scottish landscape as a source of inspiration:

> Lead me to yonder craggy steep. The murmur of the falling streams; the whistling winds rushing through the woods of my hills; the welcome rays of the bounteous sun, will soon awake the voice of song in my breast. The thoughts of former years glide over my soul like swift-shooting meteors o'er Ardven's gloomy vales.[11]

Members of the Edinburgh literati agreed they had made 'a precious discovery, and that as soon as possible it should be published to the world'.[12]

Figure 3.2 The Ossianic legends depicted within Ossian's Hall of Mirrors, Dunkeld, by Gwen and James Anderson. Photograph by Lorna M. Campbell.

Scotland had found in this poem its national epic; had found in Ossian its national bard. (Figure 3.2) And the poem would achieve worldwide recognition, being translated into German in 1764, then into French, Italian, Danish, and Swedish.[13]

The tale of Fingal also had its impact on the Scottish landscape. A sea cave on the uninhabited island of Staffa, in the Inner Hebrides, became known as Fingal's Cave during the eighteenth century. When Joseph Banks, the English naturalist and fellow voyager of Captain James Cook, visited the cave in 1772, his guide told him it was named after the Fingal of Ossian's works. Following Banks's visit, the cave became a tourist attraction, drawing such famous visitors as the composer Felix Mendelssohn (whose overture *The Hebrides* is also known as *Fingal's Cave Overture*), the poets Wordsworth, Keats, and Tennyson, the artist Turner, and Queen Victoria. In his diary, Banks wrote, 'How fortunate that in this cave we should meet with the remembrance of that chief, whose existence, as well as that of the whole Epic poem is almost doubted in England!'[14]

Banks's last point is significant. Despite the widespread acceptance of Ossian's epic, there was also broad scepticism about its 'authenticity'. Many believed that it was an English-language creation of MacPherson's, drawn from some Scottish Gaelic ballads but largely adapted from medieval Irish sources, transplanted into Scotland, put into a Homeric form, and given the sublime, melancholic tone so popular at the time.[15] There was much evidence against this poem having been translated *in toto* from a long-lost Gaelic epic preserved in the oral traditions of a few isolated storytellers. And yet MacPherson's poem was not only widely accepted but widely lauded. Why were people so ready to believe in its 'authenticity'? Because, suggests one historian, 'it provided, in instant form, everything that was most desired'.[16]

An English fairytale?

Many words have been spent defining and categorising the different types of stories we tell. Myths, fables, folktales, legends, fairytales: all are stories, but all are slightly different (although there is no unshakable consensus on where one genre ends and another begins). But let us consider fairytales. They are not tales about fairies. Granted, they are sometimes, but the presence of fairies in a narrative does not qualify it as a fairytale. In fact, the name of the genre has little to do with the content of a tale.[17] The narrative's age is also irrelevant; fairytales can be ancient, modern, and everything in between. Mode of delivery does not qualify a narrative as a fairytale, either. They can be spoken, sung, or written, and indeed it is difficult to distinguish between the different modes. Oral and written forms of storytelling are symbiotic, feeding into and off each other for so long that they are impossible to disentangle.[18] There is also no 'original' or 'authentic' version of a fairytale but, rather, myriad representations in many media forms of a vast network of narratives known as the 'fairy-tale web', to use a term coined by fairytale scholar Cristina Bacchilega.[19]

What does qualify a narrative as a fairytale, then? It is a matter of belief – or lack thereof. Unlike myths and legends, a fairytale is not meant to be believed. They are fantastical narratives, often set in other worlds, and while people may have believed in the creatures and magic that inhabited these narratives, the stories themselves are recognised as fictional by the people telling, writing, reading, and listening to them.

Unlike in Wales and Scotland, there were no great ancient English myth cycle, saga, archetypal epic, or collections of English fairytales as exercises in nationalism akin to that of the Grimms in Germany (see Chapter 13). Most English-language collections of fairytales drew on tales from other cultures. The immensely popular *Fairy Books* (1889–1913), written largely by Leonora

Blanche Alleyne but often attributed to her husband, Andrew Lang, contain over seven hundred fairytales compiled from various literary sources, but these were largely translated from French, German, Italian, and Russian, and adapted for a young, British readership.[20] They were not English fairytales. We do, however, have a historic, literary collection of fairytales and folktale motifs from the pen of a single writer, considered by many the national poet of England: William Shakespeare.

During the eighteenth century, nearly two hundred years after his time, Shakespeare was being dubbed 'the bard of all bards', his statue was being erected in Westminster Abbey, and the Shakespeare Jubilee of 1769 sparked what has been dubbed a cult of 'Bardolatry' for the Elizabethan playwright.[21] Among many other things, England's unofficial national poet was a prolific transmitter of fairytales.[22] His plays strongly recall fairytales in their plots, motifs, and characters, from the tests of love and the poor girls who marry princes to the fairy potions and the dead who come back to life. There are witches, prophecies, ghosts, good outlaws, and a wicked stepmother.[23] *The Tempest* has been described as 'a classic and early example of the fairy tale adapted to the stage'; *A Midsummer Night's Dream* as 'a veritable fairy tale from start to finish', featuring enchantments, quests for love, and the archetypal setting in a magical forest.[24]

The works of Shakespeare feature a flotilla of fairies, their various descriptions drawing on the different – sometimes contradictory – popular fairy beliefs of the period.[25] Titania and Oberon, the fairy queen and king, are human-sized, powerful beings, godlike (in a Classical sense) in their meddling with the lives and loves of mortals.[26] In contrast to their mistress, the fairy attendants of Titania are miniature beings who wear coats made of bat wings and can 'Creep into acorn-cups',[27] while the fairy midwife Queen Mab, described by Mercutio in *Romeo and Juliet*, is 'no bigger than an agate-stone ... Her waggoner a small grey-coated gnat ... Her chariot is an empty hazelnut'.[28] Most akin to the popular fairy beliefs of England recorded by folklorist Katharine Briggs (explored further below) are the descriptions of Oberon's servant, Puck, 'that shrewd and knavish sprite', who tricks and rewards as he sees fit.[29]

It is believed that most of the folkloric motifs in Shakespeare's works were adapted from established tales. This would have been an effective tactic on Shakespeare's part, appealing to his audience's familiarity with these motifs.[30] However, we do not know where he sourced the material for his fairytales, whether they were oral traditions he had heard and adapted for the stage, perhaps with surprising new literary twists, or whether they were his own inventions. The earliest reference we have of Herne the Hunter, the antlered ghost who haunts Windsor Forest, comes from Shakespeare's *The Merry Wives of Windsor* (1597), and we do not know to what extent Shakespeare repurposed a local legend or crafted one himself.

From folklore to fantasy fiction

Today, and throughout much of the twentieth century, most people's engagement with folktales comes from literary (and visual – see Chapter 11) rather than oral sources. This is partly because so many writers draw on folktale motifs, reworking them into pieces of what is now known as 'fantasy fiction'. Some works of British fantasy fiction are overt retellings, whereby authors have made use of readers' familiarity with particular narratives and tropes, and adapted them to time, place, and purpose.[31] Celtic tales have proven to be a hugely popular source of inspiration for this, particularly the Arthurian cycle, which has been described by one folklorist as a 'traditional quarry for modern fantasy writers'. The Arthurian cycle is so recognisable to people that it can be retold with the assumption that most readers will be familiar with setting and key characters.[32]

T. H. White's collection of fantasy novels published in 1938–1940 and republished as one volume, *The Once and Future King*, chronicles the life of Arthur and retells what White dubbed 'the major British Epic'.[33] White's retellings have been interpreted as an extended political allegory about power and war. The first of the novels, *The Sword in the Stone* (1938), has a young, illegitimate Arthur – known as Wart – learn about different political systems through animal transmogrification: the absolute monarchy of fish, the totalitarian communism of ants, the pacificism of geese. It is no coincidence that this was written during the interwar years, when a shell-shocked Britain was questioning its identity and role in the world.[34]

Alan Garner's *The Owl Service* (1967) is another retelling of a Celtic myth. Set in 1960s Wales, it is an adaptation of the story of the mythical Welsh woman Blodeuwedd, who was made from flowers, that features in *The Four Branches of the Mabinogi*, but enacted now by three contemporary teenagers. In 2009, the Welsh publisher Seren commissioned further retellings of tales from *The Mabinogion*.[35] In Seren's description of the series, 'ten great authors have taken the Celtic myth cycle as a starting point to give us masterly re-workings with a modern twist'.[36] Many of these reworkings can be viewed as social commentaries. *The Ninth Wave*, Russell Celyn Jones's retelling of the Mabinogion tale of Pwyll, prince of Dyfed and his marriage to Rhiannon and friendship with Arawn, lord of Annwn (the Otherworld), portrays a dystopian world in the not-too-distant future of depleted fossil fuels and endemic warfare.[37] And Lloyd Jones's *See How They Run*, which retells the tale of Manawydan, the son of Llŷr, and the enchantment that transforms the Welsh kingdom of Dyfed into a wasteland, contrasts England as a land of rich towns with Wales as a mist-shrouded, economically deprived rural land from which its population has mysteriously disappeared.[38] These are 'activist adaptations'.[39]

Gender is a significant lens through which fairytales have been viewed, retold, and politicised.[40] In the 1970s, English novelist Angela Carter reworked French, German, and Italian fairytales into feminist short stories, compiled in *The Bloody Chamber* (1979). In 'The Tiger's Bride', the tale of 'Beauty and the Beast' is subverted, with the heroine becoming a beast at the end, in celebration of otherness and sexual freedom.[41] Likewise in 'The Company of Wolves', a subversion of 'Little Red Riding Hood', when the wolf threatens to eat the girl, she laughs and proceeds to seduce him, the tale ending with the line 'See! sweet and sound she sleeps in granny's bed, between the paws of the tender wolf.'

Much fantasy fiction is not a direct retelling of a fairytale, but emulates the structure of one, particularly those designated 'wonder tales' by the structural folktale theorist Vladimir Propp.[42] Such wonder tales tend to follow a hero leaving home, facing an opponent, overcoming difficult tasks, and being ultimately rewarded with love or riches,[43] as in the many quests undertaken by Arthurian knights, for example. The *Bildungsroman* or 'coming-of-age' story is a subgenre of the wonder tale, focusing on the moral growth of the protagonist as they undertake such a journey. This structure is popular with readers because of its familiarity, but authors – readers themselves, and also accustomed to the 'cultural script' of wonder tales – may even follow it subconsciously.

Most fantasy fiction draws on well-known folktale motifs but threads them together in new narratives. We see this in what are often considered the first literary pieces designated fantasy: John Ruskin's *The King of the Golden River* (1841) and George MacDonald's *The Princess and the Goblin* (1872). We see it in works where the magical or supernatural intrudes into our own world (sometimes referred to as 'low fantasy', which contains various subgenres: urban fantasy, dark fantasy, magical realism, paranormal romance). In such fiction, folktale motifs interrupt everyday lives, thrusting the narrative into the realm of the fantastical. This is what happens in Alan Garner's Alderley Edge books, starting with *The Weirdstone of Brisingamen* (1960), and in Susan Cooper's *The Dark is*

Rising Sequence (1965–1977), to name only a couple. Tropes and characters from myth and fairytale, both national and local, force the main characters – British children living otherwise ordinary lives – into quest motifs and their own *Bildungsroman*. Likewise in J. K. Rowling's *Harry Potter* series (1997–2007), wizards, witches, and a host of magical creatures from folklore turn a set of books that begin in a suburban town in Surrey into an epic fantasy in which a young boy not only discovers that he has magical powers but that he has been prophesised to save the world from a powerful villain.

Within these works of fantasy fiction, we encounter many familiar folktale motifs, as identified within *The Motif-Index of Folk-Literature*, a six-volume catalogue of (mostly European) motifs composed by American folklorist Stith Thompson in the 1930s.[44] Each motif identified by Thompson, each recurring granular element of a folktale, was given a classification number. This identifier consists of a letter categorising a broad topic, such as 'Animals' (B), then a number indicating a more specific subcategory, such as 'Dragon' (B11), and then decimal numbers giving the motif even further granularity: 'Breath of dragon kills man' (B11.2.11.2). Although there has been some criticism of Thompson's *Motif-Index*, ranging from its Eurocentric focus to its gender biases,[45] it remains a valuable tool for folklorists today seeking to analyse and compare folktales. Thompson's revised and expanded *Motif-Index* (1955–1958) contains over forty-five thousand motifs.

Rowling, who stated in a 2005 press conference, 'I have always been interested in folklore', draws on these motifs overtly and profusely.[46] For example, among many other creatures found in Thompson's *Motif-Index*, Harry Potter encounters dragons (B11), a basilisk (B12), centaurs (B21), a phoenix (B32), hippogriffs (B42.1), destructive pixies (F360), and shrieking mandrakes (F992.1).[47] Harry Potter also finds himself in many of the environments designated as folk motifs: a forbidden forest (C612), underground passages (F721.1), dungeons (R41.3), and captivity under water (R46). To overcome the many challenges he faces, Harry receives magical knowledge from the dead (D1810.13), help from witches (G284) and giants (N812), and wisdom from teachers (J152), has recourse to magical transportation (D2120), and draws on myriad folkloric tools: a wand (D1254.1), a flying broomstick (G242.1), a cloak of invisibility (D1361.12), a magic sword (D1081), a magic plant (D965), and many other items received from witches and wizards (D812.6).

Folktale motifs have long been drawn on to create new ('secondary') worlds: Lewis Carroll's Wonderland, C. S. Lewis's Narnia, Terry Pratchett's Discworld,

Philip Pullman's alternate Oxford. They increase the accessibility of these worlds – thereby increasing believability and the reader's investment.[48] Because so much fantasy literature traces a protagonist's literal journey – a central element of the wonder tale and quest motif – secondary worlds need believable landscapes and, to be further stabilised, convincing maps. British cartographic fantasy has a long history dating back to the sixteenth-century maps of Thomas More's island, Utopia. Maps add depth and detail, fostering understanding of the world and 'weighing it down'.[49]

For British fantasy, the British landscape – the 'ancestral ground' – is often drawn on as foundation for maps and descriptions of the secondary world, much more so than in American fantasy.[50] Garner's *The Weirdstone of Brisingamen* (1960), for example, is anchored narratively within the Cheshire countryside, at the iconic red sandstone escarpment of Alderley Edge and the labyrinth of copper mines beneath, where the young protagonists encounter dwarves and goblins.[51] Fantasy author Susan Cooper writes of Garner that 'the myth that he makes is carved out of the land to which he belongs, the land from which he and his people came, the land in which he lives ... He is above all a writer of place'. Neil Gaiman opined that in Garner's books 'the landscape of Alderley Edge is the strongest character'.[52] But writers have a history of presenting a biased perspective of landscape, drawing on the features that fit their literary vision and ignoring the rest. Garner does not, for example, mention the pharmaceutical laboratories that had been on the outskirts of Alderley since 1950.[53]

The most prolific world creator was Tolkien, who, through his *legendarium* (his poems, *The Hobbit, Lord of the Rings, The Silmarillion*), created the world of Arda, and within that, Middle-earth. Tolkien drew on real place names in his map of Middle-earth. Tolkien's Northfarthing has a Nobottle, just as Northamptonshire does; Tolkien's Buckland has a Newbury, just as Berkshire does – and Oxfordshire has a Buckland, too.[54] Many sites across England have been claimed as inspiration for places in Middle-earth, some with Tolkien's acknowledgement (Cheddar Gorge as inspiration for Helm's Deep) and others without (The Bell Inn, Moreton-in-Marsh, as the original Inn of the Prancing Pony).[55] Certainly Tolkien cast the Shire, a metaphor for home, as an old-fashioned, idyllic, rural England.[56] Scholars generally agree that Tolkien was striving to create that previously lacking 'mythology for England'.[57] Not finding it in historic texts, he created one, drawing on Celtic mythology, Christian theology, and sources such as *Beowulf* (from which his dragon Smaug was inspired), the *Gawain* poet, and Thomas Malory's chronicle of the Arthurian legend. But the folkloric influences on Tolkien's work were far from exclusively English.

Tolkien drew widely on medieval myth and legend in his *legendarium*. He drew on Finnish in his creation of the Elvish language, and took elements from Elias Lönnrot's Finnish epic *Kalevala*, incorporating them into his characters Tom Bombadil and Treebeard. He found much inspiration in Old Norse mythology, such as equating the End of the Third Age with Ragnarök. The names of his dwarves were lifted verbatim from the *Dvergatal*, a section of the Old Norse poem *Völuspá*.[58] And he admitted in personal correspondence that his racialised, corrupted orcs owe 'a good deal to the goblin tradition' of Scottish writer MacDonald's *The Princess and the Goblin* (1872).[59] Perhaps he did strive to create a 'mythology for England', but his influences have been described as decidedly 'cross-cultural'.[60]

Chapter 4
Legends

> I took great delight in riding and rambling about the neighbourhood, studying out the traces of merry Sherwood Forest, and visiting the haunts of Robin Hood ... there is scarce a hill or dale, a cliff or cavern, a wall or fountain, in this part of the country, that is not connected with his memory ... I took a kind of schoolboy delight in hunting up all traces of old Sherwood and its sylvan chivalry.[1]

The above passage is from Washington Irving's 1835 book, *Abbotsford and Newstead Abbey*, which recounts Irving's nineteenth-century travels in England. The American author (well known for penning *The Legend of Sleepy Hollow*) was a fervent fan of Robin Hood, describing a collection of ballads about the outlaw as 'One of the earliest books that captivated my fancy when a child'.[2] While in England, he was therefore eager to visit Sherwood Forest. On his tour, he was shown an artificial cavern known as Friar Tuck's cell, a small cave reputed to be 'Robin Hood's stable', and a niche in some crags 'called Robin Hood's chair ... here the bold outlaw is said to have taken his seat, and kept a look-out upon the roads below'. 'As I gazed about me upon these vestiges of once "Merrie Sherwood,"' Irving wrote, 'the picturings of my boyish fancy began to rise in my mind, and Robin Hood and his men to stand before me.'[3]

Irving here is an American 'fanboying' over a British legend. The story of Robin Hood is classed as a 'legend' as opposed to a 'fairytale' because it is *possibly* true; it is often told as historical fact but its truth is ambiguous.[4] Jacob Grimm made the distinction between legends and fairytales in his 1844 *Teutonic Mythology*: 'The Fairy-tale flies, the legend walks, knocks at your door; the one can draw freely out of the fullness of poetry, the other has almost the authority of history.'[5] Stories of the folk-hero outlaw Robin Hood are legends because they are anchored in time, linked to real places (Loxley, Sherwood Forest, Nottingham), and feature historical figures, such as King John. Whether the events and characters that such tales narrate are *really true* is not important; it is their believability, the sense of possibility, that makes them legends.[6] And, as we shall see in this chapter, the forms British legends can take are many and varied.

'Precious treasures of oral literature'

As demonstrated in the previous chapter, many of Britain's literary tales are adaptations of oral storytelling traditions – or at least draw heavily on their motifs.[7] Such historic oral storytellers were dubbed the 'active bearers' of tradition by the Swedish folklorist Carl Wilhelm von Sydow.[8] The nature, status, and names of these storytellers varied by period and region. In Wales, such professional storytellers were known as *cyfarwyddiaid* (singular *cyfarwydd*).[9] In Gaelic Scotland, the term was *seanchaidh*; in Manx, *shennaghee*. In Cornwall, professional storytellers were known as droll tellers, a nineteenth-century term using the French word *droll*, referring to both a quip and a witty person.[10] Nineteenth-century Cornish folklore collector William Bottrell recorded the folktales of Cornwall as told by many droll tellers, noting their propensity for 'embellishments', adapting well-known tales to time, place, preference, and the droll teller's individual imagination. For instance, Bottrell recounted a tale of a giant's castle told by 'an old tinner' who took four winter's evenings to recount the tale because he would 'indulge himself in glowing descriptions of the tin and other treasures found in the giant's castle'.[11]

With no oral records from these earlier periods, we rely on written texts – such as those listed in the preceding section – to glean glimpses of the themes, motifs, plots, and characters of the oral traditions.[12] We also rely on the early folklore collectors of the nineteenth and twentieth centuries, such as Bottrell. In a lot of these cases, the desire to collect stories was motivated by concern that Britain was losing its oral traditions. In 1947, for example, the Folklore Institute of Scotland was established, akin to the Irish Folklore Commission, sparked by an urgent need for collecting the oral traditions of Gaelic Scotland: 'Too much time has passed already, and every day adds to our loss. Let us make haste in the matter,' came the call in *An Gàidheal*, the magazine of Scottish organisation An Comunn Gàidhealach.[13] Stories were collected and recorded by members of the Institute, one of whom was the Revd Thomas Murchison. In Murchison's editorial for the 1947 issue of *An Gàidheal*, he wrote of the recent deaths of three 'tradition-bearers' in Scotland's

Outer Isles, 'each one of them carrying to the silence of the grave a precious treasure of oral literature'.[14]

In the preceding century, the need for collecting had likewise been stressed by the Folklore Society. In 1892 the Society established the *County Folk-Lore Series*, with the aim of setting up local committees in the various counties of Britain who would collect oral folktales and legends. The oral material would then be reproduced in written form for the series.[15] In his 1890 *Handbook of Folklore*, Laurence Gomme, later president of the Society, had already outlined the challenges and provided guidance to his readers – potential folklorists in the field – on the collection of oral tales:

> It is a common experience of collectors that persons who may really be brimming over with the most curious and interesting tales will persistently deny that they know any; and it is difficult to overcome their reluctance to tell them; even after long periods of friendly intimacy. Patience and geniality are the only means ... Care should be used in taking down the stories in the very words of the teller. Stories altered, or improved, into literary form are deteriorated in scientific value ...[16]

John Francis Campbell, folklore collector from the Scottish island of Islay, stressed that 'stories orally collected can only be valuable if given unaltered'.[17] From 1859, Campbell had travelled extensively throughout the Western Highlands, collecting stories orally from 'the tellers of old stories', often in Gaelic, alongside recruiting other collectors.[18] Recording the names of myriad storytellers along with their occupations, Campbell published tales of heroes, fairies, and giants. Various versions of 'The Sea-Maiden' are given, as told him by fishermen, a farm servant, and a labourer, in which a mermaid promises an old fisherman bountiful fish in exchange for his son.

Folktale collections from Scotland are awash with sea-maidens and selkies. In 1884, the story of the selkie-bride was recorded by a Captain Clark Kennedy, told by his skipper 'old John' Heddle as they toured the coast of Hoy Island in Orkney. Upon seeing seals in a nearby sea cave, John offered the following:

> Selkies, ye ken of *course*, so I need hardly tell you *that*, have a quaint, and maybe curious, habit of coming to land on a particular day, at a stated time, once in every seven years ... should anybody discover the skin of that selkie while it is in its human form, the person so doing becomes at once, and for ever, the master of that seal ...[19]

John went on to tell the legend of when Alick, a fisherman friend of his grandfather, found a selkie skin and hid it when a beautiful naked woman appeared in his home, lamenting her loss. According to John, within a few days Alick had 'woo'd an' won her, and married her at the kirk over in Stromness, all right, an' accordin' to Scripture'.[20] As many versions of this tale tell, the selkie usually manages to retrieve her seal-skin and return to the sea, leaving her husband – and sometimes children – behind.

Although selkies are largely associated with Scotland, particularly the islands, there are several motifs in the selkie-bride tale that crop up frequently elsewhere in Britain. We find the motifs of the supernatural bride, the magic wife, and the lost wife, for example, in many Welsh tales. One of the best-known relates the marriage of the Lady of Llyn y Fan Fach (a mountain lake in the Brecon Beacons) with the only son of a widow. The Lady, sometimes described as a fairy-bride, stipulated certain taboos for her husband. Many years and three children later, the husband unwittingly broke the taboos, and the Lady disappeared back into the lake. According to the Revd John Williams in his introduction to *The Physicians of Myddvai* (*Meddygon Myddfai*), although the Lady would never return to her husband, she occasionally visited her three children to teach them the magical properties of plants. These children would become the founders of the Physicians of Myddfai, a long line of renowned, historical physicians in Carmarthenshire. The legend, combining fairytale motifs with local history, was apparently recorded from the oral testimony of three elderly residents of Myddfai in 1841.[21]

A similar legend of a Cornish mermaid ('here by us pronounced meremaid') was told by Bottrell, who recorded it from a droll teller known as 'uncle Anthony', a 'venerable wanderer'.[22] In uncle Anthony's 'Droll of the Meremaid', fairytale motifs are again combined with local history. Hundreds of years ago, the legend begins, a man named Lutey lived in the village of Cury on the Lizard Peninsula, where he would often search the sand for treasure washed ashore, but with no luck – until the day he met a meremaid. Golden haired and fish tailed, she sat on a rock, wailing piteously. When Lutey asked why she grieved, she explained that she had become stranded on the sands while searching for her husband's supper. In the absence of supper, her husband would eat their children. Lutey helped her back to the sea and, for the service, she granted him three wishes. Lutey wished for 'the power to do good to my neighbours – first that I may be able to break the spells of witchcraft; secondly that I may have such power over familiar spirits as to compel them to inform me of all I desire to know for the benefit of others; thirdly, that these good gifts may continue in my family for ever'.[23] And this wish, granted, is the reason why his descendants became known as the historical 'white witches of Cury', able to magically help people and remove bewitchments.[24] But there was a price for this hereditary gift – Lutey was eventually forced to join the meremaid beneath the waves, and so too do his descendants. Once every nine years, it is said, one of them is taken by the sea.

The motif of the dangerous mermaid who promises boons with one hand and drowning with the other is widespread. Caribbean folktales, related by immigrants to Britain of the Windrush generation, have been recorded by folklorist Wendy Shearer. 'Wherever we go,' Shearer asserts, 'the stories go too.'[25] These tales include 'The Fairymaid's Lover', recounted by a storyteller originally from Trinidad, now living in Britain. It tells of a fisherman 'bewitched' by a mermaid (or 'fairymaid'), at first beautiful and then 'grotesque', who haunts his dreams and lures him beneath the waves with promises of treasure.[26] As communities migrate, so too do their mermaids.

The migrating fairy

'I will tell you of some of the pranks of this very Boggart, and how he teased and tormented a good farmer's family in a house hard by, and I assure you it was a very worthy old lady who told me the story ...' So begins the legend of the boggart of Boggart Hole Clough, a woodland clough in the village of Blackley, which first appeared in print in John Roby's 1829 *Traditions of Lancashire*. Lancashire-born Roby was a local writer, and in his work on the tales and customs of his home county he recounted a story concerning a farmer from Blackley, George Cheetham, whose farmhouse was haunted by a boggart. This boggart, a 'strange elf ... sly and mischievous', torments Cheetham's family with pranks, from snatching the children's bread and butter and dashing their milk to the ground, to making loud noises throughout the night. 'Sometimes, however, he would behave himself kindly,' Roby tells us; the boggart might churn the cream for the family or scour the pans.[27]

Just as the British landscape contains myriad supernatural creatures (as we will see in Chapter 7), the domestic space too can be shared with supernatural inhabitants – some, welcome housemates; others, unwanted squatters. Thompson categorised these domestic occupants as 'House-spirits' in his *Motif-Index* (F480),[28] while the prolific collector of fairy lore, Katharine Briggs, classified them as 'Tutelary Fairies': 'those attached to certain families or houses'.[29] These supernatural beings will treat the household well, often helping with chores and even acting as guardians, so long as they are treated well themselves. Briggs applied 'brownie' and 'hobgoblin' as catch-all terms for these domestic fairies, but in her many publications on the topic, extensive regional variations are detailed: the Scottish bauchan, the Welsh bwbachod, the Yorkshire and Lancashire dobby, the Orkney luridan, and Billy Blind of the ballads.[30] In 1957, Briggs recalled a story of a tutelary fairy she had heard from a friend who had grown up in Northumberland in the 1890s:

> [H]er mother used to take her to call on some old ladies who lived at Denton Hall near Newcastle. These old ladies would often tell them of the silkie they had in the house. The silkie is the Northumbrian brownie. The old ladies were very fond of their silkie. It is true that she made it rather difficult to keep servants, but if they were in a strait she would do all sorts of kind things to help them, particularly cleaning grates and laying fires ready to light. They often said that they did not know how they would manage without her ...[31]

But the favour of domestic fairies, Briggs warned, can be precarious.[32] When the old ladies died some years later, a new family moved in – who were not, Briggs's friend informed her, 'the kind of people to get on with fairies'. Finding that they did not respect her, the silkie turned malevolent. Tormenting the family's son with noises through the night, she drove the family from the house. Briggs refers to this transformation as a brownie becoming a boggart, described as 'a mischievous brownie, almost exactly like a poltergeist in his habits'.[33] This fits with Roby's boggart, who lived in the farmhouse in Boggart Hole Clough, Lancashire. But it was not so much the farmhouse he was attached to but, rather, the family.

So tired of the boggart's pranks, Roby tells us, the farmer Cheetham moved his family out of the farmhouse. But as they drove down the road with their furniture packed onto a cart, a neighbour asked if they were leaving. Suddenly 'a shrill voice from a deep upright churn, the topmost utensil on the cart, called out – "Ay, ay, neighbour, we're flitting [i.e. moving house]"'. Realising that the boggart would 'flit' with them wherever they went, Cheetham turned the cart around and returned home. It is the tale of this boggart, according to Roby, which gifted Boggart Hole Clough with its 'oddest of Lancashire names'.[34] Although this appears, at first glance, to be a local legend supplied by 'a very worthy old lady', presumed to be a resident of Blackley, this was not the case. It was in fact, by Roby's admission, pioneering Irish folklorist Thomas Crofton Croker who provided this story, having four years earlier recounted a similar tale, in his *Fairy Legends*, of a large house in Ballinascarthy, County Cork, haunted by a small, mischievous, gnomish creature known as the Cluricaune Naggeneen. Mr MacCarthy, the owner of the house, so exasperated by the Cluricaune's pranks, declares that he is moving – until he realises that the Cluricaune plans to move with him.[35]

Soon after Croker published this tale in 1825, a woman from Yorkshire, having read Croker's version and recognising traits similar to a Yorkshire tradition she herself was familiar with, contributed her own tale to the *Literary Gazette*, 16 April 1825: 'Indeed I am acquainted with the identical farm-house where the mischievous goblin … dislodged by its pranks a farmer and his family.'[36] This tale of a mischievous fairy or spirit so attached to a family that it will move with them from one home to another proves to be almost identical to Roby's account. Indeed, it features in many other local tales. In Scotland, it was a trow who stowed away on the back of the family's cart, remarking that it was a 'grand day for the flitting'.[37]

Unsurprisingly, Thompson identified this as a recurring motif:

> *Farmer is so bothered by brownie that he decides he must move to get rid of the annoyance.* He piles all furniture on wagon and starts for new home, meets acquaintance who remarks: 'I see you're flitting [i.e. moving house].' Brownie sticks his head out of the churn on top of the load, answers: 'Yes, we're flitting.' Farmer goes back to former home. England, Ireland, Wales (F82.3.1.1).[38]

In some cases, the domestic fairy or spirit emigrates overseas with their human family. A nineteenth-century Scottish tale tells of how Callum, a farmer in Lochabar who was haunted by a bauchan, emigrated to the United States. Callum 'was the first man to jump on shore. Directly his feet touched the ground, who should meet him … but the Bauchan.'[39]

What we have in these examples is not only tales of migrating fairies, but migrating tales, of the kind catalogued by Norwegian folklorist Reidar Christiansen in 1958.[40] These are stories and motifs that are repurposed and adapted for new locations. However, as we have seen throughout this and the preceding chapter, all folktales are migratory, or at least contain migratory motifs. It is in the nature of folklore to travel. Every time a storyteller told their tale to a different audience, the tale travelled – embellished, perhaps, or adapted to a different time and place, but retaining the central motifs.

Urban legends

The following legend was recounted by English writer Edith Romanes in her 1918 autobiography, *The Story of an English Sister*:

At one of our luncheon parties, Lord Halifax told us the following story. Two ladies (I think he knew them) had been hunting somewhere in Lincolnshire, and after the run they gave their horses to a groom and hired a gig. Presently they got to a bridge and saw a man looking very tired, so they either offered him a lift or he asked for one. Presently they came to an inn, and without any thanks he got off the back seat and made his way into the inn, round which a small crowd had gathered. The landlord came out to them, and as he came out the man brushed close past him. So they, a little vexed at the man's want of manners, asked who he was. The landlord said he had seen no one. 'Oh yes,' they said 'you must have seen him,' and they began to describe the man. The landlord looked very puzzled and said: 'Please will you come into the house a minute?' So they went into the inn, and the landlord took them into a room where on the bed lay the man they had seen – dead. 'This is the body of a man who was drowned,' said the landlord. 'His body has just been found, and we are awaiting the coroner.'[41]

This is an example of an 'urban legend'. Many readers will have heard of or used this term. It was first coined by American academics and was made popular by the American folklorist Jan Harold Brunvand in numerous publications from the 1980s onward, particularly his book *The Vanishing Hitchhiker* (referring to a popular trope, of which Romanes's account is an example). Brunvand defined them in simple terms as 'all those bizarre, whimsical, 99 per cent apocryphal, yet believable stories that are "too good to be true"'.[42] Believability is a key factor, and stories are usually framed by a rhetorical device, which the English folklorist Rodney Dale called the Friend of a Friend, whereby the story is made plausible because it was apparently passed on through a chain of unnamed acquaintances (Romanes's 'Two ladies (I think he knew them) …') – just as with a rumour; and, indeed, the term 'rumour legend' was briefly in vogue in the 1980s as well.

They were called 'urban' because their source environment was considered to be large, dense communities where oral rumours could spread quickly from street to street – or 'virally' as is commonly said now. But the term had its critics. These types of stories could be found in villages as well as cities (as we saw from Romanes's example) and, regarding orality – well, newspapers had been spreading such legends going back to the nineteenth century. An alternative term was coined in Britain for the same type of story, namely 'contemporary legend', and, soon after, the International Society for Contemporary Legend Research was founded. But this term, in turn, soon attracted its own criticism: such legends could be found back in history. Researchers went searching for them, finding them in newspapers, ballads, and other literary sources, such as in Charles Dickens's *Pickwick Papers*.[43] So, what was contemporary about them?

To counter the criticism regarding the 'contemporary' nature of contemporary legends it was argued that it was the issues central to the story that were of recent date and not the narrative framework; and besides, the tellers of such legends also emphasised the recentness of the events, rather than merely retelling a stale old tale.[44] A good example of this concerns food adulteration. Stories of human body parts or bits of animals being put in food for public consumption have long circulated in many cultures, and with the rise of Indian and Chinese restaurants in Britain in the 1960s it was inevitable that new contemporary legends would circulate in relation to high street ethnic food. In the early 1970s several folklorists reported the circulation of a story about someone recently taken to hospital after falling sick from eating in a Chinese restaurant and a rat's bone being found in their throat. Rodney Dale recalled hearing a story in three northern English towns where an Indian restaurant had recently been found to have Alsatian dog carcasses in the freezer: 'the public health people tried to prosecute, but the restaurant was offering "meat", and Alsatian is "meat", so they got away with it'.[45]

Contemporary legends are usually migratory, adaptable to different languages and cultures, but the long build-up to the Brexit vote in 2016 led to country-specific contemporary legends or 'euro myths', with the British newspapers playing a significant role in spreading what was, essentially, misinformation. Spurious press stories of how the 'crazy Eurocrats' were banning this and that soon circulated orally, anecdotally picked up from conversations with the likes of barbers and taxi drivers. Tied with this were other examples of 'destructive storytelling' regarding 'political correctness gone mad'. On an X/Twitter thread concerning 'monkey blood', the north-east English term for the red syrup poured on ice creams from ice cream vans, a poster related how 'in the 90s the ice cream man in Hexham always said you couldn't call it that anymore cos of the EU'.[46]

Despite the kerfuffle over terminology, it was the term 'urban legend' that became cemented firmly in popular culture. When Brunvand reflected on the cultural impact of the concept of urban legends in 2004, comparing the situation with that in the 1980s, he observed the huge influence of 'popularization, commercialization, and stereotyping' in the visual media, and noted the decline of orally transmitted urban legends, in contrast to their increasing creation and dissemination via the emergent internet.[47]

'Flying purple people eater ... or the chupacabra grew wings'

In October 2024, British newspapers ran a story about a mysterious creature spotted at Bristol Zoo. The four-legged creature caught on a night vision camera looks like a deer – except for what appear to be wings and a single horn. Rosie Sims, public engagement manager at Bristol Zoo Project, was quoted as saying: 'The sighting of this mythical-like creature is a mystery to us here at Bristol Zoo Project ... Scotland has the Loch Ness monster and Cornwall has the Beast of Bodmin Moor – have we discovered a similar mythical here in Bristol perhaps?'[48] This story exemplifies the cryptid legend. The animal photographed is a cryptid because it does not appear to belong to a species confirmed by contemporary science; it is a 'hidden creature'. As reported in a Bristol newspaper, 'the experts say the creature ... is like nothing they have spotted before'.[49] Scientist Bernard Heuvelmans, dubbed the 'Father of Cryptozoology', stated that to be counted as a cryptid, a creature must have at least one trait 'truly singular, unexpected, paradoxical, striking, emotionally upsetting, and thus capable of mythification'.[50]

The Bristol Zoo story exemplifies the cryptid legend also through its incorporation of personal memorates. Memorates are narratives about personal experiences, often told by somebody who purported to have encountered the supernatural or the unexplained.[51] 'There had been reports over the last few weeks,' the Bristol newspaper noted, 'of something unusual lurking between the trees, turning the heads of not just the staff, but also the animals that live there.'[52] It is implied here that the staff had narrated memorates of their own, of having seen or sensed something 'lurking between the trees'. In this case, we are not treated to the individual accounts, but, as we will see below, the personal memorate is a common feature of cryptid legend reporting.

The Bristol creature also fits within the cryptid legend trope because of its rapid dissemination, the enthusiastic elaborations it engendered, and the contested narrative surrounding it. Responses to Bristol Zoo's posting of the photograph on social media ranged from outright, even angry, scepticism (with observations made that the release of the image coincided with the launch of their Halloween trail, themed 'Myths and Legends') and rationalisations, to curiosity and playful explanations. 'It's a freaking baby UNICORN!' one commenter declared. 'Everybody knows that the babies have wings and can fly to the tree tops to avoid predators. I have seen them many times in the dark and mysterious forest behind my castle!' Another proclaimed it 'Pegasus', while other suggestions included 'a relative of the Jersey Devil', 'a baby dragon of course!' and 'Flying purple people eater ... or the chupacabra grew wings'.[53]

Cryptozoology is predicated on the belief that there are still isolated parts of the world where there may be animals unknown to science. Britain may not boast the same vast tracts of wilderness as North America (the cryptid world capital), but there are deep lakes, thick forests, and expansive moorlands – environments as rich with cryptid potential as they are with folklore.[54] The Folklore Society has informally been monitoring sightings of cryptids, reporting them in their newsletter (*FLS News*) since the 1990s. In 2003, Society member Gail-Nina Anderson reported sightings of Bigfoot – not in America's Pacific Northwest, but in Sussex, Lancashire, Staffordshire, and Northumberland. Anderson recounted that she was 'privileged to accompany a team of Fortean investigators tramping and squelching through the icy mud [of Bolam Lake Country Park in Northumberland]. A wisp of fur was gathered for analysis, and a dodgy footprint seen melting in the snow ... if it's a chap in a gorilla suit, I applaud his dedication in risking hypothermia.'[55] By the next issue of the newsletter, however, another Society member penned, 'I am assured, by someone who has spoken to the people involved, that the "Bigfoot" reports from Bolam Lake Country Park were nothing more than a student prank that got out of control.'[56] The supposed prank had perhaps been inspired by the media coverage of the death of Californian Ray Wallace in late 2002 and the subsequent revelation by his family that he had instigated the Bigfoot hoax in the 1950s and 1960s.[57]

The jury is still out, however, on many of Britain's cryptids. Sightings of large cats have been commonly reported; their species are not unconfirmed by science, but certainly not endemic to Britain, giving them the name 'alien big cats'. These are a subcategory of the widespread 'Out-of-Place Animal' story.[58] One sighting of an alien big cat dates back to the eighteenth century, when writer and political reformer William Cobbett was a boy. In Cobbett's book *Rural Rides*, which traces his journeys across the rural areas of Britain, he recounted an experience he had had at Waverley Abbey, Surrey. There was, he wrote, 'an old elm tree, which was hollow even then, into which I, when a very little boy, once saw a cat go, that was as big as a middle-sized spaniel dog, for relating which I got a great scolding, for standing to which I, at last, got a beating; but stand to which I still did. I have since many times repeated it; and I would take my oath of it to this day.'[59]

The second half of the twentieth century witnessed countless alien big cat sightings across Britain, most often in rural areas – the vast open moorland of Exmoor in Somerset and Devon, for instance, within which a large black cat has been sighted frequently. However, sightings are also reported in urban areas. In 1963, reports were made of a large cat in Shooters Hill, south-east London, which led to a hunting search party of over one hundred police, police dogs, soldiers, RSPCA officials, and schoolchildren. No cheetah was ever found, but those in the search party certainly seemed to enjoy it. The hunt, reported one newspaper, was 'a great day out' for the schoolchildren, while troops at the Royal Artillery barracks nearby decided that 'The Great Safari in S.E.18' was 'better than sitting in a barrack room'.[60] The common theory was that these various large cats had been imported into the country as exotic pets and then either had been let loose or had escaped. Blame was laid at their paws for the death of livestock.

Given enough sightings, the large cat gains a toponymic title and thereby a local identity: the Beast of Exmoor, the Beast of Bodmin, the Beast of Margam, the Thorganby Lioness, the Surrey Puma, the Fobbing Puma, the Beast of Pewsey Vale, the Shooters Hill Cheetah.[61] While alien big cat sightings are not exclusive to Britain, the country does appear to have a particular affinity for them – perhaps because, since the extinction of the British wolf, the island's largest native carnivore is the badger, and so the notion of a dangerous predator hidden on the moors, in the woods, the hills, or indeed the streets of London, is especially thrilling.[62] Another suggestion is the potent politicisation of cat sightings.

Having spent twelve years conducting fieldwork among the farming communities of rural west Wales, anthropologist Samantha Hurn recorded over one hundred big cat sightings – and experienced one herself while on a late-night walk with her German shepherd dog, Max. Recording her own memorate, she wrote, 'we were terrified! ... I shone my torch in the direction from which [Max] had come and caught the gleaming eyes of a large, predatory animal'.[63] It became Hurn's opinion, the more interviews she conducted, that the cat sightings in Wales had 'become metaphors for disenfranchised Welsh farmers', on the one hand symbolising unlikely survival, resistance, and freedom in the Welsh hills, and on the other hand representing common knowledge within a rural community that is refuted by the (English) official bodies.[64]

Large cats are out-of-place animals, but some cryptids in Britain are mysterious creatures unconfirmed by science – something in which the country has a long history of interest. The bestiaries of the Middle Ages, illustrated compendia of beasts used to communicate Christian moral messages, placed the mythical alongside the scientific. The 'Ashmole Bestiary' and the 'Aberdeen

Bestiary', both twelfth- or thirteenth-century illuminated manuscripts of English origin, feature unicorns, phoenixes, dragons, basilisks, griffins, manticores, alongside 'real' animals.[65] Saints' lives also contained early precursors to cryptozoology. In the 'Life of St. Columba', compiled in the seventh century by Adomnán, an abbot of Iona, an event from a century earlier is described. Irish monk Saint Columba was staying in the land of the Picts when he encountered local residents burying a man by the River Ness. The man had been swimming in the river when he was 'bitten most severely by a monster that lived in the water'. This being a hagiography, when the 'ferocious monster' emerged again with an 'awful roar', Saint Columba simply made the sign of the cross and commanded the monster, 'Thou shalt go no further, nor touch the man; go back with all speed'. The monster, now 'terrified', fled – a miracle that converted the 'barbarous heathens' to Christianity.[66] Despite water beasts being a popular trope of medieval hagiographies, this account has been pointed to as the earliest description of Britain's arguably most famous cryptid: the Loch Ness Monster.

Although there were earlier legends and alleged sightings of a large, unidentified creature living in or near Loch Ness, the account that really germinated the phenomenon was given by John and Aldie Mackay. On 28 April 1933, the managers of a loch-side hotel claimed that they had seen something 'whale-like' splashing in the water. Their sighting was reported a few days later in the *Inverness Courier*: the couple 'were startled to see a tremendous upheaval on the loch ... the creature disported itself, rolling and plunging for fully a minute, its body resembling that of a whale ... it disappeared in a boiling mass of foam'. The journalist was keen to stress the integrity of his informants, noting that the (then anonymous) husband was a 'well-known business man' and the wife 'a University graduate'.[67]

In August of the same year, the same newspaper featured another story, this one supplied by George Spicer and his wife, on holiday in Scotland from London, who reported seeing a large creature – 'the nearest approach to a dragon or pre-historic animal that I have ever seen' – with a 'long neck, which moved up and down in the manner of a scenic railway', cross the loch-side road in front of them.[68] This was the first time that the Loch Ness Monster was described as long necked, and suggestions have been made that Spicer's description was inspired by the brontosaurus in the movie *King Kong* (1933), which he had seen earlier that year. Such was the excitement prompted by these sightings, that in December 1933 the then Secretary of State for Scotland introduced 'protection in law for the "thing" living in Loch Ness'.[69]

The following year provided photographic 'evidence' of this 'thing' in Loch Ness, the iconic so-called 'surgeon's photograph', which has since been debunked but has been followed by nearly a century of reported sightings and images.[70] An 'Official Loch Ness Monster Sightings Register' is maintained online by Invernessian Gary Campbell, a chartered accountant, who began the register in 1996 following his own sighting: 'I only saw it for a few seconds ... I have spent the last 25 years trying to explain it'.[71] Ten reports were registered in 2023 and, at the time of writing, two so far in 2024, one of which reads, 'At first thought was driftwood, but slowly but surely made its way north towards the [Urquhart] castle. Looked like a head above the waves.'[72]

As one geographer has noted, 'Nessie' has become 'Scotland's international superstar fantastical creature', and hundreds of thousands of visitors have travelled to Loch Ness (producing a yearly revenue of nearly £41 million) in the hopes of catching a glimpse of the cryptid.[73] In 2019, Urquhart Castle, which overlooks Loch Ness, attracted over 447,000 visitors, while Loch Ness by Jacobite cruises took more than 321,000 people on tours where they are promised 'the opportunity to discover the secrets of Loch Ness and search for Nessie with the help of onboard sonar ... Be sure to keep your camera ready!'[74] And there are various routes advertised for the independent traveller, one dubbed 'Monster 66' incorporating 'all the great lookout points for seeing Nessie'.[75] The Scottish landscape undoubtedly adds to the cryptid's appeal or 'charisma', the deep loch surrounded by mountains being the one place in the world where this particular (toponymically named) creature may be spotted.[76]

Chasing ghosts and other legend-trips

Travelling the Monster 66 in anticipation of catching a glimpse of Loch Ness's cryptid is an example of legend-tripping. This is a term first used by folklorist Gary Hall in his 1973 study 'The Big Tunnel', which documented visits to a purported haunted tunnel in Indiana in the United States.[77] Simply, legend tripping is the act of visiting a place because it is associated with a legend, often in the hope of witnessing a phenomenon as if the visitor themselves were in the legend.[78] It is an act of ostensive play – ostension meaning 'to show'. Rather than the telling of, or listening to, a narrative, it is the physical and visual enactment of it: the performance of legend.[79] This behaviour has been heavily documented in North America, where it is interpreted as a rite of passage or ritual of rebellion for adolescents. The legend-trippers often drive to some remote, even forbidden location, in anticipation of experiencing something supernatural. Sometimes they also engage in antisocial behaviour as part of the legend-trip: vandalism, drink, drugs, and sex.[80] However, it is not only the youth who engage in legend-tripping, and it is certainly not exclusive to North America.[81]

Many places in Britain are visited by people of all ages because of their associations with legends; and the legends most inspiring of trips tend to be of the supernatural variety.[82] Places haunted by ghosts, particularly named ghosts with developed backstories, have long attracted the curious and the daring. Edinburgh's Greyfriars churchyard boasts a mausoleum said to be haunted still by the 'Bluidy Mackingie', the ghost of Sir George Mackenzie, a seventeenth-century prosecutor. Writing of the *Traditions of Edinburgh* in 1825, Robert Chambers observed,

> It used to be a "feat" for a set of boys, in a still summer evening, to march up to the ponderous doors [of the mausoleum] ... and cry in at the keyhole:-
>
> > 'Bluidy Mackingie, come out if ye daur,
> > Lift the sneck and draw the bar!'
>
> After which they would run away as if some hobgoblin were in chase of them.[83]

The Mackenzie Poltergeist and his so-named 'Black Mausoleum' still feature on the City of the Dead Edinburgh ghost tour. The tour is structured around a potential encounter with the poltergeist, acting out the legend. In the first two years of the tour in the 1990s, there were more than seventy alleged encounters, ranging from cold spots and nausea to loss of consciousness.[84] The audience then go on to tell of their encounters as legend-tripping memorates.[85] Subsequently, the tour leader adds the memorate to their repertoire, the new legend being narrated to the audiences of future tours.[86]

Supernatural legend-tripping is big business, and has been for some time. As far back as the seventeenth century, crowds would gather at alleged hauntings, and local businesses were quick to exploit them. The famous Cock Lane ghost of eighteenth-century London drew mass crowds and, as was observed in a letter by the writer Horace Walpole, 'all the taverns and alehouses in the neighbourhood [made] fortunes'.[87] Inns and pubs began advertising themselves as haunted, attracting customers who wanted to spend a night in the room of such-a-ghost.[88] Haunted travel guides proliferated, ghosts tours increased rapidly from the 1970s, and during the twenty-first century television became a popular platform for (commercial) ghost legend-tripping. The television series *Most Haunted*, for example, has been sending teams of investigators on

Figure 4.1 The Major Oak of Sherwood Forest, long promoted as connected to Robin Hood. Photograph by Ceri Houlbrook.

legend-trips to reputed haunted sites across Britain since 2002;[89] and, since 2021, Danny Robins's radio show *Uncanny* has been broadcasting the personal memorates of people who have encountered the uncanny, in one of the most popular podcasts on BBC Sounds.

Other legend-trips take place at sites associated with the (supposed) actions of legendary characters: Tintagel Castle for King Arthur, for example, and – returning to Washington Irving's tour – Sherwood Forest for Robin Hood. The folk-hero outlaw may be a hazy historical/mythical figure whose associations with particular places are (tourism-motivated, media-generated) suppositions, but the cultural connection between Robin Hood and Sherwood Forest, Nottinghamshire, is deep rooted.[90] In the eighteenth century, Major Heyman Rock was assessing Sherwood's timber resources when he saw a large, old oak which he observed could have been there in Robin Hood's day. He named it Major Oak, and it became associated with Robin Hood, romanticised as his hideout. During the nineteenth century, people began to visit the Major Oak, which still today is protected behind a barrier and propped up with stilts (Figure 4.1).

Legends

Figure 4.2 The 'young officer' dressed as Robin Hood at the Christmas party attended by Washington Irving: 'The costume, to be sure, did not bear testimony to deep research.' Illustration by Frank Dadd in *Irving's Old Christmas* (New York, 1916), p. 110.

People also began to visit the nearby town of Edwinstowe, whose parish church was old enough to become the place where Robin Hood and Maid Marian married.[91] The Robin Hood Festival has been running almost annually since the 1980s, attracting thousands of visitors to Sherwood Forest with displays of horseback jousting, axe-throwing, music, historical re-enactments, and, of course, archery at the Major Oak. And still today, legend-trippers to Sherwood Forest can become ostensive enactors of the Robin Hood legend simply by purchasing a bow-and-arrow set from the gift shop and donning a green bycocket hat –although, whether Washington Irving, fanboy of Robin Hood, whose legend-tripping was detailed at the start of this chapter, would have approved is questionable. Writing in 1876 of a Christmas costume party he had attended, Irving was particularly scathing of one costume: 'The young officer appeared as Robin Hood, in a sporting dress of Kendal green, and a foraging cap with a gold tassel. The costume, to be sure, did not bear testimony to deep research.'[92] (Figure 4.2)

Part III

Environment

Part III

Environment

Chapter 5
Folklore of the natural world

We have a rather rose-tinted view of our ancestors' knowledge of the natural world, thinking they must have had a more harmonious respect for the animals and plants around them. The immediate environment was certainly a valued resource, particularly with regard to health and protection. But it was also deemed full of perceived threats and competition. From the sixteenth through to the mid-nineteenth century, Acts of Parliament required parish authorities in England and Wales to reward the extermination of vast numbers of animals designated vermin, destroyers of crops, and stealers of fish and eggs. Payments were made for the killing of foxes, hedgehogs, otters, moles, polecats, rats, stoats, weasels, badgers, pine martens, snakes, corvids, birds of prey, pigeons, herons, woodpeckers, bullfinches, and even kingfishers. Sparrows became a particular target from the mid-eighteenth century, often trapped and killed by children.[1] Then there were the 'vermin' killing fields of the many shooting estates established by the wealthy elite in the nineteenth century.

With regard to the plant world, there had long been the notion of weeds, pernicious green invaders that stole the space and goodness from farmers' crops and poisoned livestock. The annual plant groundsel accrued the name 'ground glutton', the parasitic common dodder was called 'devil's guts', while stitchwort was known as 'devil's corn' in western England. Weeds became a metaphor for worthlessness and weakness; fields were described as 'filthy' with them.[2] Society seemed to be, at times, engaging in a full-scale war with much of nature.

In various ways, folklore played its part in reinforcing these negative attitudes towards flora and fauna. One quite widespread tradition, for instance, was to kill the first butterfly of the year to avoid bad luck. In some places the same applied to adders and wasps. James Napier (1810–1884), a folklorist of western Scotland, recalled how detested and abused the yellowhammer or 'yellow yite' was in his boyhood, because it was thought to have a drop of the devil's blood, which also explained its jerky flight. He hastened to add that the hatred was 'only local', but in other parts of northern Scotland it was also known as the 'Devil's bird', and it was persecuted in parts of northern England for the same association.[3] This was a legend-led prejudice, but others were born of misunderstanding.

We should not overestimate our ancestors' powers of observation and identification skills. Many people did not make a difference between rooks and crows, slow-worms and snakes, toads and frogs, and hares and rabbits, let alone the myriad differences of the insect world. The author of *Eggs of British Birds* (1853) expressed his frustration at the common confusion between house martins and swallows across all social levels, while the English botanist Benjamin Stillingfleet (1702–1771) complained that 'our common people know scarce any of the grasses by names'.[4] Popular knowledge of British plants and animals today is also quite limited, though in different ways. Urbanisation during the nineteenth and twentieth centuries divorced most people from experiencing the diversity of the natural world in their everyday lives, while in rural areas the massive decline of animal and plant species over the last century due to habitat destruction, intensive farming, fertilizers, and pesticides has meant the loss of regular contact with many once-common species.

The origins of British folklore regarding flora and fauna are difficult to trace, but some of it can certainly be found in the writings of ancient Rome and Greece, particularly in the works of Aristotle and in Pliny the Elder's huge, encyclopaedic *Natural History*, which was completed around AD 77. But this does not mean there was some continuous tradition of lore in Britain over the last two thousand years that was shared with the Roman world. In sixteenth-century Europe the 'rediscovery' of the Classics, combined with the print revolution, meant that notions and opinions from the ancient world gained a new influence on thinking about the workings of nature. The first partial English edition of Pliny's *Natural History* appeared in 1601 and was used as a source for popular literature, such as herbals, divination manuals, books of secrets, and almanacs, and, through these, elements percolated into British popular belief.[5] A complete translation finally appeared in 1855, just in time for the boom in nineteenth-century folklore writing about nature. Thumb through any old folklore book on British animals and plants, and you will find a liberal sprinkling of references to Pliny. But there is plenty of British folklore about the natural world that cannot be found in the ancient sources – and some cannot even be dated any further back than the nineteenth century.

Most recorded folklore about British fauna grew around a remarkably small number of animals. Our large mammals, such as foxes, badgers, and deer attracted little recorded tradition. Likewise, squirrels, weasels, stoats, and martens. Only a few insects accrued lore, and little is said about different types of fish. Even bats, which one might think would have generated a rich body of tradition, are rarely found in the annals of British folklore. It is possible that this partly reflects collection bias, and partly that folklore about these animals had been forgotten by the mid-nineteenth century. But the two main explanations concern fear and proximity, in our opinion. As we shall see, animals considered harmful to human health were a preoccupation. Think of all the wolf and bear lore in European countries, which is not relevant in Britain. Then there is the closeness of human–animal interactions, and regular observable experience in daily life, usually in and around the house or the local environment. The richness of bee folklore as compared to other insects is understandable in this respect (Figure 5.1).[6] Most wild mammals, while sometimes observable during the day (particularly hares), are much more active at dusk, dawn, and night, and disappear swiftly when disturbed.

Figure 5.1 A widow and her son inform the bees of a death in the family. *The Widow* (1895) by Charles Napier Hemy (1841–1917).

In the days before outdoor lighting, they were probably even more fleeting sights than today. How many of us encounter them mostly in the beam of car headlights at night, as roadkill, or in lit urban streets? Nocturnal animal folklore is largely based around startling noises that pierce the darkness rather than visual encounters – and bat calls are either barely audible, or inaudible to most of us.

Natural misunderstandings

Whether derived from notions found in the Classics or from indigenous folk wisdom and observation, a lot of folklore about British plants and animals was based on false knowledge of the natural world that seemed reasonable until scientific research slowly but surely began to undermine its basis. Some animals and plants were attributed powers solely on the basis of their behaviour or how they looked. On the Isle of Man as late as the 1920s the devil's coach horse beetle, or *tarroo-deyll*, was thought to be able to set fire to roof thatch with its raised abdomen. Another example is the notion that dragonflies could sting. In Dorset they were known as 'hoss [horse] adders' or 'hoss stingers' as they buzzed around livestock in the pastures of the region. Writing in 1889, folklorist John S. Udal noted that 'as a rule, the country folk are right as regard the natural attributes which their provincial names imply, but in this case it is a misnomer'.[7] Udal also noted the Dorset labourer who, when asked why he had just killed a slow-worm (which is completely harmless), replied: 'if it do sting 'ee you are sure to die within seven year'.[8] Elias Owen (1833–1899), a clergyman folklorist of North Wales, noted sadly, 'this beautiful timid creature is often wantonly cut into pieces by its cruel and mistaken captors, for they credit it with the possession of evil propensities'.[9]

Several widespread misnomers accrued around the cuckoo, particularly that it sucked eggs to improve its 'cuckoo'. The Sussex folklorist Charlotte Latham recorded in 1878 a song she heard sung by local children and which can be found in variant forms around the country:

> The cuckoo's a merry bird: sings as she flies;
> She brings us good tidings, and tells us no lies.
> She picks up the dirt in the Spring of the year,
> And sucks little birds' eggs, to make her voice clear.

Latham noted that 'it would be useless to attempt to disprove' the 'superstition' in the last line.[10] Bending a knee to 'folk wisdom' was partly a romantic gesture.

The photographer, Cambridge scholar, and chronicler of the Norfolk Broads, Peter Henry Emerson (1856–1936), received mockery in the scientific press for the nature accounts he recorded in his *Birds, Beasts and Fishes of the Norfolk Broadland* (1895) because he gave great credence, in his own words, to 'the authority of fowlers, ratcatchers, fishermen, gamekeepers, and the like'. This led him to accept and even attempt to prove some of their popular beliefs about the natural world. Cuckoos were a good example. Emerson observed that every marshman believed that cuckoos sucked on eggs to clear their voice, and numerous of them swore to him that they had seen them do so with the eggs of thrushes, blackbirds, and reed buntings. All this left Emerson 'quite satisfied' that the belief was true. Still, he drew the line at another Norfolk belief: that cuckoo chicks, once big enough, swallowed and ate their host parents.[11]

The mystery of bird migration puzzled the great thinkers of ancient Greece and Rome, generating various, now fantastical, theories that nevertheless proved enduring. In seventeenth-century England, the Oxford scholar Robert Burton (1577–1640) pondered on the matter with the ancient authors as his authoritative source, wondering whether 'they hid in caves, rocks and hollow trees, as most think', hibernated at the bottom of lakes, or 'followed the Sun'. By the early nineteenth century, naturalists had by and large plumped for migration to Africa, but hibernation theory continued widely in popular belief. The West Country mineralogist and folklorist, Robert Hunt (1807–1887), observed that in the outlying districts of Cornwall it was still a prevalent belief that the cuckoo and the swallow hid away over the winter.[12]

A venerable third theory also clung to the cuckoo, or *Y gôg* in Welsh: namely, that it did not migrate or hibernate like swallows, but transformed itself into a sparrowhawk during the winter. This was based on common observation: the two birds have a similar flight pattern and plumage, and the female cuckoo's call is similar to that of the sparrowhawk. Recent ornithological research suggests that this mimicry is an evolutionary development, perhaps to scare potential host parents from the nest so that the cuckoo can lay her egg.[13] Elias Owen remarked that in North Wales, 'the cuckoo is a sacred bird. It is safe from the gamekeeper's gun.' But this was certainly not the case elsewhere. Many were killed by gamekeepers, due to the confusion with sparrowhawks.[14] In a paper given to the British Association meeting in Newcastle in 1863, the Revd H. B. Tristram complained of the ignorance of the natural world displayed by gamekeepers and their masters, noting that a short time ago he had remonstrated with a man for shooting cuckoos, to which he received the defiant defence 'that it was well known that sparrowhawks turned into cuckoos in the summer'. As late as 1933, a Devon labourer reported that he had recently heard several men say that the cuckoo was the same bird as a sparrowhawk.[15]

Creatures of the earth

In folklore, 'worm' covered a range of animals from mythic dragons to snakes, slow-worms, and intestinal parasites. But here we focus on the humble but profoundly important earthworm, which was known more commonly by several names. The term 'mads' was for long the most widespread, but in Grose's *Provincial Glossary* (1787) we also find 'yesses', and in Hampshire the variant 'isses'. In nineteenth-century Dorset, big red earthworms were known as 'ingle dogs', the 'ingle' pertaining to 'fire' and hence referring to the red colour.[16] We now know the crucial role that worms play in nature and agriculture, but until the early twentieth century they were much maligned in popular belief, lumped together with pestilential caterpillars and grubs as the destroyer of root crops. In his *Rural Cyclopedia* (1847–1849), the Scottish minister John Marius Wilson (1805–1885) remarked with frustration that 'earthworms are generally regarded by farmers and gardeners as mischievous', noting that salt and lime water were applied to fields to destroy them.[17]

In 1837, Charles Darwin presented to the Geological Society his groundbreaking research on the invaluable role played by the humble earthworm in the formation of soils. It was much reported upon at the time, and subsequently the media tried to instruct the populace on the importance of the mads. An 1862 article in the *Scottish Farmer* ended its praise of the earthworm with the frustrated comment that 'their usefulness is seldom thought of, whereas by the many they are still ignorantly looked upon and loathed as the "wriggling tenants of the grave"'.[18] But the dislike of earthworms proved resistant to popular education. The Nottinghamshire folklorist and writer Clifford Greatorex, author of, among other books, *What the Countryman Wants to Know*, recalled how, around 1930, a local woman told him that earthworms were the gardener's worst enemy. After a warm rain had fallen she would go out and 'put salt on the nasty varmints' just as her mother and grandmother had done. He tried to explain that they were the gardener's friend, but she would have none of it.[19]

That other great toiler under the earth, the mole, received even worse treatment at the hands of the British. Indeed, it was one of the most systematically persecuted of our mammals for centuries. In the year 1829 alone, the mole catcher for the parish of Penton Mewsey, Hampshire, was paid for the deaths of 318 moles.[20] They had long been known as 'mouldwarps', and it was still a common name for the mole in northern parts during the nineteenth century, with variant dialect pronunciations, such as a 'mowdy warp' in Cheshire. In West Country England it was mostly called a 'want' or 'woont', and in parts of the Midlands a 'hunt' or 'hoont', while it was a 'cont' in Shropshire, where mole hills were known as 'conty tumps'.[21] They were associated with death and popularly thought to be blind. As a consequence, we find old cures for poor eyesight based on dead moles. According to one early modern guide to farriery, one of the remedies used to cure blindness or dimness of sight in horses was 'to take a Mouldwarp and lapping her all over in Clay, burn her to ashes, and then to take of that Powder and blow it into the Horse's Eyes'.[22] They were also unjustly blamed for destroying root crops, reducing the quality of grass in pastures, and destroying field drains.

The writer and clergyman Augustus Jessopp (1823–1914), who wrote an impassioned defence of the mole in the periodical *The Nineteenth Century*, decried the 'little bunch or collection of idle superstitions acting to the discredit of the moles', such as that 'they bring rain when it is not wanted; that they haunt the churchyard and prey upon our forefathers ... that their *earth putts* [mole hills] are poisonous to the soil around them'. The folklore surrounding moles was indeed rich.[23] In Herefordshire the first appearance of a mole hill in the garden was an omen of death, and the county's folklorist Ella Leather (1874–1928) noted her encounter with a woman and her family, in Bromyard, who all stood at the door of their home staring with dismay at the fresh 'oont' tump in their grass plot. They expressed the hope 'that it would be a very distant relative who would be "taken"'.[24]

The naturalist and surveyor of the Queen's royal parks and palaces, Edward Jesse (1780–1868), who was a friend of the mole and considered mole hills beneficial to soil quality, noted that 'there has been a very general idea among our mole-catchers, that if the smallest drop of blood is taken from a mole it occasions instant death'.[25] Even legend had them down as sinners. In 1852 a correspondent to *Notes & Queries* recounted a recent conversation he had had with an octogenarian mole catcher who lived near Bridgwater, Somerset. The old man told him that the first mole or 'want' 'was a proud woman, sir, too proud to live on the face of the earth, and so God turned her into a mole, and made her live UNDER the earth; and that was the FIRST MOLE'. The mole catcher gave proof of the story in that moles had 'hands and feet like Christians' with their five fingers and toes.[26]

Fungi: toads, ears, and fairies

In a list of fungi traditionally dedicated to saints in Europe, William Hay, in his *Elementary Text-Book of British Fungi* (1887) remarked sadly on the absence of such lore in 'fungus despising Britain'.[27] In 1878, James Britten similarly observed in his manual, *Popular British Fungi*, that 'fungi occupy a very low place in the popular estimation' and noted that the folklore was not extensive.[28] Field and horse mushrooms were certainly widely eaten, particularly in the form of ketchup. Exceptionally large horse mushrooms and puffballs were a matter of record for local newspapers. But, otherwise, there are few references to the folklore of individual species, despite some bearing names in modern nomenclature that excite the imagination, such as lawyer's wig, devil's fingers, and destroying angel.

It needs to be remembered, of course, that the term 'fungi' was not in popular use until the twentieth century, and most people referred broadly to either mushrooms (edible) or toadstools. The latter had various dialect variations with the same associations, such as 'paddock (a frog or toad) stools' in Scotland, 'toad's caps' in Norfolk, 'toad's cheese' in Berkshire, 'toad's meat' in Dorset, and 'frog's seats' in Northamptonshire.[29] Although the folklore record from the nineteenth and early twentieth centuries provides little evidence for popular opinion on the association between toads and fungi, the linking factors were clearly notions of toxicity and sliminess, and the venerable idea that life generated from the damp, rotting earth: both were 'earthie excrescences' born of decay. Indeed, it was once mooted that the 'toad' element was actually a corruption of the original meaning of 'death' from the Germanic word 'tod'.[30] The old idea that toads and frogs were venomous lived on into the nineteenth century. In his observations on the fauna of Derbyshire, Stephen Glover noted in 1831 that it was still believed that toads soaked up all the poisonous qualities in water and hence were venomous.[31] This may help to explain the idea of toad's cheese and meat. Perhaps the toad was thought to accumulate poison through eating or sitting on fungi.

Nineteenth-century cookery and fungi manuals cautioned readers about the widespread 'superstition' that placing a silver spoon or coin in fungi dishes was a good method of detecting toxicity because the silver would tarnish in contact with poison. Much cited on this matter was David Badham's *Treatise* on the Esculent Funguses of England (1847), in which he warned that it was 'an error which cannot be too generally known and exposed, as many lives, especially on the continent, have been and still are sacrificed to it annually'.[32] But this was advice for a British middle class increasingly interested in the gastronomic potential of fungi. There is no evidence of adventurous consumption among the common folk, whose aversion to anything other than the field mushroom was notorious. Writing in 1868, for instance, the fungi-eating enthusiast John Bell recalled staying at a little inn in Somerset a few years before and, having harvested a basket of fairy ring mushrooms, asking his landlady to serve them up for supper. She was extremely reluctant to cook what she called the 'pixie stools', and Bell observed that 'from her expression of countenance the next morning I believe she felt some disappointment in seeing us perfectly well'.[33]

One of the few fungi to attract a legend in Britain was a curious brown fungus that grows on trees and resembles a human ear. It was known in Latin since the Middle Ages as *auricula judæ*, or Judas's ear, due to the legend that it commemorated Judas Iscariot's act of hanging himself from an elder tree, which is one of the fungus's main hosts. The association of elder with Judas's act of suicide was common in early modern Britain and was referenced by Shakespeare, for example.[34] But it was also observed at the time, and in other countries, that there were other arboreal candidates for the fateful gallows. Besides, elder, with its spindly stems, is not exactly an ideal choice. Anyway, 'Judas's ear' then became corrupted to 'Jew's ear' in Britain, and it was popularly known as such into the twentieth century, though it is now increasingly referred to as 'jelly ear' to avoid anti-Semitic connotations.

The puffball was another fungus that had a foothold in folklore. In nineteenth-century Scotland it was referred to variously as the Devil's snuff box and blind man's ball or buff.[35] The latter term derived from an old belief that the spores, when blown into the face, caused blindness or stupefaction. Up until the mid-nineteenth century bee-keeping manuals continued to recommend burning a puffball (*Bovista*), in order to make the bees drowsy. Puffballs also had old associations with the fairies and were known as 'puck fists', or dialect variants thereof, in some parts of England, such as 'puckfousts' in Gloucestershire. The fairies' fungal associations may have derived from their supposed subterranean dwelling place and the evidence of fairy rings. Writing in 1860, fungi enthusiast Llewellynn Jewitt noted that he had heard baby mushrooms referred to as 'fairy buttons' by people in parts of Derbyshire, and the belief that when they grew old and decayed with blackened gills, the Devil had put his hand on them and chased away the fairies.[36]

References to 'fairy butter', or *Ymenyn y Tylwyth Têg* in Welsh, also appear in the folklore record, particularly in relation to northern England. In 1825, John Trotter Brockett described it in his *Glossary of North Country Words* as 'a fungus excrescence, sometimes found about the roots of old trees. After great rains, and in a certain degree of putrefaction, it is reduced to a consistency, which, together with its colour, makes it not unlike butter.'[37] It was actually either a type of yellow jelly fungus called *Tremella*, or possibly the slime mould *Fuligo septica*, which appears on dead wood and is known today as dog's vomit slime mould or scrambled egg slime mould, due to its frothy yellow consistency.[38] The old notion was that they were the remnants of fairies churning butter at night and leaving dollops around in haste before sunrise.

Udder suckers

The idea of animal milk-stealers was widespread as an explanation for why cows mysteriously dried up when they were otherwise perfectly healthy and in their lactation period. It is true that people did go out into the fields at night and illicitly milk the dairy cows of their neighbours. In 1875, for instance, a tramp named Thomas Brooks was sent to the Wakefield House of Correction after being caught sucking the teats of a cow in a local farmer's cowhouse.[39] But, more often than not, certain animals that frequented pastures were blamed. The hedgehog was the number one suspect in Britain and, as a result, it was persecuted nearly as mercilessly as the mole. Hedgehogs were sometimes called urchins, but the parish vermin payments also reveal various spellings and pronunciations of hedgehog. In Hampshire parish records we find 'hig hogs', 'hegogs', and 'hog ogs'.[40]

One reason they were considered vermin was for eating the eggs of hens and game birds, but it was mostly due to the widespread belief that hedgehogs sucked the milk from cows as they lay in the pasture, and in doing so also ulcerated the cows' udders with their spines. In 1750, for instance, William Ellis, a farmer of Little Gaddesden, Hertfordshire, recorded in his manual, *The Modern Husbandman*, 'I have cured my Cows, when one or more Teats have been sucked by the Hedge-Hog, which commonly caused Blood to follow, and a sore Dug [teat].'[41] Such eighteenth-century husbandry books perpetuated the belief, but from the early nineteenth century the hedgehog's innocence of this crime was widely proclaimed, with numerous defences published by agriculturalists and naturalists such as John Leonard Knapp (1767–1845), who pointed out in 1829 that it was obviously impossible for the small mouth of the hedgehog to accommodate a cow's teat. He noted further that it was difficult to dissuade people of the belief and so to 'spare the life of this most harmless and least obtrusive creature in existence'.[42]

Once again, the notion was based on understandable but false observation. Hedgehogs obviously found freshly cow-patted fields good hunting grounds for insects, and so it was not surprising to see them scuttling between cows' legs or around cows in repose. The naturalist John George Wood (1827–1889) wrote in 1865 that he had received several accounts from trusted observers of hedgehogs lapping up the milk that oozed from the overflowing udders of cows lying in the field shortly before milking. But it was made clear that they never touched the teats.[43] In popular belief, the hedgehog's supposed capacity for imbibing milk bordered on the supernatural. A correspondent to a Cornish newspaper in 1884 reported his conversation with a woman of Falmouth who knew as a 'fact' an occasion when, one night, a solitary hedgehog sucked fifteen cows dry. When he tried to explain the impossibility of a little hedgehog consuming so many gallons of milk, she stuck adamantly to her story.[44] The debate over the issue was so hot in the parish of Ash, Surrey, that in 1908 the Parish Council wrote to the Board of Agriculture for clarification. The Board's Secretary responded:

> I am directed by the Board of Agriculture and Fisheries to inform you that your letter has been referred to their zoological adviser, and the Board are informed that the statement that hedgehogs take the milk of cows that are lying down is unfounded in fact.[45]

But the belief remained widespread well into the twentieth century, with contemporary legends disseminated in the press. For instance, in 1922 the 'Town and Country' column of the *Derby Daily Telegraph* reported sceptically on a story circulating around Sheffield that a farmer had, only the other day, caught 'a hedgehog fastened on to a young cow whilst it lay in a shed'. According to the rumour, not only did the hedgehog drain the cow of milk, but it nibbled her teats so badly that the local vet ordered the cow to be put down.[46] And dubious personal testimony, so important to the rumour mill, also continued. In 1928, someone wrote to the *Derbyshire Times* stating that he had once seen seventeen hedgehogs sucking milk from ten cows.[47]

The snake's supposed love of milk was a widespread and ancient notion, though memorates about it are fewer in Britain than those concerning hedgehogs.[48] In 1910, the village of Oddington in Oxfordshire became something of a media sensation when it was reported that two cows, owned by a Mrs

Rice, had been sucked dry by snakes. The farm bailiff had initially suspected that the Romani or tramps had been milking them at night, and instructed a cowman named George to set watch over the animals. One day he found one of the cows lying down in the meadow with two grass snakes on her teats, which he promptly killed. A journalist from the *Birmingham Gazette* went to the village to investigate and interviewed 'Jarge': 'Don't tell me they was hedgehogses as milked her 'cos I don't believe in no such foolishness,' declared George. 'If I hadn't a seed the two snakeses with my own eyes I'd never believed that neither.' Soon after he had killed the snakes the cow miraculously started giving milk again. Rumours swirled that the snakes had reached a ginormous size from gorging on the milk, but, despite the best efforts of the journalist, the dead snakes were never produced as evidence of their crime.[49]

From 1940s Sussex we hear of a middle-class man who bought a house and kept a couple of cows in his meadows as pets. He employed a local farm labourer to maintain them. One day he saw two dead grass snakes hanging from a wall and asked the labourer what they were doing there. The labourer replied that he had killed them for sucking the cows. When the owner pointed out the impossibility of the snakes consuming milk in this way, the labourer replied that he did not how they did it, but 'kept saying that they had done it somehow or other'.[50]

The nightjar, a ground-nesting bird whose habitat was and is highly localised, was also widely referred to as the 'goatsucker' by naturalists, journalists, and folklorists, following a belief that they sucked the udders of livestock. Yet, look in nineteenth-century regional dialect studies and you won't find the term used in popular idiom. It was known as the 'churr owl' in Aberdeen and 'scissor grinder' in East Anglia, due to its magical nocturnal call; as 'dor hawk', due to one of its prey being the dor beetle, which also buzzes around at dusk; as 'fern owl' in Somerset, and 'gapmouth' in Dorset, while 'night-crow' or 'night hawk' were used in parts of northern England and elsewhere.[51] The goatsucker actually derives this name and reputation not from British folklore but from its Latin name *Caprimulgus*, meaning 'goat milker'. This was coined by the Swedish naturalist and 'father of taxonomy', Carl Linnaeus (1707–1778), who based it on accounts of the bird by Aristotle and Pliny the Elder. This was then reinforced in the early nineteenth century by dubious reports from the British colonies of similar nightjar behaviour. In 1853, the author of *Goldsmith's Natural History* suggested that 'The superstition has probably originated from its being often found in warm climates under cattle, capturing the insects that torment them.'[52]

The hare is the fourth of our udder suckers and takes us firmly into the territory of the supernatural. While legends of witches turning themselves into hares to do their mischief, and sometimes being shot in the process, are widespread in British folklore, the witch-hare as milk stealer is largely a tradition of north-eastern England and Scotland, allied to the strong milk-hare tradition in Scandinavia.[53] In the 1840s, a young man of Tain, in the Highlands of Scotland, who was imprisoned for assaulting a woman for being a witch, declared in his defence: 'she has been seen a hundred times milking the cows in the shape of a hare'.[54] The Revd John Atkinson (1814–1900), author of *Forty Years in a Moorland Parish* (1891), noted similar accounts told by his North Yorkshire parishioners, including one instance of a farmer of Commondale who set one of his labourers to watch his cows to see who was stealing their milk: 'each night he had noticed a hare that came in through a gapway in the dike, and that seemed to be feeding about, and mostly right in amongst the cows where they were feeding or standing the closest together'. The direction of the hare's entry was suspiciously close to where there lived a suspected witch named 'Au'd Mally'.[55] Dateable accounts expressing concern about the hare's depredations are rarely found beyond the mid-nineteenth century, though.

Animals respected ... sometimes

While wild mammals were rarely considered to have any folkloric virtues that gave them protection from human persecution, there were a clutch of birds that were given venerable respect. The robin was one. Legend had it that the robin's red breast derived from its having attended Christ on the cross and thereby received some drops of his blood. But eighteenth-century commentators reckoned that its sacred status was more to do with a very popular ballad that had been circulating since the late sixteenth century called 'Children in the Wood' or 'Babes in the Wood'.[56] The story concerned an evil uncle and the abandonment and death of two children in a forest. As a version from 1800 relates:

> No burial these children did,
> Of any man receive,
> Till robin red-breast carefully,
> Did cover them o'er with leaves,
> And now the heavy wrath of God,
> Upon the uncle fell.

In the early 1860s in Suffolk there was a blunt saying, 'you must not take robins' eggs; if you do, you will get your legs broken'. The contributor of this information also recalled asking a boy in his local parish school why one of his hands shook so uncontrollably that he had difficulty holding his pen. 'Have you been running hard, or anything of that sort?' He asked. 'No,' replied the boy sadly, 'it always shakes; I once had a robin die in my hand, it will always shake.'[57] Over in Cornwall, Robert Hunt, writing at the same time, recalled: 'I remember that a boy in Redruth killed a robin: the dead robin was tied round his neck, and he was marched by the other boys through the town.' As they marched, they sang a well-known rhyme:

> Those who kill a robin or wren,
> Will never prosper, boy or man.[58]

The wren, as mentioned in the couplet above, was also afforded some protection, in part due to its association with the robin, and was sometimes referred to as its wife. On the other hand, there was the ritual killing and display of wrens on St Stephen's Day (26 December) or Twelfth Night on the Isle of Man and in the western regions of Wales and Scotland, most likely due to cultural exchange with the heartland of the custom in Ireland.[59] The general association between the two birds dates back to at least the mid-eighteenth century, as the Sussex landscape painter, George Smith (1713/14–1776), mentions them in his poem about two young lads mucking about in the countryside and catching birds:

> I found a robin's nest within our shed,
> And in the barn a wren has young ones bred.
> I never take away their nest, nor try
> To catch the old ones lest a friend should die.
> Dick took a wren's nest from his cottage side,
> And ere a twelvemonth past his mother dy'd.[60]

While crows, magpies, and ravens had long accrued negative associations with death and misfortune, the rook had a more nuanced place in popular belief.[61] The Hampshire gentleman farmer Edward Lisle (d. 1722) wrote in his posthumously published *Observations in Husbandry* that: 'It is a common proverbial saying of the countryman, that at whatsoever country-farm a colony of rooks planted themselves, and made a rookery, it is a sign of good luck and good fortune attending that man.' This belief that a rookery was lucky was widely recorded across the country by folklorists in the following century.[62]

The Welsh folklorist Elias Owen recalled a case where a gentleman was so concerned when he saw the rooks deserting the rookery on his land that he told his servant to go and destroy the new rookery they were building so that they would return to his place and ensure no bad luck befell him. But the rooks persisted and gathered up the sticks from their destroyed nests and carried on rebuilding.[63]

But let us not be under any false illusions that this folkloric tradition shielded them from persecution, for, as the folklorist Charlotte Burne noted sadly, while the rook was something of a 'sacred bird' in British folklore, nevertheless 'no superstition protects their lives'.[64] Farmers like Lisle considered them as a crop pest and their empty nests a 'harbour' for the detested sparrow, and so rooks were systematically destroyed for centuries as vermin. Looking through numerous accounts, it is clear that those who respected the lore about rookeries were usually the owners of large parks or of small private mansions with a leisure garden, rather than farmers – and certainly not the ruthless owners and gamekeepers of shooting estates. For example, in 1915 the local newspaper for Broughty Ferry, Dundee, reported that a new rookery had appeared nearby in a clump of trees close to a mansion house, and that the owner, adhering to the old adage, had instructed that his new feathery neighbours were not to be disturbed.[65] Some amateur ornithologists even tried to force the creation of a rookery on their land. One such was the Revd Robert Hawker (1803–1875), a Devon antiquarian and eccentric, who helped to create the modern Anglican harvest festival. He so desired a rookery next to his home that one day he 'went to his chancel, and kneeling before the altar, besought God to give him a rookery where he wanted'.[66]

Unlike rooks, swallows were not categorised as vermin, but their nests, and those of house martins, were sometimes considered unsightly excrescences by those preoccupied with the aesthetics of their well-to-do homes. A widely reprinted note from a correspondent to *The Globe* in 1877 moaned of the 'minor annoyances' their nests and droppings caused 'to life in many country houses' and recommended greasing the areas of the house where they nested to frustrate their nest building. It was reported in 1888 that in parts of Berkshire people were careful to preserve martins' nests for good fortune, but if there were signs that sparrows had colonised the nests, then 'a long pole is brought and the mud structures poked to pieces'.[67] But the spoilsports were outnumbered by those who welcomed swallows and martins as bringers of spring joy and good luck. One such was the Yorkshire *Wetherby News*, which, in 1879, argued:

the swallow is a friend who seeks us out in cities, who will build in market places, upon railway stations, and under the corbels of factories where great steam hammers make the very room vibrate. It can do our children no harm to let their nurses teach them the pretty, old superstition that the swallow brings good luck, and that ill fortune will befall us if we scare them away.[68]

There was an element of class *Schadenfreude* when things went wrong for affluent nest disturbers. In 1895 it was reported that, sometime since, a Yorkshire farmer had ordered his labourers to remove all the swallows' (martins') nests from under the eaves of his house. They expressed reluctance to do so as it would bring bad luck, but he forced them. Not long after, a friend of the farmer for whom he was bound in the sum of £4,000 went bankrupt and he had to break up his farm to pay it. A newspaper reported that 'everybody said they knew what would happen, for the birds' nests could not be removed with impunity'. The observance of this belief continued into the twentieth century. When, in the 1940s, ornithologists went around East Lancashire farms to ring swallows for migration research, they met several farmers who were anxious that the ringing would disturb the nesting swallows and make them leave.[69]

The notion that the British salute a solitary magpie can be found all over the internet as a national eccentricity, and it is sometimes described as an ancient 'superstition'. Yet, intriguingly, the belief is not prominent in the various early county folklore surveys, even though many record the old magpie rhyme that begins 'one for sorrow, two for mirth (joy)', though the earliest published mention of this is still only from the 1780s.[70] The earliest mention we can find of saluting magpies is from an exchange in *Notes & Queries* in 1866, where a correspondent recalled that, when recently travelling along a road near Reading,

> I saw a country fellow walking in the same direction, about fifty yards ahead. He suddenly pulled off his hat, and made a sort of bow, though there was no one in his sight, we being behind him. On asking the reason for this strange proceeding, my companion pointed out a magpie which had just quitted a wood, and was flying across the road, and told me it was a general practice there to pull off the hat to the magpie 'for luck.'[71]

The correspondent asked readers whether this was a common thing and received one reply that suggested 'it would be shorter, I think, to say where this did *not* prevail', and reeled off a number of counties up and down the country where the respondent had come across the practice, noting that in the high peaks of Derbyshire people usually bowed.[72]

The relationship between birds and humans altered with the arrival of the automobile. As early as 1925 an article appeared in *The Scotsman* on 'Bird Victims: The Toll of the Motor Car'.[73] It is no surprise, then, that we catch a few glimpses of how this impacted on the old traditions. In 1931, newspapers reported evidence from a Surrey inquest that during her fateful journey the deceased woman motorist had struck and killed a robin that flew out of a hedge. She commented to a passenger at the time that it was a bad omen, and a few hours later she was killed in a car crash. Viewing birds of ill-fortune out of the car window could also work in other ways. In January 1934, the women's section of Matlock Royal British Legion gathered to discuss dreams and omens. One of its members said that she felt magpies 'worked her ill' and that 'if she saw one whilst in a car there was sure to be a breakdown'.[74]

While spiders had some recorded lucky associations here and there, in the insect world the ladybird was the only one to accrue widespread respect. It was known by a variety of regional names, such as a 'doody cow' in parts of Yorkshire, 'lady lanners' in lowland Scotland, '*Y fuwch coch fach*' (the little red cow) in Welsh, and 'lady cow' in various other places.[75] The 'lady' aspect is thought to refer to the Virgin Mary, though some early folklorists linked the beetle to Germanic goddesses. The 'cow' element in ladybird folk names is widespread across Europe, which led to suggestions that it has ancient origins.[76] Yet, no convincing explanation has been put forward. One nineteenth-century theory was that its value as a destroyer of crop aphids had been known 'time out of mind' and so it was thought to be doing God's or the Virgin's work in providing bounty, like the cow that gives life-giving milk.[77] In parts of East Anglia it was known by the curious name 'Bishop-Barnabee', and writing about it in 1830 the Revd Robert Forby observed that the beetle was 'one of those few highly favoured among God's harmless creatures, which superstition protects from wanton injury'.[78] Its reputation as a good omen was given a national boost when it was adopted as a piece of mass-produced lucky jewellery in the early twentieth century.

Nature's prophets

Most old county folklore surveys had their ample sections on natural omens, which, as noted in the Introduction, often present a mass of contradiction and confusion when considered in the round. But some omen traditions were consistent and common. With regard to the numerous portents of death, birds tapping at the windows or shutters, or birds and bats flying against them or entering the house, were widespread omens.[79] Other prevalent heralds of death included seeing bees swarming on a dead branch or a hedge stake, and also the act of bringing spring blossoms into the home, such as those of blackthorn, fruit trees, and furze.[80] The name 'mother-die' was given to cow parsley and other umbellifers as a portent of impending maternal death if brought into the home, though research suggests this is a largely twentieth-century belief. It may derive from the popular association with the flowers of hemlock.[81]

Perhaps the most ingrained fears concerned uncanny noises in the night. None have been so consistently recorded over the centuries as those emanating from the appropriately named deathwatch beetle. The ticking or tapping sound it makes is rarely heard these days, but in the past this small wood-boring beetle (*Xestobium rufovillosum*) was common enough in building timbers and furniture, where its larvae fed on decaying wood. There are several references to the omen in seventeenth-century sources.[82] The English intellectual Thomas Browne (1605–1682) observed that 'Few ears have escaped the noise of the Dead-watch', and opined that 'He that could extinguish the terrifying apprehensions hereof, might prevent the passions of the heart, and many cold sweats in Grandmothers and Nurses, who in the sickness of children, are so startled with these noises.'[83] The beetle and its sinister sound wormed its way into the words of poets and fiction writers in subsequent centuries, and continued to cause nocturnal dread. Sussex folklorist Charlotte Latham observed in 1878: 'How often has the sound made me start and tremble in my childhood when heard at night, in consequence of my having had this belief instilled into me by my nurse.'[84]

The prophetic fear of the deathwatch beetle could be self-fulfilling. In March 1907 newspapers reported on the recent death of a farmer's wife named Bellamy, of Ramsey, Huntingdonshire (now Cambridgeshire), due, in part, to the ghastly tick of a death watch beetle. A look at the censuses and death registers reveals this to be Sarah Bellamy, aged sixty-six, wife of John Bellamy. According to John, his wife was severely frightened by a knocking noise coming from an old wooden deed box in the farmhouse. She awoke John one evening and exclaimed: 'It's knocked! You know that's the warning!' 'I knew what it meant,' recalled John, 'my wife was to be taken from me!' The same noise had been heard when his father died. 'The message which the box gave us brought such dread on my wife,' explained John, 'that she took to her bed and gradually pined away.'[85]

The harsh night-time call of the barn owl (screech owl) was another long-established and widely held omen of impending death.[86] Seventeenth-century authors referred to the tradition when depicting the popular credulity of their time. In the satirical verse account of a 'Country cunning Man' in *More Knaves Yet* (c. 1613) we hear how:

> Wise Gosling did but hear the Scrich Owl crie,
> And told his Wife, and straight a Pigge did die.[87]

In his *Agriculture improv'd*, William Ellis noted that, 'according to the Notion of County Dames, it is this Screech-Owl that forebodes Death, or Sickness'.[88] Up and down the country, nineteenth- and early twentieth-century folklorists recorded similar opinions about the barn owl and ill fortune. During a Carlisle Bankruptcy Court proceedings in 1944, the person concerned, William Frederick Westmorland, when asked how he accounted for the failure of his farm at Ainstable, Cumbria, replied: 'I had the misfortune to kill a white owl [barn owl] and I have never had any luck since.' As he explained, 'a white owl was nesting in my barn, and while forking hay I accidently struck and killed it'.[89] In general there does seem to have been a diminution in severity, from omen of death to mere omen of bad luck, by the early twentieth century.

Several plants had widely held divinatory properties based on observation.[90] The closing of the flowers of the scarlet pimpernel was a well-known harbinger of rain, and so it was also known as 'shepherd's warning' or 'poor man's weather glass'. Its reputation was as much literary as 'folk', though, as the satirical couplet from a poem on 'Signs of Rain' (1810) by Dr Edward Jenner, the inventor of the smallpox vaccine, was much repeated in print:

> The walls are damp, the ditches smell,
> Closed is the pink-eyed pimpernel.

There was also what one local newspaper called 'the portentous race between oak and ash'.[91] This had numerous recorded variant sayings, but all with the same advice: 'oak before ash in for a splash, ash before oak in for a soak'. A more elaborate version was recorded in 1874:

> If the oak opens before the ash,
> T'will be warm and dry with good wheat to thrash;
> But if ash leaves open before the oak,
> There'll be cold, and of rain too great a soak.[92]

Chapter 6

Folk medicine

The Scottish antiquarian and lawyer William George Black (1857–1932) declared in 1878 that he was the first to coin the term 'folk medicine': 'It is meant to comprehend the subjects of charms, incantations, and those habits relating to the preservation of health, or the cure of disease, which were and are practised by the more superstitious and old-fashioned.'[1] A book on the subject followed in 1883, published by the Folklore Society. But the study of British folk medicine soon got bogged down. How to make sense of such a hodgepodge of often undatable, inexplicable, eclectic, and sometimes bizarre accounts? It did not help that some early folklorists used the archaic Old English term 'leechcraft' instead of the newly coined 'folk medicine', implying thereby that it was a fragmented survival of outdated medieval understanding and 'superstition'. But this vast, accumulated jumble of knowledge can be unpicked by combining historical and folkloristic approaches to healing beliefs and practices.

The study of British folk medicine requires the careful tracking of influences over time. Some of the lore can be found in Anglo-Saxon leechbooks (medical manuals) and later medieval texts; other notions and cures derived from early modern orthodox medicine, and new formulations and inventions were generated throughout the modern era according to developments in science and pseudo-science, as well as new environmental conditions. Folk medicine was never a fixed body of ideas and knowledge. It was adaptable and could become near unrecognisable from its original conception. Consider what we call 'cure accretion', where a healing item or recipe originally for one specific ailment became multipurpose over time, the original, obvious relationship between cure and illness vanishing in the process. We need to recognise that a lot of folk medical knowledge was introduced and passed down through literary sources as well as orally. During the seventeenth and eighteenth centuries there was a boom in herbals and self-help 'domestic medicine' manuals. The likes of Robert James's *Medicinal Dictionary* (1743) provided an expanding literate populace with a huge compilation of centuries of medical knowledge that drew heavily upon ancient sources and the ideas of physicians in other European countries. Folk medicine was not just about people, either. Until the early twentieth century, in numerous ways, veterinary healing was closely aligned with human medicine.

It is also important to recognise the role of astrology, religion, and magic in medical cultures over time. The severity of sickness could be affected by astrological influences, the waxing and waning of the moon in particular. Even in the early twentieth century it was still quite widely believed that whooping cough got worse during a waxing moon. While astrological herbalism was largely discarded by medical officialdom in the eighteenth century, it continued to influence popular medicine long after. The saying of prayers, recitations from the Bible, and 'amens' were integral to some healing traditions. The diagnosis of witchcraft as a cause of sickness was a significant aspect of folk medicine until the early twentieth century. A wide range of conditions were blamed on witches, from eczema to epilepsy, though the most common were mental illnesses and chronic conditions, such as internal cancers, for which orthodox medicine could do little. An illness might be considered natural at first but became recategorised as supernatural by the sufferer over time. The cure usually required magical retribution and the wearing of charms and talismans, though herbal remedies were also prescribed.

There were many regional and local healing traditions, and numerous foreign influences were introduced over time, so the construction of a distinct British, English, Welsh, or Scottish tradition needs to be treated with caution. Consider, for instance, the popularity and promotion of the medical treatise known as the *Meddygon Myddfai* in the nineteenth century. This was a dubious, 'rediscovered' indigenous Welsh healing tradition attributed to the legendary twelfth-century Physicians of Myddfai. It was attractive from a nationalist perspective. As one nineteenth-century Welsh herbal compiler, William Williams, grumbled, 'if a Welshman seeks health he has to go to an Englishman, or one brought up in English ways ... if one dares to seek the ancient means that gave health and long life to our ancestors, then English physicians dub him an empiric or quack'.[2]

While much folk medicine was concerned with self-diagnosis and cure, there had always been thousands of male and female folk healers who offered their specialist services, such herbalists, bonesetters, wen cutters, worm doctors, cancer curers, cunning-folk, and charmers. Cunning-folk were the most important in folkloric terms and will be discussed in the next chapter. Charmers and charming were a separate tradition. Charmers either employed simple oral or written verse healing charms, often based on apocryphal biblical stories, or possessed a healing object for specific ailments. Key to the tradition was that they must not charge for their services. There were also casual healers, who were thought to know a 'bit more' than others. Blacksmiths and butchers were prominent in this category, and so were itinerant outsiders like tramps, tinkers, and the Romani. In popular culture the title of 'Doctor' or 'Doctress' was also sometimes applied to such folk healers who had no official training. Seventh sons and seventh daughters, for instance, were sometimes called 'doctors' by birthright.[3] The resort to such people was not an either/or situation. Most people over the last few centuries both visited licensed physicians and resorted to folk medicine.

What caused sickness?

Before germ theory – in other words, our modern biomedical understanding of disease as being caused by pathogenic micro-organisms such as fungi, bacteria, and viruses – there was still a long-held, general notion that some sickness was contagious, that you caught it from someone or something else. The plague and syphilis are obvious historical examples. Our modern scientific notions of 'infection' were little present in this concept, though. Contagious sickness could be supernatural or environmental. In folk medical theory there was a further notion that the cause of the sickness could not be destroyed or cured by medicine; it could be removed only by passing it on to another person, animal, or inanimate object. We will return to this shortly. And today, as folklorists have shown, old notions of contagion and contamination continue to mix with modern understanding of infection in popular culture, through urban legends and social media rumour. Psychologists have also shown how fundamental cognitive processes are at play, with experiments showing how we still make irrational decisions based on physical associations of contamination, such as not wanting to touch the clothing of a mass murderer, or declining to drink a can of drink placed next to a plastic dog turd.

The ancient notion of humours dominated orthodox medical thinking until well into the eighteenth century. Although we do not find the language of 'humours' in popular usage, traces of the theory can still be found in folk medicine. The idea that health was governed by the balance of the four humours in the body – phlegm, blood, yellow bile, and black bile – goes back to the Greco-Roman world, and its enduring hold over Western medicine was due in large part to the medical writings of the Roman Greek physician Galen (AD 129–216). Central to Galenic medicine were treatments that ensured a harmonious balance between the humours by applying hot and cold or wet and dry treatments, and using purges, emetics, and blood-letting to expel humoral excesses. Then, in seventeenth-century Britain, Galenic medicine was challenged by the 'chemical medicine' espoused by the Swiss physician and alchemist Paracelsus (d. 1541). External chemical influences were deemed as primary causes of ill health, and so cures were likewise based on metals, minerals, and compounds. As a consequence, mercury and sulphur became particularly important ingredients in the chemical physician's arsenal.

Traces of both medical systems can be found in the subsequent folk medicine collected by folklorists and can still be detected today in how people understand and cure their illnesses. The adage 'feed a cold, starve a fever' derives from humoral theory, for instance. In 1978, a North London general practitioner conducted a study of folk medical notions concerning colds and fevers among his patients and found that the elderly ones born before the Second World War still widely expressed the view that colds were caused by environmental effects on the body. They caught colds because they did not 'dress properly', went outside after washing their hair, walked barefoot on a cold floor, got 'one's feet wet', walked 'around with damp socks on', went 'out into the rain, without a hat on', or stepped 'into a puddle'.[4]

Let us also introduce here the concept of 'culture-bound syndromes', in other words, troubling health experiences or strange behaviour that often have localised names and are considered to be a distinct category of illness within a specific culture, though not necessarily recognised as a condition by orthodox medicine. A good example in the history of British folk medicine was a condition known in eastern Scotland as the 'leaping ague' or 'louping ague', which affected humans and sheep. Some described it as a 'melancholy disorder', while others put it down to the effect of intestinal worms. In 1792 it was described as having prevailed occasionally in the area of Lethnot for more than sixty years, and five years later the Revd John Jamieson said of the parish of Tannadice that it was common some twenty to thirty years before. One of the last reported cases occurred in 1818.[5] Fits could be triggered by noise such as the clanging of tongs or the ringing of bells. Dr Farquison of Dundee described seeing two girls succumb to the condition as follows:

I was in the house, one of them was attacked with this disorder, and immediately fell upon her knees; with her head bent back betwixt her shoulders, her neck projecting outwards and very turgid, her eyes not at all disordered nor fixed in this posture, she remained half a minute; after which she got up in great confusion, ran to a large table, leaped up to it at once, though three feet high; her tongue making a circle in her mouth and producing a confused, blubbering noise.[6]

Farquison was told that the pains began in the little finger of both hands and then spread to the head. The condition was heard of no more by the mid-nineteenth century.

Another example is 'hag-riding'. This is related to a now clinically recognised sleep disorder known as sleep paralysis, during which sufferers often experience disturbing hallucinations and a pressure on the chest as well as the inability to move. Up until the mid-twentieth century, in the West Country, it was sometimes thought to be caused by witches or hags riding on the sufferers, who sometimes claimed to see witches on top of them. Several court cases arose in the nineteenth century from sleep paralysis victims assaulting suspected witches after their nocturnal ordeals.[7] These days, examples of culture-bound syndromes in Britain are mostly associated with 'first world' anxieties or the medical traditions of recent migrant communities, such as psychological conditions blamed on *jinn* in some British Muslim communities.

Animal invaders

As the Scottish doctor and folklorist David Rorie (1867–1946) observed from his own patients, people often talked about illness as a vague entity which they called 'the trouble' that could be fed, starved, or transferred. The trouble could be 'got out' through the placement of poultices, for example, which were then destroyed.[8] But there was a widespread and enduring popular medical fear, fuelled by folk misnomer, that the various openings in the body were prone to unwelcome entry from small animals that then caused a range of symptoms. Take worms, for example.

People regularly got intestinal worms, such as threadworms and tapeworms, in the past from ingesting their eggs in infected meat or drinking sewage-polluted water. But worms were also thought to be in places where they certainly were not, such as teeth. Writing in 1876, a correspondent to the *St. Andrews Gazette* noted that in Aberdeenshire and other parts of Scotland the toothache was still called 'the worm', though he observed: 'I never heard any one seriously allege that the decay of the tooth and the gnawing pain by which it is so frequently accompanied were produced by a worm.' In other words, the name was a relic of a redundant belief.[9] Other sources suggest the notion lingered for a few more decades. What seemed like an implausible idea was made real by quack doctors and medical charlatans. In 1778 the respected London surgeon John Coakley Lettsom (1744–1815) noted that there was currently in London a celebrated toothache doctress who, by sleight of hand, removed the 'worms' from her clients' teeth. She kept silk moth eggs and took the larvae from them 'which she artfully exhibits after using certain operations'.[10]

Several decades later, the author of the *Yorkshire Cattle-Doctor* (1834) complained of similar tricks when it came to a condition he called the 'Felon', where cows walked stiffly, went off their food, and looked generally unwell: 'many people affirm that there is a worm in the beast's tail, and cut it, pretending to take out the worm. This is a mean juggling trick.'[11] An old glossary explained that the object extracted was sometimes just a piece of sinew that looked a bit like a worm.[12] Such tail cutting due to supposed worms carried on for another century, leading to the occasional intervention of the RSPCA and ensuing court cases, such as one dealt with by the Isle of Ely Police Court in 1902, when a farmer was charged with animal cruelty. The court heard how an emaciated cow was thought to have tail worm, so a hole was cut in the tail and salt put in it to kill the worm. The RSPCA inspector complained that 'it was an old woman's or an old man's superstition'.[13] In 1938 the Bridgend police court, Wales, dealt with what a Cardiff veterinarian called a 'very old, barbarous custom'. A dairy farmer of Porthcawl was fined £1 and three guineas' costs for animal abuse after a hay-cutter, Archie Phillips, declared a sick cow had a worm in the tail and cut it. In his defence, Phillips said he had been born and bred on a farm and seen tails cut hundreds of times for the worm: 'It was an old custom among farmers.'[14]

In 1929, a Norfolk GP wrote how he had recently seen a patient who had been discharged from Norwich Hospital for neuritis and diabetic gangrene. The woman explained to him the cause of her neuritis (nerve inflammation). Years before she had an open head wound and a neighbour helped to bind it up. But before it was fully sealed a centipede, known locally as a 'forty-foot', had got into the wound and thence had free passage around her body for years. It used to 'arsle to and fro' (move back and forth), she explained. Then, one day in hospital, she saw the 'forty-foot' run across her bed counterpane with two young ones: 'Beauties they were, too. They'd have took a prize anywhere.' Since then, she had been free of her discomfort.[15]

The earwig was a more common intruder. In 1829 it was reported as a matter of fact in Welsh papers, for instance, that twenty-five live earwigs were extracted from the head of a young woman of Henllis, Newport, who had been suffering from terrible headaches.[16] But the defence of the earwig was growing. In 1830 the *Bucks Gazette* complained of the 'unfounded popular prejudice' against the insect. Although it suggested that they might occasionally attempt to shelter in the ear, the odour of earwax would drive them away, and besides, they could not pass the ear drum. A domestic manual called *The Housewife's Reason Why* (1857) likewise condemned the idea of earwigs causing madness or death as a 'vulgar error', and by way of reassurance gave an anecdote about how several regiments were camped in fields near Winchester some years earlier that were swarming with earwigs. Yet, in the entire season only one soldier reported having an earwig crawl into his outer ear while asleep and it was easily removed without any inconvenience.[17] Despite such attempts at popular instruction, the belief continued to have currency into the early twentieth century. An inquest on a twelve-year-old boy from Southwark in 1913 heard the father state that his son had gone off to work in the Kent hop fields in good health, but when he returned home he could see from his son's face that an earwig 'had got into his head and poisoned him'. He stated, intriguingly, that he had read that they caused such brain trouble in a Sunday newspaper.[18]

At the inquest of Mary Rogers, wife of a Wolverhampton blacksmith, in 1919, it was heard how she was convinced she had earwigs in her head and an adder in her stomach. During her stay in an asylum she once asked the medical superintendent for a glass of milk. As he told the inquest, she put it by her bedside and told him that she hoped that during the night, while she was asleep, the snake would emerge to drink the milk and she would be cured.[19] Such an idea was not a figment of an insane mind.

The notion that reptiles and amphibians could grow inside human and animal stomachs, depriving the victim of nourishment, had been reported for centuries and was alive and well in Britain into the twentieth century.[20] How were they thought to get there? People concluded that they had swallowed tadpoles, spawn, or baby snakes when drinking from rivers, streams, and ponds. The Scottish folklorist James Napier recalled that in his childhood the belief was widespread in western Scotland and 'this gave boys a great fear of stretching down and drinking from a pool, or even a running stream'.[21] Another explanation concerned people or animals sleeping out in the open air with their mouths open and the snakes or newts taking advantage. In 1889, for instance, it was reported that John Hammon, of Stanford, Kent, had recently bought a calf from a farmer named Bowes of Elham, which soon fell poorly and seemed at death's door. He gave the calf a drink and was amazed to see a dead snake nearly three foot long emerge from the calf's mouth. The calf soon recovered, and it was supposed that the snake had been attracted to the drops of milk in the calf's mouth shortly after suckling, and slithered in while the calf lay dozing in the fields.[22]

When people were convinced that they had such 'bosom serpents', they drew upon their physical ordeals, the chronic gastric gnawing pains, hunger, and belly discomfort they felt, which no doctor had successfully cured. It was the actual experience that reinforced the notion and continuation of the belief. After apparently vomiting up a four-inch lizard one day in 1904, George Biggins, aged seventy, of Shrub End, Colchester, suspected that there was another. 'I am not yet well,' he said. 'When I sit quietly I can still feel something moving just as the first lizard did.'[23]

Although folk ideas were often reported as instances of popular medical ignorance, the boundary between them and medical orthodoxy was still blurred at the end of the nineteenth century. In 1892, newspapers reported that after a woman named Jane Rowe of Marazion, Cornwall, vomited up a lizard, the local doctor named Mudge preserved it and reckoned it had been living in her stomach for years.[24] A search through the census records reveals that he was a licensed surgeon and general practitioner named James Mudge. Three years later, regional newspapers reported soberly on a case of newt extraction from Silvertown, East London. A woman was thought to have swallowed a newt tadpole hidden in some insufficiently washed watercress she had eaten. Terrible intestinal pains and diarrhoea ensued as the tadpole developed into an adult newt in her stomach. All this was surmised because a West End physician apparently witnessed her extracting an immense eight-inch-long newt from her throat after severe vomiting.[25] As well as tempting snakes out with bowls of milk, folk cures for stomach intruders included swallowing a salted herring or salted pork and then lying by a stream. The amphibian or reptile would get so thirsty that it would crawl up the throat and out of the mouth to reach water.[26]

Later in the twentieth century, popular understanding of germ theory still showed signs of this old folk notion. Instead of animals there was a new cohort of bodily invaders – 'germs', 'bugs', and 'viruses'. But people talked about them in the singular. The common phrase 'I've got a bug' is clearly an echo of the old animal intruder. In the 1978 London study mentioned earlier, patients referred to being attacked from the inside by one 'germ' or 'bug' moving around their bodies like in the old descriptions: 'I've got that Germ doctor, you know – the one that gives you dry cough.'[27]

Curing sickness

We begin by acknowledging that magic and religious faith played an important role in British folk medicine in the cure of both naturally and supernaturally inspired ailments. Sometimes cures were overtly magical, using written charms, for example, but in many instances there is just a pinch of magic, a bit of ritual. Prayers or amens might be said. A herbal remedy might involve triplication – taking three of something or doing something three times or nine times. An ingredient might also have to come from a symbolic place in order to be effective, such as herbs plucked from a grave, or picked at certain times. In this section the focus is on other broad categories of curative method, some of which still had porous boundaries with the world of magic. One of them was the *law of sympathy*, which was central to folk healing.

The law of sympathy, broadly defined in medical terms, is that 'like cures like', either symbolically or physically, and that things can have an invisible healing influence over other things that have at one time been in contact, however briefly. The healing power of some plants was based on their resemblance to the body part that was afflicted. God had given it a 'signature'. This was an ancient notion given renewed vigour in Paracelsian medicine. So, some plants with yellow flowers, such as celandine, were good for jaundice, which caused a sallow complexion. The 'hair of the dog' for the cure of hydrophobia (rabies) is another classic example of sympathetic association. Cases can be found into the early twentieth century of people plastering hairs from the aggressing dog onto the bite wound. There are several examples of people eating the fried liver of the dog as well. To break the sympathetic association, the dog could also be killed, and several court cases arose from this practice in the 1870s and 1880s.[28] A good example of symbolic sympathy concerned the practice of curing inguinal hernias by splitting a young tree and passing the patient through the tree and then binding the tree back up. As the tree healed, so the hernia would disappear.

Transference was another key concept of folk medicine, being related to folk contagion theory and the law of sympathy. Certain ailments could be cured by transferring them to another living thing or inanimate substance. If a living thing, it would eventually die and ensure that the ailment left this world. In

1895 a Mr Cuthbert of Clun, Shropshire, wrote to the professional journal *The Lancet* under the heading 'Strange Remedies', telling of a local case he knew where to treat a young boy of oral thrush a frog was hung head downwards into his mouth until it died. One man boasted that he had 'worn out' four frogs curing his own child of the same.[29]

In another Shropshire account from the 1870s, an elderly woman who performed the cure for others did express some sympathy for the frogs: 'we used to hear the poor frog whooping and coughing, mortal bad, for days after; it would have made your heart ache to hear the poor creature coughing as it did about the garden'.[30] This was of course proof, though, that the disease had been transferred. Thanks to this cure, thrush was known as 'the frog' in some parts of England. One of the most widely recorded examples concerned the transference of whooping cough to a dog by taking some hair from the affected child's head and placing it in either a piece of meat or bread and butter and feeding it to a dog. It was still recommended and occasionally practised into the early twentieth century. A letter writer to a Northamptonshire newspaper in 1925 noted that, eight years before, an elderly woman in West Haddon had advised her to do this on hearing that her children had whooping cough.[31]

Afflictions could also be transferred to inanimate substances. Although rare in the folklore surveys of the late nineteenth century, Scottish witch trial records reveal the widespread ritual of washing the shirts of the sick in running water to wash away the disease. The macabre practice of rubbing wens (large sebaceous cysts on the head) with the hand of a freshly hanged man was also likely an act of transference. This was practised in England up until the mid-nineteenth century, providing executioners with pocket money for leading distressed wen sufferers onto the gallows platform minutes after hangings. The wens were likely destined for Hell with their new host.[32] Rituals to transfer sickness to *living* humans were rare, presumably for moral reasons. The main exception was a wart cure whereby each wart was rubbed with a pebble, the pebbles were then placed in a bag or wrapped in a parcel and left at a crossroads or on a footpath. The first person to pick up the package would get the wart. Voluntary transference is also evident in the tradition of buying and selling warts.

The wearing of curative objects was integral to folk healing. Some were overtly magical in purpose, while others were considered to work on sympathetic or scientific principles. Ancient archaeological artefacts that were thought to be the result of natural or supernatural forces rather than human manufacture made up one category. The snakestone or adder stone bead is one of the oldest recorded examples, used variously to assuage childbirth pains, whooping cough, teething, and malaria (ague), and either was worn or was dipped in water that was then drunk. These were usually decorated Romano-British or Anglo-Saxon glass beads found in the fields, but in popular belief they were thought to be formed from the spittle or froth of snakes. The tradition was strongest in Scotland and was known in Wales, but was little mentioned in English folklore. In Scotland, prehistoric spindle whorls were likewise interpreted as adder stones formed from snakes sloughing their skins. Prehistoric flint arrowheads were considered to be the work of elves or fairies and were imbued with healing properties.[33]

Plants could also be worn as amulets. Vervain is a good example, which was used in religion and medicine in ancient Rome and mentioned in the Classics. The use of the root as an amulet for scrofula was widely promoted in a cheap pamphlet written by a gentleman farmer and healer of the poor named John Morley, of Halstead, Essex. Entitled *An essay on the nature and cure of the King's Evil, deduced from observation and practice*, it went through some forty-two printings between 1760 and 1824.[34] The basis of the cure was borrowed from earlier printed sources, but Morley added his own flourishes, and went on to explain:

> When I put this Root about the Patient's Neck, I am not ashamed to say, 'Pray God give his blessing to this my Endeavours,' or some such short Ejaculation; not by way of Charm, or such like Nonsense, but to remind the Patient of our Dependence on the divine Help.[35]

This vervain charm can be found repeatedly cited, usually unacknowledged, in twentieth-century newspapers and folklore books as a traditional folk cure for a variety of ailments.

Chronic pain was particularly likely to attract amuletic medicine as a long-term preventative rather than cure. Rheumatism, for example, accrued an array of healing amulets over the last few centuries, with a strong emphasis on the supposed innate chemical properties of the material worn. Lodestone or magnetic amulets were used for centuries for this purpose. In 1835 a Lambeth doctor wrote in *The Lancet* that 'many of the poorer class of people carry a piece of "stone brimstone" in the pocket as a charm against that complaint'. He had recently talked to a sailor who put sulphur powder in his boots to keep the rheumatics at bay.[36] Nearly a century later, Edward Lovett interviewed the proprietor of a London chemists who sold hermetically sealed phials of mercury as a rheumatism cure.[37] Paracelsian medicine alive and well!

Persistent leg cramps was another such condition, which led to the wearing of small animal leg bones, such as sheep patella, as a sympathetic or transference cure. A correspondent to the *Gentleman's Magazine* in 1826 related: 'I remember, when I was a boy, finding in the pocket of an octogenarian domestic, a part of the bone of a leg of mutton. On inquiry, I found it was considered to be a charm – a sure and certain remedy against the cramp!'[38]

Those animals feared, despised, or considered unlucky while alive were often considered medically useful in death. Before the rabbit's foot became a popular lucky charm in the twentieth century, a hare's foot was carried as a curative amulet, recorded from the sixteenth century onward as a charm for cramps, colic, and rheumatism.[39] Although eating hare meat was something of a taboo, hare's brain was a well-recorded cure for fractious infants into the early twentieth century, most likely due to the law of sympathy. The hare was associated with melancholy, and so would have a calming effect on restless infants. In 1877 physician Edward T. Blake instead rationalised that the phosphorous and fat content of a hare's brain would have been beneficial for atrophied children.[40] Snake skins or sloughs were worn to prevent headaches. The association is not clear, but possibly based on humoral notions of the coolness of snakes and that the hotness of the head caused headaches. In 1894 a correspondent to the *Illustrated Sporting News*, who wrote of his fascination with snakes in southern England, noted that he had frequently 'seen snake skins taken from the lining of an agricultural labourer's working hat' as a headache preventative.[41]

The mole has also played a significant role in British folk medicine since at least the early modern period. The blood was used to cure epilepsy, while the foot of a mole was carried as an amulet against multiple ailments. Lieutenant J. A. Walker noted in 1839 that around Minehead, Somerset, it was still practised that the left forefoot of a mole suspended in a silk bag from the neck was a charm against toothache. Writing at the end of the century, the vicar of Alford, Lincolnshire, confirmed that there were still two people in his parish who wore a mole's foot around their necks as a preventative for the fits from which they suffered.[42]

When the London journalist Henry Mayhew (1812–1887) interviewed collectors and market vendors of live frogs and toads, he found the toad trade was near non-existent, with one vendor complaining that there was demand for only around twenty a year, though he knew some 'real stunners' around Hampstead and Willesden. What little demand there was, was from herbalists: 'I don't know what they're wanted for,' said one toad collector, 'something

Figure 6.1 Amuletic dried toad or frog that was carried in a silk bag, 1901–1930, south Devon. Science Museum Group.

about the doctors, I believe.'[43] This tiny trade in toads for London's herbalists was probably to do with the long-established amuletic use of toads into the early twentieth century (Figure 6.1). The cure had two medical bases. One was the toad's supposed poison-drawing property. Hence, according to the London physician John Pechey (1655–1716) in 1697, 'Externally Toads are of excellent Use in the Plague, for Preservation and Cure. The whole Toad may be worn for an Amulet in the Plague, or they may be applied to the pestilential Bubos; for they are said to draw out all of the Venom, and so cure the sick.'[44] The other modus operandi was sympathy. In his *Country Housewife's Family Companion* the farmer and agricultural writer William Ellis (c. 1700–1758), of Little Gaddesden, Hertfordshire, related the instance of an eleven-year-old girl from his village who was cured of the King's Evil in her feet by the toad cure recommended by a passing beggar woman:

> If they would cut off the hind Leg, and the fore Leg on the contrary Side of that, of a Toad, and wear them in a silken Bag about her Neck, it would certainly cure her; but it was to be observed, that on the Toad's losing its Legs, it was to be turned loose abroad, and as it pined, wasted, and died, the Distemper would likewise waste and die.[45]

While the wearing of such animal amulets largely died out by the early twentieth century, several other simple traditions remained. Carrying a nutmeg for sciatica, lumbago, and rheumatism remained popular. In 1937 a Warwickshire newspaper correspondent got chatting to a group of businessmen on the train and found that, of the ten, three carried a nutmeg and believed fully in its power.[46] Potatoes continued to be kept in pockets for the same reasons. It was reported from Calderdale in 1932 that young children still wore red silk thread around their necks as a preventative against colds.[47] New, cheap, mass-produced charms and amulets also came into vogue, though they rarely lasted more than a few years, disappearing once stock dried up or the fashion dwindled.

One of the more enduring amulets was the blue bead necklace, worn to prevent bronchitis. Indeed, such was their popularity that in 1914 Edward Lovett conducted a major street investigation across London, enquiring about the beads at sixty 'poor class' shops and sixty 'fancy' shops that sold beads and trinkets. Every working-class shopkeeper knew about or sold the blue beads, but not one of the posher shops said they knew anything about them.[48] They were apparently mass produced in Austria and sold wholesale to vendors in Britain for three shillings per gross of necklaces. In 1926 a contributor to *Folklore* noted the continued popularity of strings of blue beads worn under their clothes by children and old women as a protection against chest ailments.[49] When she asked her South London 'char lady' about them, the woman replied that her granddaughter, who was living with her, wore one. 'Do you ever take it off, say, when you wash her?' 'Oh no! Then she'd catch cold.'[50] But by the 1940s the fad was largely forgotten.

From 1954 to 1955 there was a brief, unfortunate enthusiasm for asbestos rope as a cure for lumbago. Wilfred Perkins, a manufacturer of such rope in Hurstpierpoint, Sussex, was a very happy man, though he made no claims as to its healing properties: 'now scores of people all over the country are going to sleep with two eight-foot lengths of asbestos rope under their mattresses,' he told the *Daily Mirror*.[51] Then, in the 1960s, came the more enduring, widespread vogue for wearing copper bracelets as a cure for rheumatism. It was not a new tradition. In the early twentieth century an old fisherman of Scarborough fabricated and sold copper bangles and rings for the condition.[52] But copper bracelets became a national item following a clever advertising campaign between 1959 and 1961. In September 1961, the *People* newspaper carried out an investigation under the sceptical headline: 'Would you fork out a quid for this curious "cure"?' The company behind the product and advertising was the recently founded Sabona Rheumatic Relief Company Ltd (still in existence), which claimed in its marketing that various celebrities, such as the actor Kenneth More and the Marquess of Bath, wore their bracelets.[53] Others jumped on the bandwagon, with one firm claiming in their adverts that their bracelets were a 'centuries old remedy, so well known to gipsy folk'.[54] In 1978, Michael Mason, a consultant rheumatologist and medical secretary of the Arthritis and Rheumatism Council, complained that most of his patients wore one when they first came to see him.[55]

Our healing categories so far have relied mostly on ritual actions or external influences, but, as today, many medicines were taken orally and ingested, including some plants with sympathetic properties. There was an element of 'if it tastes bad it must be good for you' in folk medicine, though sweeteners like honey or sugar were common in remedies to counteract bitterness. There were also remedies that 'worked', at least in part, by overcoming feelings of disgust. This was probably partly the case with 'worm water', made from boiled earthworms, which seems to have been mostly used for intestinal complaints. There was also, perhaps, an element of 'sympathy' – worms to cure worms in the innards. A Yorkshire cure for heartburn, or 'water springs' as it was known in local dialect, consisted of a handful of earthworms from a churchyard boiled with calcined, powdered shells from mussels, oysters, or cockles. The shells would have acted as an antacid, but there was no need for the worm water. Folklorist William Henderson remembered a fireside conversation at Sprouston, in the Scottish Borders, in 1863 during which he expressed scepticism about worm water, and was promptly rebuked. Had he not heard of the local woman at death's door and given up by the doctors? Her friends 'houkit a pint o' worms, and biled them in fresh water, and gaed her the broo to drink. Frae that hour she began to mend.'[56]

The 'hold your nose and swallow' element was also partly in play with regard to the ingestion of small frogs for ailments of the throat or those that caused respiratory discomfort, such as consumption, whooping cough, and asthma. The farmer and agricultural writer William Ellis wrote that one Daniel Watkins of Long Marston, near Aylesbury, told him that he had successfully cured himself of asthma by swallowing young frogs. Ellis also recommended putting three small frogs down the throat of a sheep that is unable to regurgitate its cud. Occasional reports of the practice can be found up until the late nineteenth century. There was also a physical curative aspect to the frog cure in that the sliminess of the frogs, as also with frog spawn water, was thought to act as a lubricant to ease the passages, and also as an expectorant. A magical element was sometimes present. For whooping cough, the Yorkshire folklorist Richard Blakeborough 'was assured that nothing was better than to walk along a road until you found nine frogs; these had to be carried home and made into a soup'.[57]

In early twentieth century north-east Scotland, 'oil of white slugs' was still used as a cure for consumption, but snail soup was the most widespread of these sorts of slimy cure.[58] In his *Family-Physician* (1678), Gideon Harvey criticised the 'London snail water' being sold as a consumption cure by apothecaries in the capital, and instead provided a recipe for his own 'Liquor of snails' for the same purpose. As he explained (in humoral terms), 'the cool, clammy, and glutinous substance' cooled consumptive fevers, repaired the 'consumed' parts, and acted as an expectorant. Well into the eighteenth century, domestic medicine guides provided similar snail water recipes for chin coughs and consumption. Sarah Harrison's *The house-keeper's pocket-book* (1755) recommended for consumption twenty snails boiled in a quart of water along with daisies until reduced to a pint. A spoonful of this was to be taken every morning in some milk.[59] By the nineteenth century it had been dropped from such literature, but it lived on in folk medicine. A newspaper reported in 1874 that there was a lively trade in common snails at Covent Garden Market for the cure of chest complaints. Even as late as 1961 a correspondent to *Folklore* noted that some seven years before she had found that in several parts of Berkshire bad coughs were still treated by dissolving snails in water to form a liquor, which was then swallowed as an emulsion with cream and a sweetener.[60]

There were numerous modest, home-made mundane treatments based on the natural properties of plants, of course, such as herbal teas and tonics. Mint tea was generally used for digestive problems, and taken for coughs and colds in southern England. An infusion of betony was drunk variously for indigestion and headaches. It was mentioned in 1863 that the lichen lungwort (*Sticta pulmonaria*) was still used for consumption in the New Forest, and that people would ask at the chemists for 'a pennyworth of lungs of oak'.[61] Then there were poultices, balms, ointments, and creams for topical application. House leek, for instance, was quite widely used to assuage scalds and sunstroke, herb robert for skin complaints, and greater plantain for piles, rashes, and sores. Numerous plants were used in wart cures.[62] Most such remedies can be found in the old herbals and recipe books, but there was quite a lot of regional diversity, suggesting that some folklore records captured mutable oral tradition at play, with one plant having different purposes from one region to another.[63]

Industrial-urban folk medicine

It would be wrong to consider folk medicine as some ancient rural heritage in exorable decline over the last two centuries. Druggists and herbalists were important perpetuators of folk medicine in expanding urban areas, stocking herbs and chemicals that had long been used in folk cures. The markets of industrial cities also sold ingredients. In 1860, for instance, the fungologist Miles Joseph Berkeley (1803–1889) reported that 'Jews ear' was still sold at Covent Garden Market, London, 'in consequence of some supposed healing properties'.[64] This was probably not the fungus but, rather, liverwort (a cure for hydrophobia), at a time when rabies panics still periodically erupted in London and elsewhere. A century before, the English botanist John Hill (c. 1714–1775) had observed that the fungus version was 'out of repute' as a remedy, but that a different plant was then commonly sold at Covent Garden Market under the same name, noting that it was collected from the water pipes at the New River head at Islington, which was a crucial source of water for London.[65]

New environments bred new opportunities. The treatment of whooping cough by breathing noxious air led to afflicted children being taken to lime kilns and down coal mines. In 1902 one newspaper wryly observed that 'it is well known that gasworks are regarded as first-class health resorts for children suffering from whooping cough'. The comment was occasioned by an article written by Edward A. Harman, an engineer at Huddersfield gasworks. Harman had seen many children being brought to tour for an hour around the purifier boxes and tar syphons, 'the more sulphurous and ammoniacal the smells were, the greater the relief the children obtained'.[66] David Rorie suggested that the pyridine in the gasworks air acted as an antiseptic and germicide.[67] There are also reports of children being taken to sniff the tarmac of newly laid roads during the first half of the twentieth century.

For a few decades around the turn of the twentieth century, railway 'tunnel air' also became a quite well-recorded adaptation of the cure for whooping cough. Charlotte Burne, writing in the 1880s, knew a gentleman travelling from Whitchurch to Tutbury on the North Staffordshire line, who witnessed a woman lifting her child to an open window as the train passed through the Harecastle Tunnel. A decade or so later, another such encounter happened on the train from Peterborough to King's Cross. In 1902 it was reported that a guard on the London Underground was told by a young East End woman travelling with her baby that they had done two complete rounds on the Inner

Circle because a herbalist and bone setter had told her that a sulphurous atmosphere was a good treatment for her baby's whooping cough.[68] With the advent of passenger aeroplanes, another new folk formulation of 'curative air' appeared in Britain in the 1930s, inspired by pseudo-scientific research in Germany – namely, that the special atmospheric air conditions during high-altitude aeroplane flight would cure whooping cough. In January 1939, children Audrey and Malcome Brooke were put on a plane at Leeds-Bradford aerodrome and taken to a height of 14,000 feet. Their father was hopeful of a successful cure, as he reported that neither of them coughed during the flight. The Second World War obviously interrupted further such attempts, but in 1949 a special whooping-cough flight was arranged from Croydon airport by Rose and Edward Davis, the parents of two young children suffering from the malady.[69]

The advent of the telegraph and electricity in urban streets and homes brought new folk health concerns over external influences and bodily intruders. While this is not evident from folklore sources, the asylum records are rich in information. In 1910, Lancashire patient William Moores, aged forty-eight, was tormented by an electricity testing station across the street from where he lived, which he blamed for the pains in his limbs and head and his wife's miscarriage. Some people were very suspicious of wiring and complained that evil influences were being sent into their home and bodies through electrical or telephone wires. One patient explained that his neighbour sent electricity through the walls to persecute him, giving him pains in the head and making 'the oil boil out on his scalp'. Many such cases show how some people initially saw electricity as an invisible malign force akin to witchcraft.[70] We find echoes of the same health concerns in contemporary beliefs about the spread of mobile phone masts and 5G broadband.

A new age of folk medicine

William Black's view of folk medicine as the work of the 'superstitious and old fashioned' is now old fashioned itself. The use of animal parts in folk medicine may have largely died out by the early twentieth century, but herbalism has maintained a firm place in British alternative healthcare. In the early 1990s the *Flora Britannica* project, a crowd-sourced ethnographic survey about British wild plants, found that a half dozen or so species were regularly reported as still being widely used across the country in folk-medical ways, including feverfew for migraines, comfrey for bruises, dandelion as a diuretic and laxative, and greater celandine for warts. Roy Vickery's decades of crowd-sourcing contemporary plant lore have revealed a similar picture.[71]

The term 'Western herbal medicine' was coined in the UK in the 1990s to make a distinction between herbalism based on this venerable European tradition and the growing popularity in the country of non-Western medical systems. Around this time there were over nine hundred registered 'medical herbalists' of the European/British tradition. A study published in 2001 found that 4 per cent of people had consulted such a herbalist in their lifetimes, but many more, 32 per cent, had used over-the-counter herbal remedies.[72] There has also been a renewed enthusiasm among pharmaceutical companies to use traditional medicinal plants, such as drugs derived from the yew tree, wormwood, and goat's rue, and the production of plant extracts such as valerian for insomnia, squill as an expectorant in cough medicines, and St John's wort for depression. Overseas plants have also been marketed, such as evening primrose, first grown in Britain in the seventeenth century, its oil being used for various conditions such as post-menopausal symptoms and eczema.[73]

Herbalism is just one sector in what is now known as Complementary and Alternative Medicine (CAM), although a study published in 2010 found some reservations among those who professed to be traditional British 'folk healers' about being marginalised due to the growth of the much broader CAM market. The 2005 Health Survey for England revealed that over 50 per cent of asthma patients, around one-third of arthritis sufferers and cancer patients, and 35–69 per cent of dermatology patients had tried some form of CAM, often motivated by the personal experience that mainstream medicine had proved ineffective.

Other surveys have also shown that sufferers of other conditions, namely obesity, anxiety, and depression, were also more inclined to try alternative therapies.[74] Among these alternative therapies are an interesting mix of ancient non-Western medical traditions, such as South Asian Ayurvedic medicine, which includes humours and humoral imbalance in its conception of body and spirit, and uses herbs, minerals, and metals in its cures. Although it was likely practised by Indian migrants in Britain for a couple of centuries, it garnered much wider British interest from the 1980s.[75] Traditional Chinese medicine has also attracted non-Chinese British patients. Like Ayurvedic medicine and Western humoral theory, it is based on holistic notions of bodily health, with good health corresponding to the right balance of energy flows in the body. Herbal remedies and acupuncture provide the means of controlling excesses of 'hot', 'cold', 'wet', and 'dry' energies.[76]

Part IV

Spiritual life

Part IV
Spiritual life

Chapter 7
Living with a supernatural world

The term 'supernatural' pervades popular culture today. It is used to cover everything from elves to extrasensory perception, from haunted houses to Ouija boards. But it comes with a lot of historical baggage and has accrued multiple meanings. Anthropologists, sociologists, historians, psychologists, folklorists, and mass media have contributed to a stew of definitions, usages, and approaches. Go back five hundred years, though, and 'supernatural' was a basic theological term denoting things above or beyond God's natural world. This was sometimes presented as a dichotomy between material and non-material or spiritual existence. Much debate centred on whether miracles were natural or supernatural. Demonologists argued that the Devil did not have supernatural powers; he could work only within the order of nature, and thereby used tricks and illusion – wonder – to fool people into believing that he and his demons worked in supernatural ways. The term 'preternatural' entered intellectual discourse to denote phenomena that were not supernatural but could not necessarily be explained in natural terms – in other words, the hidden or occult workings of God's creation. In theory, the more that humans came to understand natural processes, the more redundant became the term preternatural.

By the nineteenth century, the category of preternatural was largely forgotten as a way of understanding inexplicable phenomena. Orthodox Protestant religion and biblical interpretation became increasingly rationalised, while fringe science came up with new theories of invisible natural forces at work in the world, such as animal magnetism, hypnotism, and odic force.[1] Still, debates over natural and supernatural categories were reinvigorated by the rise of spiritualism, leading to the coining of new terms such as 'supernormal' and 'psychical'.[2] Meanwhile, 'supernatural' developed a baggier meaning, becoming a catch-all term for inexplicable experiences, magical happenings, or spooky sensations, leading the London Evangelical Alliance to reject the term in 1896 because of its increasing occult associations, and to replace it with the word 'spiritual'.[3]

The supernatural was not a separate category of study for early British folklorists. It was included in the title of only one article in the journal *Folklore* before 1938, and it was only from the 1970s onward, with the term becoming part of popular language, that it appeared on a more regular basis. That does not mean it was absent from the folklorist's vocabulary all this time, just that it was usually used in a casual rather than conceptual way to describe 'superstitious' beliefs, the spirit world, or magical powers generally.

Come the current millennium, and psychologists have reflected critically on the range of related terms they now use. As the authors of one article put it: 'What's in a Term? Paranormal, Superstitious, Magical and Supernatural: Beliefs by Any Other Name Would Mean the Same'.[4] The authors argue that their discipline needs to provide much more precise conceptual definitions. Folklorists might also want to look again at the way they have used such terms, particularly in light of the increasing adoption of the term 'paranormal' in folklore studies.

'Paranormal' was first used in English literature in 1905 and was a translation from a French publication. At that stage it was basically used as a synonym for the term 'supernormal', or preternatural, and was defined in 1906 as 'powers which at present transcend those of other men, but at which may at some future phase of evolution become themselves the rule rather than the exception'. It started to be used regularly in psychical research literature only in the 1920s, and subsequently the definition began to broaden. In contemporary mass culture it has, like supernatural, expanded hugely to cover a wide set of unconnected phenomena, including UFOs, ghosts, monsters, and psychic powers, thereby spawning the concept of 'paranormal cultures'. It has been suggested, indeed, that 'folklorists are the academics best suited' to explore people's experiences of the paranormal.[5] Let us see.

Magical people

The figures of the witch and the magician have two entwined identities in folklore – the real and the legendary. They were sometimes the subject of 'once upon a time' stories that were 'told as true' and which reinforced local and national identities.[6] Take, for example, the Cornish legend of Lord Pengerswick the Enchanter and his battles with the Witch of Fraddam, related by Robert Hunt in his *Popular Romances of the West of England*. Think also of the celebrated Yorkshire prophetess, Mother Shipton, born of the union of her mother and the Devil, whose story was made up and first published in the seventeenth century. Yet, most witches and magicians in the folklore record were very real people – once. We can sometimes build up quite detailed pictures of these characters as they flit in and out of folklore sources, parish archives, newspaper reports, and criminal records.[7]

We referred to magicians just now, but what we really mean in a folkloric sense are men and women known as cunning-folk or, on a regional basis, conjurors, wise-women and wise-men, wizards, and *dyn hysbys* in Wales. Historians have also described them more broadly as 'service magicians' in that they provided magical expertise for paying clients, as distinct from magicians pursuing a personal esoteric tradition. As well as often being proficient herbalists they offered a range of magical services, including thief detection, love magic, and fortune-telling; but most important of all was their role in identifying witches and countering their spells. Whether in legends or trial material, roughly two-thirds were men, though cunning-women could have equally prominent reputations.[8] We often find them mentioned as having been consulted by the bewitched in early modern witch-trial narratives and they were occasionally prosecuted for witchcraft themselves. The 1736 Witchcraft Act, which denied and decriminalised the existence of witchcraft, kept penalties for those who pretended to have magical powers, so we also find them being prosecuted into the twentieth century, though usually under the Vagrancy Act, which penalised those 'pretending or professing to tell fortunes, or using any subtle craft, means, or device, by palmistry or otherwise, to deceive and impose on any of his Majesty's subjects'.[9] They were also the subject of popular biographies in the eighteenth and early nineteenth centuries and were figures in rural romantic novels.[10]

Becoming a 'living legend' was important for attracting a clientele and making their magic 'work'. The stories that circulated about successful cases of magical thief detection, for instance, were instrumental in how the practice actually worked. If word got around that a victim of theft had gone to a cunning-person to identify and deal with the thief, it sometimes led to the thief quietly returning the stolen goods to avoid magical punishment. Mystery solved! The circulation of legends also bolstered the relevancy of the cunning trade more generally, particularly in the nineteenth century, when there was greater competition from orthodox medicine, new alternative healers on the scene, and increased legal jeopardy. But legends around cunning-folk were occasionally also negative, and more witch-like personas could develop after death.[11] For instance, the son of a celebrated Herefordshire conjurer was considered 'as clever as his father, but his cleverness was not always exercised for good'. He could change 'hisself to anything', and according to one legend he stole a horse one time and was taken to Hereford gaol, but when the time came for his trial he magically disappeared.[12]

The legends told about the famed *dyn hysbys* Dr John Harries of Cwrt-y-Cadno, Carmarthenshire, were overwhelmingly positive. There were, in fact, two of them, father (c. 1785–1839) and son (c. 1827–1863). It is not always clear to which the legends refer, though most are likely about the father.[13] The many stories recorded decades after his death are respectful in tone, most of them matter-of-fact accounts of his successes that have little embroidery; but there are also a number of more tale-like, fantastical accounts. It was thought, for instance, that he could mark out thieves by making a horn grow on their heads. There is a lengthy account of a farmer who hid in some straw and saw Harries conjure up seven demons in succession to ask who had stolen the farmer's cows. Only the seventh was able to give an answer.

In other legends Harries was an upholder of moral values, taking it upon himself to punish meanness and cheating. On one occasion, when visiting Swansea, he was overcharged by a butcher for a joint of meat. Harries put a spell upon him so that he could not stop dancing and capering – a common folktale motif. The butcher's wife found her husband singing 'Eight and six for meat! What a wicked cheat!' Then their servants came under the spell and the household became a public laughing stock. Harries returned to withdraw his malediction, telling the butcher, 'That will teach you not to overcharge honest people again.'[14]

On the other side of the country, the Yorkshire wise-man John Wrightson of Stokesley accrued a similar body of legends and memorates. As one folklorist said of him in 1898, 'although he died about seventy years ago, [he] has left such a record behind as few men in his position ever build up to their credit' – or, as the Revd Atkinson put it, 'the hundred and one stories told of "Au'd Wreeghtson"'.[15] Many were matter-of-fact memories or memorates, but other stories were 'of an entirely different cast', observed Atkinson. 'Namely, that we have a good deal of embellishment, addition, exaggeration, perhaps even fiction, connected with them.' There was the tale of two men on their way to a hiring fair when they decided to have 'a bit of sport' with old Wrightson. More fool them. He received them politely and asked them to sit near the fire. He piled on the logs and it got hotter and hotter, but the two men found themselves magically fixed in their seats. The heat was unbearable, and just as they felt they were melting to death Wrightson removed his spell, warning them, 'mebbe, ye'll think tweea tahms afore making spoort wiv Au'd Wreeghtson. And noo, Gude deea tiv ye!'[16]

There were three types of witch-figure in Britain's folklore record: the conflict witch, the accidental witch, and the outcast or folkloric witch.[17] Someone became a conflict witch due to feelings of jealousy, envy, and suspicion arising from neighbourly, family, or work tensions and disputes. These usually led to an accusation following some mysterious misfortune, followed by the need to identify who had the motive to inflict such supernatural harm. In the era of the witch trials, it was this sort of scenario that led to most prosecutions in Britain. Memorates played a significant part in the build-up to accusations, with surviving trial depositions showing how witnesses recalled strange and suspicious experiences that sometimes stretched back twenty years or more. The conflict witch could potentially be a woman or a man, young or old, though other factors, such as misogyny, patriarchy, social environments, narrative traditions, and theology, determined that there was a predominance of women – some 90 per cent – among those accused and abused over the centuries.[18]

When referring to the witch trials we need to be regionally precise. Lowland Scotland witnessed the most intense prosecutions in Britain, with nearly four thousand accused between the mid-sixteenth century and early eighteenth century. England, which has a patchy survival of criminal records for the period, making comparisons difficult, certainly had significantly fewer trials per head of population. Highland Scotland, Wales, and the Isle of Man experienced only a tiny number of prosecutions by comparison. Drawing upon early modern material and folklore sources, the reason for this has been put down to shared cultural traditions in Celtic countries concerning the role of cursing, the strong belief in witches as milk stealers rather than diabolic death dealers, and the deep belief in harmful fairies.[19]

Accidental witches were often those unfortunate neighbours who happened to be in the wrong place at the wrong time. This could happen to anyone, but in the working rhythm of life in the past, women were more likely to be tapping at the doors of neighbours. Arbitrary divination techniques suggested by cunning-folk or fortune tellers were a major factor. In one instance an Exeter cunning-man told an 'ill wished' client that she should return home, salt the house, and sit there without speaking to anyone for a certain period of time, and then she was to go outside and the first person she saw was the one who had bewitched her pig. She duly carried out this ritual and the first person she caught sight of was a farmer's wife who lived nearby. Unblemished reputations and long-standing friendships were no protection from such accusations, and the accidental witch could turn into a conflict witch thenceforth. In the case related here, the author of the account, writing for the folklore section of the *Transactions of the Devonshire Association* in 1935, observed that the woman identified was subsequently 'bullied by the whole family. The poor old soul, a great friend of ours, was greatly upset when she told us, a day or two later.'[20]

The outcast witch was shaped more by folklore than by human relations. She conformed to stereotypes of how a witch looked, behaved, and lived, based on representations in fairytales and legends. The simple illustrations in English witch trial pamphlets and later forms of cheap literature reinforced the stereotype. In a society where the majority were illiterate the image had to be instantly recognizable as a 'witch'. The woman or 'witch' of Endor in the Bible was a much-referred-to archetype and continued to be cited as proof of the existence of witches in nineteenth-century folk culture. Sermons and cheap engravings depicted her as a hag-like crone, despite the Bible saying nothing about her age or appearance.[21] The outcast witch in the folklore record was, as a consequence, nearly always elderly, solitary, marginalised, with characteristic physical features or peculiar behaviour. The distinction between the outcast and conflict witch has been noted elsewhere in Europe in historical and ethnographic studies, though the terms 'village witch' for the former and 'neighbourhood witch' for the latter have been used instead.[22]

These women were remembered in legend when simple conflict witches rarely were, and the stories of their exploits became more fantastical in nature after their death.[23] A good example of using historical research to illuminate the folkloric life and afterlife of outcast witches concerns the Shropshire fortune teller Ann 'Nanny' Morgan (1791–1857), whose murder was reported in the press. By the time Charlotte Burne came to record her exploits in *Shropshire Folk-Lore* (1883), a body of legend had built up depicting the diviner as a classic wicked witch. 'I've 'eerd things on 'er as would make yore flesh creep', observed one local.[24] The Revd Atkinson recorded first-hand stories of another two such legendary 'Nanny' or 'Mother' witches in his Yorkshire patch around Danby. Atkinson was at pains to point out that, although the local legends he was told were of a fantastical nature, the witches were very real people whom he refrained from naming: 'forty years ago, a very noteworthy proportion of these witch stories were not only localised, but the names, the personality, the actual identity of the witches of greatest repute or notoriety were precisely specified and detailed'.[25]

The outcast or folkloric witch was an enthusiastic shapeshifter, usually transforming herself into a hare or cat, but rarely a dog, which was a form more commonly adopted by wholly supernatural beings. While such shapeshifting was rarely reported in early modern witch-trial accusations in Britain, it was common in the legends collected later by antiquarians and folklorists.[26] The discrepancy may be because such legends often accrued around witches after their death, and, frankly, we know hardly anything about the folkloric afterlives of those accused during the trial era. We have already come across the witch hare as a milk stealer in a previous chapter, and cats were another favourite guise. The Scottish Revd William Ross, writing in 1885, talked to an old Fife woman once who recalled an 'ancient crone' she had known in childhood who had a limp. She explained that the old witch had been out and about in the form of a black cat, and when she was about to return home in her feline form by slipping through a broken window, a man passing by with a billhook spotted her and struck her on the leg, hence causing her to limp ever after in human form.[27]

Similar legends were told about shooting hares and the telltale drops of blood that were then found leading to the local witch's cottage. There were other variants of the motif. The Welsh antiquarian Edward Hamer (1840–1911), son of a Llanidloes shoemaker, was told by a friend that one of her women factory hands had confided to her that a local witch visited her in the form of a hare while she lay in bed. One night she hit it on the head with a hammer, and the next morning she saw the witch with a black eye.[28]

The many supernatural legends of shapeshifting witches were within the bounds of possibility in folk belief, but stories of them turning victims into animals were a category shift in lore and can be firmly situated in the realm of the folktale. It was always an experience of unnamed people in the past. Such were the stories concerning the exploits of a celebrated witch named Betty'r Bont (Betty of the Bridge), told by a landlady of Dolfawr, Ystrad Meurig, to her lodger the Revd T. Lloyd Williams of Wrexham. She recalled how, some years before, a servant had laughed at Betty's powers and one night found himself in the form of a hare being chased by greyhounds.[29] Similar tales can be found elsewhere of legendary witches turning people, often farm servants, into horses and saddling and riding them.[30] Witch believers reported that witches were able to move about in a supernatural or spiritual fashion, and so pass through doors, come down chimneys, or hover at upper-floor windows at night, but rarely stated having seen witches *physically* flying on broomsticks, hurdles, sieves, or in eggshells, as in folktales. When an old Essex woman was asked whether she had ever seen a deceased local witch flying on a broomstick, she admitted that she had not and replied matter-of-factly, 'but then, you see, she lived right at the other end of the green'.[31]

Denizens of other worlds

Witches and cunning-folk were flesh and blood of the terrestrial world, but they had connections with the supernatural beings of other realms, one way or another. There were the denizens of the heavens, the subterranean or 'middle earth' inhabitants, and the dwellers of the watery depths. Let us begin with that much-travelled meddler between heaven and earth, the Devil.

While in the era of the witch trials the theological Devil was portrayed as the great conspiratorial leader of witches and a grave threat to Christendom, references to his relations with witches are minimal in nineteenth-century folklore. He played different roles in popular belief, where he was a more down-to-earth, familiar figure, as is suggested by his various names. Rather than being called Satan or Lucifer, he was known as Old Nick, Old Scratch, Old Harry, the Owd Lad, and the like.

Familiarity with the Devil's presence was also imprinted on the landscape, with legends of how he moved churches, threw boulders around, and dug great ditches.[32] The Devil had a split personality as both a moraliser and a trickster. In legends he was sometimes a terrifying, gory death-dealer ripping bad people apart, such as card players who gathered on a Sunday. This did not prevent a lively tradition among schoolboys that they could call up Old Nick by running around a church or graveyard tomb seven or nine times.[33] But at other times his mere presence was enough of a warning.

The folk Devil was also a shapeshifter, appearing mostly in demonic black dog form, but also in other animal guises, such as a crow and a horse. Several asylum patients in the late nineteenth century described seeing the Devil in beastly form. Mary Fishleigh explained that he had horns, hoofs, and big eyes. John Henry Kirk in Prestwich asylum told a medical attendant that the Devil followed him about as a big black dog.[34] He also manifested as a mysterious stranger who walked among the people, rather than acting as the invisible, spiritual tempter of Puritan and evangelical preoccupation. As in other parts of Europe, he usually appeared as a gentleman in black. In this he mirrored the guise of the clergyman, and in some legends clergymen were, indeed, mistaken for the Devil.

In one account from Lincolnshire a bishop entered a barn while two men were threshing. When they looked up and saw a man before them dressed in black and wearing a shovel hat they fell to their knees and cried out, 'Oh! Mr Devil! Mr Devil! Have mercy on us and don't take us away so soon.' When the bishop explained who he was the two men exclaimed, 'How was we to know you was our Bishop if you dressed up like the Devil.'[35] Although he looked like a man, there were sometimes tell-tale signs, as in the migratory legend of playing cards with the Old Gentleman on a bridge (usually one that exists in the landscape). A card falls into the water and, in looking over the bridge the card player sees in the water's reflection that the stranger has either horns or hooves. Sometimes it is a card dropped under a table that reveals the cloven foot.[36]

The Devil also gave entertainment value as a thwarted trickster, with stories of how he was outwitted by a poor man circulating for centuries in ballads and chapbooks. One seventeenth-century example entitled 'A Merry Song' from a popular collection, *Merry Drollery Compleat*, tells how a poor man was walking to the market one day when the Devil, that 'Grisly Ghost', hailed him and asked him to be his servant for seven years.[37] The Devil offered to release him after this period of servitude if the poor man brought to him a strange animal he could not name. The man agreed to the pact. When his seven years of prosperity were over, though, the man confessed his diabolic relations to his wife. This clever woman devised a cunning plan. She was covered all over in feathers and lime and her husband led her on all fours to the Devil. Old Nick was nonplussed and admitted defeat:

> Thou hast beasts enough to scare both me,
> And all the evils in hell.

'The Devil and the Feathery Wife' became a widespread folktale type, and it was still current in oral song tradition in Scotland into the twentieth century, and it has also been taken up by contemporary folk singers.[38]

After noting the many legendary accounts of the Devil's appearance, folklorist Wirt Sikes observed in his *British Goblins: Welsh Folk-Lore, Fairy Mythology, Legends and Traditions* (1880) that 'it is somewhat surprising so little is heard of apparitions of angels'.[39] He was quite right. Angel legends and memorates are scarce across the three nations, compared to other supernatural beings. Was this a result of collection bias by folklorists? Perhaps the answer can be found in folk religion. While the Devil had a legendary life and persona of his own, angels were more generic entities and explicitly tied to orthodox religiosity. Go back to early modern and eighteenth-century sources, and angelic visions were recorded either as part of magical conjuration or as Nonconformist spiritual experiences related to death and ardent solitary devotion.

The evangelical Independent minister Edmund Jones (1702–1793) was one of the few to discuss angel visions in relation to other spirit beings. In his remarkable *Relation of Apparitions of Spirits in the Principality of Wales* (1780),[40] he described the appearance of angels as 'a sign of good', and countered scepticism that they still appeared on earth by asking, 'what sort of friends and servants should Angels be, and never appear to any of their friends and those they serve?' But Jones also grappled with the tricky task of determining if an apparition was an angel or other spirit, including the Devil. He knew a man of Mynyddislwyn, Monmouthshire, who one day saw the apparition of an angelic old man in a cloud, but Jones doubted it, as 'Angels do not appear like old men ... because there is no decay in them'.[41]

But if we turn to other nineteenth- and early twentieth-century sources, we find more examples of angelic encounters in everyday life. The case notes of asylum patients contain numerous examples, such as Mary Ann Anleyark, in Prestwich Asylum, who frequently saw angels who beckoned to her. In 1882 a labourer named Hugh Mills said that while working near Liverpool he saw 'a number of angels with wings and dressed in long robes. These angels and men ... were working under the direction of God. In whom they were engaged in turning several fields into a flower garden.'[42] Angel sightings were also recorded during the Welsh evangelical revival of 1904–1905, and also in the trenches and on the home front during the First World War. In 1917, newspapers reported visions of angels over the towns of Waltham Abbey and Dundee. The famous accounts of the appearance of the Angel of Mons provide a fascinating example of how a piece of fiction was transformed into a mass-reported angel legend through rumour and friend-of-a-friend stories circulating from the battlefield back to Britain.[43]

The richest and most enduring body of supernatural lore concerns ghosts. They can be understood as an aspect of folk eschatology (death and the afterlife). Reformation theologians denounced the belief that the souls of the dead returned to the living as a Catholic superstition. Some argued that when people thought they saw a ghost it was really the Devil playing his tricks. As a Protestant country, then, Britain should really have become ghost free. History has proved otherwise,[44] for ghosts also roamed free of theological bounds. In legends they sometimes had affinities with the fairies and boggarts, while in the twentieth century new theories emerged that ghosts were not spirits per se but residual energy fields left by human bodies after death in certain environments.

While there are consistent themes in ghost belief and encounters with ghosts across the centuries, there are also significant differences between lore in the past and in the present.[45] From the medieval period to the twentieth century, for instance, there was a strong tradition of purposeful ghosts, who, like the Devil, played an interventionist, moral role in society. The ghosts of the murdered or the swindled returned to right the wrongs done to them in their human past by appearing at the incriminating location and making gestures to direct the ghost-seer. If justice prevailed, they returned no more. Today, ghosts are purposeless, by and large, with no apparent reason as to why they appear. That said, people do report the 'sense' of the presence of a deceased loved one, sometimes detectable as a familiar odour such as perfume or tobacco, without necessarily describing the experience as ghostly. They feel that the loved one is around to comfort them. In folklore, ghosts were sometimes tied to traditional landscape locations. They hung around silent pools where people had drowned themselves, crossroads where the executed lay buried, and churchyards. These are no longer popular locations where people claim to see ghosts, which are now primarily concerned with the built environment. Neither do people usually report seeing the headless ghosts or phantom horses and coaches of legend.

The most widespread type of legend *about* ghosts, as distinct from memorates or personal experiences, concerned ghost-laying. Numerous are the stories of clergymen, or occasionally cunning-folk, laying ghosts by sending them to the depths of the Red Sea for a long period. The idea dated back to at least the mid-seventeenth century and lived on into the nineteen hundreds.[46] In 1896, a Wiltshire folklorist recorded that he had heard many such legends from locals, including an old woman of Crockerton who told him that Longleat House was no longer haunted because 'they had the passon, and he laid the ghost in the Rid Say (Red Sea)'.[47] Sometimes the ghost was sealed in a bottle and physically taken there. Charlotte Burne observed that 'the rustics will gravely tell you how such and such an old country parson of bygone days, who probably was never out of England in his life, actually threw the bottle in which a ghost was imprisoned, into the Red Sea'. Yet, she added with a hint of exasperation, 'No notion of the long journey which such a feat would entail seems ever to cross their minds.'[48] Why the Red Sea? Folk knowledge of it derived from the Bible story of the drowning of the pharoah's army after the parting of the Red Sea. The many souls lost in the waters provided a fitting community of the damned to which other nasty ghosts could be sent.

If legend put a term limit on the Red Sea banishment, then its expiration could cause a flurry of gossip. In 1855 it was recorded in the *Gentleman's Magazine* that, about fifty years before, the ghost of a reputed murderer of Beoley, Worcestershire, had been sent to the Red Sea by a band of clergymen for fifty years. Then, two or three years ago the term of exile expired, and some locals were concerned that he had returned to the murderer's house to torment its current inhabitants by slamming doors. The correspondent reported that he had talked to the beadle, a minor parish official, who said he dared not now pass by the house at night.[49] In 1894, newspapers reported that a village in the Mendips was in a state of excitement due to recent sightings of a ghost near the churchyard. A local elder had apparently put it about that his grandfather had once told him that thirteen parsons and a woman had laid the spirit of a local squire in the Red Sea for 150 years. He reckoned that the time had expired and the squire's ghost had returned.[50]

While the heavens were the preserve of the religious otherworld, the earth had its portals to the subterranean realm of the fairies. They had various regional characteristics and dialect names. They were pixies and piskies in the south-west of England, and the 'pharisees' or 'farisees' in East Anglia and elsewhere. In Welsh they were the *tylwyth teg*, and in Gaelic the *sìth*. In Scotland there was also the fairy community known as the seelie wights, meaning 'blessed' or 'magical beings'.[51] There were folkloric links between the fairies and the Devil, angels, ghosts, and witches. They could all shapeshift, for example. In popular belief it was also a quite widely held view that fairies were either fallen angels or the ancient spirits of the dead. Several Scottish people who claimed to have entered the fairy realm said they saw deceased people they had known when alive now living among the fairies.[52] Folkloric witches and fairies also shared the legendary behaviour of dancing in rings in the fields at night and riding horses, leaving their manes tangled.

Folklorists like Katharine Briggs endeavoured to list and categorise the many forms taken by the fairy figure from the medieval period onward, and two broad categories emerged – the solitary fairies and the social fairies. The former included the 'tutelary' type we heard about in Chapter 3, and also the more frightening, shapeshifting, solitary figures encountered at night in the countryside, such as the mischievous northern boggart, the bull-beggar, or the

Welsh *pwca* that leapt upon the shoulders of travellers.[53] What concern us here are the social fairies and what has been described as the 'social supernatural', which paralleled aspects of human social structure and behaviour.[54] Attempts have been made to trace the origin of the British conception of a fairy society, with its king and queen, music, dancing, and processions. It appears to take full shape in the late medieval and early modern period, drawing upon earlier beliefs about elves as well as new literary and cultural influences.[55]

The witch trials certainly provide glimpses of a vibrant folk belief in fairies at this time, particularly in Scotland.[56] Indeed, it was the seventeenth-century Scottish clergyman Robert Kirk (1644–1692), minister of Aberfoyle and Balquhidder, who gave us the most absorbing account of the fairy realm or 'secret commonwealth'. Kirk was a learned man who saw nothing irrational in the world of spirits of whatever shape or form. He wrote down his thoughts on the fairies in 1691, but it was not until 1815 that the manuscript was first published, thanks to the novelist Sir Walter Scott.[57] Kirk explained that these 'Subterranean Inhabitants' had 'chamaelion-lyke Bodies' of 'congealled Air' that could 'swim in the Air near the Earth' and so enabled them to slip through the crannies and cracks in the earth to reach their homes. These were 'large and fair' dwellings, though usually imperceptible to 'vulgar eyes'. 'What Food they extract from us is conveyed to their Homes by secret Paths', he noted.[58]

The portals to the fairy realm, which were most commonly small hills or ancient burial mounds, were liminal places. Liminality is an important term in folklore studies that basically refers to permeable, symbolic boundaries or thresholds between two different states of existence. Human relations with the denizens of other worlds usually occurred as liminal experiences, which can relate to certain physical spaces, emotional states, specific times (think midnight), or moments of the year (Halloween or St Mark's Eve, for example). And it is important to note that urban areas have their liminal spaces in this respect as well as the countryside.[59]

The social fairies were not the only denizens who lived under the earth's surface. There was a race of subterranean fairy beings, called knockers in Cornwall and other parts of England, and the *coblynau* in Wales, who worked away in the mines. Little is said of such beings in Scottish folklore. They were generally imagined to be diminutive, bearded beings, and in nineteenth-century folklore the Cornish knockers were said to be the spirits of Jews exiled to work in the mines in ancient times. The knocking sounds they made either acted as warnings or indicated the location for profitable veins of metal ore or coal.[60] The Welsh antiquary Lewis Morris, who was also the superintendent of the king's mines in Wales, wrote in 1754 of his fascination with the knockers, noting that in the mine at Llywn Llywyd, Ceredigion, 'they frightened away some young workmen. This was when we were driving levels, and before we had got any ore; but when we came to the ore, they gave them over, and I heard no more of them.' For Morris they were 'good natured impalpable people' made by God. He was adamant that they were not 'supernatural' because all beings were natural, including angels, and he likened their existence to an extinguished fire, 'invisible and impalpable'.[61]

The Revd Elias Owen (1833–1899) talked to several Welsh miners who had neither seen nor heard the *coblynau* but nevertheless believed in their existence and named mines where they had been heard. Owen also made the useful observation that, unlike other fairies, he had never heard it said by anyone that they had seen the *coblynau*. In other words, it was largely an acoustic occupational tradition. The inquiry into the mine disaster at the Morfa Colliery in 1890 heard evidence that before the explosion happened rumours had circulated among the miners of uncanny sounds emanating from the pit. They were apparently interpreted by some as a prophetic warning. Several of the miners gathered to discuss the matter shortly before the disaster, but witnesses before the inquiry were very reluctant to talk about it.[62]

Deep water was the other obvious place to find fairy beings. We have already heard of the Red Sea as an exotic watery other world, but Britain had its many traditions of river and lake dwellers. Scotland with its lochs was, not surprisingly, particularly rich in such lore. There was the shapeshifting, shaggy man-horse known as a kelpie, or nuggle in Shetland and Orkney, who lived in rivers and streams. Numerous legends and tales have been collected about them being bridled by humans for good or ill – a reversal of witches bridling humans in horse form. The kelpie horse was a cousin of the water bulls and water cows found in remote lochs. Some legends tell of hunting parties to kill the beasts. Around 1840 the proprietor of Loch-na-Beiste tried to get rid of one by draining the loch, but when that failed he tried to poison it by adding quicklime to the water.[63] Northern England had several sinister, female water dwellers who attacked the unwary and dragged them into the unknown depths. In the nineteenth and twentieth centuries there was Jenny Greenteeth in the Liverpool area, a children's bogey figure who inhabited ponds and was associated with duckweed – indeed Jenny Greenteeth was the dialect name for the plant, while for some the presence of duckweed indicated the presence of Jenny. Peg o' Nell was another such watery bogey, who haunted the River Ribble in Lancashire.[64]

By the last third of the nineteenth century, popular belief in continued human encounters with the fairy realm was regional, fragmented, and in decline. Recent sightings of and exchanges with the fairies became rare. Welsh fairy belief remained vibrant for longer than in most of England, but, come the early twentieth century, and Jonathan Caredig Davies noted in his *Folk-Lore of West and Mid-Wales* (1911) that the belief in fairies had 'almost died out', contrasting it with the vibrant belief in ghosts. A survey of asylum patients in north-west England and Scotland from the 1860s to the 1910s reveals that fairy beliefs were restricted to Irish migrants and Scots.[65]

Still, across the country, legends continued to be told, places in the landscape continued to be associated with the fairies, and people still talked of being pixy-led or led astray by the fairies at night, without any fairies actually being seen or heard. An element of fairy faith never went away in a few areas. When, in 1990, Scottish folklorist Margaret Bennett interviewed the residents of Balquhidder, the home of the Revd Kirk, she left convinced that the belief in fairies was still alive in the village, although primarily among the local children.[66] Yet, fairies have actually made a return in the twenty-first century with numerous sightings in Britain, though few such reports now come from Britain's rural working-class going about their agricultural lives as in the old works of folklore.[67]

Finally, we come to a modern fourth realm – outer space. The belief that there was life on other planets dates back centuries, but descriptions of extraterrestrials are more recent. In the 1890s, the French medium Catherine-Elise Müller (Hélène Smith) said that she had visited Mars in spiritual form and described its inhabitants and their Martian language. The nascent science fiction genre also created its own visions of inhabited planets. But eyewitness accounts of physical human contact with aliens or sightings of their flying saucers on Earth first appeared in late 1940s America and became a popular phenomenon in Britain the following decade.[68]

With witness accounts piling up in the 1950s and 1960s, researchers began to note the similarities of alien encounters with stories of the fairy realm. The connection was first made at length by the French writer Jacques Vallée in his *Passport to Magonia, From Folklore to Flying Saucers* (1969). As he later recalled, the book was initially ignored in the United States but was well received in Britain and other European countries, where, he suggested, there was 'a greater appreciation of history and of the importance of folklore in defining culture'.[69] Vallée relied heavily on a book entitled *The Fairy-faith in Celtic Countries* (1911) for his fairy comparisons. Its author was Walter Evans-Wentz (1878–1965), an

American anthropologist who studied folklore and mythology at Oxford University and, as part of his academic studies while there, collected oral and written testimonies of fairylore from people across Cornwall, Scotland, and Wales, as well as Ireland and Britanny.

Since Vallée, others have also explored the similarities from multiple perspectives, usually drawing upon fairy and alien encounters from a range of countries.[70] Shared motifs in narratives include the appearance of strange lights before the close encounters, and time distortion – that is, when the person thinks they have been among the fairies or aliens for minutes, when hours or days have passed. Stories of the abduction of humans to the fairy realm or to a spaceship have attracted the most scholarly attention. They share a similar sequence of events, beginning with capture or enticement and proceeding through examination, gathering, otherworldly journey, return, and aftermath consequences. The idea that aliens replaced fairies is seductive chronologically in that aliens appeared on the horizon as fairies were thought to have disappeared into the twilight. But this does not work from a social supernatural perspective. Aliens are brief visitors and unnegotiable. They are intruders, and humans rarely get to travel to their realms (beyond the confines of the spacecraft). In contrast, people lived with the fairies as uneasy neighbours, they shared the Earth, and sometimes they mingled with each other's societies. Relations were transactional. Fairies could be gift givers as well as takers. In other words, aliens and fairies are two distinct categories of the supernatural that share motifs, just as fairies did with other beings.

Folklorists were quite late to take a more general interest in UFOlogy.[71] The American folklorist Linda Dégh (1918–2014) wrote one of the first papers on the subject in 1977, provoked, in part, by annoyance that no folklorists had been asked to participate in a major meeting of scientists and social scientists in 1972 to discuss the subject. She suggested that the contribution of a folklorist would have had a 'sobering and stimulating effect'. If invited, she would have told them that UFO accounts 'fall into well known traditional folklore categories, based on systems of folk religion, and that the "eyewitnesses" were nothing but folklore informants whose testimonies can be classified according to standard folklore genres'.[72] Case closed!

In terms of source material, Britain has much to offer. The United Kingdom National Archives holds hundreds of records of personal experiences of UFOs reported to the armed forces, police, and government agencies since the 1950s. These have been analysed from a folklore perspective, and they show the role of the media in shaping personal narratives and legends, and how people have sought to 'live the legend' by going in search of places where UFOs might be seen, just as with ghost investigations.[73] This was exactly what happened in the spring of 1977, when numerous sightings of fiery airborne disks, space robots, and extraterrestrials in silver suits were reported, particularly by children, in south-west Wales, leading to the area being called the 'Welsh Triangle' and the 'Dyfed Enigma'. It was folklore in the making.[74]

In related matters, Britain gave the world the crop circle phenomenon in the 1980s. What started out as simple circles trampled in cereal crops developed into highly complex fractal and symbolic crop patterns that became a striking addition to the summer landscape of southern England. They have been described as a new addition to the country's mythic landscape, and the flocking of people, many from around the world, to these circles in the 1980s and 1990s can be likened to a pilgrimage, or legend tripping, though the pilgrims were a diverse bunch including UFOlogists, New Age spiritualists, occultists, conspiracy theorists, paranormal 'frontier' scientists, and the merely curious. While, for some, the circles were a physical manifestation of the supernatural, for others they were paranormal Earth mysteries, or proof of alien visitation.[75] (Figure 7.1)

Figure 7.1 'Plucked from the Fairy Circle'. A man saved from dancing with the fairies. Wirt Sikes, *British Goblins: Welsh Folk-lore, Fairy Mythology, Legends and Traditions* (London, 1880), p. 74.

Spiritual life

As with UFO sightings, people avidly sought evidence of continuity in the folkloric past. Links were inevitably made between fairy rings and crop circles, and an old seventeenth-century wonder pamphlet called *The Mowing-Devil: or, Strange News out of Hartford-shire* (1678) which depicted the Devil scything down (not flattening) a cereal crop became a crucial but dubious piece of evidence for historical crop circles. Once again in history, debate opened up as to the nature of evidence and the search for proof on the boundary between the supernatural, preternatural, and the scientific. In this respect, the folklore of the supernatural should not, perhaps, be presented as something 'strange or extraordinary' but as a reoccurring expression of cultural inquiry about the nature of existence. Are we really alone?[76]

Chapter 8
Ritual in the landscape

The British Isles have been inhabited by humans continuously since the end of the last Ice Age. So, for around fifteen thousand years people have been leaving their marks on the landscapes of Britain. Many of these marks reveal ritual practices, offering us valuable insights (or enigmatic glimpses) into religious or magical beliefs. Some of these marks are prominent features in a landscape, from Stonehenge and Bath's Aquae Sulis to St Paul's Cathedral and London's Baitul Futuh mosque. But most ritual traces are more subtle, speaking less of large-scale communal efforts and formal religion, and more of personal, sometimes quite transient engagements with Britain's landscapes.

Palaeolithic cave etchings of a deer and stylised human females or birds in Creswell Crags, on the Nottinghamshire and Derbyshire border, may be the earliest surviving physical traces of storytelling in Britain, as theorised in Chapter 3, but they could also be the earliest surviving physical traces of ritual on the island. The beliefs and motivations behind these drawings remain a mystery to us, as does much prehistoric material – but we do like to speculate. We also like to assign ritual to any evidence of a practice not obviously practical (to our modern gaze). For instance, the red-deer stag skullcaps found at the Early Mesolithic site of Star Carr, North Yorkshire, gave rise to theories of shamanic headdresses. Likewise, when over 150 Iron Age, Roman, and medieval objects, ranging from swords to jewellery, were found in the River Witham, Lincolnshire, it was designated a site of ritual deposition. And when five thousand Iron Age coins, alongside a Roman cavalry helmet and animal bones, were discovered on a hilltop in Hallaton, south-east Leicestershire, 'ritual' was the resounding cry.

We should be wary of using 'ritual' as a default explanation for evidence that defies 'logical' explanation. We should also be careful of sensationalising finds, of preferring to cite magical thinking rather than mundane pragmatism.

We may, for example, like to interpret a horseshoe embedded in the trunk of a tree as evidence of ritual behaviour, given the horseshoe's association with luck. But we should consider the likelier explanation that it was a makeshift hitching post, used to tether horses. We may spot some historic graffiti and think 'witch-mark'; but could it have been a carpenter's mark, simple decoration, or the doodle of a bored child? We may see a padlock attached to a bridge and instantly think of the romance ritual love-locking, but we should also explore the possibility that it had a practical function, attaching one thing on the bridge to another. After all, sometimes a padlock is just a padlock.

However, sometimes a padlock *is* a love-lock. And, as we survey Britain's landscapes, past and present, there can be no denying that this is a land rich in ritual. From the forests and the fields, the villages and the cities, we find objects that speak of customs practised and beliefs held. The rivers are saturated with them, the trees festooned, the bridges bedecked. And we can use this wealth of material culture to glean insights into the myriad ways people in Britain have performed rituals in worship, in entreaty, in remembrance, and even in protest.

In worship and entreaty

It is estimated that the United Kingdom has over 200,000 km of watercourses across 1,500 discrete river systems. Add to these figures the fact that the UK has around forty thousand lakes and 12 per cent of its land coverage is wetland, and it is little wonder that Britain's watery places yield much of our material evidence for ritual.[1] It is also unsurprising, given that water has a long and cross-cultural history of ritual significance. As a vital element for life, water symbolises fertility, sustenance, and abundance. Its cleansing properties grant it potency for ritual purification, and the liminality of rivers, lakes, and wetlands as 'not quite of the land' has long meant they have been designated as gateways to the Otherworld. Most significantly, many of Britain's waterways are associated with, or personified by, deities. The River Dee in North Wales, for example, was presided over by the Celtic goddess Aerfen, while Yorkshire's River Wharfe is represented by the goddess Verbeia.

A lot of the ritual material from British waterways has been discovered by mudlarks. This is a term used to describe people who search for items of value from the banks and shores of rivers. In the eighteenth century, it applied to the poor who scraped a living from the practice, selling what they found in the unsanitary muddy banks of the Thames.[2] By the twentieth century, however, mudlarking had become a hobby for those with an interest in history and archaeology. In the 1970s, the Society of Thames Mudlarks was founded, and since then have reported thousands of finds to the Museum of London and the Portable Antiquities Scheme. While most of these objects found their way into the Thames by accident or as a convenient form of discard, many of them look to have been ritually deposited in the river. Flint tools and bladed weapons are interpreted as ritual sacrifices or offerings, potentially in worship of, or thanksgiving to, the river's presiding gods. After all, the Thames has a veritable retinue of deities and saints attached to its 215 miles, from Father Thames, conceived as a reclining bearded river god in eighteenth-century sculptures, to seventh-century Saint Birinus, who baptised converted Saxons in the waters of the river.[3]

Many medieval pilgrim badges, purchased as souvenirs from religious pilgrimage sites in Britain and overseas, have been found in the Thames. They would have been purchased to wear on clothing as a sign of a successful pilgrimage and to bring some of the power of the shrine back home. However, judging by the amount of these small pewter badges that have been discovered in the Thames, it is has been proposed – although not proven – that they were also offered to the river by returning pilgrims in thanksgiving for their safe homecoming.[4] Particularly popular are pilgrim badges from the shrine of twelfth-century, London-born St Thomas Becket in Canterbury, four days' walk from London. It has been suggested that these were deposited from the chapel devoted to Becket that was built in the middle of Old London Bridge.

Lara Maiklem, who has been mudlarking in the Thames since 2012, published details of a diverse range of ritual objects she has recovered from the river's shores. These include an Islamic prayer, folded and tied to a stone, asking for help with unrequited love, and a (possibly Wiccan) 'spell jar' wrapped in black plastic.[5] Spell jars are spiritual tools of the pagan community. Essentially, these are sealed containers enclosing the ingredients of a spell. A similar find is held by the Museum of London: a plastic pill bottle containing slivers of metal, seventeen adult human teeth, a 1982 halfpenny, a US dime, and a phial of oil of cloves. Given that oil of cloves is often used to treat toothache, it has been suggested that this was a 'spell jar' deposited in the hope of gaining relief from toothache – or to cause it in someone else?[6]

Spell jars have their historic precursors: 'witch-bottles'. This is the name given to stoneware and glass vessels believed to have been used as a cure for bewitchment. We have written records of this practice from the seventeenth century, when cunning-folk and astrologer-physicians prescribed them for patients suspected to be suffering from bewitchment. 'Take your Wive's Urine as before, and Cork, it in a Bottle with Nails, Pins and Needles, and bury it in the Earth; and that will do the feat,' advised a cunning-man in seventeenth-century Suffolk for a woman believed to have been bewitched.[7] Archaeological evidence of this folk cure survives, with bottles having been recovered containing pins and nails, as well as a variety of other items, many of which will have created a sympathetic link with the patient, such as urine, hair, and fingernails. While many have been found within the fabric of buildings, a significant amount have been recovered from the landscape, in keeping with the stipulation that the bottle be buried 'in the Earth': in fields, ditches, gardens, churchyards, and riverbanks. One was found in the riverbank at Paul's Pier Wharf, London, containing rusty nails, a heart-shaped piece of felt pierced with brass pins, and possibly some human hair.[8]

Many Hindu ritual objects have also been found in the Thames – indeed, in rivers across Britain. Rivers carry significant spiritual power in Hinduism as sites of purification and blessings, with India's Ganges being especially sacred. *Visarjan* refers to the Hindu ritual practice of depositing a sacred object in flowing water, whether religious idols following a festival or cremation ashes (*asthi visarjan*). For Hindus in Britain, who may not find it easy to travel to India for *visarjan* rituals, rivers of the British landscape have been adopted as substitutes.[9] In 1970, the Thames was officially sanctified as a holy Hindu river by Pramukh Swami Maharaj, president of a major Swaminarayan denomination, whose ashes were later scattered in the river in 2017.[10] In 2004, Leicester's River Soar was anointed with water from the Ganges, making it an official site of *asthi visarjan*.[11]

Murti are clay idols depicting Hindu gods such as Ganesh, Vishnu, and Shiva. They are immersed in rivers following festivals as a way of releasing these powerfully sacred objects back into the celestial realm. Such immersion ceremonies have seen *murti* submerged in the Thames at Hounslow, in Liverpool's River Mersey, and in Slough's Jubilee River.[12] Maiklem reports that she has found 'scores of statues and images of Hindu gods' on her mudlarking adventures.[13] The Museum of London houses several such finds, including a metal statuette of Vishnu and a card in a plastic wallet depicting the Hindu leader Sri Swaminarayan, both found on the foreshore of the Thames.[14] Many more are recorded by the Portable Antiquities Scheme, such as the stone model of Ganesh discovered in the intertidal zone at Hunstanton, Norfolk, and the votive model of Shiva found in the intertidal zone at Skegness,

Ritual in the landscape

Figure 8.1 Offerings, mostly natural (pebbles, shells, feathers), placed within the Neolithic burial tomb on the Welsh island of Anglesey. Photograph by Ceri Houlbrook.

Lincolnshire. *Diya*, Diwali lamps, are also found in many British rivers. These lamps, which would have been filled with oil or ghee, are used in vast numbers to celebrate the Hindu festival of light. Three are held by the Museum of London, having been found in the Thames.[15]

There are many traces of contemporary pagan worship in the British landscape. Both natural and historic sites across Britain have been identified as sacred by pagans, attracting pilgrimages. The age of such sites is often considered significant. The Ankerwycke Yew, Berkshire, is the focal point of pagan ritual because it is one of the oldest trees in Britain, while prehistoric sites such as the Nine Ladies stone circle, Derbyshire, and the Neolithic tomb Bryn Celli Ddu, on Anglesey, attract much activity (Figure 8.1). Perceived (rather than evidenced) continuity is central here, ancient sites being viewed as prominent markers of the pre-Christian belief systems that inspire contemporary paganism.[16]

Pagan engagement with such sites can leave material traces, particularly after significant events in the pagan calendar – the solstices and equinoxes.[17]

Practitioners may leave ritual deposits – ribbons, crystals, candles – as offerings to the spirits of the places. However, many pagans view such ritual offerings as environmentally problematic. Decomposable or natural offerings are often deposited instead: flowers, food, liquids, stone, shells, bundles of sprigs and plants.[18] And where candles are used in pagan rituals, many practitioners take them away, potentially leaving only drips of candle wax as material evidence of the ritual.[19]

In healing and wish-making

As well as rivers, Britain's landscape is also richly endowed with springs and wells. Sometimes entirely natural features, at other times marked or sheltered by an artificial structure, these small bodies of water have a long ritual history. Dedicated to local saints and believed to have curative properties – often because legend has a saint create or bless the water – they were important pilgrimage sites for medieval Christians. Estimates of how many holy wells dot the British landscape reach the thousands and are probably not exaggerated.

One of the longest-revered wells in Britain is St Winefride's Well in Holywell, Wales, which was designated the National Shrine of England and Wales by the Catholic Church in 2023.[20] According to the twelfth-century hagiography, St Winefride was a seventh-century virgin martyr, who was decapitated by a refused and vengeful suitor and then miraculously restored to life. Healing water sprung up from where her head had hit the ground. A church had been built on the site since the eleventh century, at the latest, and by the fourteenth century the well was receiving royal visits. During the English Reformation the veneration of Catholic saints was prohibited. Despite this, pilgrimages to St Winefride's Well continued.[21] In 1579 Elizabeth I, concerned that people were still visiting the well 'in great numbers ... after a superstitious sort and manner of pilgrimage', ordered a trial of the waters to determine whether they were actually curative. If the water was proven to possess medicinal properties, then access to the well was to be restricted solely to 'diseased persons'. If the waters did not have 'such virtue', then local officials were instructed to 'deface' and have 'taken down' the structure around the well. It is unknown what the result of this trial was, but the structure remained standing, and pilgrimage continued.[22]

Recorded in hagiographer Carolus de Smedt's 1887 'Documenta de S. Wenefreda' are many pilgrimages conducted by people rich and poor, Catholic and Protestant, from across England and Wales, to St. Winefride's Well through the second half of the sixteenth century and well into the seventeenth. The pilgrimages largely consisted of prayer, bathing in the water of the well, and subsequently being cured of conditions ranging from blindness, infertility, and leprosy to possession by a 'weeked spirite'. Through these records, we learn how the pilgrims may have left their marks on the landscape through ritual deposition. In March 1623, a man from Denbighshire suffering from sciatica was brought a 'relique of S. Wenefride inclosed in a stone crystall and silver case' and advised to press it against the place of pain. He did so, vowing 'to go in pilgrimage to the Well of the holy Saint, therein to bath himselfe, and moreover promised an offering there'. We are not told what this offering was or whether he fulfilled his vow, but he was cured. We get more details from the record of a man from Shrewsbury, bitten by a venomous spider, who instructed his mother to 'offer a candle to the shrine' and 'made a vowe to St Wenefreide, that if he mighte have life and healthe, he would make an image of silver and offer to her. Thus he amended much day by day, unto the time that he was whole: and then he did make an image of silver, as he had vowed, and offered it to the shrine.'[23]

Also in these records, we read of crutches being left at St Winefride's Well. In 1624, twelve-year-old Jane James from Monmouthshire was taken to the well three times for ailments blamed on witchcraft. On her second visit, she 'left the croutches on which she had gone all the yeare before'. In 1640, thirty-four-year-old Elnor Calve from Warwickshire likewise left the well no longer needing her crutches, as did William Jeffrey of Anglesey in 1668. In 1674, Wenefride Dodsworth of Yorkshire visited Holywell several times. On her second visit, 'she left one of her crutches', and on her third pilgrimage, 'cast away her other crutch'.[24] The crutches are not described as votive offerings, left in exchange or thanks for the cure. Instead, their presence in the landscape of the well is testament to the claimed successful results of a spiritual entreaty. However, when folklorist Janet Bord visited the well in 1993, she designated the crutches '*ex-votos*', offered in fulfilment of a vow to the saint. Bord was informed by the site's custodian that, until the 1960s, crutches were piled around the well, many with labels detailing the cures claimed by their former owners. By 1993, there were none at the well itself, but Bord details how, in 'the cellars of an adjoining disused building ... we saw a collection of old crutches and surgical boots piled up in a dusty corner'.[25] By 2023, the crutches had been moved to a corner of the small on-site museum.

In 1993, Bord was also informed that coins were frequently deposited in the well – and routinely removed by the site's custodian.[26] Returning to the sixteenth- and seventeenth-century records, we do witness coins acting as oblations in the healing ritual. In 1627, Lewis Pritchard from Merioneth was swept away in a ford. While being carried in the water, he took out a threepence coin from his purse and, 'bending it, offered it to God in the honour of S. Wenefride, with a full resolution to bestow it on some poor body, if he should then escape drowning'. On being washed up on shore, the bent coin still with him, 'he delayed not to fullfill his promise' and went immediately to Holywell. In around 1660 Elizabeth Barnes, a baby less than a year old, from Flintshire, had a painfully swollen eye. Her mother was advised 'to send an offering of two pence to S. Wenefrides Holy-Well, there to be given to some poor body, that should take up some of the water of the sayd Holy Well to be brought home to her to wash the childs eye therewith'. The mother sent the 'oblation', received the water, and the child was cured. In around 1667, Alice Jones from Montgomeryshire 'gave her ... neighboure some little money, desiring her to bestowe it to some poore att the Well to goe into the Well for her', in order to cure her lameness. Alice found herself cured at the very time her neighbour 'distributed her little oblation to pray for her'.[27]

The coins detailed in these records are oblations, offered to the saint or God, but, unlike in the 1990s, they are not deposited in the water of the well. They are intended to be given to 'some poor body' as an act of almsgiving, redistributed as charity in exchange for the powers of the water. Even the threepence coin bent by Lewis Pritchard – a common practice for physically designating a coin an ex-voto – potentially retains its monetary value. In his 1710 essay, 'The Adventures of a Shilling', poet and playwright Joseph Addison narrated the biography of a shilling. The coin's travels put it into the possession of a milkmaid who:

> bent me, and gave me to her sweetheart, applying more properly than she intended the usual form of, 'To my love and from my love.' This ungenerous gallant marrying her within a few days after, pawned me for a dram of brandy, and drinking me out next day, I was beaten flat with a hammer, and again set a running.[28]

Of importance here is the continued economic use of the coin after being ritually bent. While some coins were dropped into the water of wells with no intention of retrieval, most people will have considered coins worth too much economically to be entirely surrendered, and so they were more often given as alms, where they could re-enter the economy.

The more popular item for ritually dropping into water in exchange for a cure was the common pin. In 1893, antiquarian Robert Charles Hope published a book on *The Legends and Lore of Holy Wells in England* and an article on Scottish wells, observing that 'pins may be collected by the handful' at many such sites.[29] Rags were another common votive offering at holy wells, but, rather being than dropped into the water, they were more often tied to the branches of nearby trees (known as rag-trees). In some cases, having been cured by the sacred water, the pilgrim might leave a torn strip of their clothing as a token of thanks. But the rag was also a medium of healing magic, linked to the notion of contagious transfer. A person's clothing was believed to contain the illness of the wearer through physical contact and a metonymical link. As explained by Hartland in 1893, the belief was that if a strip of fabric was taken from the garment and attached to a tree, then the illness transferred to the tree, leaving the wearer cured.[30] Another belief held that the tree, partaking in the sanctity of a nearby holy well, had curative powers which transferred back to the pilgrim.[31]

Describing a holy well in Perthshire, Hartland exhibited surprise upon discovering coins deposited there: 'Sometimes [participants] go as far as to throw away their halfpence,' he exclaimed, demonstrating that surrendering a coin in these rituals was seen as an extreme form of participation.[32] There is a shift, though, as the value of coins lessens and as the nature of these sites alters in response to societal changes. We can witness these changes by taking a longue durée look at specific sites, one of which is a tiny island in the north-west Highlands of Scotland.

Isle Maree is one of about sixty islands on Loch Maree, named after Saint Maelrubha (or Maree), who Christianised that region of Scotland in the eighth century. Saint Maree is purported to have built his hermitage and consecrated a well on the island, and the well gained a reputation for curing insanity. When eighteenth-century naturalist and antiquarian Thomas Pennant visited the island in the 1770s, he noted that beside the well was a tree that was being used as an 'altar'; pilgrims who sought a cure from the holy well would deposit their tokens of thanks to Saint Maree on this particular tree.[33] Originally, these tokens appear to have been rags, but during the nineteenth century pilgrims began depositing other objects such as pins and nails. These metal objects had originally been employed to hold the rags in place on the branches and trunk of the tree, but had gradually become offerings in and of themselves. By the late nineteenth century, coins had replaced rags, nails, and pins, and had become the predominant offering at the site.[34]

Spiritual life

When Queen Victoria visited Isle Maree on her tour of Scotland in 1877, she described the tree in her diary, in an entry dated 17 September 1877, as follows:

> The boat was pushed onshore, and we scrambled out and walked through the tangled underwood and thicket of oak, holly, beech, etc., which covers the islet, to the well, now nearly dry which is said to be celebrated for the cure of insanity. An old tree stands close to it, and into the bark of this it is the custom, from time immemorial, for everyone who goes there to insert with a hammer a copper coin, as a sort of offering to the saint who lived there in the eighth century ...[35]

The original rag-tree had become a coin-tree – possibly Britain's first – and it was no longer receiving offerings for the cure of insanity. People were leaving their coins to make wishes. On fieldwork conducted at the site in 2012, over 1,600 coins in the (now dead) tree, surrounding boles, and on the ground beneath them were recorded, ranging in date from 1875 to 2010.

Given that less than half of the population of England and Wales now consider themselves Christian, and that most people in Britain can access modern medicine, it is unsurprising that sacred sites are less frequently resorted to for the curative powers of Christian saints. More generic wish-making or good luck are now the primary motivations behind most ritual offerings in Britain. Since the 1990s, hundreds of trees (mainly prone boles) across the country have been subject to the insertion of coins in exchange for wishes. These wishing-trees are much like the one on Isle Maree, only there is no known history of spiritual or ritual significance to the sites. They are mainly situated beside well-trodden footpaths in popular woodland areas, and the coins are largely the result of day-tripping families who have stumbled upon the coin-trees by chance. Some particularly well-established examples are a large bole along Ingleton Waterfalls Trail, North Yorkshire, which contained more than forty thousand coins in 2012, and a log along the trail leading to Aira Force in the Lake District, Cumbria, with at least twenty thousand.[36] Neither of these trees contained coins prior to the 1990s.

In promotion and charity

The twentieth century saw the widespread use of public fountains as wishing-wells. Although we know that coins were being thrown into some holy wells prior to the twentieth century, the custom of tossing coins into fountains was popularised by the 1954 film, and associated Frank Sinatra song, *Three Coins in the Fountain*, in which the main characters throw coins into the Trevi Fountain in Rome, a ritual which will supposedly ensure their return to Rome. The film was shown widely in cinemas across Britain in 1954 and 1955, and the Italian custom clearly entered British consciousness. Two fountains were installed at the Regent Cinema, South Shields, to coincide with the showing of the film; 'Patrons are invited to follow the idea of the film and throw coins in these fountains.'[37] Likewise at the Playhouse in Perth and in the Regal Cinema, Lincolnshire, fountains were constructed to promote the film, and patrons were invited to toss their own coins into them.[38]

Kinematograph Weekly, a trade magazine about the British film industry, reported in 1954 and 1955 on the widespread promotional 'fountain collection idea', describing it as an element of 'the usual pattern established by many ... managers for this film'. In a foyer display described by them as a 'good press angle', the Essoldo Cinema in Newcastle created a 'large-sized replica of the Fountain of Trevi [which] faced patrons as they entered and they were invited to throw a coin on it and make a wish ... the first three coins were thrown in by leading ladies of local live theatre'. *Kinematograph Weekly* also reported of the Embassy in Bristol that 'Again the fountain collection idea was used, but this time with a difference', the theatre partnering with the local council to use a public fountain in their promotion of the film. This was described as 'A STUNT that brought the greatest number of press inches in the history of the theatre ... and every press mention was another plug for the film. No wonder phenomenal business was reported.'[39]

The coins tossed into these fountains were put to good use. With the National Fund for Poliomyelitis Research as the charitable recipients, the Regal Cinema raised £33 5s and Perth's Playhouse raised £130 6s. A newspaper advertisement for the showing of the film in Regent Cinema, South Shields, stated: 'The Infantile Paralysis Fellowship will be pleased to accept your COINS in the FOUNTAIN in the Stalls Foyer at the Cinema', while the coins thrown into the fountain in Bristol went to a charity for the blind.[40]

The popularity of the custom spread beyond the cinema, generating new customs. In the year of the film's release, the mayor of Birmingham encouraged people to throw coins into a city-centre fountain, announcing, 'Rome has a fountain custom – why not Birmingham?' A local vicar was reported as critical of the mayor, condemning the practice as 'unchristian ... to look for a blessing from a fountain is to revert to the level of idol worship'. In 1955, the Lord Mayor of Leeds took things one step further by inaugurating a wishing fountain in Leeds City station by pouring in a jug of water from the Trevi Fountain, flown over by British European Airways.[41] In 1957 it was reported that:

> FOREIGN VISITORS to London this summer have created a legend around the Queen Victoria Memorial fountain, which stands opposite Buckingham Palace. The legend ... that a coin thrown into the fountain will bring a girl a rich husband and make any wish come true. It has caused a shower of money to be thrown into the water since the holiday season began. Every day young foreign girls have tossed English and foreign coins into the basin of the big memorial, with its formidable statue of Queen Victoria glowering above. The legend has grown up that the fountain has the same lucky properties as the famous Fountain of Trevi in Rome, featured in the film *Three Coins in a Fountain*.[42]

In 1962 – seven years after the *Three Coins in the Fountain*'s UK cinema release – a newspaper credited the film and song with the growing custom of throwing coins, 'mostly in threepenny bits and sixpences', into the goldfish pool and fountain in the cloister-garth of Chester Cathedral.[43]

The philanthropic uses of the custom, inspired by those earlier temporary cinema installations, became well established. In 1956 the singer Vera Lynn was photographed throwing three coins into a fountain in the forecourt of a fashionable Kensington coffee place to help raise money for a holiday home for children with cerebral palsy.[44] In 1962, a nationwide 'coins in the fountain' appeal was launched for the Freedom from Hunger campaign. New fountains were created, or existing ones promoted, as the collection points of charitable giving. 'There are more than three coins in the fountain at Trafalgar Square,' reported one newspaper. 'Indeed, the blue and white tiles at the bottom are all but covered with silver and copper. The cash thrown in – with or without a wish – will go to the Freedom from Hunger Campaign.' In Walsall, £90 worth of coins were collected from the fountain beneath Sister Dora's statue to aid this campaign, while in Biggleswade a children's plastic paddling pool was proposed as the 'mock "fountain"' erected in Market Square for the cause.[45]

In remembrance

'A wise bear always keeps a marmalade sandwich in his hat in case of emergency.' These words were spoken by Paddington Brown, the bear immortalized in the 1958 children's book *A Bear Called Paddington*. Sixty-four years later, this phrase was repeated by Paddington Brown in CGI (computer-generated imaging) form as he sat having tea with Queen Elizabeth II of the United Kingdom.

In a television comedy sketch celebrating Elizabeth II's Platinum Jubilee in June 2022, Paddington offers the Queen a marmalade sandwich from his hat. She responds by revealing a similar sandwich in her handbag: 'I keep mine in here. For later.'[46] The scene, which originally aired as part of the BBC's *Party At The Palace*, was only two and a half minutes long, but had a significant impact – watched over nineteen million times on YouTube, it also won the 2023 Memorable Moment TV Bafta award. That the popular image of the British monarch was subsequently intertwined with that of the talking bear and his beloved marmalade sandwiches would be demonstrated only three months later, when, on 8 September 2022, the death of Elizabeth II was announced.

Within two hours of the announcement, unofficial memorials had been created across the country, with members of the public laying commemorative deposits at sites associated with the late queen, such as Buckingham Palace, Windsor Castle, and Sandringham Estate. Memorials spread to Hyde Park and Green Park in London, where the Royal Parks charity began managing them; when one site became full, a new one would be introduced. Most of the deposits were flowers, with some handwritten notes and cards. However, many people chose more personalised offerings. These included black handbags – an iconic accessory of the late queen's – and hand-drawn pictures of corgis, alluding to her favoured pets. Most of the personalised deposits referenced the television sketch with Paddington Bear: Paddington toys and marmalade sandwiches, accompanied by messages: 'For later xxx', 'Save this for later, Thank you for everything ma'am xxx' (Figure 8.2).[47] Among the tributes were reproductions of artist Eleanor Tomlinson's 2022 drawing of Elizabeth II walking hand in hand with Paddington, which became a viral meme following the monarch's death.[48] These printed reproductions of the touching scene demonstrated Paddington's apparent metamorphosis into a psychopomp figure: 'Paddington will guide you home' and 'I've done my duties Paddington, please take me to my husband' (referring to Prince Philip, Duke of Edinburgh, who had passed away in 2021).

The creation of memorials and the public deposition of commemorative offerings are common responses to mourning, in both the past and the present.[49] These grieving rituals leave their marks on the British landscape. We see this with public war memorials, which have been erected on a wide scale for the mass memorialisation of war dead since the Boer Wars (1899–1902). The Imperial War Museum contains records of over one hundred thousand UK war memorials, many of which were designed and funded by local communities,

Spiritual life

Figure 8.2 Handbags and Paddington Bear toys placed among the ubiquitous flowers as memorial offerings for Queen Elizabeth II, Hyde Park, London, September 2022. Photograph by Ceri Houlbrook.

rather than by the central government.[50] Through them we can see shifts in the form, imagery, and placement considered appropriate at grassroots level for public remembrance. There was, for example, a gradual shift from memorials constructed within built places of worship to those in open spaces, such as parks and village greens. Boards, plaques, windows, and organs in churches made up the majority of Boer War memorials, with the erection of crosses increasing throughout the two world wars and the Korean War. Inscriptions also changed: while memorials for the First World War spoke of those who died having fought for God, King, and Country, less sense of a higher cause is evident in the wording of Second World War memorials.[51]

People's engagements with memorials also leave their tangible marks on the landscape. The most commonly reported item left at war memorials is the wreath of flowers or evergreens. Following the First World War, it was estimated that three hundred to four hundred wreaths a week were being placed on the Cenotaph in Whitehall, London (constructed in 1920).[52] Flowers were also laid in abundance. In 1928, the Whitehall Cenotaph was described as surrounded by flowers and wreaths, 'richer and more numerous than ever, the cenotaph from plinth to capital being almost hidden from view in a wealth of colour and beauty'.[53] By 1921, poppies had become the official flower of remembrance. Canadian doctor Lieutenant Colonel John McCrae, inspired by the sight of poppies growing in the battle-scarred landscape of Flanders, penned the poem 'In Flanders Fields' in 1915: 'In Flanders Fields, the poppies blow / Between the crosses, row on row... if ye break faith with us who die / We shall not sleep, though poppies grow / In Flanders fields.' The poem, published in *Punch* magazine in 1915 and then widely reproduced, inspired American War Secretary Moina Michael, who sold poppies to raise money for servicemen in need after the war. In 1921 French fundraiser Anna Guérin implemented 'Inter-Allied Poppy Day' in the United States, selling cotton and silk poppies made by the war widows and orphans of France, and the Royal British Legion adopted the same soon after.[54] By 1928 it was being reported that thirty-two million poppies were being sold across Britain.[55] Today, poppies are the most common offerings at war memorials, alongside wooden crosses.[56]

Not all public memorials in the British landscape honour the war dead, and not all of them are official. These unofficial memorials are variously and contentiously referred to as 'grassroot memorials', 'makeshift memorials', or 'spontaneous shrines'.[57] They can be devoted to individuals following a sudden, tragic, and often public death. A prominent example is the roadside memorial created at the site of a fatal car accident.[58] In other cases, individuals mourned by unofficial shrines in the British landscape are public figures, from musicians to monarchs. The shrines tend to be set up by admirers or supporters of the individual, at sites significant in their lives, their works, or their deaths, with objects associated with their tastes. Following her death in 2011, fans left cigarette packets at the shrine built to singer Amy Winehouse, a smoker, outside her former residence in Camden Square Gardens, London. Football scarves were left at the United Trinity statue at Old Trafford stadium, Manchester, in memory of footballer Bobby Charlton.[59]

Such mourning practices are also frequently adopted for fictional characters. When an actor dies, it is not unusual for fans to create shrines in places and with objects associated with a character they played. Following the death of Alan Rickman, cast as Professor Snape in the *Harry Potter* films, fans and mourners deposited notes addressed to Snape at 'Platform 9 3/4' in London's Kings Cross train station, some simply bearing the character's most heart-breaking line: 'Always'. In other cases, it is the fictional death of a character who inspires the creation of shrines. Following the 2009 death of character Ianto Jones from BBC science-fiction television series *Torchwood*, an assemblage of flowers, notes, and photographs formed at a site close to the fictional Torchwood headquarters in Mermaid Quay, Cardiff.[60]

In support and protest

'Take pride in knowing that your struggle will play the biggest role in your purpose.' These words, attributed to professional footballer Marcus Rashford, member of England's national team, are painted on a mural of Rashford in Withington, Manchester. Painted in 2020 by street artist Akse P19, it honoured Rashford's campaign work fighting against racism and child hunger in the UK. Following England's loss in the UEFA Euro 2020 Final in July 2021, the mural was offensively defaced. It was not long before the vandalism was covered up – not by paint, but by hundreds of paper hearts, England flags, and written tributes. Messages for the Manchester-born footballer included, 'We all stand with you, love will always win', 'You are an inspiration', 'Keep your head held high young king', 'heart of the nation', 'son of Manchester', 'Brother', 'Community together', 'Thank you for being a great role model', 'Rashford for PM'. One message quoted the Qur'an: 'So surely with hardship comes ease.' Many of the messages also allude to the interpretation of the vandalism as racist, given that it was specifically targeting three Black British players on England's national team: 'Black Lives Matter' and 'we stand with you all of us united to fight the devastating hateful racist views held by a small but sickening minority'. These messages are offerings as well as concealers, in that they are intended to cover up or conceal the vandalism. They are tokens of thanks and of support, demonstrating that ritual in the British landscape can be socially and politically driven, intended to endorse, to champion, to protest, to enact.

Many other spaces in the British landscape have been occupied by politically charged objects. The objects themselves may not be overtly provocative but, brought together in a specific way, can be as disruptive or inspirational as a march or rally. The masses of floral tributes left for Diana, Princess of Wales, after her death in 1997, did more than commemorate. It is reported that the sheer volume of flowers pressured the royal family into bending protocol and publicly expressing (some) grief at Diana's death. Some of the notes accompanying the flowers were explicitly political, critical of the press and the Royal

Figure 8.3 A mural of photojournalist Motaz Azaiza in Gaza, painted in Manchester in 2023 by street artist Akse. Photograph by Ceri Houlbrook.

Family, with one note left outside Kensington Palace addressed to the queen with the words: 'Why did you treat Diana so badly? You should be ashamed.' The grieving ritual thus became a form of social action.[61]

British responses to international issues are also ritually evident in the British landscape. The most recent is the Israel–Hamas war (2023–present). Personal support for Palestine is publicly declared in Britain through murals. In Manchester, Akse, the artist behind the Marcus Rashford mural, painted a portrait of photojournalist Motaz Azaiza in 2023 (Figure 8.3), while in London a street mural project entitled Heroes of Palestine was launched by Creative Debuts in 2024, aiming to raise awareness of the medical professionals and journalists risking their lives in Gaza. Four large murals were created in Tower Hamlets, depicting Palestinian journalists Motaz Azaiza, Wael Dahdouh, Plestia Alaqad, Bisan Owda, Hind Khoudary, and Doaa Al-Baz, and one of the last remaining doctors in Nasser Hospital, Mohammed Harara.[62]

Both sides of the conflict are represented in the British landscape. In February 2024, a Jewish community centre in North London, JW3, installed a Lovelock Hostage Bridge. One hundred padlocks were attached to the bridge leading into their centre, each one inscribed with the name of a hostage held by Hamas-led militant groups (Figure 8.4). More padlocks were subsequently added, including those signed by high-profile figures: magician Uri Geller, political strategist Alastair Campbell, actor Maureen Lipman, historian Simon Schama, and comedian David Walliams. On their website, the JW3 centre

Spiritual life

Figure 8.4 The Lovelock Hostage Bridge set up outside JW3, a Jewish community centre in North London, in 2024. Photograph by Matt Brown.

implores visitors to 'Show your love and solidarity towards the hostages, re-awaken the media to their desperate plight, and participate in displaying a powerful message to the world. Add your own signed padlock to the newly launched Lovelock Hostage Bridge.'

The Lovelock Hostage Bridge is a very recent adaptation of the love-lock custom, which involves inscribing names on a padlock before attaching it to a bridge.[63] The custom reached Britain in the 2010s, when it was practised largely by couples as a declaration of their love, the padlock representing strength and durability. Although there are earlier examples of the ritual deposition of padlocks on public structures, the concept of locking your love onto a bridge came from Italy – specifically, an Italian teenage romance novel. In 2006, novelist Federico Moccia published *Ho voglia di te* (*I Want You*), in which a pair of lovers declare their romantic commitment by attaching a padlock to the Milvio Bridge, Rome. This ritual was imitated by the many fans of the novel, who were legend-tripping to re-enact the scene on the Milvio Bridge. Fans initiated the custom elsewhere, and tourists began imitating the fans. By the power of accessible international travel and social media, the custom spread worldwide, cementing love-locking as an international ritual declaration of romantic commitment.

Love-locks inscribed with names, initials, and messages of love can now be found in nearly all cities and towns in Britain. Some large-scale love-lock landscapes include the chain-link fences along the Albert Docks, Liverpool; the weir bridge in Bakewell, Derbyshire; and a purpose-built 'love' sculpture in Gretna Green. Love-locks at these sites number the thousands. Elsewhere, such as on a wire fence in Shoreditch, London, quantities are more in the hundreds, while single and small collections of love-locks can be found on bridges and other structures scattered throughout Britain. They have not, however, remained exclusively a token of romance. Over the 2010s, they developed different purposes. Family and friend groups would attach love-locks together. Love-locks began to be inscribed and deposited to celebrate a rite of passage, with inscriptions speaking of significant birthdays, the birth of babies, and trips abroad. Most notably, they have developed commemorative functions, linking us back to the section above on memorialisation.

Some love-locks are deposited after a person's passing, evident by their commemorative inscriptions: 'With Deepest Sympathy', 'Forever in our heart', 'In memory of mum', 'Treasured memories R.I.P', 'Grandad miss you', and one in Stonehaven, Scotland, that was accompanied by laminated paper printed with the funeral poem 'Don't cry for me'. Others, less overt, may still be commemorative, such as those dedicated to individual family members: 'Daddy', 'Grandma', 'To our godmother'. In Newcastle, a local newspaper reported on a set of locks on High Level Bridge which were deposited in memory of a man who had died of cancer, locked by several members of his family. The article quotes a local resident who regularly crosses the bridge: 'These locks are like little memorials to so many people. They are there because they mean so much.' Another love-lock on the same bridge was attached by a man to commemorate his cousin: 'we put a padlock on the bridge in memory of him ... that lock means a lot to us'.[64] Love-locks have – like so many offerings in the British landscape – been deposited in declaration of love, in celebration of special events, in commemoration of loved ones lost, and, returning to the Lovelock Hostage Bridge, in support of social and political causes.

Part V

Intimate life

Chapter 9
Childlore

'Brexit means Brexit.' This was the mantra of Theresa May, British prime minister from 2016 to 2019, referring to the withdrawal of the UK from the European Union. The referendum for Brexit was held in 2016, but it was a highly contested and long-drawn-out affair. The phrase 'Brexit means Brexit,' repeated several times by May in public speeches, was her assurance that the UK would leave the European Union – despite claims that the country would suffer because of it. What has this to do with childlore? Eight years after May first used the phrase, it is still being used – not by politicians, but by children. 'Brexit means Brexit,' is shouted on the children's football pitch when somebody takes out another player, potentially getting hurt or sent off the pitch in the process, without getting the ball. Reporting on this in 2024, teacher and journalist Lola Okolosie remarked: 'By adopting "Brexit means Brexit" and transforming it into a symbol of almost dangerously rough play, you get the sense that children are holding up a mirror to the adult world. They're using it as a joke'.[1]

Children are a folk group distinct from adults – but not separated from them. Indeed, children mine the adult world for material, imitating what they see. Records from the fifteenth and sixteenth centuries reveal that children were re-enacting battles and revolts, from Henry IV's overthrowing of Richard II to Wyatt's Rebellion of 1554. In one such re-enacted skirmish at a school in Bodmin, Cornwall, in the sixteenth century, 'one of the boyes, conuerted the spill of an old candlesticke to a gunne, charged it with powder and a stone, and (through mischance, or vngraciousnesse) therewith killed a calfe'.[2] In Aberdeen, trench warfare was re-enacted in 1924 when a group of boys built a 'dug-out' in a back garden and stole fifty sticks of dynamite, forty-nine detonators, and several hundred rounds of ammunition from a powder-magazine in order to play 'soldiers' (they were consequently placed on probation). During the Second World War, a newspaper journalist observed children playing at aeroplanes in the street, shooting each other down: 'how extraordinary it is, that with real, grim war being fought – sometimes even above their heads – ... children should have to "play war"'.[3] However, drawing on the horrifying and exciting elements from the world in which they live for inspiration is not, contrary to the journalist's belief, extraordinary. It is entirely natural.

It was not only war that was imitated. In 1913, a 'Gossip of the Day' newspaper article described how a father witnessed 'his very young daughter steal dramatically on to the grass plot and proceed to toss handfuls of torn paper over its surface. While he gazed, the actress's slightly older brother suddenly emerged from cover of the shrubs, collared the little girl and sternly led her away. It appeared that the game was "suffragettes".'[4] The torn paper was apparently symbolic of the damage done to several British golf greens in protest by the suffragette movement during the 1910s. The early 2020s saw many variations of COVID-themed touch-chase games, with names such as Coronavirus Tag, Corona Tip, and Covid Tiggy. In these contamination games played during the global pandemic, the chaser was infected with COVID and transmitted the infection to those they caught.[5]

Children impact on the adult world as much as they are impacted upon by it. We see this in our domestic folk customs (see Chapter 10), many of which are implemented for the sake of children. Carving pumpkins, writing letters to Father Christmas, exchanging teeth for money with the Tooth-Fairy. Although associated with children, these customs are largely instigated by adults who encourage and facilitate the participation of children. Likewise, most nursery rhymes and fairytales are taught to children by adults, whether orally or through popular media. These are not, therefore, examples of childlore. Childlore is the lore of children: the customs, stories, and beliefs taught, implemented, and enacted *for* children *by* children. Some may term this child-led play, and it is – but only insofar as adults' folklore is adult-led play. 'Play' may work as a term to some extent, but it risks downplaying how earnestly some of the lore is believed in, how seriously some customs are observed. Also, the term 'childlore' in itself is an oversimplification. Given that a child's beliefs and customs will be influenced by their gender, age, ethnicity, religion, and environment, not to mention personality, British childlore is certainly not a case of 'one size fits all'. Childlore is a topic as large and complex as folklore itself.

Over the decades, pioneering folklorists of childlore have used various methods of collecting. An early example drew upon a network of adult correspondents. In the 1890s, founding member of the Folklore Society Alice

Bertha Gomme collected details of around eight hundred games played by children across England, Scotland, and Ireland, sourced from around seventy-six correspondents. In 1892, a highly original project was conducted when Edward Nicholson organised a school prize competition on folklore in the village of Golspie, Highland Scotland. The essays of seven girls and boys were subsequently published verbatim. He urged other schools across the country to do something similar.[6] Then, in 1951, Iona and Peter Opie developed their own network by printing a request for assistance in *The Sunday Times*, which garnered 151 responses from across Britain, including many teachers. Over time, the teachers in the Opies' network gathered examples of games and rhymes from around twenty thousand children.[7] However, there were limits to this type of collecting, most notably that any childlore was still filtered through the adult collector. A teacher gathering their schoolchildren's lore for a publication may be inclined to omit any improprieties and obscenities – indeed, a child may be unlikely to share them with a teacher.[8]

A child's reluctance to share their lore unfiltered with a teacher or adult researcher is a barrier many folklorists have come up against. Collecting examples for his 1916 publication *London Street Games*, travel writer Norman Douglas tried to overcome this by bribing children on the street with sweets, coins, and small toys – very questionable ethics by today's standards.[9] Even when Iona Opie began conducting research in the field from the 1960s onwards, spending time in school playgrounds and interviewing children, there is a high chance that the games played and songs sung were tempered for her adult ears. Visual sources may likewise be biased. Watching the 18-minute film produced by Edinburgh-based teacher James Ritchie of the games his students played in 1951, we see what the children were willing to share with their teacher and what the teacher was willing to share with his audience – largely skipping-rope games, ball games, dancing, singing, and whistling (the latter was not even performed by the children, but by poet Norman MacCaig).[10]

Paintings and sketches of children's games and customs, produced by adults, are often highly idealised. We see clean, innocent children playing with clean, respectable toys. Photographs are more candid, particularly where they appear to have been taken surreptitiously – again, ethically problematic. Humphrey Spender, project photographer for Mass Observation – a large-scale investigation into the customs of the people of Britain – photographed the children of Bolton as they played. The two young boys targeting a puddle with jets of pee seem unaware that their actions are being caught on camera.[11] You are unlikely to find this scene in a painting or in an edited film. However, where the photographs are taken overtly, they often feel choreographed; not fake, but posed. Autoethnography is another method researchers of childlore draw on; after all, we were all once children, so we all have a pool of childlore data to mine. However, our memories give us a narrow view of the beliefs and customs of children, restricted to personal perspective and tinted by time.

One of the least biased windows into childlore is material culture; the physical evidence of children's customs, beliefs, and stories, on which this chapter largely focuses. Of course, objects are not entirely objective – we all interpret them differently – but they have a valuable ability to candidly capture a child's engagement with the world around them, much like the covert photographs (without the questionable ethics). This material culture reveals the creative adaptability of childlore, the rich but changeable resources they draw on, and the complex relationship between two distinct folk groups: children and adults.

The folk art of toys

The material culture of childlore is most vividly captured in toys, those objects that can reveal what games children played and what narratives they acted out. However, many children's toys are designed, made, and purchased by adults. From the nineteenth century, mechanical push toys and toy musical instruments were being mass produced, and since then the toy market has grown exponentially, adult hands being replaced by manufacturing machines.[12] These toys mainly demonstrate what adults wanted children to play, or at least what they believed children enjoyed playing. Far more insight can therefore be gained into childlore by examining that other category of toys: those made by the hands of children, with little or no intervention or instruction from adults. Historically, these far outnumber the adult-crafted and mass-produced toys. After all, children have a great propensity to shape the world to their play, transforming objects – literally and conceptually – to suit their needs.[13] These toys are examples of children's folk art. However, few child-crafted toys tend to survive.

Lyn Stevens, curator of Edinburgh's Museum of Childhood, noted regretfully, 'We don't have a large number of items in the collection made by children as they do not tend to survive as well as the mass produced items ... what a child makes might be precious to them, but not necessarily valued by an adult and therefore it doesn't get preserved.'[14] Occasionally, though, we get lucky. In 1988, a hoard of over two hundred small seventeenth-century toys were discovered within a long-blocked stairwell in a church in Market Harborough, Leicestershire. It is believed that they were swept into the stairwell, perhaps having been accidentally dropped by children or discarded (confiscated?) by adults. Referred to as 'street toys', these objects are made of small pieces of wood and animal bone – readily accessible materials – and many of them could have been shaped into toys by children.[15]

Among the Market Harborough Hoard were sap whistles or pea shooters crafted from lengths of young wood, their cores removed, and small balls made from flint nodules. These demonstrate very clearly children's capacity to shape toys out of the natural materials available to them. There is evidence of this from the medieval period, with literary sources describing how children would play with sand, sticks, stones, and flowers.[16] For instance, in 1152, five-year-old William Marshal, later earl of Pembroke, was staying with King Stephen at Newbury, Berkshire. In his thirteenth-century biography, the following game, reminiscent of conkers (see below) is described:

> William wandered about picking plantains. When the boy had gathered a fair number, he asked the king to play 'knights' with him. Each of them would take a 'knight' or plantain, and strike it against the one held by the other. The victory would go to the player who with his knight struck off the clump of leaves that represented the head of his opponent's champion.[17]

A London reporter in 1915 described how the children of the city 'utilise everything within reach for their games – lamp-posts, stones, discarded tins, the divisions in the pavement, and their own caps'. By 1940, London's children were described as playing with shrapnel among bomb craters. At times, this enthusiastic repurposing can prove dangerous. In 1970, five children aged between five and seven were found playing with sticks of explosives, used for blasting in mines, in a Redditch coal yard. In other instances, danger comes from the law. In 1939, two boys (aged eleven and fourteen) in Sheerness, Kent, appeared in a juvenile court and were fined over what a newspaper reports as 'Malicious damage to trees' – in other words, breaking a branch to acquire a stick. The chairman at the case was quoted as saying: 'The trees are there for the community at large, and if you have not enough commonsense to know that they should not be cut about, we shall have to teach you.' For sourcing a different type of stick to play at being Robin Hood and his merry men, five London children in 1953 were seen at a juvenile court for breaking into a store-house to take five broom handles – 'The broom handles were "just ideal" substitutes for swords', the court was told.[18]

Despite these examples, sticks are usually easily accessible, which is why they are a perennial favourite. We see their popularity in the images of 1950s Edinburgh captured by photographer Adam Malcolm. Two images show a group of boys on waste ground behind tenements, each of them carrying a stick. At least one has been fashioned to resemble a sword, two others have been turned into flagpoles, and the others seem to be being brandished as spears (Figure 9.1).[19] Sticks are versatile.

The most frequent objects in the Market Harborough Hoard were 117 short, sharpened sticks. These were from the game tipcat (also known as 'tipcats', 'cat and dog', 'piggy and stick', 'billet and stick', and 'tip-cheese'), which involved two sticks, one large and one small (the 'cat'). The 'cat' is hit into the air with the longer stick, and then hit a second time, distance being the aim. Perhaps unsurprisingly, all the 117 swept into the stairwell were 'cats'. We can easily imagine the irritation of adults as the sticks were launched across the church by bored children.

Tipcat was considered a dangerous nuisance, frequently leading to complaints. In 1884, an article in the *British Medical Journal* decried tipcat an 'evil and dangerous game ... a number of persons lose their sight every year owing to this game, as the pointed "cat" is capable of inflicting severe injuries'.[20] Evocative language was also used in a 1904 description of this 'gutter game' in *Pearson's Magazine*: 'When the game of tip-cat spread like an epidemic over the land it is said to have originated in a small way in the country, to have carried in a few days to all the towns, until within an incredibly short space of time every boy in the street was playing it. More windows have been broken in London by this game than by any other method.'[21]

During the nineteenth and early twentieth centuries, local by-laws came into effect, banning tipcat in the streets – and fining those who were caught participating.[22] In 1923, a group of children in Kenilworth were summoned and fined for engaging in this 'old-standing nuisance', which had apparently led to several young children being injured and windows being broken. The game was still being played in Yorkshire and parts of Scotland in 1937, when a journalist noted that the danger of such by-laws was that they could 'draw the attention of any young rascal who is old enough to read about it to the fact that it is considered dangerous, and therefore, a commendable amusement'.

The game of tipcat was considered more dangerous in the twentieth century, apparently because there were fewer open spaces and more motorcars. By the second half of the twentieth century, the by-laws were still in place – but

Figure 9.1 Children playing with sticks on some waste ground behind tenements, Edinburgh, 1959. City of Edinburgh Council – Edinburgh Libraries.

they were now banning a game many people had not heard of. In Llanfyllin, Montgomeryshire, when the by-laws were updated in the 1960s, the fine for playing tipcat was raised from a maximum of 40s to £20, but the town clerk was quoted as saying 'I have no idea how to play tipcat'.[23] However, it did survive in some areas of Britain, albeit by different names. In 1993, folklorist Steve Roud recorded two Bangladeshi boys in West Yorkshire playing a game called 'Eeteedanda', involving hitting a short stick with a long stick to see how far it went.[24]

'Conker vandals'

In the game of conkers, the shiny brown seeds of the horse chestnut tree are foraged, pierced with a hole, hung on a string or bootlace, and then launched at another person's conker until one of them breaks. Various methods were employed to increase the strength of the conker, from baking it, to soaking it in vinegar, to placing it up the chimney.[25] Children's author – and conker enthusiast – Roald Dahl recommended storing it in a dry place for at least a year and letting it mature, condemning other methods as 'short cuts that less dedicated players take'.[26]

The name 'conkers' possibly comes from an eighteenth-century game, 'conquerers', which involved squeezing snail shells, hazelnuts, and, later, marbles together until one broke. At some point in the nineteenth century, horse chestnuts began to be used; possibly, the horse chestnut tree, first introduced to Britain in the seventeenth century, was not very widespread before then. One of the earliest references to the use of horse chestnut in this game appears in the 1856 *Every Boy's Book*, describing the marble version of conquerers: 'Nuts, chestnuts, and other similar objects are also employed in this game, only they are fastened to a string, and swung against the opponent, instead of being thrown.'[27] Contributors to *The Athenaeum* in 1899 recalled the game in the 1840s on the Isle of Wight, and in the 1850s in Loughborough and Blackburn. At this time, it was still very localised – two of the contributors noted that the game was played with walnut shells in Faversham and Brighton.[28]

Contrary to the popular perception of the horse chestnut game of conkers as a 'traditional' and perennial game – one newspaper in 1957 describing it as 'one which ... has never lost its charm in the passing of centuries', while another in 1944 referred to it as 'ancient'[29] – it was not until the twentieth century that it became popular across Britain. And almost as soon as it became popular, it became controversial. As early as the 1930s, efforts were being made to curb the game. In 1936, it was being reported that '"Conkers," as the schoolboy calls the horse-chestnut, are to be banned from London parks, for boys endanger not only their own limbs but those of the tree in their quest of the now forbidden fruit.' How did they attempt to ban it in 1936? By planting a type of chestnut tree that does not bear fruit!

It was likewise the activity of acquiring the conkers, rather than the game itself, that led to concerns in the 1980s. Mothers with young children in a village in Lincolnshire were apparently 'living in fear of the annual invasion by "conker vandals"' who use 'bricks, chair legs, a mallet, steel bars, bricks and rocks' to knock conkers from the trees. One woman had 'taken to keeping her three-year-old son indoors at weekends to safeguard him from the barrage of flying missiles'. It was also being banned in some schools during the 1980s and 1990s because of the 'ill-feeling that can, and does, erupt into belligerence as the result of the shattering of a cherished' conker. And by the 1990s, British schools were banning the game because of the damage a launched conker could potentially inflict – and the subsequent compensation claims made by parents, one newspaper referring to it as 'the march of compensation culture'.[30]

Conkers was a relatively short-lived example of childlore. Not because adults tried to ban the game (when has that ever worked?) but because adults now actively encourage it. In 1969, Opie and Opie noted, 'More recently a conker championship has been arranged annually at the village of Walton-on-Trent in Derbyshire. But happily the season is too short for much adult exploitation.'[31] What they refer to as 'adult exploitation', however, has proliferated, and now there are conker championships held up and down the country. In 1984, when the mothers in the Lincolnshire village were shielding their children from the 'conker vandals', one official response was to instigate a conker contest, at which baked conkers would be banned and parks staff would 'help collect the conkers in an effort to stop children and their parents breaking branches of trees'.[32] The World Conker Championships, held in Northamptonshire nearly every October since 1965, provides players with official conkers and laces, and strictly enforces a set of rules, specifying for example the length between knuckle and conker on the lace.[33] Although children do still forage for conkers, the game is little played in twenty-first-century playgrounds. Indeed, a journalist in 2013 scathingly denigrated one Cambridgeshire head teacher's attempt to revive conkers in the playground as 'misty-eyed nostalgia for "traditional playthings"'. Noting her own children's indifference to the game, she asks, 'could it be that ... by the standards of 21st century children, the game is a little bit crap?'[34]

The versatility of paper

You are designing a new sign for a pub. Take a piece of paper and draw a triangle, then draw a smaller triangle within it, with a thin gap between them. Along one of the narrow gaps between the triangles write 'BEER IS BEST'. On the opposite gap, write 'WHISKEY IS GOOD'. Then on the bottom gap, write 'WHAT DID THE GROOM SAY TO THE BRIDE ON THE WEDDING NIGHT?' Can't get it in? Exactly. This was a child's joke recorded in Durham in 1987, and it demonstrates two significant elements of childlore.[35] The first is that children can be – and often are – rather crude. Just like adults, their games, customs, stories, and jokes can incorporate sexual themes and obscenities, as well as misogyny and racism. Some COVID-themed touch-chase games, for example, seemed to cast Chinese children in the playground as the contagious chasers.[36] There is, as folklorist George Monger asserts, 'a nasty side of childlore' – but one that is often overlooked by folklorists, who prefer to perpetuate an idealised image of the innocent child.[37] Opie and Opie's assertion that it is only 'the ogre child [who] acquires his strange salacious prescriptions, taking criminal pleasure in ... inscribing them on the walls of the school lavatory' links back to the earlier point about filtered childlore and, as shown below, is contradicted by the material evidence.[38]

The second interesting element of the pub sign game is the use of paper. Paper became widely used in schools only during the twentieth century. As it became cheaper and more accessible, a material even more versatile than the stick became available for children's games and folk art. Not only was it canvas for art but, when it was rolled or folded the right way myriad artefacts could be created: a hat, a boat, a ball, a looking-glass. Fold it in a particularly intricate style, and you have a fortune-telling device. Variously termed fortune-tellers, tellers, chatterboxes, wiggle-waggles, and 'those paper things', one particular device involves creating flaps marked with numbers and colours. Following a series of opening and closing movements, one flap is lifted to reveal a message or a prediction for the future.[39] A journalist in 1985 described her son making such a paper fortune-teller and moving 'round the household right royally, distributing largesse. Richard, he read, smelt like roses, and I was to expect a horse.'[40]

The epitome of children's folk art is the paper aeroplane – known as the paper dart before the word 'aeroplane' entered everyday parlance. The skilfully folded paper projectiles have certainly been in Britain since the eighteenth century, when comic actor Charles Mathews was a schoolboy in London. Writing of his headmaster's 'huge powdered wig' in 1786, he recalled: 'It invited invasion, and we shot paper darts with such singular dexterity into the protruding bush behind, that it looked like "a fretful porcupine."'[41] Much like tipcats and conkers, paper planes were a cause of some friction between children and adults. In 1910, a servant in Dover was accused of assaulting a nine-year-old boy who had been throwing paper aeroplanes into her employer's garden. During the case, the mayor asked, 'Surely it does not hurt you?', to which the defendant replied, 'No but it is not very nice'. In 1923, a case was heard in Nottingham when a schoolmaster whipped a boy for 'flipping a paper aeroplane across the classroom' – and was subsequently slapped by the boy's mother. The magistrates deemed the schoolmaster's punishment justified, but fined the mother.[42]

The writing on the wall

Children do not only write on paper. The world around them is a potential canvas, and children leaving their marks on public architecture is far from a modern phenomenon. Archaeologists have identified 161 examples of children's graffiti in the Roman towns of Pompeii and Herculaneum, most prominently drawings of animals. Much of this graffiti was in spaces within homes, bath houses, and public outdoor areas, where a child would likely have been under less adult supervision. This is unsurprising, given that graffiti is often seen as a deviant activity.[43] There is much evidence of this in the British context. A newspaper's vague reference in 1892 to 'the scrawl of a nineteenth century errand boy upon the gate-post, be it to only announce to the passer-by that the owner of the gate-post is an old fool or a blooming ass' may provide more insight to adult stereotyping than the reality of children's graffiti at the time.[44] However, the material evidence of graffiti tells us much.

Within medieval schoolbooks, we see children graffitiing each other's pages. In Devon, the schoolbook of Walter Pollard contains a sentence not in his own handwriting: 'Walterus Polard non est but a dullard.' Pollard dismissed this with, 'Y saye that Polard yis none wery dullard.'[45] It has been suggested that the Viking-style longboats carved into a church wall on the Argyll island of Luing during the late medieval period were crafted by children because they were so low down on the wall.[46] Seventeenth-century graffiti was found in the Old Magnus Building in Newark, originally a grammar school. Names and dates are daubed into the walls of the attic, which was used as a dormitory. The inscribed 'R. Disney 1608' has been claimed to be the work of Walt Disney's ancestor, whose family came from that area. It has been suggested that this may have been a 'last day' ritual, to which we will return.[47] And nineteenth-century graffiti was found on the inside of a cupboard door in a boys' boarding house in Kent. Etched into the wood were names and initials of the boys, alongside dates ranging from 1880 to 2009.[48]

Graffiti, a form of folk art, is a cultural expression that can reveal much about the folklore of children, from the games they play to the stories they share.[49] We see this from the example recorded in a farm building in the Yorkshire Wolds: 'GENERAL WATSON CAPTURED TUNNEL TOP APRIL 6TH 1921. GENERAL J WATSON SURRENDERED TUNNEL TOP AFTER HOURS BOMBARDING AND WAS AWARDED THE V.C. OLD SOLDIERS NEVER DIE THEY FADE AWAY.' This is referring to a war game, akin to 'king of the castle', played on the nearby mound of a railway's air-shaft – the First World War in recent memory for the two Watson children. Other early twentieth-century graffiti in Yorkshire farm buildings featured drawings of cowboys, an inscription of 'Liverpool FC', and many examples of basic strategy games: 'noughts and crosses', 'merrills', and 'fox and geese', perhaps evidence of older (and bored) farm labourers as well as children.[50] The First World War also features in the graffiti made by two children at a farm in Lincolnshire, who inscribed a stable door with the date of the start of the war along with images of a bicycle, horses, ploughs, names, and initials. With research, the children have been identified as two boys, one from the farm and the other from the pub next door.[51]

Those involved in the Mass Observation project recognised graffiti as a form of expressive art. Humphrey Spender captured many examples of what he identified as children's graffiti in Bolton in 1937. As well as names and initials, the graffiti features the cartoon character Popeye, who first appeared in 1929; a skull and cross bones beneath the word 'DEATH'; several figures; a couple smoking, one holding an umbrella; muzzled dogs; a cowboy; and chalked words 'This Egg was' added to the inscription of a foundation stone 'Laid by Joseph Holden'.[52] A series of photographs show children peeping through a hole in the fence on a railway bridge which is covered in graffiti – a boundary has been colonised by the very people it was designed to keep out.[53]

The last-day ritual

Last-day rituals mark the rite of passage from school pupil to the next stage of that person's life, be it further education, employment, or something else. Some of these rites of passage are instigated by adults – school staff or the children's guardians – such as graduation ceremonies, proms, or 'last-day' photographs to be posted on social media. These are not examples of childlore. Childlore refers to those last-day rituals enacted by children without adult intervention, permission, approval, or even awareness. Leavers' shirts are one example of this. These are the children's school uniform shirts, covered on the last day with names, messages, and drawings by their peers – ideally in permanent marker to ensure that they cannot be washed out.[54] On an online forum for parents in the UK, a discussion in 2008 attempted to answer the question: 'When did the shirt signing thing start?'[55] Some parents could remember the custom from the 1960s and 1970s: 'I've still got mine, from early 70s', recalled one parent; 'We did our school summer dresses. Mine was 1972 and certainly this was a school custom in 1960', stated another. However, many parents believe it made a later appearance in their schools, in the 1980s and 1990s. Certainly it was well established in British schools by the start of the 21st century, and treated in the media as an expected element of children's last days in school.[56]

That the leaver's shirt signing was a ritual conducted in defiance of adult authority is evident in the reminiscences on the parents' online forum. 'We weren't allowed to at our school – it was a suspendable offence', noted one person, while another remarked, 'we weren't allowed to either, so we *all* did it. It would've been really embarrassing for them to have to suspend the whole year!' Some parents also disapproved of the custom. 'My Mum probably would have washed my shirt and bleached it to get another few years out of it had anyone written on it', and 'I'd have been in serious trouble ruining a shirt!' This 'ruining' is central to the custom, signifying that the shirt is no longer needed. It is akin to the other last-day rituals detailed on the online forum, from 'burning the awful tie' to trying to 'rip off as many front shirt pockets as possible'.[57] However, the leaver's shirt is not simply destroyed; it becomes a memento, again demonstrating children's propensity for adapting material culture to suit their needs.

Some of the disapproval over leavers' shirts is about the nature of the messages. While most of the writing on leavers' shirts was, and is, the names of the people penning them, along with messages of love and good luck, some of it is cruder, particularly for those leaving secondary school. One person on the online forum remembers the rude poems written by their friends on their last day in the 1960s. A contemporary example from a secondary school leaver in 2024 includes drawings of male and female genitalia.

Interestingly, the example in Figure 9.2 was a shirt produced with the purpose of being a leaver's shirt, professionally printed with the pupil's

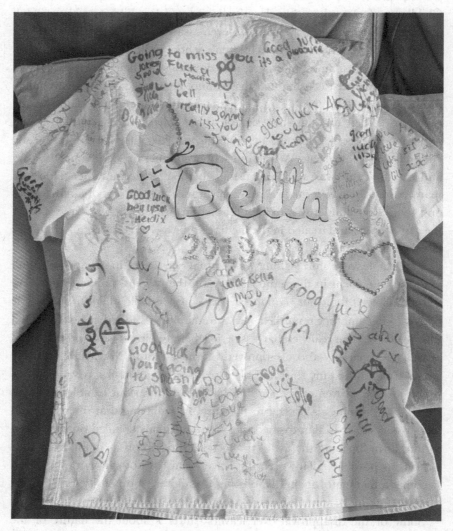

Figure 9.2 An annotated school leaver's shirt, bearing names, messages, and drawings, Manchester 2024. Photograph by Ceri Houlbrook.

name – and given as a gift to the pupil by their school. The custom has not only gained acceptance from adult authority, but is now being encouraged – indeed, instigated – by teachers and parents. The year 2024 even saw the 'Leavers' design of a Fred Perry polo shirt, costing £120 and described on the designer's website as 'A celebration of the rites of passage of youth and the obligatory leavers shirt at the end of school'.[58] Given the adult involvement in this custom now, can the leaver's shirt still be regarded an example of childlore?

The folk group of children in Britain has a long history of customarily disrupting the school environment in what one historian has termed 'rituals of misrule'.[59] Throughout the early modern period, many schoolchildren, particularly in Scotland and the northern counties of England, participated in the custom of barring-out. This involved locking the schoolmaster out of the school or classroom as a form of protest, interrupting adult authority and temporarily inverting the hierarchy. As school holidays were not standardised – nor even assured – many cases of barring-out were enacted to demand a respite from lessons. Schoolchildren tended to use this ritual of misrule to secure holidays at certain times of the year, such as in the run-up to Christmas or on Shrove Tuesday.[60] In late sixteenth-century Edinburgh and Aberdeen, barring-out was sparked when the town councils abolished the Christmas holidays, and it became frequently practised thereafter. A *History of the High School of Edinburgh* (1849) gave the following description:

> Having fixed upon a leader, they pledged their honour to stand by him to the last, and, supplying themselves with provisions and weapons of defence, they took possession of the school-house, of which they barricaded the doors and windows. For several successive days have they been known to remain voluntary prisoners, till they were either extruded, or attained their object by a reluctant and ungracious grant of additional holidays.[61]

By the end of the nineteenth century, school holidays had become largely customary, growing increasingly standardised and negating the need for barring-out – although other disruptive last-day rituals continue into the present.

Today, the last day at school is sometimes referred to as 'Muck-up Day', a term that migrated to Britain from Australia, having featured in over twenty episodes of the popular soap *Neighbours* from 1997 to 2017.[62] Muck-up Day often involves flour bombs, water pistols, and eggs, but can sometimes go too far. In 2008, a boy was expelled from a school in Wimbledon for letting off a smoke bomb which scorched the rugby pitch, and in 2019, the final year pupils of a school in North Ayrshire were sent home after rotting fish were placed around the school grounds.⁶³ In 2024, a school in Moray was apparently plagued by locusts, the school leavers having let the insects loose in the school building.⁶⁴

Adult-baiting

Deliberate disruption by a folk group of children to a folk group of adults takes place outside the school environment as well. Folklore collected from children by Opie and Opie details various pranks, which they term 'adult-baiting'. One from Ipswich, Suffolk, from c. 1952–1953, divulges: 'At night we often play at this game. First of all you hang a nail near a window then get a big ball of wool with a button on the end, and hang the button over the nail get a long way away from the window unwinding the wool then you pull and then it hits the window then the people come out after you.'⁶⁵ A boy from Forfar, Angus, gave a similar description of the loser of a game having to 'go and fetch a milk bottle full of water and sand and place it on a high place, tie a piece of string round it and also to the door. Then we knock and shout in the door something to make them come out so that the bottle will fall and make a terrible mess.'⁶⁶ These descriptions take us back to the talent of children for creatively repurposing objects. But, as times change, so do our objects – and, by necessity, the pranks of children. Blocking chimney tops with turf was a game that ceased as chimney stacks became less accessible and more children grew up in flats and tenements – where a new game in the 1950s involved tossing people's doormats over the banisters.⁶⁷

In an autobiographical episode entitled 'The Great Mouse Plot', author Roald Dahl details a prank he and four of his school friends played in 1923, targeting the mean-spirited owner of their local sweet shop in Llandaff. Dahl describes a space beneath a loose floorboard in their classroom, which he and the other boys used as a 'hiding place for sweets and other small treasures such as conkers and monkey-nuts and birds' eggs'. One day, upon finding a dead mouse inside it, Dahl proposed that they slip it inside one of the shopkeeper's jars of sweets:

> 'Then when she puts her dirty hand in to grab a handful, she'll grab a stinky dead mouse instead.' The other four stared at me in wonder. Then, as the sheer genius of the plot began to sink in, they all started grinning ... I lifted the glass lid of the Gobstopper jar and dropped the mouse in. Then I replaced the lid as silently as possible. My heart was thumping like mad and my hands had gone all sweaty ... I felt like a hero. I *was* a hero.⁶⁸

Unfortunately for Dahl and his friends, the shopkeeper reported the prank to their headteacher, who punished them with the cane.

The youth organisations of Scouts and Guides, which have been hosting adventure camps for children since the early twentieth century, had a well-known pranking culture in Britain, with tricks often aimed at the leadership team. One woman recalled her time as a guide in the 1980s: 'that was one of the cruel things, toilets. You know, you'd throw all sorts of things over when you knew they [leaders] were in the loo. I think our Guide leader got to the point where she'd always got her feet up so nobody actually knew which cubicle she was in.'[69] This former guide also remembered one leader being reduced to tears by the pranks of the children. Again, we see how children, as a folk group, are distinct from adults but not separated from them. As childlore is more likely to be reported when it impacts on adults, we see folk groups of children deliberately disrupting the adult world. Through material culture, however, we also see how children draw on the adult world for inspiration, whether to imitate or to mock, *à la* 'Brexit means Brexit'.

Chapter 10
Domestic life

Home is a place. It is also a space, a feeling, a set of practices, and a state of being.[1] Scholars across anthropology, sociology, psychology, human geography, architecture, history, and philosophy have long tried to conceptualise 'home', but there remains no agreed definition. What there has been, though, is a set of categories that attempt to capture the meaning of home to its inhabitants. It is not just about walls, but about personal perceptions. These categories include the concepts of home as: security and control; reflection of one's ideas and values; permanence and continuity; centre of activities; refuge from the outside world; indicator of personal status; material structure; place to own; and relationships with family.[2]

The word 'family' itself is highly contested and used in many ways. For this chapter, it refers to a group of people communally sharing a space they perceive as home, regardless of whether or not they are related through consanguinity or affinity. Through their shared space, the family is a folk group, and this chapter is concerned with how these folk groups do what they can to maintain the safety and prosperity of what they call home, and how they mark rites of passage and observe calendar customs together within this space. And, consequently, how the home can be viewed as a microcosm of the wider community, reflecting both continuing and changing beliefs, ideals, and needs across time.

From birth to death

The home has traditionally been the physical space in which the life cycle was bookended by rituals of birth and death. But with modern healthcare, hospitals, and care homes this is certainly no longer the case. In 2020 only 2.4 per cent of births in England and Wales took place at home, and in 2016 only 23.5 per cent of people died in their own home.³ Go back a hundred years and the situation was very different, and, with much higher infant mortality and much lower average life expectancy, folklore naturally accrued around the experience of domestic birth and death.

Apart from omens and divination rituals about future births, recorded folklore surrounding the event of childbirth is not rich, presumably due to coyness among early British folklorists and reluctance on the part of women to discuss matters outside their family or friendship group. The authors of the only systematic survey of birthing customs, conducted in the 1930s, said bluntly that 'the collection of data is difficult', though later oral histories have captured more detail and insight about ritual in the birthing room.⁴ Apocryphal letters from Jesus, or 'Saviour's Letters', which had circulated for centuries in manuscript and print, were still pasted on the walls of British cottages in the nineteenth century to ensure successful childbirth. Red coral was also thought to ensure a healthy birth and prevent infant sickness. In 1882, mail-order fraudster and fortune teller James Hartland, who was arrested in Birmingham, sold charms and talismans for a variety of purposes, including for 'safe delivery in childbirth'.⁵

From early modern sources, in particular, we know that possible entries into the room were blocked to prevent ingress by evil spirits and witches. In parts of Scotland, concerns about fairy abduction of newborns persisted into the nineteenth century. Iron objects or silver sixpences placed in the bed, the Bible kept close by, and day and night vigils over mother and child helped to fend off potential fairy interference. The dried caul of a newborn child was highly prized in folk magic, and particularly sought by sailors as a protection against drowning. They were at a premium during the First World War, due to the dangers posed by German U-boats, with 'for sale' advertisements appearing in local newspapers.⁶

Early folklorists and anthropologists were fascinated by a childbirth tradition they found in cultures across the globe, namely the *couvade*. This was a condition where a father experienced the pains of pregnancy and childbirth, mirroring the mother's real-time labour. Examples were recorded in Britain, notably by Ella Leather in her *Folk-Lore of Herefordshire* (1912). One midwife told her of attending a birth and then going to tell the husband the good news, but, on hearing it, he thought of himself, moaning, 'why I thought as my poor back was being sawed in two all the morning'.⁷ In the 1930s, several folklorists attended a meeting of the London Nursing Association where attendees revealed that such 'husband's pains' was still a widespread belief and was particularly associated with male toothache during childbirth as well as male morning sickness. Nurses and midwives present at the meeting 'were in full agreement with the truth of this belief'. A follow-up survey of East Anglian midwives revealed a similar picture, with one respondent reporting having attended a couple where the father was also in real pain and commenting that 'she did not know which of the two required her services most'.[8] While such old beliefs faded as home births declined, new rituals have been generated in the form of baby showers, which spread from the United States in the mid-twentieth century, and, more recently, gender-reveal parties – a by-product of the technology of prenatal sex discernment. The rise and global spread of the latter is thanks to social media, with the first footage of a party being uploaded to YouTube in 2008. Now there are many thousands of such videos.[9]

There is a richer seam of folklore around death in the home. As well as death omens there was also lore about ensuring a good or easy death by arranging the room of the dying person in certain ways. In one part of Dorset the bed needed to 'go with the boards', that is, not to be oriented crosswise to the floorboards. Similarly, the bed and its incumbent should not lie under a beam. In 1891, an old woman of Symondsbury was taking longer to die than expected, and it was observed by neighbours that if she remained under a beam 'her'll never die so hard'.[10] In contrast to birthing custom, the practice of leaving windows and doors open to avoid a 'hard death' by allowing the soul easy ascent without hindrance was widespread. The Welsh folklorist and Oxford professor, John Rhys, related that a farmer of Ystrad Meurig, Cardiganshire, told him that when his mother died a neighbour's wife, who had been attending her dying days, tried to open the window of the room. But it would not open, so she smashed one of the panes to ensure there was egress.[11] Equally widespread was the need to tell the bees of a death in the household. A Berkshire folklore collector recalled how, when his father died in 1855, the old family nurse told his brother, 'the bees should at once be waked, sir'. The brother pooh-poohed the idea, but she insisted. She went to a hive in the kitchen garden, tapped it three times, and said, 'Wake, your master is dead!' Relieved, she explained that the bees from that hive would tell the others, and all would be well.[12]

A scour through old folklore literature reveals numerous 'small sayings and superstitions' associated with marriage.[13] One such was the notion that May was an unlucky month to be married. But, as a statistical analysis of historic data revealed, there is no factual evidence for it being observed, and it was just another of those 'it is said' nuggets of folklore endlessly repeated, rather than some guiding folk principle in life.[14] Marriage was a ritual controlled by the church and state, yet folklore reveals another informal world of tying the knot. In England and Wales, irregular forms of marriage were no longer recognised, following an Act of 1753, but they continued in Scotland. Irregular marriages did not require publicised banns, church ceremony, or a priest as a presiding celebrant. People could be married by a declaration of mutual consent between both parties in front of a witness. Sometimes this was also recorded in writing. While the practice appears to have declined in Scotland during the mid-nineteenth century, it rose again between 1870 and 1939. Several places on the Scottish border, as well as Edinburgh, also attracted English couples wanting to get married without parental consent, the most famous being Gretna Green, with its blacksmith 'anvil priest'. Between 1926 and 1928, for instance, 365 marriages were recorded in the blacksmith's register. The ease of irregular marriage caused some concern south of the border. As a Scottish advocate observed in the 1890s, 'it is commonly believed in England that there is a considerable risk in Scotland of being married without knowing it'.[15]

As well as this Scottish legal tradition, there was a widespread popular belief in England and Wales that a marriage could be enacted simply by a couple jumping over a broomstick together.[16] We know from court cases that this was occasionally performed seriously, as references crop up in trials regarding sexual assault and deception among servants. In 1823, a servant named Anne Frost, residing in the home of an Exeter gentleman, prosecuted a nineteen-year-old male servant, Timothy Siliant, for sexual assault. She said in court that the day after the attack 'she jumped over a broomstick' and told him 'now, Tim, we are married'. In an 1850 court case, a poor servant girl from Ireland, in service in Hoxton, London, was duped by a young man who 'induced [her] to jump over a broom, and go through other mock ceremonies of marriage, under the impression that it was legal'.[17] Jumping the broom has been particularly associated with the Romani, though interviews around the 1920s with Romani families produced a mixed picture, with the evidence suggesting that it was an adopted Welsh and English tradition rather than a Romani one. It also became clear that 'jumping the broomstick' was used metaphorically for any relationship that was not registered by church or state.[18] In 1900, William Wombwell, aged seventy, and Catherine Heley, fifty-seven, of Crowle, Doncaster, adopted the 'gypsy custom' simply because 'they objected to paying marriage fees'.[19]

Divorce was not really an option for most people until legal changes in the twentieth century. As a consequence, bigamy was much more widespread in the nineteenth century than records suggest. Mass migration and rapid urbanisation made it easy for people to 'disappear', reinvent themselves, and marry again far from the community in which they originally married. But people also occasionally resorted to folk tradition in the form of wife selling. Although the practice has been recorded for over five centuries, its heyday was during the first half of the nineteenth century, an era of huge industrial-urban expansion, before petering out by the end of the century. Depending on different calculations, somewhere between two hundred and three hundred or so cases have been documented between 1760 and 1880, though it is likely many more went unrecorded.[20] While examples can be found across the country, the custom was concentrated in London (centred on Smithfield Market), and northern and midland England. Although the practice was basically illegal under the Marriage Acts of 1753 and 1836, the authorities rarely arrested the parties concerned unless the public sale caused a crowd disturbance. The press uniformly denounced the practice as disgraceful and barbaric, in part because of the ritual placing of a halter around the woman's neck to symbolise ownership.

The divorce could be instigated by either of the estranged spouses, and the public sale at the market cross or an inn was sometimes pre-announced by a town crier or by word of mouth. Few sales were genuine auctions, and, in the numerous cases where the divorce was occasioned by a wife's adultery, the transaction was sometimes planned with the other man. This was the case with William Holmes, a farm servant of Newland, North Yorkshire, who sold his wife at the marketplace in Selby in 1862. His wife had left him for another man two years before. She then returned to him, but they fought and she summoned him before the magistrates for assault. Then they hit on customary divorce as the solution.

> He bought a horse's halter, and, taking hold of his wife, placed it round her neck. In this manner he took her to the Cross, in the Market Place, and having mounted the steps, offered her for sale, and ultimately sold her to her old paramour for a pint of beer. A large concourse of people assembled to witness the proceedings, which caused no little amusement.[21]

In other cases where no adultery was evident and the divorce was occasioned simply by bad relations for one reason or another, a neighbour or friend of the couple sometimes stepped in to make the purchase and so release them. The sums involved were usually small and symbolic, a few shillings, a pound, or even just a pint of beer. Although early folklorists mentioned the tradition, usually in the past tense, our main source for the practice comes from regional and local newspapers. It was also recorded in broadside ballads of the period, which likely helped to maintain knowledge of the custom and its procedure.

Good fortune in the home

There was a general decline in protecting buildings against witchcraft from the late nineteenth century onward as the fear of witches and other supernatural threats receded. But horseshoes and holed hag-stones, which were powerful talismans against witchcraft, were not necessarily discarded – instead, their purpose changed. When Herbert Toms, curator of Brighton Museum, collected hag-stones in southern England in the 1920s and 1930s, there was little reference to their old witchy associations among the locals. Most were hung in the home or outside by the front door merely for luck. The same shift can be observed with horseshoes, which gradually shed their apotropaic function over the course of the nineteenth century.[22]

A distinction needs to be made between *protection* and the promotion of *luck*, as the two functions are often conflated. Both were employed to ensure the wellbeing of the home, but they *do* very different things: one prevents or repels the bad, while the other ensures or attracts good fortune. This distinction is exemplified by concealed shoes, the most common ritual deposit within the fabric of a building, hidden within walls, at the backs of fireplaces, up chimneybreasts, and in the roof. Over two thousand British finds are recorded in Northampton Museum's Concealed Shoe Index, most of which are single, heavily worn shoes, dating to the eighteenth and nineteenth centuries. Thirty-four per cent of concealment locations were in hearths, fireplaces, and chimneys.[23] While shoe concealments are often interpreted in museums and the media as apotropaic devices, the literary evidence suggests that shoes were concealed for promoting domestic luck. In 1937, for instance, E. J. Rudsdale, assistant curator of Colchester and Essex Museum, wrote a letter to *Folklore* noting three examples of shoes of sixteenth-century date being found up or behind Elizabethan fireplaces in the district. 'I have always understood that this was intended to bring good luck to the house,' he observed.[24] Rudsdale's explanation is supported by an article published in 1906 on 'Old Shoes for Good luck', in which it was stated that 'to keep old shoes that are past wearing about the place will surely bring good luck'.[25]

The hearth was a popular place for the concealed shoe because of its pivotal role *within* the home in a time before central heating and television:

so, not necessarily because of its liminality, but because of its centrality. The centrality of the hearth was emphasised at the start of the twentieth century by German architect Hermann Muthesius in his *Das englische Haus*: 'To the English, to remove the fire-place from the home would be like removing the soul from the body.'[26] The placing of a Yule log in the hearth is well documented: to keep it lit over the Christmas period until it burned away was considered good luck. Charles Dickens's Christmas short story 'The Cricket on the Hearth' (1845) popularised a long-held belief that a cricket chirping near the fire brought good fortune to a household. New hearth traditions also emerged in industrial-urban Britain. During the nineteenth century, a lump of coal became a lucky charm in working-class belief.[27]

In 1930, a letter to Herbert Toms explained that keeping a particular holed stone on the mantelpiece ensured that 'while it remains there' the occupier 'would never be in want'.[28] Although the hearth is obviously an ancient feature of British homes, the mantelshelf is a far younger addition to domestic architecture, entering living rooms across the class spectrum only in the nineteenth century. Once it became ubiquitous, the mantelshelf was a feature to be adorned. It facilitated the transition of objects such as horseshoes and holed stones from apotropaic devices to domestic mascots. In 1937 the Mass Observation survey team, recognising the ritual significance of the mantelshelf, issued a directive to new researchers to record the objects on their and their neighbours' mantelpieces. Some 158 reports were forthcoming.[29] Objects included religious items, such as a fourteenth-century ivory Madonna and a wooden figure of St Margaret. Also displayed were 'a horse-shoe, picked up at least three years ago', and 'a "Good Luck" mascot consisting of a black cat framed in a silvered (cardboard) horse-shoe. It is propped against the wall for support. It was a wedding gift.'[30]

Across all the major faiths, more or less, the wellbeing of the home was and is dependent on private religious devotion. The idea of the Catholic 'holy household' goes back to the Renaissance, when the rise of printing and mass production of cheap religious objects enabled more elaborate physical devotion in the home as well as in church. The desire to display domestic devotional objects such as crosses, pilgrim badges, images, and miniature statues of the saints and the Virgin Mary, served and still serve to promote the spiritual health of mind, body, and home. While Protestant theologians denounced icons as idolatrous and dismissed the display of devotional objects as 'superstition,' in Protestant homes folk religion could still hold sway. The Bible in the home could have a protective as well as a devotional function, and the use of Saviour's Letters has already been noted.

In 1944 it was reported in the press that in the Marchmont district of Edinburgh the purchaser of a house had found small, raised strips of metal fixed to several door jambs. On prising them open little scrolls were found with 'meaningless hieroglyphics'.[31] They were, in fact, *mezuzahs*. These are written passages from the Torah attached to the entrances of Jewish homes from at least the medieval period as a form of devotion and protection. In 1899 it was observed as common practice in London's Jewish communities, and, although it has declined in British households over the ensuing decades, the placement of *mezuzahs* is a live tradition. When, in 1986, Rabbi William Wolff took up his post at the Newcastle Reform Synagogue, a *mezuzah* was nailed to the door of his new home in Kenton.[32] Muslim households may also have a *taweez* in the home. These are small, folded pieces of paper containing Qur'anic texts or mystical number squares, kept in little containers.

In some British Hindu homes you may find lemons employed as protective objects. According to Hindu belief, the lemon (known in Sanskrit as *Nimbu Phala*) is a sacred fruit, ritually offered to deities, and used to heal and cast away negative energies.[33] In India, lemons – sometimes paired with chilli peppers – are hung on walls, from doorways, and inside cars to avert the evil eye.[34] Their potency and versatility led to significant inflation in the price of lemons in India in 2022, amid police investigations into the possible hoarding of lemons. Kavi Pujara, a British-Asian photographer, has photographed the Golden Mile, a road of Indian businesses and residences in Leicester. Many of his photographs provide glimpses into the domestic spaces of British Hindus, a couple of which include lemons placed on furniture or hanging on the wall above the kitchen door.[35]

Many households in Britain today also contain shrines to gods and spirits. As well as devotional items in Catholic households, Hindus have their miniature home shrine, known as a *ghar mandir* or *puja (pooja) mandir*, and there is a thriving online market for mass-produced and bespoke examples. An ethnographer studying Vietnamese communities in East London in the 2010s observed how individuals incorporated ancestor and deity worship in their domestic spaces. Altars, usually consisting of photographs of deceased relatives, offerings of food replenished daily for the ancestors, flowers, statues of Buddha or Guanyin, incense holders, and candles or electric lights to light the ancestors' way home, are situated in many London living rooms. However, the practicalities of life in modern-day London have required some people to adapt their practices. Ngọc, living in a shared house near Mile End, decided that she would not have the time to properly maintain a shrine for her ancestors and so had only an image of the Buddha on her mantelpiece altar; and Minh, who had a whole room for ancestors in Vietnam, could have only a statue of the Buddha in her London home because 'we don't have the space'.[36]

First-footing

In Chapter 1 we heard about collective house-entry customs concerned with the request for charity. First-footing was another, more intimate, custom of crossing the threshold. It was practised particularly, but not exclusively, in Scotland and north-east England and involved a person, known as the 'first-foot', coming to the house on New Year's Eve or New Year's Day and bringing with them a gift of coal, which would be placed in the hearth.[37] This ensured the luck of the household in the coming year. As with most British customs, there are myriad regional variations about who was considered an appropriate first-foot. In some places it was considered unlucky if a female was the first to enter the home in the new year, and in some places a red-haired first-foot might bring death to the household. A first-foot with a squint, eyebrows that met in the middle, or flat feet was also an ill omen. To many, a dark-haired man or boy was the ideal first-foot, but some believed fair hair was luckier. You cannot be your own first-foot: a journalist in 1987 observed that 'there are people who would rather sit outside on their doorstep than first-foot themselves'.[38]

People would orchestrate the best possible first-foot. In 1881, Robert Hunt noted, 'I knew a lady who sent a cabman before her into her house [at new year], after promising him a glass of whisky'; this would avoid a female being the first-foot. In 1902, a man's landlady in Durham was told if he went out on New Year's Eve he must be back before midnight, his hair being far too fair for him to be her first-foot.[39] And a 1960 newspaper article noted that New Year's celebrations could not commence until the admittance of a suitable first-foot: 'perhaps until the arrival of the raven-haired milkman in the morning'. Ideally, an appropriate first-foot would be admitted into the house, bringing with them offerings such as bread, spirits, sprigs of evergreen, and – most importantly – coal as a symbol of warmth and 'harbinger of prosperity', or 'to replenish the waning Yule-log'.[40] Interestingly, a 1913 article specifies coal for first-footing 'to keep in touch with the fairy that brings good luck to a house'.[41] The first-foot sets the coal in the hearth, stirs the fire, and may say something along the lines of 'Peace to this house'.[42] In 1962, an advert for a National Coal Board automatic vending machine in Edinburgh drew upon the custom: 'First Footing? Why not take along a 28 lb. pack of coal (with plastic carrying handle)'.[43]

First-foots would often be treated to wine, cake, or mince pies, and would sometimes be paid for their service, with the editor of *Memorials of Old Derbyshire* noting in 1907 that 'Dark-haired boys, it is said, used to obtain a great deal of money for taking-in the new year'.[44] Problems with the custom occasionally arose, especially as it so often involved alcohol. In 1897, a man 'worse for drink' in Dundee was arrested for stealing money from a house into which he had gone as first-foot; and in 1959, when a man was arrested in Hartlepool in the early hours of New Year's Day for 'shouting, banging and kicking on a door', the accused claimed that 'he had been drinking a lot that night and was first-footing'.[45] By the start of the twentieth century, alcohol appeared to be replacing coal as the central element of the custom. A journalist in 1907 remarked that 'Formerly, a lump of coal was nearly always carried by those who visited their friends in the first hours of the new year ... Now it is seldom carried. Some first footers carry a piece of firewood but many from what I hear carry the bottle.'[46]

The use of coal in first-footing has declined for more practical reasons as well. With the spread of domestic gas heating, and then electrical appliances, from the 1930s, the introduction of the Clean Air Act in 1956, and the advent of high-rise flats, the presence of the open coal or log fire had declined significantly in British homes by the 1970s. A journalist in 1997 remarked, 'During all the preparations for New Year's Eve the thought struck me: where, now, would you find a bit of coal to go first footing with? ... It was everywhere when we were children.'[47] Some households have found ways to adapt. Richard Bradley, growing up in Derbyshire in the 1980s and 1990s, detailed his family's persistent observance of first-footing even when they lacked a coal fire. They would move their electric fire to one side and place a piece of coal in the original grate behind. When they transitioned to a gas fire, they would remove and then replace one of the flame-retardant simulated pieces of coal instead.[48]

Celebrating in the home

People have long celebrated their birthdays, but in the distant past it was a practice largely reserved for those of high rank. We find references to birthday cakes in nineteenth-century Britain, but only in relation to royalty or members of the aristocracy. Queen Victoria 'always has a birthday cake', reported one newspaper; it 'is a triumph of the confectioner's art'. In 1847, the Prince of Wales had a 'splendid birth-day cake … On the top of the cake, upon a crimson cushion, was the crown of his Royal Highness the Prince of Wales, surmounted by a plume of marabou feathers.'[49] A particularly elaborate confectionery creation is illustrated in an 1857 article on the festivities surrounding the coming of age of a Mr J. H. Greville Smyth. The 'birthday cake' pictured in the newspaper looks more akin to a three-tiered landscaped garden, with foliage, dancing figures, and Grecian-urn planters.[50]

Many British people in this period, however, may have been unsure – and perhaps indifferent – about their actual birth dates. People may also have celebrated their saint's day (the saint they were named after) rather than the anniversary of their birth.[51] Time and influences from the Continent changed this. It is during the nineteenth century that we begin to see the middle classes adopt the birthday celebration, and having your own chef prepare a saccharine masterpiece was no longer the only way to source a birthday cake. By the mid-nineteenth century, we begin to see confectioners advertising their birthday cakes in newspapers.[52] And many families produced home-made cakes, particularly for the children of the household, as is evidenced in British fiction. In 1905, the author E. Nesbit described the birthday celebrations of Bobbie, a middle-class child, in *The Railway Children*. 'There was a cake on the table covered with white sugar, with "Dear Bobbie" on it in pink sweets.'[53]

When did the birthday cake come to be decorated with candles? Our earliest British sources attribute the custom to Western Europe. 'Swiss superstitions', recorded in *The Folk-Lore Journal* in 1883, included a description of how a 'birthday-cake must have lighted candles arranged around it, one candle for each year of life. Before the cake is eaten the person whose birthday it is should solemnly blow out the candles one after another.'[54] In 1891, a newspaper article describes 'the lovely way they have of keeping birthdays in Germany … There is always a birthday cake, of course, and if the birthday to be celebrated be that of a boy or girl who has not yet arrived to the age to be confirmed, round about this cake are placed lighted tapers, one for every year of the little life.'[55] Birthday candles numbering the age of the celebrant seem to have reached Britain by the start of the twentieth century. In 1926, a morose Eeyore was wishing for a birthday cake with three candles on it in *Winnie the Pooh*.[56]

Enid Blyton describes several candled birthday cakes in her novels and short stories – for instance, in 1931: 'There were seven coloured candles on the cake, one for each of Mollie's years. "Won't they look lovely when they are lighted!"'.[57] In some descriptions, it is blowing out the candles that grants the celebrant's wish. We see this in 'Ned's Birthday Wish', a poem published in a newspaper in 1909:

> The birthday cake was beautiful,
> A mountain high and white,
> All trimmed with name and age in red,
> And candles burning bright.
> 'Now, children, wish!' said mother dear,
> 'And blow the candles out!
> I see Ned is thinking hard,
> What can it be about?'
> 'I wish – I wish –' said Ned, and
> Another look to take,
> 'I wish,' he finished, solemnly,
> 'It was a bigger cake!'[58]

During the Second World War, birthday cakes had to adapt to heavy rationing and supply issues. But adapt they did, and birthday cakes continued to be made, 'Despite the exigencies of the war', noted one journalist. There are many references to 'war-time birthday cakes', products of people collecting ingredients over long periods of time or creatively cobbling together substitutes.[59] They exemplify the 'make-do' mentality of life in wartime Britain. Joan Edwards, sharing memories of her third birthday party in Woodside Park during the war, describes how her 'war-time birthday cake had pink icing – made from beetroot juice!'[60] Anne Rosa Coward from Portsmouth, turning six during the war, recalled how her mother and grandmother ensured that she had a birthday party complete with cake:

> My mother was vigorously attacking something in a brown paper bag with a rolling pin. She had filled the bag with a week's ration of ordinary granulated sugar, and was pounding it into icing sugar ... she had squandered two ounces of margarine to make an eggless sponge cake, stuck together with the universal 'plum' jam ... She must have used a week's supply of rations for five people for that party.

Anne's grandmother also fashioned six pink candles 'from gas tapers cut into three-inch lengths and with the wax scraped off to form wicks. She had dyed them pink with cochineal.'[61] A Mass Observation diary from 1943 tells of how the grandmother of a girl turning six 'has made her the best possible cake, with a sort of filling inside, and a pseudo-chocolate icing on top. Very passable substitute.'[62] In other cases, it was a matter of communities working together. A short story published in 1943 tells of how a bride-to-be shared her wedding cake with a neighbour celebrating her birthday: 'No sugar icing of course, but richer still with love.'[63]

Birthday celebrations are still a staple in many British households – although not uniformly. Different cultural groups have adopted and adapted the customs associated with birthdays. Conducting fieldwork among the Punjabi community of London in the 1980s, anthropologist Gerd Baumann noted that individual birthdays were not celebrated in the Punjab, but Punjabi families living in Britain incorporated them into their domestic rituals.[64] Observing the joint birthday celebration of two young Sikh brothers in Southall, Baumann highlighted similarities with the British customs of the time: a large birthday cake, the family singing 'Happy Birthday', and the children being guided by the mother in cutting the cake. Baumann also noted some interesting differences. Instead of the children distributing the sliced cake to their guests, the guests lined up and fed the cake to the birthday boys. After 'the feeding ritual', the women and children at the party danced the *bhangra beat*, a 1980s British Punjabi creation which combines traditional Punjabi music and folk dance with commercial disco.[65]

Calendar customs keep the fabric of a home in flux. Christmas decorations are a prime example. The Christmas tree came to Britain from Germany, where it had been in the homes of German Lutherans since the sixteenth century. It entered the English court via Queen Victoria's German-born grandmother, Queen Charlotte, who married George III in 1761. Setting up the first known Christmas tree at Windsor, Queen Charlotte began a trend among the aristocracy.[66] Beyond the court, though, the custom was popularised by German immigrants: 'The German families in Manchester have introduced this custom of the Christmas-tree and it is spreading fast among the English there – pine tops being brought to market for this purpose, which are generally illuminated with a taper for every day of the year,' reported one newspaper in 1844.[67]

It was, however, Prince Albert and Queen Victoria who made the Christmas tree widely fashionable. This was through an 1848 etching and detailed description of the royal family's Christmas tree at Windsor in the *Illustrated London News*, which had a wide, middle-class readership.[68] This would have been the first time many people had seen a Christmas tree, and it resulted in the custom's introduction into many British homes.[69] In the etching, we see the royal family assembled around an angel-topped evergreen, its branches hung with elaborate ornaments and pinned with lit candles. Candles were a ubiquitous addition – but they were also a fire hazard, causing some serious incidents. As early as 1897, a journalist was advising that 'A pan of water should stand near the tree'.[70]

With the introduction of electricity, a safer alternative to candles became available: electric string lights. In 1882, Edward Johnson, vice-president of Edison's electric company, became the first person to put electric lights on a Christmas tree, as a publicity stunt in New York City.[71] It was not until the twentieth century that we begin to see electricity widely illuminating the British Christmas tree, again starting with the royal family in 1909.[72] Over the first half of the century, as electricity became more affordable, electric lights replaced candles as Christmas decorations across Britain. In the village of Marykirk, Scotland, it was later: 'Many local people have been attracted by the Christmas tree, with coloured lights flickering out and in, in an upstairs window of the Marykirk Hotel. With electric light only recently introduced, the illuminated tree is the first of its kind in the district. It can be seen from as far as Craigo.'[73] It is difficult to overestimate the visual effect that such an illuminated tree would have had in a district only recently electrified.

The shift from candles to electric lights, for safety reasons as well as for the dazzling effect it offered, can be seen in how British Hindus and Sikhs decorate their homes for Diwali. The Festival of Light, which celebrates the triumph of good over evil, is marked in the domestic space by candles and lanterns in the windows and doorways. As with Christmas tree candles, these can be hazardous.[74] Fairy lights were therefore used as Diwali decorations on Hindu temples in Britain in the 1960s; for example, a temple of Krishna in Liverpool was described as 'festooned with fairy lights' in 1963.[75] But they became much more popular as domestic adornments, strung on the outside of people's homes, during the 1990s.[76] Today, effort is made by traders to market fairy lights as suitable for all occasions, including Diwali, Christmas, and Eid.

Greetings cards also adorn the British home during periods of festivity. The Christmas card was born in Britain. In 1843 – notably, the year Dickens's *A Christmas Carol* was published – Henry Cole, the founding director of the Victoria and Albert Museum (V&A), commissioned his friend, the artist John Callcott Horsley, to produce a picture of three generations of the Cole family sitting festively around a table, with images of charity on either side.[77] Cole was reforming the British postal system and, to encourage the sending of

Figure 10.1 Europe's first Diwali cards, depicting the Bhakti saint Meera and Hindu god Krishna, produced by Leicester-based artist Kamal Koria in the 1980s. Reproduced with kind permission from Kamal Koria.

seasonal greetings, he posted Horsley's card out to his friends and colleagues. As with electric Christmas tree lights, what started as a publicity stunt accrued widespread popularity and became a cultural 'tradition'.[78] By the twentieth century, the commercial symbolism of Christmas had become well established, with cards featuring evergreens and winter flowers, robins and churches in snowy landscapes, and – of course – Father Christmas. Britain now has a multi-million-pound retail industry, with roughly a billion Christmas cards bought every year.

The greetings cards industry was slow to reflect a diverse Britain, but it gradually gained ground, thanks to pioneering artists who wished to see their cultures represented. Kamal Koria was one such artist. When he moved from Gujarat, India, to Leicester in 1976, he observed that 'greeting cards for the Asian community were not available. I was quite lucky to come across some pioneering printers in Leicester who commissioned the production of Europe's first Diwali cards.' Pipi Printers commissioned Koria to produce the two Diwali cards shown in Figure 10.1, depicting the Bhakti saint Meera and Hindu god Krishna, and they became commercially available in the 1980s.[79]

Figure 10.2 West African-inspired Christmas cards by Georgina Fihosy, a British-born Nigerian, founder of AfroTouch. Reproduced with kind permission from Georgina Fihosy.

It was not until the 2010s, however, that we also began to see greater inclusivity within the Christmas card industry. Georgina Fihosy, a British-born Nigerian, founded AfroTouch Design in 2015 – 'out of frustration around the lack of representation in the greeting cards industry' – and now has her West African-inspired cards on sale in major high street retailers such as Waterstones and John Lewis. Her Christmas designs include a black ballerina and nutcracker, an 'AfroSanta', and Christmas trees and stockings patterned with African fabrics (Figure 10.2).[80]

Feasting in the home

Food is bound up in culture and history. It is little wonder, then, that folklorists often delve into people's cooking and eating habits to explore concepts of identity, especially in the cases of migrant communities and individuals negotiating new and different climates – cultural, political, and even meteorological. Christmas dinner can shed valuable light on how these negotiations play out within domestic spaces. Ethnographic fieldwork conducted in the Ghanaian communities of London in 1999 and 2001 revealed the scale of food adoption and adaptation. An Ashanti immigrant recalled their Christmas meals as a child in the 1980s: 'corned beef stew with yam' and 'fufu and chicken soup'.[81] Fufu is a West African pounded meal, traditionally made in Ghana by boiling and pounding the cassava plant with plantains or cocoyams. In the 1960s, when Ghanaian migrants began coming to Britain in larger numbers, poor availability of African foodstuffs meant there was a need for creative alternative ingredients. A substitute for fufu was made by mixing instant 'mash' with potato starch and water.[82] Other families, however, adopted what they identified as an 'English Christmas dinner', particularly towards the end of the twentieth century: 'a normal turkey, potatoes, sausage you know the small ones'.[83]

Food traditions travel. In Polish households, carp is a popular Christmas dish, to the extent that, from the 2000s onward many British supermarkets have included carp in their festive offers. In 2007, supermarkets reported a 50 per cent increase in fish sales during the Christmas period – a figure attributed to Polish communities.[84] However, by 2017, many Polish delicatessens in Britain were reducing the amount of carp they stocked at Christmas. The owner of a delicatessen in Middlesex explained: 'A lot of people are going back to Poland, or moving out of London because of Brexit. It's difficult, people don't have money and their kids are growing up and want takeaway fish and chips.'[85]

Many households in Britain do not celebrate Christmas, but still choose to prepare a special family meal on 25 December. In 2005, the BBC ran a piece on 'A British Christmas', interviewing non-Christians about how they celebrate the day. A Jewish Rabbi in Maidenhead explained that 'In a religious sense, Christmas has absolutely no significance for me ... In our family we wouldn't have the lights or the presents, but we have had turkey.' A Hindu woman from Milton Keynes notes that while some Indian families have 'samosas and Indian foods' on Christmas Day, she has what she identifies as a 'traditional' meal, with 'parsnips and carrots and gravy', but with a vegetarian alternative. Vegetarian substitutes are also described by a Chief Druid, who pointed out that the '25th of December was originally a Pagan festival', and that they celebrate by preparing a meal with 'whatever is in season'. A Muslim man from Bradford explained that 'we do Christmas without all the pomp and circumstance, but we will have the Christmas meal with a halal turkey, Brussels sprouts and roast potatoes'.[86] A 2018 survey of South Asian Muslims living in Manchester revealed that this meal often includes meat – lamb, turkey, or chicken – and involves the extended family coming together.[87]

Even among British families who celebrate a 'Christian Christmas', there is no uniform Christmas dinner – and there never has been. Turkeys are native to America and were introduced into Britain only in the sixteenth century.

Although, in 1557, Suffolk farmer Thomas Tusser was already reporting that turkeys were commonly served as 'Christmas cuntrie fare', he also listed 'Beefe, mutton, and porke, shred pies of the best, pig, veale, goose and capon'.[88] And even though, three centuries later, Isabella Beeton, known for her *Book of Household Management*, was declaring that 'a Christmas dinner ... would scarcely be a Christmas dinner without its turkey', she also lists boar and goose as popular fare.[89] It is generally assumed that as turkey became more affordable and available, it established itself as the standard fare for Christmas dinners, but this is not the case.

In 1989, the Folklore Society conducted a survey on festive foods. Respondents from across Britain recalled the foods they had eaten at Christmas both in their childhoods and as adults. Christmas pudding and cake were listed repeatedly from the 1920s ('using an old recipe handed down from her mother') up to the 1980s, and rituals surrounding them were recounted across the decades. The importance of communally stirring the mixture was specified – a custom which dates back to at least the nineteenth century. Regarding 'Stirring the Christmas pudding', recorded in *Notes & Queries* in 1861, 'Every one in the house should do this "for luck." This also, I suppose, causes merriment.'[90] This continued into the twentieth century. One family in 1960s Manchester would make their Christmas cake in October every year 'with great ceremony ... all the family had to have a stir of mixture for good luck'. However, by the 1980s, many families were microwaving their Christmas puddings or buying them pre-made, the need for stirring redundant.[91]

Even with this 'traditional fare' there was variation across Britain and across individual households, subject to availability, family history, and personal taste. Should the poultry be turkey, chicken, duck, goose, or pheasant? Should the Christmas pudding be eaten with custard, rum sauce, or brandy butter? Well-known folklorists Iona and Peter Opie disagreed on what should go into their Christmas pudding, with Iona divulging that 'he thought silver charms in the Christmas pudding were "suburban" (a favourite epithet) and insisted on a real thimble, a real bone button, and a threepenny piece'. The family from Manchester noted above would buy their Christmas pudding and insert silver threepenny bits, which would then be 'removed from finders, kept for use again following year'.

Most households kept their own 'traditions', the Folklore Society survey revealing significant variety and, again, much influence from other cultures. 'Home-made pork pie for breakfast' for one family in the 1920s. Scotch broth, cock-a-leekie, or 'old brown Windsor soup' in the 1930s. And for something sweet, Turkish delight, butterfly cakes, 'sugar mice off the tree'; *Pfefferkuchen* and *Stollen* for a family with German heritage; pumpkin pie (if pumpkin was available – squash if not) for someone who had moved from the United States to Britain in the 1960s. A few households were choosing nut roast by the 1980s, with vegetarianism on the rise. Norfolk dumplings were chosen by one family instead of Yorkshire pudding ('We may, of course, have had them during the war because they didn't take eggs'). The most suitable accompanying sauce was open to debate: mint sauce, bread sauce, apple sauce; cranberry sauce for one person originally from Canada; parsley sauce for another whose father was German; and 'salad', which was described as a 'vegetable sludge' consisting of mint, lettuce leaves, spring onions, sugar, and vinegar, apparently popular among 'northern families'.

Pandemic times

The home is a folkloric microcosm. It reflects changes in how communities protect themselves – and in what they seek protection from. It demonstrates shifts in the forms of prosperity and wellbeing that they seek, and the means employed to secure it. It (quite literally) exhibits the occasions celebrated, from calendar customs to personal rites of passage, and how communities mark those events. The home proves very malleable, adapting to these protean beliefs, ideals, and needs as times change. Nowhere do we see this adaptability more clearly, and more abruptly, than during the COVID-19 pandemic. On 23 March 2020, the British Prime Minister announced the first lockdown in the UK, ordering people to 'stay at home'. Lockdowns were lifted and resumed, locally and nationally, but, essentially, many people in Britain were restricted to their homes for extended periods until March of the following year. Suddenly 'home' took on a very different meaning and function. The home became both a haven and a prison. 'Stay home and stay safe', was the order, or 'Stay home. Save lives.'[92] Home was deemed a space physically fortified from the infectious disease. Simultaneously, it was a space in which people were legally confined, threatened with fines if they left unnecessarily for more than one mode of exercise a day. And so, for about a year, the home became many people's worlds – and it had to adapt to this immense shift in its significance. Suddenly, communal events needed to be transferred into the private home. Festivals moved online. Rites of passage and calendar customs, usually celebrated with friends and extended family, were observed with the immediate household only – or through a computer screen.

Another way the home was adapted during lockdown was through harnessing the communicative power of windows. In 2017, a team of sociologists conducted research into the domestic windows of Glasgow, noting that 'windows are good to look through, sociologically speaking'.[93] Although they perform mundane functions – letting in light but keeping out weather and intruders for most British homes since the Industrial Revolution[94] – glass windows are also aesthetic objects allowing for curated displays. What you choose to put in an outward facing window is the part of your private, domestic space that you would like, or allow, others to see. Flags, campaign posters, and seasonal decorations are all part of the window display curated to convey a message or even perform identity.[95] During the pandemic, at a time when people were separated long term from the outside world by the walls and closed doors of their homes, this communicative role of the window was abruptly heightened.

Throughout lockdown, creative messages of hope could be seen in many windows across Britain. Many of these took the form of painted rainbows, a long-standing symbol of hope and unity.[96] The custom began in Italy, the first European country to be hit drastically by the pandemic. Handwritten Post-It notes containing the phrase 'Andrà tutto bene' (All will be well) began appearing on front doors in the Lombardy region of Italy, and soon after, families were reproducing the phrase on large signs and adding brightly coloured rainbows. The custom, shared online and in the news, spread worldwide, reaching British windows in force. Many families in Britain, especially those with children, crafted their own signs. The Italian phrase was replaced by 'stay strong', 'this too shall pass', and messages of thanks to the National Health Service and other key workers. Many of the signs contained no words at all, the rainbow itself becoming an instantly recognisable symbol of enduring hope in the shadow of the pandemic. The V&A Museum of Childhood collected thousands of these pieces of folk art, recognising their significance as a symbol of the times.[97]

Other items in lockdown window displays included teddy bears, aimed at giving children something to look for (*à la* 'going on a bear hunt') while on their daily walks.[98] Messages specifically between neighbours entered these displays, with written conversations forming across windows.[99] Seasonal decorations adapting to lockdown also featured: surgical face masks worn by carved pumpkins and Christmas elves, along with signs warning Santa to 'socially distance'. New rituals formed, while old ones were adapted. Some were short lived. Once a week, at 8 p.m. on a Thursday evening, people were encouraged to stand in their open windows or doors and 'clap for carers', a ritual that brought the socially distanced country together in paying tribute to the National Health Service and key workers. As one newspaper described the ritual, 'The exuberant din of hand clapping, cheering, hoots and whistles resounded along streets that had been eerily hushed for most of the day ... Children banged on pots and pans, dogs barked, and handbells rang out.'[100] This ritual lasted only a few weeks in many areas of Britain, though.

Other changes made in response to the pandemic may prove more durable. One takes us back to the birthday cake. Increased fear of spreading germs led many families to forgo blowing out the candles on the cake (which would then be distributed for eating, potentially spangled with the celebrant's saliva). So established is the custom, however, that creative adaptations were sought. The 'wish cake' was invented – a much smaller birthday cake, such as a cupcake, solely reserved for the celebrant. A candle would be placed on the wish cake, the celebrant would blow it out, make their wish, and eat the cake – while a larger cake, candle and saliva free, would be cut and distributed to the guests. Another alternative is to blow candles out one by one, apparently reducing the amount of saliva – and possibly increasing the number of wishes allowed, as one journalist suggested. In the United States, new inventions have been marketed as the solution, such as the 'Blowzee' – a tube with a battery-powered propeller at the end that expels spit-free air when blown into – and the 'No Blow Candle', containing a microphone and a LED light that responds to singing and clapping.[101] Whether these prototypes will reach Britain, and whether the various adaptations will prove long lasting, only time will tell.

Part VI

Modern media

Part VI

Modern media

Chapter 11
Broadcasting folklore

In 2023, a small community in the Forest of Dean, Gloucestershire, made some 'controversial changes' to their calendar custom of Eel Day. They had long celebrated their local delicacy of eel by crowning an 'Eel King' in an annual parade, but to make the festivities more inclusive, this year they crowned an 'Eel Queen' instead. Specifically, they chose a fifty-year-old woman named Linda. 'Baptised' in a natural pool within the forest, 'sharing these magical waters with the eel', Linda was cleansed before the festival. As one of the organisers worded it, this was to represent 'death of the old, birth of the new'. Linda was then bedecked with a large radial headdress of wheat, flowers, and foliage, and the ceremonial robe, worn by the Eel Kings before her. Accompanied by community members wearing various animal costumes, including eels, the Eel Queen paraded through stations – from one marked 'puberty', through 'menopause', and ending at 'rebirth'. At each, a member of the community would be garlanded, the words 'may all your transitions be joyful' were chanted, and Linda would throw an eel over her shoulder to the cheering crowd.

This is not an account of a real custom observed by a real community. It is a piece of fiction, created by British comedian Bridget Christie for the Channel 4 comedy drama series *The Change* (2023). The six-part series is an insightful, evocative commentary on evolving folklore in a changing world. As we saw in Chapter 1, festivals and calendar customs adapt to survive. Eel Day – no doubt inspired in part by the Ely Eel Day festival in Cambridgeshire, which itself has only a short history, dating to 2004[1] – is one such example of an adapting calendar custom. The gender dynamics of previous Eel Days (and folk customs in general) are overtly critiqued by some of the show's characters; the line 'from time immemorial, we women have had masculine iconography and phallic symbolism shoved down our throats' provokes reflection as well as laughter. Another custom problematised in *The Change* is that of

Morris dancing and blackface, with the leader of the local troupe noting that 'it's a minefield for white people ... all this blackface stuff'. 'No it isn't,' comes the simple response. 'Just don't do it.'

As well as commenting on the nature of folklore, *The Change* demonstrates how folklore can be adapted to the screen. And, garnering praise from critics, winning several national television awards, and renewed for a second season, it also demonstrates how popular folkloric content is with modern audiences. But it is not a new-found popularity. Folklore has fascinated British broadcasters, filmmakers, and screenwriters for as long as Britain has produced broadcasters, filmmakers, and screenwriters. And, as this chapter demonstrates, folklore does not become fixed by appearing on screen. Indeed, it proves more malleable than ever.

Recording folklore: early film, radio, and television

In the early years of moving pictures, when short films were toured around fairs and music halls by travelling showmen, the screening of local crowd scenes proved to be one of the most popular genres. There were footage of workers leaving factory gates, busy street scenes, and football matches, but commercial filmmakers also captured processions and community traditions.[2] There are records of some sixty shorts concerning local festivities and calendar customs, including fairs and Whitsun walks.[3] Beyond the initial sensation of seeing motion pictures in the first place, the crowd films also played on the pleasure principle of 'seeing yourself' on screen, and the greater the number of people captured in the film footage of an event, the greater the number of local punters who would turn up and pay to see themselves, family, and friends. Such moments may have also helped to reinforce community bonds and bolster the value of folk performances – if it was worth someone recording and viewing it, it was worth doing it.[4]

In 1904 the crowning of the Knutsford May Queen, and attendant Morris dancing, was filmed and then shown to the public just two days later at Manchester's St James' Hall. The same year, showman George Kemp filmed the Buxton well-dressing ritual for one of his travelling bioscope shows, which also included footage of young girls maypole dancing.[5] In the surviving stock of Lancashire filmmakers and showmen Sagar Mitchell and James Kenyon, who founded their film company in 1897, there is footage of egg rolling in Preston around 1901, and the May Day processions and crownings in the Lancashire towns of Bootle (1903) and Leyland (1905), and the Welsh town of Llandudno (1907). There is also footage of a carnivalesque Whitsuntide procession.[6] With early photography it was difficult to capture the dynamism of folklore because of exposure times. Participants had to stop and pose for the camera. Moving pictures can be a more valuable historical document, as in the minute or so of footage we get a much better sense of the social composition of crowds, the nature of dance moves, and the emotions of those present. By and large, though, these early films captured the Victorian revival version of customs, rather than the earthy rambunctiousness of a Guy Fawkes celebration or Plough Monday.

With the development of the cinema and the advent of the British newsreel industry in 1910, when French film company Pathé set up a British subsidiary, the filming and distribution of news shorts about local customs and traditions became a national and even international enterprise. The challenge was to know what might attract the attention of a general rather than local audience for a minute or two while waiting for the main feature to start.[7] The heyday for such news shorts was in the interwar period, and a search through the British Pathé and British Film Institute archives reveals a clear set of customs and traditions that were deemed 'newsworthy' for the cinema audience during the 1920s and 1930s. There was some overlap with the older showground shorts, with Rose Queen and May Queen ceremonies, and Charter and Mop Fairs (Stratford-on Avon Mop Fair in particular, due to the Shakespeare connection) being filmed and shown regularly. But new subjects came into vogue. One was the revived, civic beating the bounds tradition. Pathé filmed, for example, the big beating ceremonies in St Albans (1913), St Clement Danes (1923), Okehampton (1928), and Hereford (1933). It is worthy of note that they were introduced to audiences as 'revivals' of an ancient custom.

Then there were the 'quaint' or 'picturesque' calendar customs. Well dressing at Tissington and Buxton were filmed on several occasions. The Helston Furry Dance, which was and is held on 8 May and involves decorous couples dancing through the streets of the town, was filmed as a news item at least five times between 1921 and 1933. They captured the children's dance, which was first added to the custom in 1922. The Dunmow Flitch was another favourite, with five surviving news clips from the 1920s. The thing is, though, that the Dunmow Flitch fell into abeyance with the advent of the First World War and started again only in 1930. What the news companies filmed in the 1920s was an upstart imitation organised by the East London town of Ilford, some thirty miles away. It grabbed all the headlines, apparently leading to some discontent back in Dunmow. Still, Empire News was there to record the revived Flitch

Figure 11.1 Abbots Bromley Horn Dance, Staffordshire, 1982, one of the many photographs of British customs in the Doc Rowe Archive. Photograph by Doc Rowe.

at Dunmow in 1930. Otherwise, some now well-known calendar customs were also commercially filmed on one or two occasions. The Padstow Oss was captured with sound by Pathé in 1932, with the introductory title card explaining that its 'origin is buried in oblivion & has been held from time immemorial to welcome in summer'. The Abbots Bromley Horn Dance was filmed in 1926 and 1927, with the latter's title card joking, 'No saxophone – only horns, which the dancers carry, in four-hundred-year-old custom.' (Figure 11.1)

BBC radio began broadcasting locally in 1922, and a few years later formed six regional services as well as the national service. Although it was sometimes accused of being a centralising or homogenising cultural force, the BBC's regional programme teams tried to reflect the diversity of art, culture, and traditions within Britain.[8] The search for content led the programmers to draw upon folklore to interest their listeners and prove their 'regionalness'. It is no surprise that calendar customs remained a popular topic, but of course the nature and experience of them had to be evoked through sound only – which was something of a challenge. In 1934 the news that the BBC was going to record the Haxey Hood game caused some excitement in the local press. As it turned out, they were not able to record it live, for technical reasons, and instead they broadcast a twenty-minute talk on the custom by the Lincolnshire playwright and editor Herbert Green, which went out between 6:30 and 6:50 p.m. on 7 January 1936. The BBC were back again in 1950, with a *Yorkshire Post* journalist reporting that: 'A BBC commentator found himself in the centre of it all and of his microphone there was nothing to be seen save a length of trailing cable. As I watched with amusement his attempts to escape, a crowd of scarlet-clad figures suddenly descended on me.'[9] The BBC understandably returned to the Dunmow Flitch repeatedly, as the custom was based on a mock verbal trial that could be recorded and broadcast as an oral performance.

Where radio could innovate, as compared to early film, was in the coverage of a broader range of folklore topics in the format of talks and interviews. In August 1927, Major C. J. Evans explored 'Welsh Folk-Lore – Coblynau, Gomes or Knockers'. A few years later, in October 1931, Regional Programme Scotland broadcast a documentary on 'The Folklore of Hallowe'en' presented by Alexander Polson, who had recently written a book, *Our Highland Folklore Heritage* (1926); and in 1936 it broadcast a fifteen-minute Gaelic-language programme on the folklore of the Western Isles. In 1932–1933 Regional Programme Midland produced a series of talks on county folklore. There was 'Tales of Old Derbyshire', for instance, presented by Laurance Ramsbottom (Organizing Secretary of the Derbyshire Rural Community Council), while Mrs. M. M. Priestley (editor of *The Woman's Leader*), talked on 'Worcestershire Customs, Sayings and Folklore'. The *Radio Times* observed, regarding the latter, that 'Universal education, broadcasting, the cinema, the motor-bus, and other cheap means of transit – all these are tending to abolish purely local characteristics and to induce uniformity. In Worcestershire, chiefly in the rural parts, some old customs are still, or have been till very recently, practised, old sayings are in use, and folk-lore is remembered.'[10] The creation of the BBC's mobile recording unit in 1935 offered new possibilities for capturing live events. As the *Radio Times* for May 1936 explained: 'The Padstow and the Helston ceremonies have both previously been broadcast … but of necessity the performances had to some extent to be "staged". This year, with the help of the mobile recording unit, it is hoped to record the ceremonies exactly as they occur.'[11]

In November 1936, the BBC launched its television service for parts of England, though transmitters serving Scotland and Wales began to be established only from 1952. The founding of Independent Television (ITV) followed in 1955. There is little evidence that there was much folklore reportage in the early decades of BBC television, but from the 1950s onward more content appears to have been created as the BBC founded regional television units and ITV created regional franchises such as Anglia Television. Just as with local and regional newspapers a century before, regional television was keen on calendar customs to fill out the news content. Shrove Tuesday pancake racing was one such popular item. Gaumont had first filmed the famous race at Olney back in 1927, and it had been shown in newsreels subsequently, but from the late 1950s onward, through the 1960s and 1970s, Associated Television (ATV), which held the ITV franchise for the Midland region, regularly reported on the races at Olney and also at Ironville, Whittington, Bulkington, and elsewhere in the region.[12] In the same period, ATV's *Midland News* returned repeatedly to the now internationally known cheese rolling at Coopers Hill, Brockworth, Gloucestershire.[13] ATV *Today* also covered the traditions of the growing ethnic population of the region, with a report in 1969 on the celebration of the Bengali Hindu festival of Durga Puja, dedicated to the goddess Durga, by residents in Birmingham. It was thought to be the first such ceremony in the city.[14]

In an article on the decline of Hogmanay, one Scottish newspaper observed approvingly in 1932 that old customs had recently been 'vigorously "revived"' by the BBC and other organisations.[15] It is evident that the BBC contributed to a renewed national observance of Hogmanay, for instance, but as light entertainment rather than as a night of first-footing and boisterous ritual begging. From 1923 it began its annual Hogmanay concert and, on occasion, it also broadcast talks about traditional Hogmanay customs. These broadcasts had national reach, which was further reinforced when, at the outbreak of the Second World War, the regional services gave way to one national Home Service. On 31 December 1939, the Glasgow *Sunday Sun* gave over nearly a quarter of its front page to the Home Service schedule, observing that 'a strong Scottish flavour will permeate the BBC programmes today'. At 5 p.m. the Scottish writer and broadcaster John Allan (1906–1986) gave a talk on Hogmanay celebrations and reckoned that the English were now paying more attention to marking the New Year. At 9:15 p.m. there was a programme entitled 'For Auld Lang Syne', and then the Hogmanay BBC Theatre Orchestra got into the swing of things at 10:20 p.m.

A study of Scottish fiddle music broadcast by early BBC radio has also explored how the BBC shaped the way such music was performed for its listeners. At first the BBC employed classically trained violin players, and when it began to use folk players and dance bands it still acted as a gatekeeper as to how the music was performed.[16] Even in its early days the BBC stood accused of promoting a particularly English and patrician view of the culture and tradition of Britain and the three nations.[17] A London broadcast on the 'Scottish character' in 1934 attracted the ire of a Scottish correspondent to the *Dundee Evening*

Telegraph. Its depiction of the Scots 'might have been true 50 years ago', he grumbled, 'but it has certainly no connection with our life today'. He also mocked a Scottish BBC official who had mistakenly referred to Scottish children hanging up stockings on Hogmanay.[18]

In the 1950s the BBC become more deeply involved with collecting and not just reporting or broadcasting, thanks to the advent of the portable tape recorder. A five-year scheme of recording folk song, dialects, folktales, and customs was initiated with the support of the English Folk Dance and Song Society. Most of the 150 hours or so of recording were folk songs and ballads from Britain and Ireland, but there were two hundred children's singing games, rhymes, riddles, and descriptions of calendar customs by local informants.[19]

April Fools' Day is one of the best examples of how early television could also shape folkloric tradition. By 1850, the editor of the *Sherborne Mercury* considered it a relic of an uncouth past, stating that 'it is now confined to the lower class of society'. He welcomed that 'probably in a few years it will so completely have passed away as to be remembered only as a matter of history'.[20] It is certainly the case that early folklore collectors made little mention of April Fools' Day, and by the early twentieth century newspapers were reporting that its practice had become restricted to school children.[21] In 1914, the *Dundee Courier* suggested that although 'not fallen completely into abeyance, the occasion has been shorn of much of its glory by the stress of modern life'.[22]

It was during the later twentieth century that modern media reinvigorated April Fools' Day as a national moment once again. It all began in 1957, when the BBC current affairs programme *Panorama* aired its now celebrated hoax report on the spaghetti tree harvest in southern Switzerland, presented by respected broadcaster Richard Dimbleby. As one national newspaper explained in an article headed 'What a Dish – with Dimbleby Sauce!': 'Under blossoms which, he explained, were a fortnight early this warm Spring, he showed us girls gathering 18-inch lengths of spaghetti from trees.' Hundreds phoned into the BBC after the broadcast wanting more information about growing spaghetti or to know whether it was a hoax. In 1965 the BBC *Horizon* science television programme interviewed eminent physics professor Samuel Tolansky about his latest discovery – Smellyvision, by which he could transmit odours from the studio through the television and into people's homes. He duly proceeded to 'transmit' the smell of chopped onions and roasting coffee, causing viewers to ring in and say the onions had made their eyes water.[23]

April Fools' pranks became something of a BBC institution, embraced by its radio shows as well. On All Fools' Day in 1970 the popular *Jimmy Young*

Show on Radio 1 included a recipe for 'half a gallon of kangaroo's milk and "one large larrop stump"', causing listeners to call in asking if he was serious. Earlier in the day, Pete Murray fooled his listeners by asking them 'to turn on their TV sets ... and watch his Radio 1 show in colour'. ITV and the British print media jumped on the bandwagon. In 1962, a year after it received its regional franchise license from ITV, Westward Television did an April Fool on its viewers with a feature on the notional Dartmoor village of Nutcombe, where could be found a rare nut called a 'duff' that had amazing healing properties. The *Guardian* became the national newspaper most associated with the day in modern British journalism, with its 1977 travel guide to the non-existent island of San Serriffe causing a media sensation. The *Guardian* website includes a list of every April Fools story it has run since 1974.[24]

Using all these twentieth-century visual media, plus more recent footage on YouTube, it is possible to observe a few calendar customs periodically, in an ethnographic way. This can provide useful insights, over a century or more, regarding the composition and number of participants and audiences, changes in costume, and crowd behaviour. A good example is the Haxey Hood, for which there is surviving footage from 1929, 1938, 1954, 1962, and 1967, and then numerous videos on YouTube for the 2000s (Figure 11.2). For instance, one can observe the greater role of young boys in the game in the early footage. As well as these sources there is the nationally important archive of the folklorist Doc Rowe, who has been photographing, recording, and filming calendar customs and folk song and dance across the country since the 1960s, including making annual documentation visits to Padstow May Day since 1963.

Folklore as folklure

On 15 May 1969, folklorist Tom Burns watched nineteen hours of American television, taking notes on any examples of folklore or 'traditional material' alluded to. He gathered a significant amount, ranging from traditional music and song to beliefs, gestures, narratives, proverbs, and customs.[25] Similar levels of rich material would no doubt have been revealed from a survey of British television at the time. By the end of the 1950s, there were more British households with television than without. In 1987, twenty-four-hour broadcasting was introduced. By 2022, around 27.3 million households in the UK had televisions, and by 2023, over 70 per cent of those televisions were able to access the internet – and consequently, unlimited on-demand streaming services.[26] Today,

Figure 11.2 The Haxey Hood game, Lincolnshire. The 'Fool' addresses the crowd from the Mowbray Stone before the game begins. Photograph by Doc Rowe.

nineteen hours of television offers substantially more options – and substantially more diverse folkloric material – than it would have done in 1969. However, folklorists have done more than survey folkloric material and motif-spot: we have asked what function folklore serves in television and film.

Another American folklorist, Priscilla Denby, writing on 'Folklore in the Mass Media' in 1971, divided the three months' worth of examples she had recorded into three categories: folklore as an aside, folklore as folklure, and folklore qua folklore.[27] Folklore as an aside refers to examples of folklore that appear or are referred to briefly on screen, possibly without the producer knowing its folkloristic content. This reflects the unremarkability of such content in everyday life. Take wedding customs, for example. When Joan wore a white dress and veil for the first wedding in the British television soap opera *Coronation Street* in 1961, and when we saw the ensemble again in the 1994 film *Four Weddings and a Funeral*,[28] the folkloric custom of a British bride wearing a white dress and veil did not need explanation for a twentieth-century British audience; it was a cultural given.

The category of folklore as folklure encapsulates those examples where folklore is harnessed for its selling power. Before television, stock folklore characters were used in advertising because of their relatability and immediate association with magic, from witches and wizards to genies. Fairies were particularly popular. From the end of the nineteenth century, winged children and women promoted the purity and cleansing power of Fairbank's Fairy Soap (evolved today into the washing-up liquid Fairy). A search through the Intellectual Property Office's records and newspaper advertisements reveals that fairies were used to advertise all manner of commodities, including lights, lamps, toffees, warmers for babies' bottles, and sewing machines.

The trend of using folkloric figures continued in 'spot advertisements' in British cinema from the 1910s, followed by the first advertisement broadcast on British television in 1955 (for Gibbs SR toothpaste). We see it also in early adverts for electricity, when there was still awe – and fear – about this new source of power. A 1934 promotional film for Western Electric Company, by London Film Productions, compared electricity in the home to a genie and a wizard: 'And so', the father in the film proudly boasts to his family, 'our genie turns out to be not only a powerful little wizard, but a good little wizard, who gives us all comfort and serves us in our homes. A real wizard in the wall.'[29]

Stock folkloric characters can be employed to communicate all manner of messages. In 1986, Clifford the dragon was used to advertise the strength of Listerine antiseptic mouthwash, selling the idea that even the breath of a dragon who smokes, guzzles beer, and eats knights can be appealing to a beautiful damsel – so long as they use Listerine.

Fairytales are often the first stories people hear, are relatable to many in a modern audience, and have clear staying power – so advertisers were quick to capitalise on them.[30] People's familiarity with folkloristic narratives meant that television adverts could be condensed to thirty seconds and the promotional message would be instantly understandable for a British audience, adults and children alike, without any need for explanation. For example, in the 1990s, the porridge oats brand Ready Brek featured a shot of three bears departing their cottage, leaving behind bowls of porridge, while a small red dragon (the brand's mascot) tells the viewer that the bears made a big mistake by going for a walk to let their Ready Brek cool down, because 'Everyone knows, and I mean everyone' – the dragon gestures to a young girl with ringlets who has entered the cottage and begun to pour syrup onto the porridge – 'that Ready Brek's yummiest when it's hot'. Also in the 1990s, a Mini Cheddars advert showed a man dressed as a wolf opting to eat the savoury biscuits rather than the woman in a red cape, who seemed to believe that the wolf was her grandmother. We know the fairytales these adverts allude to without any need for explanation.

The folklure advertising trend continued into the twenty-first century. In 2014, an advertisement for the Thomson travel company showed 'Simon the Ogre' shedding his horns and fangs and turning into a human through the magical restorative effects of a family holiday: 'It's amazing what our holidays can do.' And in 2024, the real estate company Rightmove advertised the vast range of dream properties they sell via fairytales – described by an advertising news website as 'familiar stories firmly based on place' which have the power to 'fire up the imaginations of potential customers'.[31] One Rightmove advert featured a red apple and the words 'Thatched cottage. In the woods. 7 bedrooms', while another had a background of long, blonde hair, and the line 'Palatial rooms. With a tower. Staircase optional.' Again, these adverts rely on the audience's familiarity with the folkloristic content.

Fairytales are often subject to modern twists when used in advertisements. Jack and the Beanstalk is a case in point. In the 1980s, Jack is played by the griffin from the Midland Bank logo, who plants coins instead of magic beans – and finds a cash machine at the top of the beanstalk: the 'happy ending' of a good savings account! In 1985, Jack has great success growing his beans because he plants them in Levington Multi-Purpose Compost, while in 1986 he steals a colossal roll of Andrex ('the legendary toilet tissue') from the giant rather than the goose and makes his riches through the 'giant saving' of using Andrex. In 2003/2004, Jack's mother is more concerned with the stains on his clothes: whether mud or giant's blood, at least 'Persil's new tablets fizz into action on any stain imaginable'. In 2011, Jack swaps his (toy) cow for a tin of Heinz baked beans, but his mum is not mad because their 'magic' is their healthfulness; and in 2017, the giant runs away from Jack because he has just eaten Weetabix – such were the cereal's strengthening properties. In the 2024 advert for Sky Protect, rather than atop a beanstalk, the giant lives at the top of a large block of flats.

'The magic ... takes on visual form in Technicolor'

Along with folklore as an aside and folklure on screen, another category is folklore qua folklore. This is where folkloristic content is broadcast explicitly as folklore – interesting because it is an example of popular belief, narrative, or custom. This category refers to those examples above, where folklore as enacted 'in real life' was documented, recorded, and broadcast in early film, radio, and television. However, as was seen in Chapter 3, folkloric motifs and narratives are also popularly adapted for fiction – and this translates well to the screen. The screen also has great potential for ostension: the physical, visual enactment of a narrative.[32]

As early as 1946, Stith Thompson recognised that 'cinema, especially the animated cartoon, is perhaps the most successful of all mediums for the presentation of the fairytale'.[33] It was the animated cartoon's unprecedented scope for constructing the creatures and characters of folklore, giving them lifelike qualities, that so impressed Thompson, who cited the 1937 Disney production of *Snow White and the Seven Dwarfs*. Following its commercial success, Disney continued to adapt the works of early folklore collectors, such as *Cinderella* (1950) and *Sleeping Beauty* (1959). The early animated films may have largely been American productions, but they certainly reached British audiences. By the 1930s there were four thousand cinemas across the UK, and about a third of the country's population were estimated to have watched *Snow White* in 1938.[34] Additionally, many of these folkloric films were based on British literary works: *The Adventures of Ichabod and Mr. Toad* (1949), *Peter Pan* (1953), *The Sword in the Stone* (1963), *Bedknobs and Broomsticks* (1971), and *The Lord of the Rings* (1978), to name only some. Clearly, British literature was viewed by American production companies as a rich source material.

The British audiences' responses to Disney's 1951 adaptation of English author Lewis Carroll's 1865 *Alice's Adventures in Wonderland* demonstrate an appreciation for the ostensive power of film animation. A Scottish reviewer noted in 1952 the 'difficulty of translating the Carroll fantasy to the screen. Most people will agree that Disney has made a remarkable attempt at something which was, perhaps, in the nature of things impossible!' Other British newspaper reviews in the year of the film's release raved about how 'The magic of Lewis Carroll's "Alice in Wonderland" takes on visual form in Technicolor' and 'the result is the brilliant combination of two kinds of genius; Disney's superb technique does not cramp Lewis Carrol's characters at all ... the issue is a fairy-tale entertainment at its beguiling and bewitching best'. One reviewer opined, 'The story of Alice belongs exclusively to those long lost lazy Victorian afternoons when a sleepy haze made every garden a wonderland. And if Hollywood's cartoon genius has managed to capture something of this then he has given us something valuable.'[35]

Although less prolific than their American competitors, British production companies also adapted folktales into film, as well as relishing portraying ghosts on screen. In the days of silent cinema, it was the more generic folkloric tropes that were drawn upon. In 1901, Walter R. Booth and Robert W. Paul – both pioneers of British cinema – produced the silent film *The Magic Sword; or, A Medieval Mystery*, which featured a knight saving his beloved by wielding a sword gifted by a fairy and battling a witch and an ogre. The film was only two minutes long, but it harnessed multiple trick effects to show the magical elements of the narrative. Novel, complex double exposures and superimpositions enabled the witch to take off on her broomstick and be turned into a magic carpet, and the giant ogre to grab the damsel from the castle ramparts.[36]

European folklore was the inspiration for other British films, such as *Tom Thumb* (1958), based on the tale 'Thumbling', by the Brothers Grimm, and *The Snow Queen* (1995), inspired by Hans Christian Andersen's 1844 fairytale. British films also drew heavily on British folklore-themed literature, such as in the 1978 semi-animated fairytale film *The Water Babies*, filmed in Yorkshire and based on the 1863 book by Charles Kingsley. And in 1991, Wales produced its first animated feature, *The Princess and the Goblin* (produced by the Welsh television station S4C), which was based on the 1872 novel by the Scottish author George MacDonald. This film, following a princess and a miner's son battling villainous goblins, enjoyed the largest US release of any Welsh film of the time. The film's producer was quoted in 1994 as saying, 'It is very gratifying to think that Welsh goblins will be popping up in the minds of thousands of American children.'[37] The fact that the original source material was written by a Scot went unmentioned.

Adapting Arthuriana

Some folk narratives and characters prove to be particularly popular material for filmmakers, adapted and re-adapted myriad times. Robin Hood is one such character, portrayed on screen time and time again, while King Arthur is another. Indeed, the Arthurian legends have been retold so many times, first on page and then on screen, that one historian has observed that 'the modern cult of King Arthur can be said to be an industry all unto itself'.[38] The appeal of these legends is easy to understand. The historical murkiness of the legends and associated figures is liberating for filmmakers, who can cherry-pick which of the many conflicting sources to draw from, interpreting and adapting them to suit their creative and commercial aims. Through these Arthurian films, we can therefore trace changes over time in what these creative and commercial aims were.

It was the American company Edison Films who first brought the Arthurian legends to life on screen in their 1904 silent version of Wagner's *Parsifal*. By the second half of the twentieth century, British filmmakers, often in collaboration with Hollywood, were producing prolific Arthurian material, each with their own slant and their own brand of historical inaccuracy. In 1953, the British MGM film *Knights of the Round Table* focused almost exclusively on the tragic love triangle between Arthur, Guinevere, and Lancelot, following the trend for Hollywood melodrama. A year later, the British-American film *The Black Knight* (1954) centred on the conflict between Christianity and paganism, and has been interpreted as pro-West, anti-communist propaganda, so prevalent in the 1950s. Americans and Brits are represented by the Christian Arthurian knights, who promote working hard to better your position, while the pagans (i.e. communists) send spies to infiltrate the Round Table.[39]

Political commentary colours another adaptation of the Arthurian legends: *Monty Python and the Holy Grail* (1975). This British satirical comedy does not attempt historical accuracy ('Holy Hand-Grenade of Antioch' and 'Castle Arggh!', for example), is an irreverent amalgamation of different Arthurian traditions, and parodies cinematic techniques. It does, however, make some insightful statements about academia's attempts to historicise Arthurian legend; the labelled 'famous historian' who attempts to narrate the story quite tellingly has his throat slit by a charging knight.[40] The political commentary of the film is overt through dialogue and the many anti-authoritarian scenes. King Arthur's right to rule is challenged in a Marxist speech by a character named Dennis – a king rules through 'our dated imperialist dogma, which perpetuates the economic and social differences in our society' – and is questioned by one of Arthur's peasant subjects who does not know who the 'Britons' are and did not know they had a king. This encounter with the peasant is played for laughs, but is no less insightful for its entertainment value. That there has never been a unified British identity and countrywide recognition of a single authority figure, even in the mythical age of Arthur, is the most historically accurate message of any Arthurian film. As one historian has commented, 'As the Britain of the 1970s revealed its multiculturalism while the British Empire receded into a burnished memory, the Pythons found the right comic but intelligent tone to critique imperialism and authoritarian rule.'[41]

The magical elements of the Arthurian legends are handled very differently across seventy years of filmmaking. Some omit magic entirely, aiming for a sense of realism, rationality, and historical accuracy. *Arthur: The Young Warlord* (1975), originally a twenty-four-episode British television series (1972–1973), adopts a documentary style, with Arthur as narrator debunking many of his own legends. The film *King Arthur* (2004) situates the legends within a historical theory, the Sarmatian Hypothesis, which proposes that Arthur was a Roman military leader named Lucius Artorius Castus who commanded a group of Sarmatian warriors in Britain. Despite marketing itself as 'the true story', however, most elements are more Hollywood than history. The characterisation of Guinevere, played by British actor Keira Knightley, as a warrior rather than a damsel in distress is in keeping with feminist trends of the decade, but is less consistent with the historical evidence for fifth-century Britain. As one historian opines, 'it is wish-fulfillment for contemporary film audiences, though wrapping the slight teenage Knightley in leather bikini-top "armor" hardly seems an advance for feminism'.[42] *The Last Legion* (2007) provides the backstory of Arthur and Merlin within the context of the collapse of the Western Roman Empire. Merlin, who goes by the Latin name of Ambrosinus, is a Druid performing sleight-of-hand tricks rather than real magic. He is seeking the sword of Julius Caesar, made for 'he who is destined to rule', i.e. Arthur, who appears at the end of the film as a young boy.

On the other hand are the screen adaptations that make no pretence at historical accuracy. BBC's television show *Merlin* (2008–2012) has magic at the centre of most of its plot lines. Following the humorous exploits of a young Merlin as he tries to conceal his power in a kingdom where magic is outlawed, viewers encounter spells, potions, curses, magical weapons, alchemy, telepathy, and such folkloric creatures as dragons, griffins, unicorns, goblins, and trolls. It is unabashed fantasy, made to entertain children as well as adults. Likewise, the 2019 film *The Kid Who Would Be King*, targeted at families, features myriad magical abilities, demons, and dragons. It also comedically modernises the Arthurian legend. The bearer of Excalibur becomes a twelve-year-old boy called Alex; his knights – also pre-teens – are named Bedders (Sir Bedivere), Kaye (Sir Kay), and Lance (Sir Lancelot); and their battle with Morgan-le-Fay is set in a twenty-first-century London suburb. Despite being targeted towards children, *The Kid Who Would Be King* has also been interpreted as delivering a modern political message, locating the story within the tumultuous late 2010s. The background references to authoritarianism, political instability, and economic crisis can be viewed in contrast to the time of honour, unity, and equality as described under the rule of King Arthur. The premise of the film, that the villain Morgana will return 'when the land is lost and leaderless', certainly does not reflect well on twenty-first-century Britain.[43]

In the same decade, the notion of English nationhood is again problematised in a film with implicit allusions to the Arthurian legends: Ben Wheatley's *Kill List* (2011). In what has been described as an urban folk horror, the audience follows Jay, purposeless and disillusioned, across the barren, isolated landscapes of a northern English city as explicit parallels are drawn between Jay and his friend Gal (Galahad?) and Arthurian knights (through a bedtime story, the naming of pets, and the toy sword Jay gifts to his son). But the parallel is distorted, because Jay and Gal's crusade is one of violence and murder, and the England they are shown to live in is derelict and abandoned, any past sense of nationhood having crumbled. *Kill List* is a deliberate inversion of the nostalgic, hegemonic nation normally promoted by retellings of Arthurian legends. It is, as one literature scholar observed, a deconstruction of mythical England.[44]

The next decade brought us the 2021 film *The Green Knight*, featuring British actor Dev Patel as Gawain, the immature, inexperienced nephew of the King (never named, but assumed to be Arthur). Gawain's quest to face the Green Knight, known to us from a fourteenth-century poem, is retold here by director David Lowery to communicate an ecofeminist message, equating toxic masculinity with environmental extraction.[45] The centralised female characters lead Gawain on a journey of what one environmental studies scholar describes as 'environmental enlightenment'.[46] Films have longed played a role in ecocritical, geopolitical messaging ('eco-cinema'). In 1989, for example, ITV Cymru Wales (then known as Harlech Television) pitched the environmental tale *A Furling's Story* – which would later be renamed *Once Upon a Forest* (1993) – to an American cartoon studio. This animated film follows three young forest animals ('furlings') as they seek a cure for their friend, who is dying from poisonous gas emitted from an overturned fuel truck. On their journey, they navigate many dangers, including 'yellow dragons' – which are, in fact, yellow construction vehicles. The environmental message of the film is clear: humans are the enemy.

Once Upon A Forest is one film that feels folkloric – a noble quest, a great evil, 'yellow dragons' – but is not actually based on a single folkloric source. It is therefore an example of the folkloresque, a term coined by folklorist Michael Dylan Foster to describe a product not 'based on any single vernacular item or tradition; usually it has been consciously cobbled together from a range of folkloric elements, often mixed with newly created elements, to appear as if it emerged organically from a specific source'.[47] There are many examples of the folkloresque in British cinema and television. *Yellow Submarine*, the 1968 musical fantasy adventure film featuring the songs and personas of the English rock band The Beatles, is highly folkloric in plot – the utopia of Pepperland is attacked by a race of blue-skinned, clawed, humanoid creatures who throw magic apples at the residents, turning them to statues and draining all colour from the land – but is not based on any specific folkloric source. Many of the plot lines in the British television series *Doctor Who* (1963–present) are also folkloresque, placing folkloric creatures – ghosts, werewolves, sirens, minotaurs, and headless monks, to name only some – within new narratives. The long-running series also incorporates many folkloresque creatures: cybermen, weeping angels, chumblies, mire beasts, alpha centaurans, drashigs, chronovores, and swampies, are just some of the many monsters, creatively conceptualised for television – but also the products of various folkloric elements having been 'consciously cobbled together'.

Of wicker men and Pooh-sticks: performing and producing folklore

Hundreds gathered in rural Scotland to watch the 'torching of a human effigy'. One account records how 'a procession of torch-bearers led the way around the complex and up the hill to the looming effigy of the wickerman. Then, just as the sun was setting behind the distant hills and to the beat of drums, the wickerman was set alight.' 'With flames leaping some 50ft into the twilight', another source accounts, 'the 400-strong crowd were hushed until giving a hills-echoing roar as the giant figure suddenly collapsed in a final inferno.'[48] Although these descriptions intimate a historical account of a historical custom, they all date to the twenty-first century – and all refer to twenty-first-century events. These events, which took place in the Scottish countryside of the early 2000s, ranged from a celebration at a prehistory-themed tourist attraction to a family-friendly music festival – and they all drew on the 1973 film *The Wicker Man*, set and filmed in Scotland.

This British film, inspired by David Pinner's 1967 novel *Ritual* and often viewed as the quintessential folk horror film, centres on the many ritual customs of the people of a fictitious Scottish island, Summerisle, culminating in the burning of a colossal wicker human effigy. The religion of this community is presented as a revival of 'Celtic paganism', but there is no acknowledgement of how problematic of a concept 'Celtic paganism' is. The rituals performed as part of this fictional religion are formed from a miscellany of disparate folkloric motifs, cherry-picked from various periods and cultures, from maypoles and fire jumping to standing stones and human sacrifice. Whether or not director Robin Hardy and screenwriter Anthony Shaffer intended to create a film consciously critiquing the harnessing and editing of customs, or whether they believed they were accurately portraying 'Celtic paganism', is still open for debate.[49] Either way, *The Wicker Man* is a folkloresque film; it is the product of amalgamating a twentieth-century novel with a melange of stereotypical motifs rather than a single folklore narrative. *The Wicker Man* has also become a popular inspiration for ostensive play, with communities not just in Scotland but worldwide re-enacting the burning of their very own wicker man – *sans* human sacrifice – to celebrate various calendar customs or local festivals. Often these rituals are presented as historical re-enactments, and the burning of a wicker effigy has entered vernacular belief as an authentic pagan custom. The folkloresque has thus created folklore.

Folklore travels easily from the screen or page to people's lived experiences, entering general consciousness, shaping customs, and becoming folklore in reality.[50] For example, fans seek connections with fictional characters and narratives by making pilgrimages to particular sites or performing actions as a form of embodied play.[51] It is embodied play that is behind people's visits to a specific bench in Oxford's Botanic Garden. This is where the two main characters of Phillip Pullman's fantasy series *His Dark Materials* agree to meet beyond the end of the books, and fans not only sit on the bench but have carved it with the characters' initials.

Embodied play is also behind people's visits to a fake platform at London Kings Cross train station. Here, fans of the vast *Harry Potter* franchise queue at the staged 'Platform 9 3/4', don Hogwarts scarves, and grasp hold of the handlebars of a half-disappeared luggage trolley. Embodied play inspired by the *Harry Potter* books and films can also be seen in the home and on the playground. Sticks repurposed as wands, dressing gowns as Hogwarts school robes, blankets draped around shoulders as invisibility cloaks, and shampoos and herbs used as potion ingredients are all examples of embodied or 'fantasy play'.[52] Verbal spells from J. K. Rowling's universe have entered popular knowledge – *wingardium leviosa, accio, expecto patronum* are the closest things to Latin that we hear in most British schools today. And the casting of these spells, as a form of fantasy play, has been designated a form of 'folk performance'.[53]

Embodied play inspired by popular culture is not a new phenomenon. Children playing cowboys in the first half of the twentieth century no doubt drew some of their inspiration from the many cowboy films being produced – the earliest of which, *Kidnapping by Indians*, was actually made in Blackburn, England, in 1899.[54] In the 1950s, we also find references to children playing at Robin Hood. The children referred to in Chapter 9 who were remanded in London for stealing broom handles to make swords had 'wanted to play at being Robin Hood and his merry men'.[55] The year was 1953. Had these children watched Walt Disney's *The Story of Robin Hood and His Merrie Men* (actually filmed in Sherwood Forest), widely released in cinemas across Britain just the year before?[56] In the twenty-first century, fantasy play and children's folk performances often centre on the superheroes of the comic book franchises Marvel and DC.[57]

Popular culture also has a long history of creating folk customs. In 1928 'Poohsticks' entered vernacular knowledge. This was a game first mentioned in children's book *The House at Pooh Corner* (1928) by A. A. Milne, and it was depicted in the 1983 Disney animation, *Winnie the Pooh and a Day for Eeyore*. It involves the players dropping sticks on the upstream side of a bridge and seeing whose stick first appears on the downstream side. By the 1960s, Poohsticks had become a popular game. In 1968, 'player of Pooh-sticks' was being used as a synonym for daydreamer. In 1969, a newspaper was reporting on the dangers the game was causing in a town in the West Midlands: 'The noble sport of Poohsticks is causing a road hazard ... Children are throwing sticks into the river on one side of the bridge, then running across the road to see which emerges first.' Following some near misses between children and motorists, a guard rail along the pavement was planned: 'Which would ruin the Poohsticks but perhaps save a life.'[58] But it was not only children who played. In 1966, students at Hull University challenged Sheffield University to a Poohsticks contest, and in 1984 the World Poohsticks Championship was inaugurated in Oxfordshire (regulation sticks only), drawing competitors from around the world.[59] In 2015, the director of engineering and education at the Royal Academy of Engineering published a scientific formula for identifying the optimum Poohstick, involving factors such as cross-sectional area, density, buoyancy, and the drag coefficient.[60]

With the examples of wicker men, Poohsticks, and Platform 9 3/4 in mind, to return to the opening paragraphs of this chapter, how long will it be before a British 'Eel Queen' is being baptised, garlanded, and paraded through the stations of puberty, menopause, and rebirth, chanting 'may all your transitions be joyful' and tossing eels over her shoulder?

Chapter 12
Digital folklore

British digital folklore does not exist. But that is not to say that digital folklore does not exist. Of course it does, and folklorists have long recognised the internet's unprecedented efficacy in transmitting folklore.[1] Why? It offers a rapid and effective dissemination mechanism: computer-mediated communication allowing for the quick (indeed, instant), widespread, and easy exchange of information, unrestricted geographically.[2] First introduced to the British home in the 1990s, nearly all households in Britain now have internet access. By 2020, adults were spending more than a quarter of their waking day online, and online messaging platforms such as WhatsApp and Facebook Messenger have largely replaced other forms of non-face-to-face communication.[3] Now that the internet is the main means of communication throughout the world, the role it plays in the transmission of folklore cannot be overstated, and what we have on the internet is a vast, unintentional archive of folklore.[4]

But still, *British* digital folklore does not exist. This is because digital folklore, by its very nature, is global; it belongs to the *World Wide* Web. Because it is not geographically nor nationally bound, the internet has altered not only how the 'folk' share folklore but also what constitutes the 'folk'. A folk group can be separated by continents but still be in constant communication. Also, because of the rapid transmitting potential of the internet, a piece of digital folklore may start out as British, but rarely remains limited to Britain. What this chapter is concerned with, therefore, are the examples of digital folklore that seem to particularly resonate with the British.

Even on the surface, the digital world is entangled with folklore. It pervades the digital world's vernacular language. 'Trolls' write insulting or offensive messages on other people's social media accounts. 'Ghosts' cut off digital communication, vanishing without explanation, or lurk on social media without engaging. 'Zombie' computers have been compromised by a virus and are in the control of a remote hacker.

The internet has also vastly increased our exposure to folklore and our ability to research it. The online encyclopaedia *Wikipedia* hosts 43,261 freely accessible articles featuring the term 'folklore'. There are countless blogs and podcasts exploring folklore themes, and there is massive interest on social media to share folklore content. The hugely successful 'Folklore Podcast' by Mark Norman and hashtag #FolkloreThursday by Willow Winsham and Dee Dee Chainey are cases in point.[5] However, the internet is not only a place for sharing and archiving folklore. It is a place for generating it. And, as this chapter demonstrates, many (if not all) genres of British folklore have found their place online, adapting and thriving in a digital world.

Transformative storytelling online

'Going on a curse-spree <3', declared the chair on 9 August 2012. The day before, the chair had mused on '#10ThingsIGetAlot How do you curse people if you're only a chair ...?', while the day after, it was lamenting, 'I almost miss the days when I wasn't cursed, people sat on me all the time'. Some of the chair's complaints were more prosaic – broken legs and 'The moths are chewing at my upholstery' – but it mainly seemed to be preoccupied with cursing. This was the Twitter account of the Busby Stoop Chair, currently held by Thirsk Museum in North Yorkshire. According to legend, it is haunted by the ghost of Thomas Busby, a local murderer who was executed in the eighteenth century. The chair had come from the Busby Stoop Inn, where it gained a reputation for being cursed and causing the deaths of those who sat on it. In the 1970s it was donated to Thirsk Museum, where it is 'hung out of harm's way', preventing anyone from sitting on it.[6] And, for a brief period in 2012, it took to social media to ruminate and vent.

That a cursed chair had its own Twitter account should come as no surprise. The internet is awash with the magical, the supernatural, and the folkloric. The Loch Ness Monster has several (parody) social media accounts (@RealNessie, @Loch_NessMonsta, @therealnessie): 'World's Hide & Seek Champion and Scotland's oldest resident', reads one bio. The boggart of Boggart Hole Clough, whom we met in Chapter 4, has his own X account, @boggartmcr, with the bio: 'I'm a Boggart, a northern sprite that lives in dark holes and garbage bins ... I eat tadpole jelly and sweaty sock slime.' Fantasy fiction characters, too, have their accounts. Tolkien's Frodo Baggins, for example, has over eight thousand followers on his X account @FrodoBaggins: 'Legendary Hobbit from Middle-earth (a.k.a. The One Ring Wonder)'. In March 2024, Frodo posted, 'Took a "Which Middle Earth Character Are You?" quiz on @BuzzFeed. Got Gollum. Twice. 👀 #IdentityCrisis'. An aged Harry Potter has his own Instagram account, chosen1, where he posts nostalgic photos from his childhood for 'tbt' ('Throwback Thursday'), which are liked and commented on by other wizards and witches. Even Rowling's The Sorting Hat has several X accounts.

The creators of such social media accounts are engaging in digital ostensive play. They are digitally embodying a character or creature to parody its story, also often exploring hypothetical scenarios beyond the bounds of its established, canonical narratives. In doing so, these digital ostensive players expand on the stories, becoming storytellers themselves. This is also the case with fan fiction, whereby fans of a published narrative (a book, film, television series, game) expand on and reinterpret the material for other fans to read. This process has a long history; Tolkien himself was technically a 'fan fiction' writer, drawing heavily on *Beowulf* and Old Norse poetry.[7] But it was in the 1960s that fan fiction became a recognised genre, with fans of the television show *Star Trek: The Original Series* (1966–1969) adding their own material to the canon in unofficial publications known as 'fanzines'.[8] Tolkien too had fans reinterpreting his legendarium in this period, the first documented so-called 'Tolkienfic' appearing in the fanzine *I Palantír* in 1960.[9] However, with the rise of the internet came an unprecedented social platform for sharing fan fiction with fellow fans. Vast repository websites were formed to house these self-published pieces of literature, from FanFiction.Net in 1998 to Archive of Our Own (AO3) in 2008, currently containing more than 13,990,000 works of fan fiction.[10]

Much fan fiction reinterprets works identified in Chapter 3: fairytales or pieces of fiction that draw on fairytale tropes.[11] For example, AO3 archives over 490,000 literary reinterpretations of J. K. Rowling's *Harry Potter* and 109,000 of Tolkien's works. These often look beyond the canonical narrative. In 2016, a fan fiction writer penned a five-thousand-word epilogue to Garner's *The Owl Service*, set nine years later, when two of the novel's protagonists, Roger and Gwyn, reunite in London.[12] Another, written in 2022, is set immediately after the ending of *The Owl Service*, addressing the questions 'will Roger and Alison reconcile with Gwyn? What will their future relationship look like?'[13] This is communal storytelling. Online fan fiction therefore harks back to a time before copyright, when stories were multi-authored and perpetually transformed to suit new purposes.[14] Such stories all add to Bacchilega's transnational and transmedia 'fairy-tale web', demonstrating that the network of fairytale representations grows even vaster online.[15]

Fan fiction writers have been described as 'the latest in a long line of transformative storytellers'.[16] AO3 currently has a user base of over 7,723,000 such people, forming a participatory subculture online – or, indeed, a folk group. The project 'Fanlore', linked to fan fiction archives, recognises this. Their multi-authored website states that the project's mission is to 'engage fans from a wide variety of communities that create and enjoy fanworks, to provide them with a platform to record and share their histories, experiences and traditions'.[17] Included in the website is a glossary of terms used by fan fiction writers – the vernacular language of this folk group. Examples include 'to hit the backbutton', which means to exit a page without finishing a piece of fan fiction, having given up on reading it. An 'anonymouse' is somebody who comments on a fan fiction thread anonymously. 221B refers to a form of constrained writing that imposes a word limit of 221 and specifies that the last word must begin with 'B' (unsurprisingly, this originated with Sherlock Holmes fan fiction writers).

It has been observed that a significant proportion of the folk group of fan fiction writers identify as female and/or queer, and they reinterpret tales to make them more relatable or appealing.[18] In this way, fan fiction is reparative literature, allowing marginalised groups to establish more queer, female, and person-of-colour presences in popular (largely white, cis-male dominated) tales.[19] We witness this reparative motive in 'shipping' trends, whereby fans desire – and pen – romantic relationships ('ships') between fictional characters. As with Captain Kirk and Spock in the early fan fiction of *Star Trek*, much fan fiction shipping features characters of the same gender. In Tolkienfic, for example, such 'ships' include Frodo and Samwise, Legolas and Gimli, Aragorn and Legolas, and Bilbo and Thorin. In a 2019 study, an online Tolkienfic writer stated: 'Writing fan fiction helps me to correct problems with race, gender, and sexuality that I see in Tolkien's books.'[20] Likewise, the many fan fiction pieces of *Harry Potter* featuring transgender characters may have been written in response (to 'correct problems') to the ongoing debate of transphobia surrounding J. K. Rowling.

Folkcore: folklore as internet aesthetic

The internet is made up of countless online subcultures (i.e. folk groups). Subcultures are created in digital spaces when users engage with other users with mutual interests and values. One way they can locate these mutuals is through metadata tagging. A user-generated tag, commonly known as a hashtag, is a word or phrase incorporated into a social media post (microblog, photo, video), identifying a theme or topic covered by the post. By including a hashtag, the content creator allows other users to search for it by this theme or topic, and thus online communities can emerge. There are also certain online platforms that allow other users, besides the content creator, to tag the content, drawing other users into the subculture. Interestingly, the term used to describe this form of collaborative tagging is folksonomy. This is a portmanteau word of 'folk' and 'taxonomy', the information architect who coined the term in 2004 having explained, 'I am a fan of the word folk when talking about regular people'.[21]

All online subcultures are interesting from a folklore perspective, but of most relevance to this book are the subcultures that draw on British folklore in the crafting of their collective identity. One way in which identities are crafted online is through so-called internet aesthetics. Internet aesthetics are a form of categorisation; labels, often tagged, situate images, art, clothing, music, and other forms of popular culture as belonging to a particular subculture's visual (and often ideological) identity. They establish the style, the genre, of a person's online persona, many of which evoke folklore.[22] #Fairycore is one particular internet aesthetic, with images and videos drawing on fairytale imagery, creating fantastical digital spaces through costuming, landscapes, filters, and music.[23] It has become such a well-known trend that the V&A's collection of online 'creative quizzes and videos that celebrate art, design, fashion, film, music, pop culture trivia' includes a quiz on 'How well do you know your fairycore aesthetic?' Questions range from 'Which of these is a classic fairycore plant? Palm trees, tulips, holly trees, bluebells' (bluebells, apparently) and 'You have to plan a fairycore party – what food are you serving?' (cupcakes drizzled with dandelion honey, naturally).[24]

There are various folklore-themed aesthetic subcultures, such as #mermaidcore, #elfcore, and #pixiecore. #Spriggancore draws on the Cornish folkloric creature the spriggan, with the user-generated 'Aesthetics Wiki' stating that this internet aesthetic employs 'darker and moodier imagery' with fog, horns, antlers, and deep forests.[25] #Selkiecore aestheticises Scottish marine folklore, with darker and more neutral colours than in #mermaidcore, featuring cloudy skies, rocky shores, and seal imagery.[26] And #goblincore, which became popular on the social media platform Tumblr in the 2010s, celebrates 'the danker, gnarlier side of nature', with images and videos drawing on moss, mushrooms,

Figure 12.1 #goblincore images from mossgoblingrrl's Instagram account, aesthetically celebrating 'the danker, gnarlier side of nature' on social media. Reproduced with kind permission from mossgoblingrrl.

and insects in their aesthetics through clothing, make-up, and natural settings (Figure 12.1). A *Guardian* article in 2021, noting that #goblincore was on the rise again, theorised that it was motivated by anti-capitalist values, a post-COVID lockdown desire to retreat into the wild, and a childlike appreciation for nature's imperfections.[27]

Witchcore is another trending internet aesthetic, involving dark colours, occult symbols, plants, candles, and semi-precious stones. As well as an aesthetic, however, it is also a religion. Communities of contemporary Pagans and Wiccans are so prevalent on social media that a new term was coined: Witchtok. This term, playing on the name of the video-sharing site TikTok, denotes a substantial digital subculture of self-identified witches and Wiccans who use digital platforms to share details of their beliefs and craft.[28] Videos posted on TikTok and YouTube are often instructional, detailing spells and rituals derived in large part from the twentieth-century works of the English Wiccan author Gerald Garder and Anglo-Indian folklorist Margaret Murray – but often with contemporary twists and carefully crafted aesthetics. @TheCityWitchUK joined the video-sharing platforms YouTube in 2019 and TikTok in 2021, and has since accumulated over eight thousand followers/subscribers. Her diverse spells are aestheticised as per their purpose (Figure 12.2). The 'Love spell for a

Modern media

Figure 12.2 Various aesthetics employed by @TheCityWitchUK on YouTube and TikTok, reflecting the diverse spells detailed in her online videos. Reproduced with kind permission from @TheCityWitchUK.

couple' video features two pink, torso-shaped candles, flickering brightly against a hazy backdrop of pink flower petals and herbs, with the accompanying music described as 'Romantic Piano'.[29] The video on 'Total Destruction Curses' features a black backdrop, black candles – including some shaped as poppets and pierced with pins – a silver dagger, and battle-themed 'Viking' music.[30]

The memeification of British culture

Keir Starmer, Prime Minister (PM) of the United Kingdom (2024–?), wears a green hood, holds a bow and arrow, and sings 'Everything I do, I do it for you'. Theresa May (PM, 2016–2019) as the Asgardian goddess of death in a skin-tight suit of black leather, battles Thor, god of thunder. A stern-faced, tuxedoed Daniel Craig walks beside Queen Elizabeth II. 'All of Parliament ma'am?' he asks. 'Yes 007,' she replies, 'the whole bloody lot of them.' Tolkien's hobbit Pippin asks, 'What about Brexit?' and a bemused Aragorn points out, 'We already had it'. 'We've had one, yes,' Pippin explains, as if it is obvious. 'What about second Brexit?' Winnie the Pooh and Piglet walk together through the woods. 'How did you vote?' asks Pooh. 'Leave,' said Piglet. 'I voted remain,' said Pooh. 'Are we still friends?' 'Yes.' 'Good,' said Piglet. 'Let's go and get pissed.'

Politics and popular culture make for a potent (and often humorous) mix, and nowhere do we see this more clearly than in the viral meme. The word 'meme' was coined in 1976 by the evolutionary biologist Richard Dawkins. As a portmanteau word of mimesis and gene, it refers to a 'unit of cultural transmission, or a unit of imitation', which propagates itself by 'leaping from brain to brain'.[31] It is used today to describe online user-generated content – often images and videos – which replicates and gains influence through online transmission, 'leaping' from e-mail to e-mail (funny cat memes were some of earliest) and then from social media account to social media account (where cat memes remain popular). A meme becomes 'viral' if it is duplicated and disseminated at an exponential rate. Described as 'prominent examples of vernacular creativity', memes are examples of folklore and folk art.[32] They are a common means of online expression, communicating polyvocal cultural ideas and public discourse through creative remixing of popular culture and current affairs. It is unsurprising, therefore, that educators who teach English as a foreign language recommend memes as visual aids in learning aspects of British culture, ranging from etiquette, festivals, and food and drink, to language and humour (offering insights into wordplay, irony, sarcasm, parody, satire, spoonerisms, and banter).[33]

Political feeling is a significant element of British culture that memes can shed light on; the phenomenon has been described as the 'memeification' of political discourse, whereby memes not only reflect a nation's (often conflicting) political feelings but influence them. But to fully grasp the message and appreciate the humour of these memes, some contextual knowledge is needed. Memes are vernacular objects of specific folk groups, often obscure to 'outsiders'. To understand why Keir Starmer is dressed as Robin Hood in this doctored TikTok video, and to understand why the caption reads 'He steals from the old to give to his masters', we also have to understand the criticisms of the PM for policies that are perceived to benefit big business and disadvantage pensioners.[34]

Likewise, to understand why Theresa May's face has been superimposed onto Hela, goddess of death, you also have to recognise that the man whose face replaces Christopher Hemsworth as Hela's adversary Thor is Jeremy Corbyn. You also need to understand that this YouTube video was released at a time when May and Corbyn were rivals in the 2017 UK general election.[35] This also helps our understanding of why so many memes of this period feature May as a robot, alluding to perceptions of her as robotic and 'square', while Corbyn is portrayed as 'cool' and 'authentic', his face superimposed onto popular grime artist Stormzy, or, with a lightsabre, as sage *Star Wars* character Obi Wan Kenobi.[36] And to appreciate why British actor Daniel Craig is in serious but discrete conversation with Queen Elizabeth II, you have to know that Craig was currently cast as James Bond, a fictional British secret agent who would perform covert missions 'for Queen and Country' – potentially including the 'handling' of all of Parliament. You would also need to be aware that this meme was created at a time when the British Parliament was in disarray.[37]

Online challenges

In August 2014, English actor Sir Ian McKellen took a break from playing Sherlock Holmes on a London film set to lead a group of actors and dancers in pouring water over their heads from plastic buckets. He had been tasked with this by the Welsh actor Luke Evans, among others. On the same day, another English actor, Benedict Cumberbatch, sat in his garden and let somebody empty a bucketful of water over his head. He had been challenged to do this by yet another English actor, Tom Hiddleston, who had been soaked with a bucket of water in his London garden a few days before. Cumberbatch then challenged the British racing driver Lewis Hamilton, who had two people throw buckets of water at him while in his riding suit. Hamilton then challenged the British fashion model Naomi Campbell, who took a splashing while lying in a bikini. Scottish actor James McAvoy challenged politicians Alistair Darling and Alex Salmond, rivals in the Scottish independence referendum, who submitted to having buckets of ice water thrown over their heads a few days apart. Salmond proceeded to challenge British PM David Cameron – who declined to have a bucket of ice water poured over his head and wrote a cheque instead.

This chain of British celebrities was participating (or not) in a ritualised act known as the Ice Bucket Challenge. This was a challenge aimed at promoting awareness of the motor neuron disease amyotrophic lateral sclerosis (ALS) and encourage donations to research. It was instigated in North America but became particularly popular in Britain, with Charities Aid Foundation estimating that 30 per cent of young people, and 17 per cent of the UK's total population had participated in the Ice Bucket Challenge, drawing around £10 million of donations.[38] Various elements made this campaign so successful. Firstly, the platform. This was specifically a *social media* campaign. It was not enough for the challengees to submit to a bucket of ice water being poured over their heads. They had to be filmed doing so, and that video had to be publicly posted on their social media accounts. This meant the campaign was not geographically bound. The challenge became viral and, despite commencing in the United States, it spread quickly to other countries worldwide.

A second reason for the campaign's success was the endorsements of well-known actors, artists, sportspeople, and politicians. These undoubtedly encouraged public participation – and because of the social media platforms, celebrities and members of the public could interact with each other much more openly and freely. The challengees 'volunteered' others within their videos, so the challenges became public. And thirdly, the performative enactment of the meme allowed for modifications, so the videos could be personalised without losing their central, familiar elements – their 'invariant memic structure', as one marketing semiotician described it.[39] This meant that British theoretical physicist Stephen Hawking, a sufferer of ALS, could nominate his family to undertake the challenge on his behalf for practical reasons, but it was still viewed as Hawking having completed the Ice Bucket Challenge. The actor Patrick Stewart performed his challenge with characteristic suavity, writing out a cheque, pulling a silver ice bucket towards himself, then pouring ice and some liquor into a glass and taking a sip.

Challenges, as the ritualised, performative enactments of memes, pervade social media. Many are instigated in the United States, but reach Britain rapidly, with countless online videos circulating which detail how to play these 'ritual games'.[40] One British TikTok user, @syl_k_smooth, shares frequent 'creepy kids games' with her forty-two thousand followers. One video, posted in 2022, describes 'Baby Blue', with @syl_k_smooth directly addressing the camera:

> Have you ever played Baby Blue? If you haven't, then I'm going to tell you how to play. You go to the bathroom on your own and lock the door behind you. You look into the mirror and you act as if you're holding a baby in your arms. You then have to say the words 'Baby Blue, Blue Baby', whilst rocking your arms. You have to say that thirteen times over ... you will feel the weight of an invisible baby in your arms and it will keep getting heavier ... you must take the invisible baby before it gets too heavy and flush it down the toilet. You should then quickly leave the bathroom. However, if you don't do this fast enough, it is said that a woman will appear in the mirror and scream "Give me back my baby!" ... Are you brave enough to give this one a go?[41]

This video generated over two thousand comments, many of which demonstrate that viewers had followed the instructions. 'It is scary but it doesn't work I tried it twice', remarked one viewer; 'gonna try it and update after', said another. One viewer admitted, 'I felt weight in my arms', and another said, 'i got my brother to do it without showing him the last part he ran out the washroom horrified but luckily he survived'. 'I did it and when I ran I stubbed my toe', bemoaned one, and another: 'SOME PEOPLE IN MY CLASS WERE PLAYING AND SOMEONE DROPPED THE BABY'. Other @syl_k_smooth's 'Creepy kids games' videos include 'The Axe Man', 'Sandman', 'Devil's Face', 'The Answer Man', and 'Charlie Charlie'. We may not know where many of these challenges originated, but through such videos they reach (and are re-enacted by) a British audience.

Many challenges invoke beliefs in the supernatural, but some, like the Ice Bucket Challenge, are simply about imitating actions for the sake of participating in an online trend. The imitated action is recorded and shared on social media, often hashtagged with the term of the challenge (#icebucketchallenge). Tagging identifies the content creator as part of the relevant online subculture. One such challenge that became particularly popular in Britain was 'happy slapping'. Gaining popularity in Britain in the early 2000s, this 'challenge' involved recording a physical assault on an unsuspecting victim and posting the video online. One newspaper article in 2005 identified it as a 'nationwide phenomenon' which 'began as a craze on the UK garage music scene before catching on in school playgrounds across [London]' in 2004.[42] There is no evidence linking it to the garage music scene, and later speculation suggests that this unfounded connection was a sign that the media were laying the blame for these random acts of violence on a particular class and a particular race.[43]

A more plausible link can be made between 'happy slapping' and the 'you've been Tango'd' phenomenon from the previous decade, born from a 1992 advertising campaign for the British soft drink Tango. As one economist observed, 'The ad itself is the kind of thing the British think is very funny, but may leave others puzzled.' A young man stands on a street corner with his friends, drinking from a can of Tango. A nearly naked, rotund, bald man painted orange runs around them and gives the drinker a double-handed slap. There is an instant replay and a *Match of the Day*-style commentary, and then another voice-over declares, 'You know when you've been Tango'd'. The advertisement won multiple awards and increased sales of Tango by 300 per cent – but it was also pulled or banned from air because of unforeseen consequences.[44]

In 1993, the *Manchester Metro News* quoted a solicitor as saying, 'We believe if you put out an advert, it is likely that children, in particular, will copy it' – and indeed they did. This solicitor was referring to the case of a ten-year-old boy from Stockport whose eardrum was perforated when he was 'Tango'd' by a friend, copying what the article described as the 'cult advert'. 'It was a craze and everybody at school was doing it,' the boy explained. Just a month later, a thirteen-year-old boy in Aberaman needed an operation on his eardrum because of this 'copy-cat prank'.[45] The Tango advert, however, was not the first to comedically employ the double-handed slap. Comedians Morecambe and Wise (also known as Eric and Ernie) had popularised it through their acts, running from the 1940s to the 1980s. Their sketches, which frequently saw Eric slapping both sides of Ernie's face, may have inspired the Tango adverts, which in turn may have inspired the 'happy slapping' video challenge.

In 2013, a psychology researcher interviewed British male adolescents from London, Birmingham, and Manchester, all of whom had watched a 'happy slapping' incident on social media. The interviews revealed that most considered the trend 'harmless', 'playing pranks', and 'more interesting than yet another boring cinema flick'. One adolescent opined, 'As long as nobody gets hurt I see nothing wrong with happy slapping.'[46] But people have got hurt. In 2008, a man in Keighley, West Yorkshire, died when his spine was ruptured in a 'happy slapping' attack, while in 2010, a man in Tooting, South London, fell and hit his head on the pavement after such an incident. He died of brain injuries.[47] In both cases, the adolescent attackers were sentenced to imprisonment, as was the person who filmed the former attack on a camera-phone.

There was recognition of this danger by the adolescents interviewed by the psychology researcher, who drew a distinction between 'real happy slapping', viewed as harmless pranks, and 'morons going beyond the limit and causing injury'. But this is not the only example of a social media challenge that reached dangerous levels in Britain. The UK Safer Internet Centre, a collaboration between various charities aimed at making the internet a safer place for children and young adults, outlines their stance on 'challenges' that 'are often created to cause alarm and have been designed to seem enticing or exciting for young people'. One of the key pieces of advice for anyone concerned about a social media challenge is: 'Don't name it: Warning others about an online challenge may seem like the smart thing to do but naming it can inadvertently direct other people towards it.'[48] Frighteningly and tragically, online challenges in the 2020s frequently involve self-harm, and the deaths of many British adolescents have been blamed on such incidents. Following the advice of the UK Safer Internet Centre, we will not detail them here.

Haunted digital space

Alongside such challenges as potentially dangerous online content, the UK Safer Internet Centre also lists 'viral stories, hoaxes, or digital ghost stories'. Alluded to on this safety website but not named is the creepypasta. This is a term coined around 2007, derived from the portmanteau word copypasta (copy-and-paste), relating to memes and other viral online content that is intended to be frightening. These can take the form of digital urban legends. Some legends are created specifically for online repositories such as Creepypasta Wiki, which boasts on its home page, 'Proudly hosting 13,030 of your worst nightmares since 2010'. Akin to fan fiction, the narratives on such websites (dubbed 'pasta' by the community) are original pieces of writing by members of the subculture, shared publicly and open for comments and discussion. Akin to urban legends, they are told as if true.

Creepypasta Wiki is global in scope, but, as is the case with urban legends, each narrative creepypasta is location specific. The English examples lean heavily into their 'Englishness', drawing on landscape tropes and international perspectives of the nation. One example is 'The Old English Village'. 'If you're ever in England,' this creepypasta begins, 'there is a place quite unlike any other place in the world. Deep in the English countryside, located in the southwest, there is a small village that time has forgotten ... It won't be on any map ...' The legend details how a person can find this village travelling by foot through a forest and how, when they reach it, they will come across a wishing-well. Into it they must throw coins and a sample of their blood. A repulsively decomposing figure will then emerge from the well, offering his maggot-infested hand. If the person stands their ground and takes his hand, they will awaken back at home, cured of any illness and immortal. Comments below the narrative creepypasta either rate the technical skill of the writer ('good pasta. 7/10', 'Like it! 8/10', 'You nailed the tempo with the wording here, and I enjoyed every second of reading this one') or participate in some digital ostensive play by engaging credulously with the content ('I want to do this!', 'were [sic] is this village', 'Yes I've been there, and yes, it's erie [sic]').[49]

Another specifically English example on Creepypasta Wiki is 'The Queen's Guard'. This one is a first-person narrative, seemingly written by a member of the Queen's Guard, although certain Americanisms creep in, such as 'cell' for mobile phone and 'mom', suggesting it was not written by a Brit. The narrator recounts a series of incidents that took place while they were stationed at the Tower of London in 2012, involving a pale, dark-haired woman haunting him at work and then at home. 'If I were a writer,' the narrator tells us, 'I'd use all these descriptive tools to paint a picture of how horrifying that woman looked that night. Let me tell you, this was the single most terrifying thing I've ever seen.' Again, comments either rate the writing or play along with the narrative: 'The woman seems paranormal', 'the woman was possessed', 'This guy should shoot this thing'.[50]

British creepypasta also takes the form of videos. In 2008, a video appeared on YouTube entitled 'Creepy fairy insect – UK'. For the first three-quarters of this two-minute, non-stylised video, the man behind the camera is given an informal tour of a British garden by his two children and their friend. They show him the pond, the trampoline, the swing and slide set, and the apple tree. It is in this tree that they see something unusual. 'What's that?' one of the children asks as the camera zooms in on a branch. Something winged buzzes, and at first the cameraman – and the viewer – think it is an insect, perhaps a dragonfly. But then a child shouts, 'Oh my God!' and we see something the size of a dragonfly – but the shape of a winged humanoid, with two arms, two long legs, and a head. It is only on camera for a second as it hovers, seemingly surveying the camera, and then flies out of shot. The cameraman makes a sound of dismay, turns, and runs; we see the children fleeing across the garden in apparent fear. The video cuts out as the camera shakily turns back to the tree.[51]

This video may be a twenty-first-century, online version of the sensational Cottingley Fairies purportedly captured on camera by two young cousins in Yorkshire in 1917, but later revealed to have been cardboard images copied from a children's book and propped up using hatpins. However, if this video is a hoax, then it is an unusual one. The video gained over four million views, but the comments function was turned off and the anonymous poster never followed up on it. He had posted only one video before this – an unrelated recording of a show – and none after. If he was seeking attention with this video, he did not claim it, neither he nor the children ever coming forward to share more of their experience. And the fairy itself was a far cry from its Cottingley ancestors; no flowing dress, no fashionable hairstyle, no dancing pose. This was a dull-coloured, insect-like creature, uncanny only for a second and then gone. If it was a hoax, it was a convincing one – although many people thought the same about the Cottingley Fairies images at the time. Cryptids evolve with technology.

Videos of haunted objects also find a receptive audience on social media. In 2010, a YouTube account was created by @TheAnguishedManOfficial – later identified as Sean Robinson, a man living in Cumbria who had inherited a painting from his grandmother. In a video that has garnered over 326,000 views to date, soundtracked by eerie, atmospheric music, Robinson shares an image of the abstract painting of a man, his mouth open in an expression of anguish. 'This oil painting has been in our family for near thirty years ...' the caption reads. 'My grandmother kept it in her attic. She said there was something evil about it ... Apparently the man who painted it committed suicide shortly after finishing it ... My grandmother told me the artist used his own blood mixed in with the oils ... I never believed in ghosts or the supernatural but I do now ...' The captions go on to detail the 'many unexplainable things' Robinson has seen and heard since coming into possession of the painting, from the phantom figure of a man to the sounds of crying. 'This painting is cursed,' the video concludes as an ominous bell tolls in the background.[52] Many of the viewers seemed to agree. 'Ok That Thing will now be engraved in my head forever ... You are in my prayers,' commented one viewer, while another declared, 'Scary! What is reflected in his eye?' Other viewers suggested, 'it might be the soul of the painter in there or maybe someone the painter killed', and, 'the artist attached his soul/spirit to the painting using his own blood! That is creepy!'

In June 2013, another 'haunted object' video went viral: this one a 25 cm-tall Egyptian statuette of an unknown, elite man in Manchester Museum (museum accession no. 9325). Having noticed that the statuette seemed to have moved position, museum staff set up a camera and filmed it over a week-long period. When they watched the video back, it was clear that the statuette was slowly spinning within its glass case.[53] The forty-two-second timelapse video, posted first on the Egypt at Manchester blog and then on YouTube, went viral.[54] Watched more than five million times, it generated mass international online discussion via social media, blogs, and comments on online news articles about what could have been causing this object to spin, seemingly of its own accord.[55] Theories proposed online included the statuette having awakened, a 'mummy's curse', the power of ancient Egyptian gods, and alien technology – the ability to move objects in this way having assisted in the construction of the pyramids. Although Manchester Museum offered a mundane explanation – that the traffic on the busy road outside was causing vibrations – many people preferred the paranormal interpretations.

Haunted spaces are visited as a form of digital legend-tripping. Paranormal investigators are increasingly using social media to document and share their investigative legend-trips. @HauntedScouse is one such team, using X and

YouTube to follow Adam and Chris 'as they investigate areas of alleged paranormal activity in Liverpool, Wirral, Merseyside and beyond'.[56] One of their taglines is 'going where others fear to go'. On investigating 30 East Drive, Pontefract – dubbed the 'most haunted house in Britain' – they share a night-vision video of themselves making their way through the house, their equipment (the 'rempod' and the 'cat balls') seeming to respond to a paranormal presence.[57] There are myriad other social media paranormal investigators, following a similar formula: investigators visit a purportedly haunted place, give some historic background and then set up their equipment, monitoring the place overnight via night-vision camera. Often something occurs, perhaps an unexplained noise, a passing shadow, or a flashing machine. These social media videos are clearly drawing on such television shows as *Most Haunted* for inspiration (see Chapter 4).

There is a different type of haunting online. This haunting manifests in places such as Scarfolk, a grim town in north-west England, and the county of Hookland, which was lost in the 1980s following Margaret Thatcher's redefinition of Britain's county boundaries. These places have their geographies, their histories, their communities, their local dialects, and their folklore. But they are not real – or at least, not physically. These places exist online, conceptualised in blogposts and on social media accounts. Scarfolk is a fictional town created by the writer and graphic designer Richard Littler, which, according to the Scarfolk Council website (Littler's blog), 'did not progress beyond 1979. Instead, the 1970s loops ad infinitum.'[58] Hookland is a fictional county, crafted primarily on X by the writer David Southwell, in which the uncanny – megaliths and standing stones, local witches and cunning-folk, and a cult of electricity pylon worshippers – exist in harmony with the prosaic of a British county trapped in the 1980s: local pubs and churches, a museum of curiosities, locally produced cheeses (Stinking Tom and Burnt Bishop), and a culinary speciality akin to toad-in-the-hole.

Scarfolk and Hookland are haunted places, and not just because they house the occasional ghost. They were born from the hauntological imaginations of their creators – and also of those who engage with the world-building online content (@HooklandGuide has over thirty-eight thousand X followers and @Scarfolk has over sixty-three thousand). The term 'hauntology' derived from French philosopher Jacque Derrida's writings on the spectre of cultural memory, specifically that of Marxism looming over post-Cold War Europe. It has been adapted to refer to a different cultural memory: of childhood in 1970s Britain. Those who grew up in this decade are considered the 'Haunted

Generation', to which both Littler and Southwell belong. This generation was the last before technology such as camcorders and videocassette recorders became available widely. It is haunted by the hazy, grainy, fleeting, unverifiable memories of places visited and television shows watched – but not recorded.

In an interview for the *Fortean Times*, Littler mused on his creation of Scarfolk as inspired by 'the sense of ill-defined "wrongness"' of his childhood TV viewing, from the sinister public information film *The Spirit of Dark and Lonely Water* to the children's show *Bagpuss*.[59] In the same issue of the *Fortean Times*, Southwell reflected on his creation of Hookland in 2012: 'I wanted to do something that dealt with the ghost soil of Britain – all the folklore, all the high strangeness that grew and bloomed in the gloriously strange TV, film and books I grew up with as a child in the 1970s. I wanted to put the weirdness back.'[60] Trying to capture the 'strangeness', that which is both comforting and unsettling, which is stored in the 'English Eerie' landscape and also in the memories of the Haunted Generation, Southwell describes his lost county on X: 'Hookland is the recovered memory that you cannot dismiss. Hookland is the recovered memory you secretly hope is true. Hookland is that place you visited once, but cannot find on any map … Hookland is ghost soil.'[61]

In the editorial of the same issue of the *Fortean Times*, the editors ask what happens to folklore, so rooted in landscape and locality, when it meets 'geography-abolishing media technologies'. They consider places like Scarfolk and Hookland, and conclude that folklore, here conceptualised as the hauntological imagination, is colonising the digital world. But, as this chapter has shown with its exploration of digital ostension, transformative storytelling, memes as vernacular creativity, ritualised challenges, and creepypasta that pervade our online spaces, it is not only in Scarfolk and Hookland that 'local ghosts lurk in the heart of the global machine'.[62]

Part VII

Identity

Chapter 13
The folklore of nations

Physical and cultural boundaries have always been porous when it comes to folklore. Ideas, stories, and beliefs have migrated via different forms of media over the centuries. Some aspects of British folklore were generated through global conflict and colonial encounters. Trade and commerce have also long been vehicles of folkloric exchange. These 'foreign' influences often remain unknown to the majority of the population and are sometimes difficult to trace over time. Additions to the rich English vocabulary are one of the more obvious examples. But people are more sensitive to folklore brought through the movement of peoples rather than via the more intangible migration of beliefs and traditions through overseas exchange, colonialism, and the spread of literature. This needs to be understood in terms of both outward and inward migration. The outward migration of the Welsh, Scots, and English to different parts of the world brought with it the movement of folklore on a large scale. Some beliefs, traditions, and customs clearly did not survive the journey, while others did, or were adapted to new social and natural environments. Exploring what customs, traditions, and beliefs continued, or were recreated by diaspora communities, has much to tell us about the development of national identities back in Britain. Distance distilled diaspora perceptions of who they were from generation to generation, and this influenced cultural change back home. Even when aspects of folklore disappeared during a first wave of migration, subsequent generations sometimes recreated and revived them.

When talking about British folklore we must also remember that *within* the country there has been huge migration and settlement over the centuries. The Romani are an important example, bringing a distinct body of lore and practices with them as they moved around the country. They have long been an integral part of British folk culture, and yet are often absent from narratives of Britishness.[1] We can also think of the Welsh and Scottish societies that formed in eighteenth-century London to promote their homeland cultures and traditions. This may not have led to the significant transfer of folklore from one nation to another, but we must not forget the continuance of individual, family, and small-community customs and beliefs over generations in Welsh, Scottish, and English diasporas within Britain. And then, of course, there are the inward migrations from overseas. DNA science has revolutionised the tracing of waves of settlement from prehistory onward. In more recent centuries, historical documents record in detail the migrations that occurred through trade, warfare, and colonialism. In the 1800s, the large-scale immigration of the Irish and, later in the century, arrivals from Italy, for example, had a perceptible influence on British culture. But when it comes to identity politics and folklore today, it is the post-Second World War migrations from the Caribbean and South Asia, and the more recent movement of East Europeans, which have raised debate about national character. This is, of course, a shifting discourse to be found everywhere across the globe. As this chapter shows, the application of a folkloric lens can help to trace a path through the polemics and soundbites, and to map ways to understanding the sharing of cultures.

Ishness

By the late eighteenth century, there was a groundswell of educated Welsh concern that the identity of the *gwerin* (folk) was on the verge of extinction, due to the twin forces of the dominant English, and the Nonconformist preachers – who were blamed for the decline of Welsh pleasure in dancing, singing, music-making, storytelling, and other old folk performances.[2] A fight back began. Societies were created to promote Welsh identity and provide fraternal support. A dedicated band of wealthy and sometimes eccentric individuals took up the challenge. One such was Augusta Hall (1802–1896), otherwise known as Lady Llanover, who was a wealthy landowner labelled as 'Dame Wales'. She tirelessly promoted the Welsh language, championed the triple harp as a Welsh instrument, and created a Welsh national costume for women based on elements of old-style folk dress, with a tall black hat and red woollen cloak, which her own female staff wore on the estate. The promotion of iconic Welshness to tourists from the nineteenth century onward should also not be underestimated. A popular guide to Wales that was printed several times in the 1830s and 1840s highlighted notable 'singular' and 'curious' customs such as the Welsh dress, jumpers, and the strewing of flowers on graves. The likes of love spoons and tea towels continue to play their part in public perception.[3]

The re-establishment of the *eisteddfod* was the key to the maintenance and promotion of this preserved, revived, and reinvented Welsh identity. This competitive bardic gathering was medieval in origin and fostered by the Welsh aristocracy, but the institution petered out under English rule in the early modern period. It was revived in the late eighteenth century, thanks largely to the Welsh diaspora in London, in the guise of the Gwyneddigion Society, which existed between 1770 and 1843 to promote Welsh culture, literature, and language. It was not the only such London Welsh organisation with these aims. The Honourable Society of Cymmrodorion was founded in 1751, and continues today in a revived form.[4] It was in the 1790s that the seeds of the *eisteddfod* as an invented aspect of druidic culture were also created by the eccentric poet Edward Williams (1747–1826), better known as Iolo Morganwg. He thought the *eisteddfod* had druidic origins and set up a society of bards known as the *Gorsedd*, whose rituals he created from a mix of Freemasonry, Christianity, and Welsh myth. These druidic ceremonies became a colourful aspect of the *eisteddfod* revival (Figure 13.1). Various local *eisteddfodau* were held

Figure 13.1 Druidic costume and regalia at the national *Eisteddfod*, c. 1905. *Sir Benjamin Stone's Pictures: Records of National Life and History* (London, 1906), Vol. 1.

during the first half of the nineteenth century, organised by the likes of Lady Llanover, and then, in 1858, the first Grand National *eisteddfod* was held in Llangollen.

The first *eisteddfod* to be organised in America was in the Welsh coal-mining community in Carbondale, Pennsylvania, on Christmas Day 1850. Over the decades, others were created in Welsh migrant communities around the globe, such as in Patagonia, South Africa, and Australia.[5] For the Welsh diaspora, the preservation of the Welsh language was important, though not easily maintained abroad, and the focus of the international *eisteddfodau* was on Welsh creativity and artistic expression. In Australia an '*Eisteddfod* of the Welsh in Victoria' was first held on Christmas Day and Boxing Day 1867 in the mining town of Ballarat. Dr David John Thomas (1813–1871), a long-settled migrant from Carmarthenshire, declared in his public address: 'I see so many bards, essayists, poets, singers, and harpists around me, encouraged in their noble undertaking by faces beaming with joy.' But there was a personal *mea culpa*: 'I must crave our indulgence for not addressing you in the language dear to us, by which for so long a time I have not had an opportunity of speaking.'[6] Several decades later, the St David's Welsh Society of Edmonton, Canada, held their own *eisteddfod*, with the programme for 1934 including a children's section with competitions for recitations in Welsh, English and Welsh solo singing, and drawing, while the adult section included male and female choirs, and the best one-act play dealing with an aspect of traditional Welsh life.[7]

The national revival also led to some early folklore collecting before the days of the late nineteenth-century Folklore movement. The constitution of the Honourable Society of the Cymmrodorion expressed the Society's interest in 'Quæries of the Invisible World', though nothing concrete came of it. There was an obvious tension between the celebration of the richness of Welsh culture in all its aspects, including fairy beliefs and customs, and the desire to show Wales as an enlightened country that had moved beyond the days of what was frequently described as 'druidic superstition'.[8] In May 1830, the outgoing president of the Carmarthen Cymreigyddion Society, Archdeacon Beynon, gave a speech to members in which he said he was 'extremely desirous that there should exist among our literature a transcript of the peculiarities and superstitions of the Welsh', and to that end proposed to offer a prize of twenty sovereigns and a medal to the best work of five hundred pages on the subject. He highlighted that Ireland, England, and Scotland had their collections of national 'superstitions', but not his own country, and he feared that it was 'doomed to want a record of those distinctive national traits which are becoming every day more faint'. An advertisement was duly placed in the *Carmarthen Journal*, and a year later William Howells rose to the challenge and won the prize with his book *Cambrian Superstitions* (1831). Howells was keen to promote the enlightened state of the country. 'The march of Intellect, has made its welcome appearance amongst hills and dales, moors and marshes, *even* amongst the mountains and valleys of Wales,' he declared. 'Almost every peasant can *now* read, and no longer dreads passing over his threshold in the dark.'[9]

By the end of the century, the collection of living folklore was considered as important as the discovery of medieval myths. From the 1880s onward, there are several examples of local *eisteddfodau* that held essay competitions exploring the relevant county or district folklore traditions. The National *Eisteddfod* in Aberdare in 1885 offered a £10 prize for the best 'original collection of the folklore of Glamorgan'. Two entries were received and were adjudicated by Professor John Rhys (1840–1915), who took the 'opportunity of appealing to the newspapers of South Wales to encourage the collecting of Welsh Folklore before it is altogether too late'. The Revd Elias Owen won the prize essay at the 1887 national *eisteddfod* held in London for his account of the 'Folklore of North Wales', which was subsequently published as *Welsh Folk-Lore* (1896).[10] In the Introduction to his collection of the *Folk-Lore of West and Mid-Wales* (1911), Jonathan Caredig Davies, who had spent many years in Welsh Patagonia, wrote that 'Welsh Folk-Lore is almost inexhaustible, and of great importance to the historian and others. Indeed, without a knowledge of the past traditions, customs and superstitions of the people, the history of a country is not complete.'[11]

In the twenty-first century the *Mari Lwyd* has become one of the most prominent folkloric symbols of Welshness at home and abroad. Performances of the *Mari Lwyd* have cropped up across England, America, and Australia, leading to concerns of cultural appropriation in Welsh social media posts, and suggestions that only performances in Wales should be recognised by its Welsh name and elsewhere it should be called something else. But, as a Welsh scholar of the tradition has put it, 'No one is trying to steal the *Mari Lwyd* from Wales, indeed, the growth, adoption and celebration of the tradition is of huge importance to keeping both the *Mari* alive, and the very concept of Wales being somewhere distinct and recognisable.' This is borne out by the self-styled 'Chicago Tafia', a small group of Welsh migrants who tour their home-made *Mari Lwyd* around local bars and pubs in the city. As one of the organisers explained, 'With the resurgence of unusual old traditions from

Identity

around the world via social media, *Mari Lwyd* is becoming nearly as well-known as Krampus or Gryla, so many of the locals in the pubs were already somewhat aware of the tradition.'[12]

Around half the population of Wales could still speak Welsh up until the twentieth century, whereas in Scotland only around 5 per cent of people could speak Gaelic in 1900. It is no surprise, then, that with a few exceptions, such as Nova Scotia and Newfoundland, language and its expression played a relatively minor role in Scottish settler identity, in comparison with the Welsh. In parts of Novia Scotia the traditional Gael *céilidh* ('house-visit') with singing, fiddle music, and storytelling continued to be practised into the twentieth century, before declining. Gaelic speaking diminished more rapidly, though dialects are still recognisable and there have been efforts to promote the language in the region. In the 1890s the *Mòd*, a Gaelic version of the *eisteddfod*, was instituted in Scotland by the An Comunn Gàidhealach (The Highland Society), founded in 1891, and several *Mòds* were organised by Gaelic societies in North America, the most enduring being that of the Vancouver Gaelic Society.[13] In general, though, there was and is an emphasis in Scottish diasporas on games, dress, piping, and dance, all of which were highly stylised and curated. The Highlands, a distinct geographical and cultural area of Scotland, became synonymous with the Scottishness of the whole country.

More than the Welsh, one can easily be identified globally as Scottish or having Scottish ancestry simply by wearing a kilt, plaid, and tartan. This ease has also led people with no Scottish ancestry to adopt Scottishness or to 'play the Scot' at certain moments in the year, such as Hogmanay, Burns Night, St Andrew's Day, and at the many Highland Games put on across the world. This has been described as a form of 'ethnomasquerade'.[14] While the kilt is an individual expression of national identity, the collective observance of Scottishness was crucial. Competitive tests of strength, Games, piping, and dancing go back a long way in Scotland, but the Highland Games as we know it today is, once again, largely a creation of late eighteenth- and nineteenth-century identity building. In the aftermath of Culloden and the impact of the clearances and emigration, Highland fraternal societies were formed at home and abroad to promote a culture under attack. The organising of Games was a highly successful vehicle for doing so, just as the *eisteddfod* was for Welshness.[15] The Inverness games of 1842 consisted of throwing the hammer, putting the stone, jumping a height, and what the local newspaper described as 'the most national of the whole' – tossing the caber. There were also awards for piping, dancing, and 'the best dressed Highlander'. The latter was 'for encouraging the use of the picturesque costume of the Celt'.[16] The proliferation of the Games at home and abroad was boosted by Queen Victoria's visit to the Braemar Gathering in 1848, along with the promotion of the Games by other large estate owners, who owned most of Scotland's landmass. Today there are hundreds of Games around the globe, attracting hundreds of thousands of people, and the phenomenon has been well studied. One example is the Glengarry Highland Games, revived in Eastern Ontario in 1948, many decades after the original Games in the county had ceased. It has grown to become one of the largest in the world, with around thirty thousand visitors.[17] This was part of a wider initiative to promote Scottishness in an area that was experiencing socio-economic change.

The collective exhibition of Scottishness at home and abroad is also bound up with three main calendar celebrations: St Andrew's Day (30 November), Hogmanay (31 December), and Burns Night (25 January). Hogmanay has been discussed in previous chapters and it is interesting how, shorn of its winter environment and community context, it could fail to migrate to the likes of Australia. As a Scottish migrant in Australia observed sadly, 'there is nothing Scottish about it [New Year today] whatsoever – no first footing, no shortbread or black bun, any of that, it was just that they got to stay up late and go into the city'. When asked, 'Have you ever tried the first footing thing in Australia?' they responded, 'No ... people wouldn't understand.'[18] Burns Night has proved much more adaptable as a gastronomic and alcoholic ceremony that is based on conviviality in small groups. One can also celebrate Burns's genius without necessarily being tied to ancestral Scottish identity.[19]

At a time in the nineteenth century when expressions of Scottishness abroad were defining identity, the day of the country's patron saint was certainly not a moment of national celebration in Scotland itself. As the *Aberdeen Evening Express* complained in 1879, 'our Patron Saint is nowadays sadly neglected by all in his own land with the exception of the societies founded in his honour'. The many St Andrew's Societies that sprung up all over the Empire certainly marked the day with an enthusiasm that was lacking back home. In 1867, two hundred Scotsmen resident in Bombay held a banquet in the saint's honour. Two years later, the day was marked by annual Games, sports, and feats of strength in Kingston, Jamaica, organised by the local Caledonian Society.[20] Singapore hoteliers became quite competitive over the lavishness of the St Andrew's Day meals they arranged. In 1908 the famous Raffles Hotel boasted that it provided 'real Haggis specially imported, [and] special Scottish music'.[21] Scottish Masonic lodges also held their annual meetings and the election of officers for the ensuing year on St Andrew's Day. Yet, St Andrew's Day was only officially made a bank holiday by the Scottish government in 2006, though businesses and schools are not required to provide a day off. Writing in 2009, the then First Minister, Alex Salmond, declared that 'we see people across our nation celebrating St Andrew's Day with new enthusiasm, a new passion'.[22]

More than the other two nations, folklore tourism has played a longer and more significant role in shaping Scottishness as a brand. The popular folkloric novels of Walter Scott (1771–1832) were an important part of the nineteenth-century English vogue for Highland tours, with guidebooks drawing upon the romantic landscape and its legendary associations. Hunting and fishing tourists kitted themselves out in the recently devised clan tartans. The mid-twentieth century witnessed the rise of Nessie tourism. Loch Ness has been described as a Scottish theme park, with shops in the region stocked with every conceivable monster souvenir. More recently, kelpie tourism has been a strategic part of the development strategies of several communities, most notably Helix Park, near Falkirk, with its spectacular pair of hundred-foot-high horses' heads, called The Kelpies. The rise of cheaper air travel from the 1970s opened new opportunities for mass Scottish diaspora tourism from North America to taste the 'authentic' experience of the ancestral homeland. But mass tourism has brought its own challenges, well demonstrated by Up-helly-aa festivals, where tensions have arisen between Visit Shetland's desire to open the festivals to more tourists and some locals who feel that it is being 'Disneyised', losing its community identity, and that there is enough tourism already.[23]

The notion of a Celtic tradition cuts across all three kingdoms, involving Cornwall (and the Isle of Man) as well as Wales and the Scottish *Gàidhealtachd*, and also Ireland, Brittany, and Galicia. But the very idea of an ancient Celticness has been effectively deconstructed by scholars. Celticism was shaped in the nineteenth century by a romantic impulse in the fields of Irish and British folklore, linguistics, medieval literature, archaeology, and history.[24] The notional Celt was a proud, cultured pagan. A shared series of cultural expressions were identified in art, mythology, fairy faith, religion, and the ritual year, and aspects could be found as survivals in contemporary customs, tales, and beliefs. Arthurian legend and druidism were other linking themes. Folklorists played their part in constructing this collective identity from a bricolage of comparative sources. One such was Alfred Trubner Nutt (1856–1910), a founding member of the Folklore Society, who suggested that the myth of the Holy Grail had Celtic origins and was convinced that he had found evidence that metempsychosis (transmigration of the soul) was at the core of Celtic religion. Another was the aforementioned John Rhys, author of *Celtic Folklore, Welsh and Manx* (1901), who also attempted to reconstruct Celtic religion and was a key figure in formulating the idea of an ancient 'pagan Celtic New Year', known as *Samhain* in the Irish language.[25]

As a concept, Celtic culture became well embedded in archaeology, folklore, and literary studies, and from the 1970s it spawned a popular vogue for Celtic art designs as well as its own publishing industry catering for the public thirst for New Age Celtic mysticism. But doubts set in about the underpinning evidence for a pan-Celtic civilisation. The idea of a Celtic religious ritual calendar was meticulously unpicked, the archaeology proved unconvincing, and mythic and folkloric motifs could also be found in non-Celtic cultures.[26] In scholarly terms today, the ancient and medieval 'Celtic world' is perhaps best understood in terms of cultural 'interconnectivity and mobility' rather than homogeneous identity.[27] But in contemporary popular culture Celticness, or neo-Celticism, has developed a validity and life of its own; the academic concerns have been shrugged off and Celtic identity has been embraced as a contemporary spiritual lifestyle with pagan and Christian paths. As one 'New Age' Christian resident of Glastonbury put it, 'it doesn't matter about strict historicity – it sets up a wonderful warm glow of hope, helps you feel more integrated. What we need in the West is a Celtic renaissance.'[28]

There is little evidence that people of non-British origin overseas have performed or are performing an 'ethnomasquerade' of Englishness, other than, perhaps, aping the English aristocracy. There are, after all, some practical challenges to the construction of folk Englishness past and present, compared to the other two nations whose own identity building was defined by defiance of English dominance, as well as the diaspora experience. There was never any need, for instance, to preserve or promote the English language as a matter of cultural survival. There was no great ancient English myth cycle, saga, or archetypal epic, nor indeed were there great collections of folktales, such as that of the Grimms in Germany.[29] Nor did England have a tradition of regional and national folk dress like other European countries, and no attempt was made to invent one. People have nothing in their wardrobes to dust off each St George's Day that states 'I am English and proud'. The St George flag does all the heavy lifting. Indeed, it has been argued that, actually, 'Englishness was invented in the Anglo-world beyond England's shores'.[30]

To focus on America, the sheer number of English migrants in the colonial era led to a dominant Anglo-American culture after Independence that smothered the need to defend or celebrate some notional English ethnicity as a national imperative. Yet, from the late eighteenth century there were explicit expressions of English identity in the form of the middle-class St George's Societies founded in America, Canada, and Australia. An American umbrella organisation called the North American St. George's Union was founded in 1873 to promote Englishness. These societies put on performances to mark St George's Day, which, once again, was a day little celebrated back in England. Events were commonly themed around Robin Hood and Good Queen Bess, with toasts to the king or queen and other national figures – chiefly Shakespeare, whose birthday was also thought to be on St George's Day.[31]

The Anglo-American middle classes were obviously not on the streets burning barrels on 5 November, or cross-dressing and capering on Plough Monday, but they predictably promoted the refashioned May Day pageants and maypole dancing as 'Old English' customs. In 1898 the Universalist Church in Manchester, New Hampshire, put on a May Party that included a May Queen, Jack-in-the-Green, Robin Hood, and children performing what was described as Morris dancing. Such events were promoted particularly in the early twentieth century by colleges and universities.[32] In 1904, the Young Peoples' Guild of Middlebury, Vermont, put on a 'tableau in costume, appropriate music and May-pole drills, all representative of an Old English May Day'. Down in Missouri in 1916, university women put on a paganesque May Day pageant based around Pan and his dancers. An 'Immortal Maid' appears picking flowers and then falls asleep, during which they transport her to 'Old English May Day time' and ask her to be their queen. She refuses at first, but then they all dance around a maypole and she changes her mind.[33] These were usually one-off events rather than attempts to establish a calendar tradition.

Traditional English *ceremonial* performances did not migrate well. There is little evidence for the continuance of mumming plays in any of the former colonies. Newfoundland is one exception. Its fishing communities, which had a strong component of settlers from south-west England, performed Christmas house-visiting mumming into the mid-twentieth century. As in England, the mid-1850s saw attempts by Newfoundland authorities to ban raucous mumming, but its eventual demise (until it was revived), has been linked to the decline of small-scale family fisheries and the industrialisation of fishing and fish processing.[34] The *revived* Morris tradition was established in North America during the early twentieth century. It was taught in New York public schools, for example, and from the 1960s adult enthusiast groups were founded, mostly in the eastern states, mirroring the region of early English colonial settlements.[35] With regard to English social dancing, the advocacy of Cecil Sharp and Mary

Neal helped to establish an ersatz version in America. It was well received by a wealthy, white, Anglo-American audience concerned with what was considered the uncouth influence of 'wilder' dance traditions brought by more recent urban migrant communities. Country dancing was thought more respectable, more appropriate for children – girls in particular – and reaffirmed the English roots of American culture.[36]

In recent years the orchard wassail has proved the most successful of English migratory customs in the contemporary world, exactly because it is fixed to a specific environment or landscape rather than to ethnic heritage. There is sometimes an impression in the journalistic accounts that it is an unbroken, continuous English tradition from the medieval period. A 2019 report on wassails in New York State bore the subheadline 'Common in England, the practice of toasting to the health of the orchard has hopped across the pond'.[37] The custom had largely died out in England by the early twentieth century, and the assumption derives from the many revivals from the 1960s onward. In the winter of 2012–2013 some 170 individual wassails were recorded in Britain, nearly all of them revivals or recreations in one way or another.[38] In 2015, a wassailing festival was founded in the Huon Valley in Tasmania, which had been a major apple-orcharding industry from the late nineteenth century till the 1950s. Promoted under the name Mid-Winter Fest, it is in part a celebration of the 'Glory Days' of the local industry, but also suggests a broader Anglo-Tasmanian nostalgia for Merrie England ancestry – with a touch of the modern 'gothic' aesthetic.[39] The parade that culminates in the wassail features participants in Morris costumes, 'pagan-style' animal face masks, a white hobby horse, and a Jack-in-the-Green. One of the New York wassails also encourages animal masks as a contemporary conflation of traditions. The New York State wassailings in the cider-making region of the Five Finger Lakes are mostly organised by cider companies. As one owner explained: 'My father had traveled abroad to visit cideries in the United Kingdom to learn more about their history. One of the instructors got into how cider is celebrated and that's how he learned about wassailing.' Another cider maker similarly stated: 'It really stems from the fact that we respect and draw off knowledge of English cider tradition ... It's another excuse to celebrate life and enjoy being outside and sing under the stars.'[40]

It was suggested in the early 2000s that folklore had never been used to construct English patriotic identity.[41] The observation was based on comparisons with the Welsh and Scottish experience. It is true that English folklorists and antiquarians were relatively quiet when it came to defining English identity, but we have seen how the nineteenth- and early twentieth-century revivals of calendar customs, and their migration overseas, were rooted in a potent mix of Merrie England and Empire. The conflation of Englishness with Britishness has also obscured English identity building. Folklorists' reluctance to explore Englishness is also to do with the explicit politicisation of folklore in the twentieth century. The Nazis drew heavily on *Volkskunde* (folklore) for their myths of Aryan superiority, and during the 1920s and 1930s English nationalist movements had their fair share of Nazi German sympathisers who shared the romantic idea of a unified Anglo-Saxon heritage that did not involve the peoples of the Celtic nations. The prominent role of the active Nazi sympathiser Rolf Gardiner (1902–1971) in the English folk song and dance revival is one such uncomfortable example. Gardiner espoused a return to untainted 'English religion' and saw the heart of Englishness in local rural life and tradition. Morris and sword dancing were the essence of Englishness and their performance was a reconnection with spiritual purity. He set up his own male Travelling Morrice troupe in 1924, and in 1936 he took a group of sword and Morris dancers to the Berlin Olympics. At his Springhead estate in Dorset he created a calendar of folk performances, such as May Day and Plough Monday, not out of antiquarian interest, he said, but so that participants could 'regain their consciousness of the year's rhythm in a fresh way'.[42]

If folklore arguably played a *comparatively* minor role in English national identity in the past, the situation has certainly changed since the mid-1990s. While for two hundred years Welsh and Scottish nationalist sentiment had been fuelled by the dominance of England, after the demise of the Empire, England began to go through its own process of introspection and a search for identity. First, Welsh and Scottish Devolution happened; then the drum beat of Euroscepticism grew steadily, fuelled by the right-wing press, fake news, fear mongering, and mythic notions of sovereignty and cultural values under threat, and culminated in the Brexit referendum (Scotland voted Remain, as did Welsh-language areas of Wales). Over this period a raft of books for the popular market, some written by television personalities, attempted to define the essence of Englishness. Anthropologist Kate Fox's best-seller *Watching the English* (2004) sold over half a million copies; in the preface to the 2014 edition she reflected that part of its success was because it had come out 'at a time when we English are having a bit of an identity wobble'.

There is, of course, a big difference between the construction of nationalism as an aggressive political ideology and the search for a cultural national identity. The former is usually exclusionary, while the latter can be inclusive. Across the twentieth century, we have witnessed newly independent European countries going through these processes, and folklore has usually played its part in both aspects of nation building – and rebuilding: we see it also in England's ongoing 'identity wobble'.

It feels like England is going through another Merrie England period.[43] The St George's flag flutters more than the Union Jack. But this time there is no Empire and the conflation of Englishness with Britishness has attenuated. Research shows that there is little confusion between the two these days, with people clearly identifying their nationality as either one or both, just as research on Scotland around the time of Devolution showed that most Scots were relaxed about identifying as both, in different ways.[44] The Victorian Merrie England harked back to 'ye olde' rural world of five hundred years ago, while the current one has two distinct identities. For some people, many of them from the boomer generation whose parents lived through the Second World War, the nostalgia is for a notional 'blitz spirit' and a post-war period of full employment and victorious national pride. There is still a strong sentimental feeling for the rural in this post-war dreamland, as encapsulated in Prime Minister John Major's 1993 speech on Britain and Europe (but which actually epitomised the conservative ideal of Englishness): 'the country of long shadows on county [cricket] grounds, warm beer, invincible green suburbs, dog lovers and pools fillers ... and if we get our way – Shakespeare still read even in school'.[45] The further right this discourse goes, the more it becomes about whiteness, 'ethno nationalism', and the promotion of the myth of the 'Indigenous English'. This narrative urges the 'Little Englanders' to defend their cultural rights like some threatened minority in the face of the European Union and migrants. Folk music and ancient customs have inevitably, but unfortunately, been championed as an aspect of this claimed indigenous purity.[46]

The alternative side of the new Merrie England is also rooted in rural folk culture – but one that is deep time, psychogeographic, aesthetic, and centred on landscape rather than ethnicity.[47] But one does not have to be white to be part of the new affinity with Englishness; it is defined by the desire to reconnect spiritually, not politically, to re-enchant the land through folklore and performance at a time of growing concern about change – environmental, not cultural, this time. While this allure is intended to restore a sense of communal wellbeing it also opens the seductive path to the paganeseque and folk horror in the imagination.[48] Yet we cannot ignore, as studies have shown over the years, that the countryside still feels an unwelcoming place for non-white citizens, though the situation is changing.

Identity

England's leading heritage organisations have recognised this trend and played their part in the 2000s, latching on to the importance of folklore and landscape. CPRE, The Countryside Charity, formerly known as the Campaign to Protect Rural England, which has origins dating back to 1926, have a page on their website recognising the importance of the 'Folklore of the land' and which asks, 'How can we honour the folklore of the land? How might we (re)connect with what's on our doorsteps?'[49] English Heritage have created a crowd-sourcing map of myth, legend, and folklore; a video series called 'Tales from English Folklore' which explores the legends associated with some of its properties; and a book, *This Our Monsters: The English Heritage Book of New Folktale, Myth and Legend* (2019).[50] The National Trust also commissioned *A Treasury of British Folklore* (2018) and promote the legends surrounding some of their English sites, such as Devil's Dyke. This renewed romantic search for Englishness through the prism of folklore has also led to new projects to record contemporary calendar customs, following in the footsteps of photographic surveys in the early twentieth century and the mid-twentieth-century folk revival. The same impulse can also be found in contemporary art and folk music.[51] The maypole has been reinvented once again as a symbol of Englishness, but now with often tongue-in-cheek survivalist talk of ancient phallus worship and fertility rites. It was reported in 2018 that sales of maypoles were growing, thanks to a revived interest in maypole dancing and due, in part, to the invention of collapsible maypoles that can be easily stored.[52]

Multifolkloric Britain

Finally, we turn to Britishness. In Chapter 1 we heard how, in the 1980s, members of the Conservative Party called for a national Trafalgar Day holiday to replace May Day. A couple of decades later, it was mooted by Labour ministers in 2007 that a 'British Day' public holiday should be instituted as part of a 'citizenship revolution'. This did not go down well in the press. The *Independent* journalist Deborah Orr thought it was 'a fake, embarrassing piece of idiocy to be avoided at all costs'.[53] The idea was born of comparisons with the likes of Bastille Day in France (14 July), Norway's Constitution Day (17 May), and Independence Day in America (4 July), though, as was pointed out, these national public holidays were born of the experience of liberation one way or another, for which Britain had no comparable experience in modern history. Something akin to Australia Day (26 January) was also suggested, but, considering that that event marks the colonisation of the continent in

1788, it was also understandably shelved as a model.[54] British Day was clearly not to be. But what does this episode tell us about the idea of Britishness in folkloric terms?

As numerous historians have observed, the idea of Britishness was constructed on the twin pillars of monarchy and empire. Britain was not just a country but was meant to represent a shared culture that extended far beyond its shores. Empire Day (see Chapter 1) was one of the ritual underpinnings of this sense of Britishness, and reinforced loyalty to it across the colonies.[55] But with the Empire gone and monarchy remaining as the last standing pillar, with serious questions being raised about the country's role in the trade of enslaved people and its present-day ramifications, and with Devolution a reality, what was there to celebrate? When the Olympic Games came to London in 2012 the *Isles of Wonder* opening ceremony was intended as a modern pageant of Britishness (inclusive of Northern Ireland), a spectacular showcase of creativity curated with a knowingness about contemporary national identity. Shakespeare was predictably cited as an inspiration. The opening tableau, 'Green and Pleasant Land', represented a Merrie Englandesque rustic world with two stone cottages, a cricket match, beehives, wheat fields, and the obligatory villagers dancing around three maypoles. Danny Boyle, the ceremony's artistic director, described it as 'the countryside we all believed existed once'. The next section, 'Pandemonium', celebrated Britain as the birthplace of the Industrial Revolution and included other notable events from the nineteenth and twentieth centuries, such as the First World War – represented by a field of poppies. There followed a pre-recorded spoof with the Queen and James Bond, and then the key tableau celebrating the National Health Service with an army of nurses in 1940s costume. At the end there was a parade of the British, including representatives of the Windrush generation, Pearly Kings and Queens, Chelsea pensioners, trade unionists, and suffragettes.

Isles of Wonder, while widely lauded, inevitably attracted criticism for what was not in it. 'Where were Nelson and Wellington?' moaned one right-wing journalist. 'Why were there so few references to the Second World War and only a fleeting glimpse of Churchill?' From the opposite political perspective, journalists and academics pointed out that the problematic role of Empire and imperialism in forging Britishness was also left out of the narrative. *Isles of Wonder* has also been described as a British national fantasy and an act of national mythologising with regard to race and society. Benedict Anderson's conception of nation as an 'imagined community' has been repeatedly invoked.[56] This is not the place to unpick the cultural politics but, rather, to present *Isles*

Figure 13.2 Leeds West Indian Carnival Procession, 2008. Harehills and Chapeltown. Photograph by 'Chemical Engineer'.

of Wonder as a snapshot in time regarding contemporary *motifs* of Britishness that were chosen as being most recognisable to the broadest number of people and in the most positive light.

The concept of Britishness certainly masks deep structural social, racial, and cultural inequalities, but it can, in terms of folklore at least, also act as an umbrella for multiculturalism in the sense of a 'community of communities' engaged in folklore of whatever origin.[57] While multiculturalism has faced politicised accusations of undermining Britishness, it can be argued that ethnic diversity actually helps to underpin the relevance of both Britishness and contemporary folklore (Figure 13.2). What makes folklore 'British' today is its heterogeneity, its long history of migration and immigration, and the twentieth-century ethnic diversification of all three nations. This multifolkloric Britain is not only defined in terms of ethnic diversity but also embraces regional and local identities, harking back to the early folklorists' sense of identity and pride in their counties or local environs. It has been suggested by the editors of a book on Celtic identity, for instance, that 'celticity can contribute to a sense of Britishness as multicultural'.[58]

The UK government's commitment in 2024 to implement the 2003 UNESCO Convention for the Safeguarding of Intangible Cultural Heritage provided a further opportunity to reflect on multifolkloric Britain. UNESCO sets out five indicative genres of Intangible Cultural Heritage (ICH): oral traditions and expressions; performing arts; social practices, rituals, and festive events; knowledge and practices concerning nature and the universe; and traditional craftsmanship. By 2024 the UK was one of only twelve countries worldwide yet to have ratified the Convention. In early 2024, however, a series of consultation workshops were held with grassroots practitioners, folk societies, heritage organisations, museums, and community groups from across the United Kingdom. While the Convention recognises that folklore is an integral aspect of ICH, the relationship between the two has been problematised by folklorists. Indeed, the Convention was based on the *1989 Recommendation on the Safeguarding of Traditional Culture and Folklore*, but the word 'folklore' was subsequently abandoned, due to concerns from former colonised countries because of its historic resonances.[59] In Britain, however, the intention to ratify has sparked a public conversation which needs to be couched in the language of 'folklore', because the term Intangible Cultural Heritage means nothing to most people.

A press release by the government invited communities across the country to nominate 'their most cherished local traditions' for a possible national register of ICH, with prompt suggestions including pantomime, sea shanties, Hogmanay, *Eisteddfodau*, cheese rolling, the Notting Hill Carnival, and steel drumming.[60] It is an interesting debating game, of course. What would your list look like? But there is a big problem with any attempt to list British folklore in this way. For one, folklore is ever changing. Attempts to judge authenticity, setting folklore in aspic, raise new concerns. How old does the folklore have to be? We are at an inflexion point in British folklore, where such initiatives as signing the UNESCO Convention present us with divergent paths. We prefer a focus on the multifolkloric, which embraces cultural diversity as part of the continuum of British folklore in ever-changing and challenging times.

Figures

1.1	The Charter Pole Fair held in Corby, Northamptonshire, every twenty years, 1902	page 29
1.2	The Biddenden dole in Kent dates back to at least the early seventeenth century	32
2.1	An eighteenth-century London scene of milkmaids dancing on May Day	43
2.2	The Whittlesea Straw Bear and 'its' handler	44
2.3	The May Queen procession at Knutsford, Cheshire	57
2.4	Chinese New Year decorations in London's Chinatown	62
3.1	Culhwch entering King Arthur's court	68
3.2	The Ossianic legends depicted within Ossian's Hall of Mirrors, Dunkeld	69
4.1	The Major Oak of Sherwood Forest	92
4.2	The 'young officer' dressed as Robin Hood at the Christmas party attended by Washington Irving	93
5.1	A widow and her son inform the bees of a death in the family	99
6.1	Amuletic dried toad or frog	128
7.1	'Plucked from the Fairy Circle'. A man saved from dancing with the fairies	153
8.1	Offerings placed within the Neolithic burial tomb on the Welsh island of Anglesey	159
8.2	Handbags and Paddington Bear toys placed as memorial offerings for Queen Elizabeth II, Hyde Park, London	168
8.3	A mural of photojournalist Motaz Azaiza in Gaza, Manchester, 2023	171
8.4	The Lovelock Hostage Bridge outside a Jewish community centre in North London, 2024	172

Figures

9.1	Children playing with sticks on waste ground behind tenements, Edinburgh, 1959	183
9.2	An annotated school leaver's shirt, 2024	190
10.1	Europe's first Diwali cards, depicting Bhakti saint Meera and Hindu god Krishna	208
10.2	West African-inspired Christmas cards	209
11.1	Abbots Bromley Horn Dance, Staffordshire, 1982	220
11.2	The Haxey Hood game, Lincolnshire	225
12.1	#goblincore images from mossgoblingrrl's Instagram account	241
12.2	Various aesthetics employed by @TheCityWitchUK on YouTube and TikTok	242
13.1	Druidic costume and regalia at the national *Eisteddfod*, c. 1905	257
13.2	Leeds West Indian Carnival Procession, 2008	270

A note on calendar reform and bank holidays

European astronomers measuring the equinoxes in the early modern period revealed that, over time, the old Roman Julian calendar had slightly overcalculated the solar year. This had an impact on the calculation of the lunar cycles that determined the date of Easter, and so, in 1582, Pope Gregory XIII (1502–1585) ordered the revision of the calendar by the omission of ten days and the reform of leap years.

The shift to the Gregorian calendar happened piecemeal across Europe, starting first in Catholic countries, for obvious reasons. Britain was quite late to make the change. By the time it did, in 1752, eleven days had to be omitted. The dates 3 September to 13 September were chosen to be expunged to minimise initial disruption to the customary and legal calendar. The legislation still allowed statutory fairs to remain on the old calendar, except those that fell at Easter, which were shifted to the new calendar, though some local authorities decided to move with the times and advertised the new 'traditional' dates. Almanack writers had to explain the changed calendar to their many readers, while also sometimes providing a reminder of the Old Style dates. The churches followed the new Gregorian calendar assiduously in its observance of religious festivals, but some customary celebrations stuck to the Old Style. To fall in line with the Gregorian calendar, in 1752 the legal New Year was also fixed as 1 January rather the previous date of 25 March.

Today there are eight bank holidays in England and Wales. The first bank holidays were created by the Bank Holidays Act of 1871, and were Easter Monday, Whit Monday, the first Monday in August, and Boxing Day. As the name suggests, bank holidays were instituted specifically to provide statutory days off for bank clerks, but within years, as some politicians feared, they increasingly applied to all workers. The four days were added to the existing customary public holidays of Christmas and Good Friday. The 1871 Act was replaced in 1971 by the Banking and Financial Dealings Act. Consequently, in England and Wales the holiday on the first Monday in August was transferred to the last Monday, and the moveable feast of Whit Monday was replaced with the fixed date of the last Monday in May. New Year's Day was added in 1974, and the early May Monday bank holiday was created in 1978. The history of bank holidays in Scotland, of which there are nine, is rather different. In short, Easter Monday never became a bank holiday, but 2 January did (second day of Hogmanay). St Andrew's Day was added in 2007.

Select bibliography

Bacchilega, Cristina (2013) *Fairy Tales Transformed? Twenty-first-century Adaptations and the Politics of Wonder*. Wayne State University Press: Detroit.
Badder, Delyth and Mark Norman (2023) *The Folklore of Wales: Ghosts*. University of Wales Press: Cardiff.
Bartels, Sarah (2021) *The Devil and the Victorians: Supernatural Evil in Nineteenth-Century English Culture*. Routledge: New York.
Bell, Karl (2012) *The Magical Imagination: Magic and Modernity in Urban England, 1780–1914*. Cambridge University Press: Cambridge.
Bennett, Gillian (1994) 'Geologists and Folklorists: Cultural Evolution and "The Science of Folklore"', *Folklore* 105, 25–37.
Bennett, Gillian (1999) *Alas, Poor Ghost! Traditions of Belief in Story and Discourse*. Utah State University Press: Logan.
Bennett, Gillian and Paul Smith (eds) (1996) *Contemporary Legend: A Reader*. Routledge: New York.
Bennett, Margaret (2019) *Scottish Customs: From the Cradle to the Grave*. Birlinn Ltd: Edinburgh.
Beresin, Anna and Julia Bishops (eds) (2023) *Play in a Covid Frame: Everyday Pandemic Creativity in a Time of Isolation*. Open University Press: London.
Blain, Jenny and Robert J. Wallis (2007) *Sacred Sites, Contested Rites/Rights*. Liverpool University Press: Liverpool.
Boyes, Georgina (1993) *The Imagined Village: Culture, Ideology, and the English Folk Revival*. Manchester University Press: Manchester.
Bradtke, Elaine (1999) *Truculent Rustics: Molly Dancing in East Anglia before 1940*. The Folklore Society: London.
Briggs, Katharine (1967) *The Fairies in English Tradition and Literature*. University of Chicago Press: Chicago.
Bro, Lisa Wenger, Crystal O'Leary-Davidson, and Mary Ann Gareis (eds) (2018) *Monsters of Film, Fiction, and Fable*. Cambridge Scholars Publishing: Newcastle-upon-Tyne.
Bronner, Simon (2017) *Folklore: The Basics*. Routledge: London.
Brown, Callum G. (1998) *Up-helly-aa: Custom, Culture, and Community in Shetland*. Manchester University Press: Manchester.
Brown, Ian (2020) *Performing Scottishness: Enactment and National Identities*. Palgrave Macmillan: London.
Bushaway, Bob (1982) *By Rite: Custom, Ceremony and Community in England 1700–1880*. Junction: London.

Select bibliography

Cheeseman, Matthew and Carina Hart (eds) (2022) *Folklore and Nation in Britain and Ireland*. Routledge: London.

Clarke, David (2004) *The Angel of Mons: Phantom Soldiers and Ghostly Guardians*. Wiley: Chichester.

Davies, Owen and Ceri Houlbrook (2021) *Building Magic: Ritual and Re-enchantment in Postmedieval Structures*. Palgrave Macmillan: London.

Dorson, Richard M. (1968) *The British Folklorists: A History*. University of Chicago Press: Chicago.

Fischer, Bob (2017) 'The Haunted Generation', *Fortean Times* 354, 30–37.

Gibson, Marion, Shelley Trower, and Garry Tregidga (eds) (2013) *Mysticism, Myth and Celtic Identity*. Routledge: Abingdon.

Griffin, Emma (2005) *England's Revelry: A History of Popular Sports*. Oxford University Press: Oxford.

Groom, Nick (2018) 'Hallowe'en and Valentine: The Culture of Saints' Days in the English-speaking World', *Folklore* 129, 331–352.

Gwyndaf, Robin (1994) 'The Past in the Present: Folk Beliefs in Welsh Oral Tradition', *Fabula* 35, 226–260.

Harte, Jeremy (2022) *Cloven Country: The Devil and the English Landscape*. Reaktion: London.

Heaney, Michael (ed.) (2018) *The Histories of the Morris in Britain*. English Folk Dance and Song Society: London.

Henderson, Lizanne (ed.) (2009) *Fantastical Imaginations: The Supernatural in Scottish History and Culture*. John Donald: Edinburgh.

Hurn, Samantha (ed.) (2016) *Anthropology and Cryptozoology*. Routledge: Abingdon.

Hutton, Ronald (1996) *The Stations of the Sun: A History of the Ritual Year in Britain*. Oxford University Press: Oxford.

Hutton, Ronald (2022) *Queens of the Wild: Pagan Goddesses in Christian Europe*. Yale University Press: New Haven.

Ironside, Rachael and Stewart Massie (2020) 'The Folklore-centric Gaze: A Relational Approach to Landscape, Folklore and Tourism', *Time and Mind* 13, 227–244.

Koven, Mikel J. (2007) 'The Folklore Fallacy: A Folkloristic/Filmic Perspective on "The Wicker Man"', *Fabula* 48, 270–280.

Koven, Mikel J. (2007) 'Most Haunted and the Convergence of Traditional Belief and Popular Television', *Folklore* 118, 186.

Leskovar, Jutta and Raimund Karl (eds) (2018) *Archaeological Sites as Space for Modern Spiritual Practice*. Cambridge Scholars Publishing: Newcastle-upon-Tyne.

McNeill, Lynne S. and Elizabeth Tucker (eds) (2018) *Legend Tripping: A Contemporary Legend Casebook*. Utah State University Press: Logan.

Menefee, Samuel Pyeatt (1981) *Wives for Sale: Ethnographic Study of British Popular Divorce*. St Martin's Press: New York.

Naithani, Sadhana (2010) *The Story-time of the British Empire: Colonial and Postcolonial Folkloristics*. University Press of Mississippi: Jackson.

Nardi, Sarah De, Hilary Orange, Steven High and Eerika Koskinen-Koivisto (eds) (2019) *The Routledge Handbook of Memory and Place*. Routledge: Abingdon.

Nicholson, Roger et al. (eds) (2015) *Contested Identities: Literary Negotiations in Time and Place*. Cambridge Scholars Publishing: Newcastle-upon-Tyne.

Norman, Mark (2015) *Black Dog Folklore*. Troy Books: London.

Opie, Iona and Peter Opie (1959 [1987]) *The Lore and Language of Schoolchildren*. Oxford University Press: Oxford.

Select bibliography

Oring, Elliott (ed.) (1986) *Folk Groups and Folklore Genres: An Introduction*. Alibris Books: Denver.

Rodgers, Diane A. (2019) 'Something "Wyrd" this Way Comes: Folklore and British Television', *Folklore* 130, 133–152.

Roper, Jonathan (2007) 'Thoms and the Unachieved "Folk-Lore of England"', *Folklore* 118, 203–216.

Roud, Steve (2006) *The English Year*. Penguin: London.

Roud, Steve (2010) *The Lore of the Playground: One Hundred Years of Children's Games, Rhymes and Traditions*. Penguin: London.

Simpson, Jacqueline and Stephen Roud (2000) *A Dictionary of English Folklore*. Oxford University Press: Oxford.

Snyder, Christopher A. (2019) '"Who Are the Britons?": Questions of Ethnic and National Identity in Arthurian Films', *Arthuriana* 29, 6–23.

Storch, Robert D. (ed.) (1982) *Popular Culture and Custom in Nineteenth-century England*. Croom Helm: London.

Sutton-Smith, B., J. Mechling, T. W. Johnson, and F. R. McMahon (eds) (1999) *Children's Folklore: A Source Book*. Utah State University Press: Logan.

Tallis, Lisa (2009) 'The "Doctor Faustus" of Cwrt-y-Cadno: A New Perspective on John Harries and Popular Medicine in Wales', *Welsh History Review* 24, 1–28.

Thompson, E. P. (1991) *Customs in Common*. Penguin: London.

Thompson, Stith (1955–1958) *Motif-Index of Folk-Literature*, rev. and enlarged edn. Indiana University Press: Bloomington.

Trevor-Roper, Hugh (2008) *The Invention of Scotland: Myth and History*. Yale University Press: New Haven.

Trubshaw, Bob (2002) *Explore Folklore*. Heart of Albion Press: Loughborough.

Vickery, Roy (1997) *Dictionary of Plant-lore*. Oxford University Press: Oxford.

Vickery, Roy (2010) *Garlands, Conkers and Mother-Die: British and Irish Plant-lore*. Bloomsbury: London.

Waterton, Emma and Steve Watson (eds) (2010) *Culture, Heritage and Representation: Perspectives on Visuality and the Past*. Ashgate: Farnham.

Wood, Andy (2013) *The Memory of the People: Custom and Popular Senses of the Past in Early Modern England*. Cambridge University Press: Cambridge.

Wood, Juliette (1997) 'Perceptions of the Past in Welsh Folklore Studies', *Folklore* 108, 93–102.

Wood, Juliette (1999) 'Folklore Studies at the Celtic Dawn: The Role of Alfred Nutt as Publisher and Scholar', *Folklore* 110, 3–12.

Young, Francis (2023) *Twilight of the Godlings: The Shadowy Beginnings of Britain's Supernatural Beings*. Cambridge University Press: Cambridge.

Young, Simon (2022) *The Boggart: Folklore, History, Placenames and Dialect*. University of Exeter Press: Exeter.

Notes and references

Unless otherwise stated, all URLs were last accessed on 20 February 2025.

Introduction

1. On debates over the definition of 'folklore' see Simon Bronner, *Folklore: The Basics* (London, 2017); Simon Bronner, 'Toward a Definition of Folklore in Practice', *Cultural Analysis: An Interdisciplinary Forum on Folklore and Popular Culture* 15 (2016), 6–27. In a British context see also the useful observations in Bob Trubshaw, *Explore Folklore* (Loughborough, 2002). Our thanks to the anonymous reviewer for comments on matters of definition.
2. Richard M. Dorson, *The British Folklorists: A History* (Chicago, 1968); Ronald Hutton, 'The English Reformation and the Evidence of Folklore', *Past & Present* 148 (1995), 89–116; Celestina Savonius-Wroth, *Visions of British Culture from the Reformation to Romanticism* (London, 2022), pp. 89–122.
3. John Brand, *Observations on Popular Antiquities* (Newcastle, 1777), p. 4.
4. Francis Bacon, *Sylva Sylvarum* (London, 1627), p. 262.
5. Jeremy Harte, 'Superstitious Observations: Fortune-telling in English Folk Culture', *Time & Mind* 11 (2018), 67–88 (67 n. 5); Alexandra Walsham, 'Recording Superstition in Early Modern Britain: The Origins of Folklore', *Past & Present*, Supplement 3 (2008), 178–206.
6. Henry Bourne, *Antiquitates vulgares* (Newcastle, 1725), pp. x, 215.
7. Dorson, *British Folklorists*, p. 5.
8. Dorson, *British Folklorists*, pp. 34–43; Simon Young, 'Folklore Collection in the English Counties, c. 1850–1950', *Tradition Today* 11 (2022), 52–54.
9. *The Bookseller*, 6 December 1862.
10. Jonathan Roper, 'Thoms and the Unachieved "Folk-Lore of England"', *Folklore* 118 (2007), 203–216; Jonathan Roper, 'Sternberg, the Second Folklorist', *Folklore* 125 (2014), 202; Gillian Bennett, 'The Thomsian Heritage in the Folklore Society (London)', *Journal of Folklore Research* 33 (1996), 212–220.
11. Sidney Oldall Addy, 'Derbyshire Folk-Lore', in J. Charles Cox (ed.), *Memorials of Old Derbyshire* (London, 1907), p. 347.
12. Stephen Miller, *The Notes and Queries Folklore Column, 1849–1947* (Cambridge, 2021); Stephen Miller, 'The Lost Publications of the Folk-Lore Society', *Folklore* 124 (2013), 226–235.

13 Henry B. Wheatley, 'Report of Brand Committee', *Folklore* 24 (1913), 111, 115.
14 Allan Gomme, 'The Collection of English Folklore: Ways and Means', *Folklore* 64 (1953), 326–327.
15 Stephen Miller, '"I have the Prospect of Going to Galloway": the Rev. Walter Gregor and the Ethnographic Survey of the United Kingdom', *Transactions of the Dumfriesshire and Galloway Natural History and Antiquarian Society* LXXXIII (2009), 211–225.
16 John Ashton, 'Beyond Survivalism: Regional Folkloristics in Late-Victorian England', *Folklore* 108 (1997), 19–23; Roper, 'Sternberg'; Juliette Wood, 'British Women Folklorists before the Second World War', *Folklore* (2013, virtual issue).
17 *Notes & Queries*, 1 July (1876), 12.
18 *Notes & Queries*, 12 February 1876; *Yorkshire Post*, 23 March 1931.
19 *Notes & Queries*, 29 July 1876; Eilee Elder, 'But Who Was Mrs Gutch?', *Newsletter of the Society for Lincolnshire History and Archaeology* 55 (1988), 23–26; see also Matthew Townend, *The Victorians and English Dialect* (Oxford 2024), pp. 206–207; Chris Wingfield and Chris Gosden, 'An Imperialist Folklore? Establishing the Folk-Lore Society in London', in Timothy Baycroft and David Hopkin (eds), *Folklore and Nationalism in Europe during the Long Nineteenth Century* (Leiden, 2012), pp. 255–274.
20 Charlotte Latham, 'West Sussex Superstitions Lingering in 1868', *Folk-Lore Record* 1 (1878), 5; Charlotte S. Burne, 'The Collection of English Folk-Lore', *Folklore* 1 (1890), 326, 322.
21 Sadhana Naithani, *The Story-time of the British Empire: Colonial and Postcolonial Folkloristics* (Jackson, MS, 2010).
22 T. Duncan Greenlees, 'Insanity among the Natives of South Africa', *Journal of Mental Science* 41 (1895), 71.
23 Gillian Bennett, 'Folklore Studies and the English Rural Myth', *Rural History* 4 (1993), 77–91.
24 P. H. Ditchfield, *Old English Sports: Pastimes and Customs* (London, 1891), pp. 1–2.
25 Edward Lovett, 'Amulets from Costers' Barrows in London, Rome, and Naples', *Folklore* 20 (1909), 70.
26 Karl Bell, *The Magical Imagination: Magic and Modernity in Urban England, 1780–1914* (Cambridge, 2012); Owen Davies 'Urbanization and the Decline of Witchcraft: An Examination of London', *Journal of Social History* 30 (1997), 597–617; Owen Davies *Troubled by Faith: Insanity and the Supernatural in the Age of the Asylum* (Oxford, 2023).
27 Our thanks to Tina Paphitis for conducting this search and for her comments on the issue.
28 J. D. A. Widdowson, 'New Beginnings: Towards a National Folklore Survey', *Folklore* 127 (2016), 264.
29 Alan Dundes, 'The Devolutionary Premise in Folklore Theory', *Journal of the Folklore Institute* 6 (1969), 13. For a critique see, Elliott Oring, 'The Devolutionary Premise: A Definitional Delusion?' *Western Folklore* 34 (1975), 36–44.
30 George Laurence Gomme, *Ethnology in Folklore* (London, 1892), p. 7.
31 Gillian Bennett, 'Geologists and Folklorists: Cultural Evolution and "The Science of Folklore"', *Folklore* 105 (1994), 25–37; Owen Davies and Ceri Houlbrook, *Building Magic: Ritual and Re-enchantment in Post-Medieval Structures* (London, 2021); Georgina Boyes, 'Cultural Survivals Theory and Traditional Customs: An Examination of the Effects of Privileging on the Form and Perception of Some English Calendar Customs', *Folk Life* 26 (1987), 5–11.

32 Oliver Douglas, 'Folklore, Survivals, and the Neo-Archaic', *Museum History Journal* 4 (2011), 223–244; Chris Wingfield, 'Is the Heart at Home? E. B. Tylor's Collections from Somerset', *Journal of Museum Ethnography* 22 (2009), 22–38. See also Tabitha Cadbury, 'Home and Away: What Was "Folklore" at Cambridge?' *Journal of Museum Ethnography* 22 (2009), 102–119.
33 P. M. 'Animal Apparitions in Lincolnshire', *Lincolnshire Notes & Queries* 4 (1896), 146–149.
34 Sabine Baring-Gould, *Book of Folklore* (London, 1913), p. 2.
35 Joseph Jacobs, 'The Folk', *Folklore* 4 (1893), 237.
36 A. R. Wright, 'Presidential Address: The Unfinished Tasks of the Folk-Lore Society', *Folklore* 39 (1928), 18.
37 R. R. Marett, 'Presidential Address: Folklore and Psychology', *Folklore* 25 (1914), 12.
38 Stephanie Lynn Budin and Caroline J. Tully (eds), *A Century of James Frazer's* The Golden Bough (Abingdon, 2025).
39 Laura Carter, 'Rethinking Folk Culture in Twentieth-Century Britain', *Twentieth Century British History* 28 (2017), 546.
40 Iorwerth Peate, 'Archaeology and Folk-Culture', *The Archaeological Journal* 91 (1934), 213.
41 Alexander Fenton and Margaret A. Mackay (eds), *An Introduction to Scottish Ethnology*, Vol. 1 (Edinburgh, 2013).
42 Carter, 'Rethinking Folk Culture', 554.
43 George Ewart Evans, 'Folk Life Studies in East Anglia', in Geraint H. Jenkins (ed.), *Studies in Folk Life: Essays in Honour of Iorwerth C. Peate* (London, 1969), p. 36.
44 Iona Opie and Moira Tatem, *A Dictionary of Superstitions* (Oxford, 1989), p. v; Steve Roud, *The Penguin Guide to the Superstitions of Britain and Ireland* (London, 2003), p. xv.
45 Dan Ben-Amos, *Folklore Concepts: Histories and Critiques* (Bloomington, 2020), p. 4.
46 Andy Wood, *The Memory of the People: Custom and Popular Senses of the Past in Early Modern England* (Cambridge, 2013); Bob Bushaway, *By Rite: Custom, Ceremony and Community in England 1700–1880* (London, 1982).
47 *Westmorland Gazette*, 28 November 1857; *Buckingham Express*, 23 September 1871.
48 See Regina Bendix, *In Search of Authenticity: The Formation of Folklore Studies* (Madison, WI, 1997).
49 Simon J. Bronner, *Folklore: The Basics* (Abingdon, 2017), pp. 154–155; Venetia Newall, 'The Adaptation of Folklore and Tradition (Folklorismus)', *Folklore* 98 (1987), 131–151; Guntis Šmidchens, 'Folklorism Revisited', *Journal of Folklore Research* 36 (1999), 51–70.
50 Cited in William S. Fox, 'Folklore and Fakelore: Some Sociological Considerations', *Journal of the Folklore Institute* 17 (1980), 246.

Chapter 1: The Ritual Year

1 Joseph Lawson, *Letters to the Young on Progress in Pudsey* (Stanningley, 1887), p. 78.
2 https://yougov.co.uk/society/articles/45291-only-5-britons-are-giving-anything-lent-2023
3 *Cardiff Times*, 9 April 1892.
4 Steve Hindle, 'Beating the Bounds of the Parish: Order, Memory, and Identity in the English Local Community, c. 1500–1700', in Michael J. Halvorson and Karen E. Spierling (eds), *Defining Community in Early Modern Europe* (Aldershot, 2008), pp. 205–227.
5 *Yorkshire Post*, 24 April 1931.

6 John K. Walton and Robert Poole, 'The Lancashire Wakes in the Nineteenth Century', in Robert D. Storch (ed.), *Popular Culture and Custom in Nineteenth-century England* (London, 1982), pp. 100–125; Steve Hindle, 'Custom, Festival and Protest in Early Modern England: The Little Budworth Wakes, St Peter's Day, 1596', *Rural History* 6 (1995), 155–178.
7 *Leicester Daily Mercury*, 9 November 1964.
8 *Leicester Daily Mercury*, 25 October 1976; *Bristol Observer*, 11 November 1950; *Southall Gazette*, 4 November 1983; *Harrow Observer*, 11 November 1983; *Southall Gazette*, 8 November 1985.
9 *Stanmore Observer*, 1 November 1990.
10 *Echo (London)*, 16 March 1896.
11 *Shields Gazette and Shipping Telegraph*, 1937; Humayun Ansari, *'The Infidel Within': Muslims in Britain since 1800* (London, 2004), pp. 139–140.
12 *Nottingham Evening Post*, 14 August 1915; *Marylebone Mercury*, 12 January 1968; www.independent.co.uk/life-style/eid-al-fitr-prayer-celebrations-park-ramadan-b2070288.html
13 Thomas Davidson, 'Plough Rituals in England and Scotland', *Agricultural History Review* 7 (1959), 27–37.
14 B. Talbot, *The Compleat Art of Land-Measuring* (London, 1784), p. 298.
15 Steve Roud, *Folk Song in England* (London, 2017), pp. 335–336.
16 See Steven King and Alannah Tomkins (eds), *The Poor in England 1700–1850: An Economy of Makeshifts* (Manchester, 2003).
17 Andy Wood, *The Memory of the People: Custom and Popular Senses of the Past in Early Modern England* (Cambridge, 2013), pp. 1–8; Bushaway, *By Rite*; Peter King, 'Gleaners, Farmers and the Failure of Legal Sanctions in England 1750–1850', *Past & Present* 125 (1989), 116–150.
18 *Nottingham Journal*, 11 September 1919.
19 William Hone, *Every-Day Book* (London, 1837), Vol. 2, Col. 1270.
20 Stephen Hussey, '"The Last Survivor of an Ancient Race": The Changing Face of Essex Gleaning', *Agricultural History Review* 45 (1997), 61–72.
21 *Uxbridge & W. Drayton Gazette*, 27 October 1950.
22 See Ronald Hutton, *The Stations of the Sun* (Oxford, 1996), pp. 56–60, 65–69, 163–167.
23 Eddie Cass, *The Pace-Egg Plays of the Calder Valley* (London, 2004).
24 *Sheffield and Rotherham Independent*, 13 January 1849.
25 Ruairidh Greig, 'Seasonal House-visiting in South Yorkshire', MPhil thesis, University of Sheffield, 1988, 71.
26 Jonathan Ceredig Davies, *Folk-Lore of West and Mid-Wales* (Aberystwyth, 1911), pp. 62–64.
27 *Aberdeen Press*, 31 December 1932.
28 Neill Martin, 'Ritualised Entry in Seasonal and Marriage Custom', *Folk Life* 46 (2007), 73–95; Trefor Owen, 'The Ritual Entry to the House in Wales', in Venetia Newell (ed.), *Folklore Studies in the Twentieth Century* (Woodbridge, 1980).
29 Tim Hitchcock, 'Begging on the Streets of Eighteenth-century London', *Journal of British Studies* 44 (2005), 484–487.
30 K. D. M. Snell, *Annals of the Labouring Poor* (Cambridge, 1985), pp. 67–104.
31 *Monmouthshire Beacon*, 14 May 1897.
32 James David Marwick, *List of Markets and Fairs now and formerly Held in Scotland* (1890), p. 11.

33 *Reports from Commissioners 1868–9. Agriculture (Employment of Women and Children)* (London, 1868–1869), Vol. 13, p. 29.
34 *Morning Leader*, 8 October 1900.
35 Elijah Bell, 'Leisure, War and Marginal Communities: Travelling Showpeople and Outdoor Pleasure-seeking in Britain 1889–1945', PhD thesis, University of Essex, 2020.
36 See Steve Hindle, *On the Parish? The Micro-politics of Poor Relief in Rural England c. 1550–1750* (Oxford, 2004), pp. 96–171.
37 H. Edwards, *A Collection of Remarkable Charities* (London, 1842), pp. 41, 100, 6; Steve Roud, *The English Year* (London, 2006), pp. 172–173; *South Yorkshire Times*, 27 February 1891.
38 Reprinted in *Jersey Independent*, 5 April 1890.
39 *Penrith Observer*, 26 April 1938; *Leeds Mercury*, 24 February 1905.
40 David Cressy, *Bonfires and Bells* (London, 1989), pp. 50–67.
41 Hutton, *Stations*, pp. 288–294.
42 *Sheffield Evening Telegraph*, 29 May 1888.
43 *Lincolnshire Echo*, 30 May 1894.
44 Jim English, 'Empire Day in Britain, 1904–1958', *The Historical Journal* 49 (2006), 247.
45 Cressy, *Bonfires and Bells*, pp. 119–120.
46 *Ayrshire Weekly News*, 3 August 1888.
47 Clare L. Tonks, 'Commemorating the Battle of Waterloo in Great Britain, 1815–1852', PhD thesis, Edinburgh University, 2021, 44–46.
48 *Leicester Journal*, 25 June 1852; *Exeter Flying Post*, 27 June 1850.
49 Miroslava Hukelova and Margaret Holloway, '"Lest we forget": The Significance and Meaning of Remembrance Sunday in Contemporary British Society', *Mortality* 28 (2023), 469.
50 *The Scotsman*, 20 April 1892.
51 Chris Wrigley, 'May Day in Britain', in Abby Peterson and Herbert Reiter (eds), *The Ritual of May Day in Western Europe: Past, Present and Future* (London, 2016); Eric Hobsbawm, 'Mass-producing Traditions: Europe, 1870–1914', in Eric Hobsbawm and Terence Ranger (eds), *The Invention of Tradition* (Cambridge, 2012), pp. 263–309.
52 Leigh Eric Schmidt, *Consumer Rites: The Buying and Selling of American Holidays* (Princeton, NJ, 1995); Jack Santino, *New Old-fashioned Ways: Holidays and Popular Culture* (Knoxville, TN, 1996); John Widdowson, 'Trends in the Commercialization of English Calendar Customs: A Preliminary Survey', in T. Buckland, and J. Wood (eds), *Aspects of British Calendar Customs* (Sheffield, 1994), pp. 23–35.
53 Nick Groom, 'Hallowe'en and Valentine: The Culture of Saints' Days in the English-speaking World', *Folklore* 129 (2018), 331–352; Sally Holloway, 'Love, Custom and Consumption: Valentine's Day in England c. 1660–1830', *Cultural and Social History* 17 (2020); Hutton, *Stations*, pp. 146–150.
54 *Eastern Daily Press*, 1 February 1888; *Hull Daily Mail*, 7 February 1930; *Western Daily Press*, 9 February 1938.
55 Hutton, *Stations*, pp. 174–176; Christina Hole, *A Dictionary of British Folk Customs* (London, 1978), p. 213; T. E. Lones, 'Worcestershire Folklore', *Folklore* 25 (1914), 370.
56 Kathleen W. Jones, 'Mother's Day: The Creation, Promotion and Meaning of a New Holiday in the Progressive Era', in Nancy F. Cott (ed.), *Social and Moral Reform* 17 (1994), 503–525.
57 *The Tatler*, 12 July 1916.

Notes and references

58 Schmidt, *Consumer Rites*, pp. 256–267.
59 *Nottingham Evening Post*, 29 February 1940; *Liverpool Echo*, 2 March 1959; *Louth Standard*, 21 March 1953.
60 Violet Alford, 'Folklore Gone Wrong', *Folklore* 72 (1961), 603.
61 Mark Warren (2024) 'How Supermarkets Utilise End-of-aisle Displays to Drive Sales', *Gus Logistics*, www.guslogistics.co.uk/how-supermarkets-utilise-end-of-aisle-displays-to-drive-sales/

Chapter 2: Performing together

1   Peter Harrop and Steve Roud (eds), *The Routledge Companion to English Folk Performance* (London, 2021), p. 1.
2   *Loughborough Monitor*, 16 January 1862; *Loughborough Monitor*, 16 February 1865; *Northampton Mercury*, 17 January 1885; *Stamford Mercury*, 11 January 1878.
3   Roy Judge, *The Jack-in-the-Green: A May Day Custom* (London, 2000).
4   W. W. Fyfe, *Summer Life on Land and Water at South Queensferry* (Edinburgh, 1851), p. 51.
5   Isabel A. Dickson, 'The Burry-Man', *Folklore* 19 (1908), 383.
6   *Stamford Mercury*, 13 January 1893; *Cambridge Independent Press*, 15 January 1887.
7   Terry Gunnell, 'Masks and Mumming Traditions in the North Atlantic', in Terry Gunnell (ed.), *Masks and Mumming in the Nordic Area* (Uppsala, 2007), pp. 290–291.
8   E. C. Cawte, *Ritual Animal Disguise: A Historical and Geographical Study of Animal Disguise in the British Isles* (London, 1978).
9   Rhian E. Jones, *Petticoat Heroes: Gender, Culture and Popular Protest in the Rebecca Riots* (Cardiff, 2015), pp. 59–81; Elaine Bradtke, *Truculent Rustics: Molly Dancing in East Anglia Before 1940* (London, 1999), pp. 12–14; Chloe Metcalfe, *Beginners Guide: English Folk Costumes* (London, 2014).
10 *Worcestershire Chronicle*, 8 June 1859.
11 Alun Howkins and Linda Merricks, '"Wee be black as Hell": Ritual, Disguise and Rebellion', *Rural History* 4 (1993), 41–53; Theresa Jill Buckland, 'Black Faces, Garlands, and Coconuts: Exotic Dances on Street and Stage', *Dance Research Journal* 22 (1990), 1–12.
12 David Taylor, *From Mummers to Madness: A Social History of Popular Music in England, c. 1770s to c. 1970s* (Huddersfield, 2021), pp. 197–214; Michael Pickering, *Blackface Minstrelsy in Britain* (London, 2017).
13 See, Emma Griffin, 'Popular Culture in Industrializing England', *The Historical Journal* 45 (2002), 619–635.
14 Emma Griffin, *England's Revelry: A History of Popular Sports* (Oxford, 2005), p. 71.
15 *Bury and Norwich Post*, 10 January 1865.
16 *London Evening Standard*, 7 November 1906; *Daily Mirror*, 1 November 1963; *Manchester Evening News*, 22 October 1992.
17 *Kentish Independent*, 18 November 1854.
18 Robert D. Storch, '"Please to Remember the Fifth of November": Conflict, Solidarity and Public Order in Southern England', in Robert D. Storch (ed.), *Popular Culture and Custom in Nineteenth-century England* (London, 1982); Hutton, *Stations*, pp. 393–407; D. G. Paz, 'Bonfire Night in Mid Victorian Northants: The Politics of a Popular Revel', *Historical Research* 63 (1990), 316–328; Chris Hare, 'The Skeleton Army and the Bonfire Boys, Worthing, 1884', *Folklore* 99 (1988), 221–231.
19 *Coventry Evening Telegraph*, 19 November 1954.

20 *Newcastle Journal*, 6 March 1878; *Kelso Chronicle*, 12 February 1864.
21 *Chester-le-Street Chronicle*, 28 March 1930; 20 February 1931.
22 Richard Jefferies, *Wild Life in a Southern County* (London, 1879), p. 102.
23 Alun Howkins, *Whitsun in 19th Century Oxfordshire* (Oxford, 1974), pp. 60–61.
24 *Northampton Mercury*, 4 October 1862.
25 *The Graphic*, 22 February 1896; *Cornubian and Redruth Times*, 24 June 1887; *East & South Devon Advertiser*, 18 June 1887.
26 *West Cumberland Times*, 2 May 1894.
27 *Aberdeen Evening Express*, 29 January 1889; *Aberdeen Free Press*, 29 January 1889.
28 Jonathan Freeman Croose, 'The Practices of Carnival: Community, Culture and Place', PhD thesis, Exeter University, 2014, pp. 75–78; Dion Georgiou, '"The Drab Suburban Streets were Metamorphosed into a Veritable Fairyland": Spectacle and Festivity in The Ilford Hospital Carnival, 1905–1914', *The London Journal* 39 (2014), 227–248.
29 Deborah Sugg Ryan, '"Pageantitis": Frank Lascelles' 1907 Oxford Historical Pageant, Visual Spectacle and Popular Memory', *Visual Culture in Britain* 8 (2007), 63–82.
30 Angela Bartie et al. (eds), *Restaging the Past: Historical Pageants, Culture and Society in Modern Britain* (London, 2020); Michael Woods, 'Performing Power: Local Politics and the Taunton Pageant of 1928', *Journal of Historical Geography* 25 (1999), 57–74.
31 See, Keith D. M. Snell, *Parish and Belonging: Community, Identity and Welfare in England and Wales, 1700–1950* (Cambridge, 2006).
32 Verity Wilson, *Dressing Up: A History of Fancy Dress in Britain* (London, 2022).
33 Callum G. Brown, *Up-helly-aa: Custom, Culture, and Community in Shetland* (Manchester, 1998).
34 Bushaway, *By Rite*, pp. 265–273.
35 David Walker, 'The Social Significance of Harvest Festivals in the Countryside: An Empirical Enquiry among Those Who Attend', *Rural Theology* 7 (2009), 3–16.
36 John Pugh, *Remarkable Occurrences in the Life of Jonas Hanway, Esq* (London, 1787), p. 234.
37 *Hastings Times*, 26 April 1879; see also Judge, *Jack-in-the-Green*, p. 75.
38 Simon Cordery, *British Friendly Societies, 1750–1914* (Basingstoke, 2003), pp. 35–38; Howkins, *Whitsun*; Bushaway, *By Rite*, pp. 259–265.
39 *Taunton Courier*, 11 June 1873.
40 William Howitt, *The Rural Life of England*, 2nd edn (London, 1840), p. 447.
41 Robert Colls, *This Sporting Life: Sport and Liberty in England, 1760–1960* (Oxford, 2020).
42 Peter Swain, 'The Origins of Football Debate: The Evidence Mounts, 1841–1851', *The International Journal of the History of Sport* 32 (2015), 299–317.
43 Anthony Bateman, '"More Mighty than the Bat, the Pen …": Culture, Hegemony and the Literaturisation of Cricket', *Sport in History* 23 (2003), 27–44; Griffin, *England's Revelry*, pp. 47–52; Colls, *Sporting Life*, pp. 171–174.
44 Lawson, *Letters*, p. 82.
45 *The Illustrated Newspaper*, 29 April 1871.
46 *Rhyl Record and Advertiser*, 4 May 1901.
47 Roy Judge, 'May Day and Merrie England', *Folklore* 102 (1991), 141–142.
48 George Long, *The Folklore Calendar* (London, 1930), p. 70.
49 *Widnes Weekly News*, 20 July 1878.
50 Sarah Maza, 'The Rose-Girl of Salency: Representations of Virtue in Prerevolutionary France', *Eighteenth Century Studies* 22 (1989), 395–412.

51 *Norwood News*, 26 June 1886.
52 *Rochdale Times*, 10 July 1889; *North Wales Weekly News*, 21 July 1899.
53 Roud, *English Year*, pp. 328–329; www.visitlytham.info/recreation-entertainment/events-featured/lytham-club-day-and-rose-queen-festival/
54 Kate Smith, 'Change, Continuity and Contradictions in May Day Celebrations in Northamptonshire', *Folklore* 119 (2008), 142–159; Catherine Bannister, *Scouting and Guiding in Britain: The Ritual Socialisation of Young People* (Cham, 2022), pp. 107–127.
55 Colin Cater and Karen Cater, *Wassailing: Reawakening an Ancient Folk Custom* (Hedingham, 2013).
56 *Bury and Norwich Post*, 23 July 1851.
57 *Suffolk Chronicle*, 21 July 1855.
58 *Bell's Weekly Messenger*, 16 October 1858; *Essex Times*, 21 August 1869; Francis W. Steer, *The History of the Dunmow Flitch Ceremony* (Chelmsford, 1951), pp. 34–59.
59 *Luton Reporter*, 2 November 1906; *Western Times*, 6 October 1921; *North Devon Journal*, 11 August 1921.
60 https://stalbanstimes.co.uk/st-albans/join-the-historic-beating-the-bounds-ceremony-this-sunday/
61 Tony Ashley, 'The Hinckley Bullockers: A Potted History and Voyage of Discovery', *The Morris Dancer* 5 (2016), 89–97.
62 Bradtke, *Truculent Rustics*, pp. 7–9; Cass, *Pace-Egg Plays*, p. 48.
63 Sue Allan, 'Merrie England, May Day and More: Morris Dances in Cumbria in the Early Twentieth Century', in Michael Heaney (ed.), *The Histories of the Morris in Britain* (London, 2018), pp. 179–203.
64 Val Parker, 'The Women's Morris Federation – from Start to Finish', in Heaney (ed.), *Histories of the Morris*, pp. 279–295; Theresa Jill Buckland, 'Liberating Tradition: Gender Politics in Late Twentieth Century English Revivalist Morris Dancing', in Daniela Stavělová and Theresa Buckland (eds), *Folklore Revival Movements in Europe post 1950* (Prague, 2018), pp. 311–331; Lucy Wright, 'Girls' Carnival Morris Dancing and Contemporary Folk Dance Scholarship', *Folklore* 128 (2017), 157–174.
65 Helen Cornish, '"Not All Singing and Dancing": Padstow, Folk Festivals and Belonging', *Ethnos* 81 (2016), 631–647; *The Guardian*, 1 May 2021; Richard D. G. Irvine, 'Following the Bear: The Revival of Plough Monday Traditions and the Performance of Rural Identity in the East Anglian Fenlands', *EthnoScripts* 20 (2018), 31.
66 https://open-morris.org/about/documents/face-paint-statement/
67 Edward Wigley, '"A Place of Magic": Enchanting Geographies of Contemporary Wassailing Practices', *Social & Cultural Geography* 22 (2021), 879.
68 https://boagreenmanfest.org/welcome/the-green-man-jack-in-the-green/

Chapter 3: Storytelling

1 W. Tecumseh Fitch, *The Evolution of Language* (Cambridge, 2010).
2 C. W. Sullivan III, 'Folklore and Fantastic Literature', *Western Folklore* 60 (2001), 283.
3 Geoffrey of Monmouth, *History of the Kings of Britain* 1.11. Translated by Aaron Thompson, revisions by J. A. Giles (Cambridge, Ontario, 1999), p. 14.
4 Monmouth. *History* 1.16, p. 20.
5 Monmouth. *History* 8.19, p. 144.

6 John J. Davenport, 'The Matter of Britain: The Mythological and Philosophical Significance of the British Legends' (manuscript, 2004).
7 Sioned Davies, 'Storytelling in Medieval Wales', *Oral Tradition* 7 (1992), 233; Brynley F. Roberts, 'Oral Tradition and Welsh Literature: A Description and a Survey', *Oral Tradition* 3 (1988), 70; Robin Gwyndaf, 'Welsh Folk Narrative and the Fairy Tale', in Hilda Ellis Davidson and Anna Chaudhri (eds), *A Companion to the Fairy Tale* (Martlesham, 2003), pp. 191–201.
8 Gabriela Steinke, 'To Boldly Go: Futuristic Retellings of Ancient Welsh Myths' (conference paper, University of Lisbon, 2017).
9 Cited in Marion Wynne-Davies, *Women and Arthurian Literature: Seizing the Sword* (Basingstoke, 1996), p. 112.
10 Hugh Trevor-Roper, *The Invention of Scotland: Myth and History* (New Haven, CT, 2008), p. 43.
11 James MacPherson, *The Poems of Ossian* (Boston, MA, 1773 [1851]), p. 28.
12 Letter of Alexander Carlyle, dated 9 January 1802, cited in Trevor-Roper, *Invention of Scotland*, p. 50.
13 Henry Okin, 'Ossian in Painting', *Journal of the Warburg and Courtauld Institutes* 30 (1967), 330.
14 Diary of Joseph Banks, 12 August 1772. Cited in Paul M. Allen and Joan de Ris Allen, *Fingal's Cave, the Poems of Ossian, and Celtic Christianity* (New York, 1999), p. 25.
15 Neil Davidson, *The Origins of Scottish Nationhood* (Sterling, VA), p. 129.
16 Trevor-Roper, *Invention of Scotland*, p. 54.
17 Elliott Oring, 'Folk Narratives', in Elliott Oring (ed.), *Folk Groups and Folklore Genres: An Introduction* (Denver, CO, 1986), p. 124.
18 Jack Zipes, *The Irresistible Fairy Tale: The Cultural and Social History of a Genre* (Princeton, NJ, 2012), p. 3. See also Willem de Blécourt, *Tales of Magic, Tales in Print: On the Genealogy of Fairy Tales and the Brothers Grimm* (Manchester, 2012).
19 Cristina Bacchilega, *Fairy Tales Transformed? Twenty-first-century Adaptations and the Politics of Wonder* (Detroit, MI, 2013).
20 Andrea Day, '"Almost wholly the work of Mrs. Lang": Nora Lang, Literary Labour, and the Fairy Books', *Women's Writing* 26 (2019), 400–420.
21 Trevor-Roper, *Invention of Scotland*, p. 43.
22 Charlotte Artese, '"Tell Thou the Tale": Shakespeare's Taming of Folktales in *The Taming of the Shrew*', *Folklore* 120 (2009), 325.
23 Kenneth Muir, 'Folklore and Shakespeare', *Folklore* 92 (1981), 231–232; Ciara Rawnsley, 'Behind the Happily-Ever-After: Shakespeare's Use of Fairy Tales and *All's Well That Ends Well*', *Journal of Early Modern Studies* 2 (2013), 146.
24 Duke Pesta, '"This Rough Magic I here Abjure": Shakespeare's "The Tempest" and the Fairy-tale Body', *Journal of the Fantastic in the Arts* 15 (2004), 50; Rawnsley, 'Behind the Happily-Ever-After', 145.
25 Muir, 'Folklore and Shakespeare', 235–236.
26 Gabriella Schuett, 'Shaping a Nation and Transforming Identity: Ovidian Mythic Allusions in William Shakespeare's A Midsummer Night's Dream and John Milton's "Lycidas"', PhD thesis, Georgia State University, 2024, p. 40.
27 William Shakespeare, *A Midsummer Night's Dream*, Act II, Scene I; Act II, Scene II.
28 William Shakespeare, *Romeo and Juliet*, Act I, scene IV.
29 Shakespeare, *A Midsummer Night's Dream*, Act II, Scene I.

Notes and references

30 Rawnsley, 'Behind the Happily-Ever-After', pp. 141–142; Charlotte Artese, *Shakespeare and the Folktale: An Anthology of Stories* (Princeton, NJ, 2019); Schuett, 'Shaping a Nation', p. 24.
31 Sullivan, 'Folklore'.
32 Sullivan, 'Folklore', 285, 281; Dimitra Fimi, *Celtic Myth in Contemporary Children's Fantasy: Idealization, Identity, Ideology* (London, 2017).
33 T. H. White, *The Sword in the Stone* (London, 1976), p. i.
34 Arthur Isaac Jackson, 'Writing Arthur, Writing England: Myth and Modernity in T. H. White's *The Sword in the Stone*', *The Lion and the Unicorn* 33 (2009), 44–59.
35 C. A. Sanz Mingo, 'Medieval World, Modern World: The Making of a Nation. The Welsh *Mabinogion* in Modern Adaptations', in Roger Nicholson et al. (eds), *Contested Identities: Literary Negotiations in Time and Place* (Newcastle, 2015), pp. 121–136.
36 www.serenbooks.com/book/new-stories-from-the-mabinogion-box-set/
37 Hynek Daniel Janoušek, 'New Stories from the Mabinogion and Pedeir Keinc y Mabinogi: Texts, Narratives and Tradition', *Prague Journal of English Studies* 2 (2023), 28–29.
38 Janoušek, 'New Stories from the Mabinogion', p. 35.
39 Bacchilega, *Fairy Tales Transformed?*
40 Bacchilega, *Fairy Tales Transformed?*, p. 70.
41 Anđelka M. Gemović, 'From Captivity to Bestiality: Feminist Subversion of Fairy-tale Female Characters in Angela Carter's "The Tiger's Bride"', *Reči (Beograd)* 11 (2019), 102.
42 Vladimir Propp, *Morphology of the Folktale* (Leningrad, 1928).
43 Merja Leppälahti, 'From Folklore to Fantasy: The Living Dead, Metamorphoses, and Other Strange Things', *Journal of the Fantastic in the Arts* 29 (2018), 179.
44 Stith Thompson, *Motif-Index of Folk-Literature*, rev. and enl. edn (Bloomington, 1955–1958). A useful online search engine has been developed by the Meertens Institute, Amsterdam: https://momfer.meertens.knaw.nl/
45 For critiques of the *Motif-Index*, see Torborg Lundell, 'Folktale Heroines and the Type and Motif Indexes', *Folklore* 94 (1983), 240–246; Alan Dundes, 'The Motif-Index and the Tale Type Index: A Critique', *Journal of Folklore Research* 34 (1997), 195–202.
46 Edinburgh 'Cub Reporter' Press Conference, 2005, cited in Samantha G. Castleman, *Inexhaustible Magic: Folklore as World Building in Harry Potter*, Master's thesis, Western Kentucky University, 2017, p. 1.
47 Sullivan, 'Folklore', 283–284.
48 Roger D. Abrahams, 'Folklore and Literature as Performance', *Journal of the Folklore Institute* 9 (1972), 75–94.
49 Tom Shippey, *The Road to Middle Earth: How J. R. R. Tolkien Created a New Mythology* (London, 1992), p. 92; Stefan Ekman, *Here Be Dragons: Exploring Fantasy Maps and Settings* (Middletown, CT, 2013).
50 Peter Hunt, 'Landscapes and Journeys, Metaphors and Maps: The Distinctive Feature of English Fantasy', *Children's Literature Association Quarterly* 12 (2009), 11.
51 Alan Garner, *The Weirdstone of Brisingamen* (London, 1960).
52 Susan Cooper, 'In the Same Room at the Same Time', in Erica Wagner (ed.), *First Light: A Celebration of the Life and Work of Alan Garner* (London, 2016), p. 35; Neil Gaiman, 'The World and the Worlds: Some Musings and Two Book Reviews', in Wagner, *First Light*, p. 85.
53 Hunt, 'Landscapes and Journeys', p. 13.

54 Shippey, *The Road to Middle Earth*, p. 93.
55 The Bell Inn – Moreton-in-Marsh, Cotswolds.
56 Hunt, 'Landscapes and Journeys', p. 11.
57 Jane Chance, 'A Mythology for England?' in Jane Chance (ed.), *Tolkien and the Invention of Myth: A Reader* (Lexington, KY, 2004) 1–16; Tommy Kuusela, 'In Search of a National Epic: The Use of Old Norse Myths in Tolkien's Vision of Middle-Earth', *Approaching Religion* 4 (2014), 25–36.
58 Shippey, *The Road to Middle Earth*, p. 87.
59 Matt King, 'Taxonomizing Goblins from Folklore to Fiction', *Folklore* 135 (2024), 87–109 (97).
60 Kuusela, 'In Search of a National Epic'; Chance, 'A Mythology for England?'; Marjorie Burns, *Perilous Realms: Celtic and Norse in Tolkien's Middle-Earth* (Toronto, 2005).

Chapter 4: Legends

1 Washington Irving, *Abbotsford and Newstead Abbey* (Philadelphia, PA, 1835), p. 184.
2 Irving, *Abbotsford*, p. 183.
3 Irving, *Abbotsford*, p. 191.
4 See, for instance, Steve Roud, *London Lore* (London, 2010), p. xii.
5 Jacob Grimm, *Teutonic Mythology*, Vol. 3 (London, 1883), p. xv.
6 Lynne S. McNeill and Elizabeth Tucker (eds), *Legend Tripping: A Contemporary Legend Casebook* (Logan, 2018), p. 4.
7 Roberts, 'Oral Tradition', p. 61.
8 Carl Wilhelm von Sydow, 'On the Spread of Tradition', in Laurits Bødker (ed.), *Selected Papers on Folklore* (Copenhagen, 1948), pp. 11–43.
9 Davies, 'Storytelling in Medieval Wales', p. 231.
10 Ronald James, *The Folklore of Cornwall* (Exeter, 2018), pp. 22–35.
11 William Bottrell, *Traditions and Hearthside Stories of West Cornwall*, Volume 1 (Penzance, 1873), p. vi.
12 Davies, 'Storytelling in Medieval Wales', p. 233.
13 *An Gàidheal* XLII/8 (An Ceitein, 1947), pp. 93–94. Cited and translated in Hugh Cheape, '"Tha feum air cabhaig": The initiative of the Folklore Institute of Scotland', in Virginia Blankenhorn (ed.), *Craobh nan Ubhal: A Festschrift for John MacInnes* (Edinburgh, 2014), p. 53.
14 Cheape, 'Tha feum air cabhaig', p. 56.
15 Stephen Miller, 'The County Folk-Lore Series (Volumes 1–7) of the Folk-Lore Society', *Folklore* 124 (2013), 327–344.
16 George Laurence Gomme, *Handbook of Folklore* (London, 1890), p. 115.
17 John Francis Campbell, *Popular Tales of the West Highlands, Orally Collected*, Vol. 1 (Edinburgh, 1860), p. xi.
18 Campbell, *Popular Tales*, p. xxviii.
19 Clark Kennedy, 'Wild Sport in the Orkney Isles', *Baily's Magazine of Sports and Pastimes* XLII (1884), 356.
20 Kennedy, 'Wild Sport', 357.
21 Gwyndaf, 'Welsh Folk Narrative', 196. Cf. Juliette Wood, 'The Fairy Bride Legend in Wales', *Folklore* 103 (1992), 56–72.
22 Bottrell, *Traditions*, p. 64.

23 Bottrell, *Traditions*, p. 68.
24 James, *The Folklore of Cornwall*, pp. 93–96.
25 Wendy Shearer, *Caribbean Folk Tales: Stories from the Islands and the Windrush Generation* (Cheltenham, 2022), p. 10.
26 Shearer, *Caribbean Folk Tales*, pp. 113–119.
27 For the most in-depth study of boggarts, see Simon Young, *The Boggart: Folklore, History, Place-names and Dialect* (Exeter, 2022).
28 Stith Thompson, *Motif-Index of Folk-Literature*, F480.
29 Katharine Briggs, *The Personnel of Fairyland* (Detroit, MI, 1953 [1971], p. 15; Katharine Briggs, 'The English Fairies', *Folklore* 68 (1957), 271.
30 Katharine M. Briggs, *An Encyclopedia of Fairies* (New York, 1976); Katharine Briggs, *The Fairies in English Tradition and Literature* (Chicago, IL, 1967).
31 Briggs, 'English Fairies', 272–273.
32 Briggs, 'English Fairies', 271.
33 Briggs, 'English Fairies', 273.
34 John Roby, *Traditions of Lancashire* (London, 1829), pp. 274–301.
35 Thomas Crofton Croker, *Fairy Legends and Traditions of the South of Ireland* (London, 1825 [1834]), p. 83.
36 Cited in Jennifer Westwood, *Albion: A Guide to Legendary Britain* (London, 1987), p. 367.
37 Donald Archie MacDonald classifies this as Migratory Legend F30: We're Flitting, in 'Migratory Legends of the Supernatural in Scotland: A General Survey', *Béaloideas* (1994/1995) 47.
38 Stith Thompson, *Motif-Index*, F82.3.1.1.
39 Campbell, *Popular Tales of the West Highlands*, p. 93.
40 Reidar Thoralf Christiansen, *The Migratory Legends: A Proposed List of Types with a Systematic Catalogue of the Norwegian Variants* (Suomalainen Tiedeakatemia, 1958).
41 Cited in Jacqueline Simpson, 'Hitchhiker Vanishes from Gig', *FLS News* 28 (1998), 14–15.
42 Jan Harold Brunvand, *Encyclopedia of Urban Legends* (Santa Barbara, CA, 2001), p. xxviii.
43 Jacqueline Simpson, 'Urban Legends in The Pickwick Papers', *The Journal of American Folklore* 96 (1983), 462–470.
44 Gillian Bennett and Paul Smith (eds), *Contemporary Legend: A Reader* (New York, 1996); Thomas Pettitt, Paul Smith, and Jacqueline Simpson, 'Contemporary Legend: The Debate Continues', *Folklore* 106 (1995), 96–100.
45 Graham Shorrocks, 'Chinese Restaurant Stories: International Folklore', *Lore and Language* 2 (1975), 30; Rodney Dale, *The Wordsworth Book of Urban Legend* (Ware, 2005), pp. 174–175.
46 Imke Henkel, *Destructive Storytelling: Disinformation and the Eurosceptic Myth that Shaped Brexit* (Cham, 2021); Owen Davies, 'A Folklorist Looks at Ice Cream Vans', *Folklore* 135 (2014), 14.
47 Jan Harold Brunvand, 'The Vanishing "Urban Legend"', *Midwestern Folklore* 30 (2004), 5–20. Our thanks to Rob Gandy for a copy of this article.
48 Jasper King, 'Mysterious Creature Spotted at UK Zoo and Experts Have No Idea What It Is', *Metro News*, 22 October, 2024, https://metro.co.uk/2024/10/22/mysterious-creature-caught-camera-bristol-zoo-21840300/; Shivali Best, 'Mysterious Four-legged Creature Spotted at Bristol Zoo Leaves Experts Baffled', *Daily Mail Online*, 22 October 2024,

www.dailymail.co.uk/sciencetech/article-13987081/Mysterious-four-legged-creature-Bristol-Zoo.html.
49 Lewis Clarke, 'Mysterious Creature Spotted at Bristol Zoo Leaves Experts Baffled', *Bristol Live*, 21 October 2024, www.bristolpost.co.uk/news/bristol-news/mysterious-creature-spotted-bristol-zoo-9647659.
50 Bernard Heuvelmans, *On the Track of Unknown Animals* (London, 1955 [1958]), p. 5; Peter Dendle, 'Cryptozoology in the Medieval and Modern Worlds', *Folklore* 117 (2006), 192.
51 Carl Wilhelm von Sydow, 'Categories of Prose-Folk Poetry', in Laurits Bodker (ed.), Selected Papers on Folklore (Copenhagen, 1948), pp. 11–43.
52 'Mysterious Creature Spotted at Bristol Zoo Leaves Experts Baffled', *Bristol Live*.
53 www.facebook.com/bristolzooproject
54 Dendle, 'Cryptozoology', 199.
55 Gail-Nina Anderson, 'Bigfoot in Britain', *FLS News* 41 (2003), 14–15.
56 Janet Bord, 'Bigfoot in Britain', *FLS News* 42 (2003), 11.
57 *The Scotsman*, 7 December 2002.
58 Michael Goss, 'Alien Big Cat Sightings in Britain: A Possible Rumour Legend?' *Folklore* 103 (1992), 193.
59 William Cobbett, *Rural Rides* (Edinburgh, c. 1912), p. 265.
60 *Daily Herald*, 19 July 1963; *Hartlepool Northern Daily Mail*, 18 July 1963; BBC Archive 1963: Shooters Hill cheetah, www.bbc.co.uk/videos/c2le24202g20 (accessed 14 March 2025).
61 Goss, 'Alien Big Cat Sightings', p. 189; J. Chandler, 'The Beast of Bodmin', *FLS News* 22 (1995), 9–10; Editorial comment to Chandler, 'The Beast of Bodmin', *FLS News* 22 (1995), 10; Gordon Ridgewell, 'Alien Big Cats', *FLS News* 50 (2006), 16.
62 Goss, 'Alien Big Cat Sightings'.
63 Samantha Hurn, 'Land of Beasts and Dragons: Contemporary Myth-making in Rural Wales', in Samantha Hurn (ed.), *Anthropology and Cryptozoology* (Abingdon, 2016), p. 207.
64 Hurn, 'Land of Beasts'.
65 Bodleian Library MS. Ashmole 1511; Aberdeen University Library, Univ. Lib. MS 24: The Aberdeen Bestiary.
66 Adomnán, *The Book of Saint Columba*, Book 2, Chapter 28, cited in William Reeves, *The Historians of Scotland*, vol. 6 (Edinburgh, 1874), pp. 55–56.
67 *Inverness Courier*, 2 May 1933.
68 *Inverness Courier*, 4 August 1933.
69 Lorna J. Philip, 'Selling the Nation: The Commodification of Monstrous, Mythical and Fantastical Creatures', *Scottish Geographical Journal* (June 2024) 13n.
70 Chris Cairney, 'Other Dragons or Dragon Others? A Cultural View of the Loch Ness Monster', in Lisa Wenger Bro, Crystal O'Leary-Davidson, and Mary Ann Gareis (eds), *Monsters of Film, Fiction, and Fable* (Newcastle-upon-Tyne, 2018), pp. 377–378.
71 Mike Merritt, 'Gary Campbell, the man who logs every credible Loch Ness Monster sighting, celebrates 25 years tracking Nessie's occasional visits to the surface, The Northern Times, 24 May 2021, www.northern-times.co.uk/news/nessie-sighting-archivist-celebrates-a-quarter-of-a-century-239248/
72 www.lochnesssightings.com/index.asp?pageid=717286
73 Philip, 'Selling the Nation', p. 6.

Notes and references

74 Enchantment | Loch Ness, by Jacobite, www.jacobite.co.uk/tours/enchantment (accessed 14 March 2025); Philip, 'Selling the Nation', p. 7.
75 'The Monster 66', *The Official Loch Ness Monster Sightings Register*, www.lochnesssightings.com/index.asp?pageid=618520
76 Philip, 'Selling the Nation', p. 12.
77 Gary Hall, 'The Big Tunnel', in Linda Dégh (ed.), *Indiana Folklore: A Reader* (Bloomington, 1973), pp. 225–257.
78 Mikel J. Koven, 'Most Haunted and the Convergence of Traditional Belief and Popular Television', *Folklore* 118 (2007), 186; McNeill and Tucker, *Legend Tripping*.
79 Linda Dégh and Andrew Vázsonyi, 'Does the Word "Dog" Bite? Ostensive Action: A Means of Legend-Telling', *Journal of Folklore Research* 20 (1983), 7–8; McNeill and Tucker, *Legend Tripping*.
80 Bill Ellis, 'Legend-Tripping in Ohio', *Papers in Comparative Studies* 2 (1982–1983) 61–73; Bill Ellis, *Lucifer Ascending: The Occult in Folklore and Popular Culture* (Lexington, KY, 2004), p. 116.
81 Bill Ellis cites several examples of British legend-tripping in his *Lucifer Ascending*, pp. 116–117.
82 McNeill and Tucker, *Legend Tripping*, p. 5.
83 Robert Chambers, *Traditions of Edinburgh* (London, 1825 [1912]), pp. 224–225.
84 Joy Fraser, 'Never Give Up the Ghost: An Analysis of Three Edinburgh Ghost Tour Companies', thesis, Memorial University of Newfoundland, 2005, p. 180. See also Julian Holloway, 'Legend-tripping in Spooky Spaces: Ghost Tourism and Infrastructures of Enchantment', *Environment and Planning* 28 (2010), 618–637.
85 Kenneth A. Thigpen, 'Adolescent Legends in Brown County: A Survey', *Indiana Folklore* 4 (1971), 205.
86 Fraser, 'Never Give Up the Ghost', 217.
87 Cited in Owen Davies, *The Haunted: A Social History of Ghosts* (London, 2007), p. 63.
88 David Inglis and Mary Holmes, 'Highland and Other Haunts: Ghosts in Scottish Tourism', *Annals of Tourism Research* 30 (2003), 61.
89 Koven, 'Most Haunted'.
90 Yorkshire also lays claim to Robin Hood *of Loxley*. See David Clarke, R. Clayton, D. Eaton, N. Humberstone, and J. Wingate, *Reclaiming Robin Hood: Folklore and South Yorkshire's Infamous Outlaw* (Sheffield, 2001).
91 Roy Jones, 'Authenticity, the Media and Heritage Tourism: Robin Hood and Brother Cadfael as Midlands Tourism Magnets', in Emma Waterton and Steve Watson (eds), *Culture, Heritage and Representation: Perspectives on Visuality and the Past* (Farnham, 2010), p. 152.
92 Washington Irving, *Old Christmas* (New York, 1886), p. 152.

Chapter 5: Folklore and the natural world

1 See Roger Lovegrove, *Silent Fields: The Long Decline of a Nation's Wildlife* (Oxford, 2007); Matthew Cragoe and Briony McDonagh, 'Parliamentary Enclosure, Vermin and the Cultural Life of English Parishes, 1750–1850', *Continuity and Change* 28 (2013), 27–50.
2 Thomas, *Man and the Natural World*, pp. 270–271; Susan Drury, 'Plants and Pest Control in England circa 1400–1700: A Preliminary Study', *Folklore* 103 (1992), 103–106.
3 James Napier, *Folk Lore* (Paisley, 1879), p. 112.

4   C. Jennings, *The Eggs of British Birds* (Bath, 1853), p. 144; Thomas, *Natural World*, p. 74.
5   Jennifer Mori, 'Prognostic Birds and Vulgar Errors: Popular Naturalism in Early Modern England, 1550–1800', in J. A. T. Lancaster and R. Raiswell (eds), *Evidence in the Age of the New Sciences* (Cham, 2018), pp. 269–293.
6   James N. Hogue, 'Folk Beliefs and Superstitions', *Encyclopedia of Insects* (2009), pp. 372–376.
7   W. Walter Gill, *A Second Manx Scrapbook* (London, 1932), p. 287; John S. Udal, 'Dorsetshire Folk-speech and Superstitions Relating to Natural History', *Proceedings of the Dorset Natural History and Antiquarian Field Club* 10 (1889), 34.
8   Udal, *Dorsetshire Folk-Lore*, p. 248.
9   Elias Owen, *Welsh Folk-Lore* (Oswestry, 1896), p. 352.
10 Charlotte Latham (1878) 'West Sussex Superstitions', *The Folk-Lore Record* 1 (1878), 10.
11 Peter Henry Emerson, *Birds, Beasts and Fishes of the Norfolk Broadland* (London, 1895), pp. 162–164.
12 Anne K. Mellor, 'The Baffling Swallow: Gilbert White, Charlotte Smith and the Limits of Natural History', *Nineteenth Century Contexts* 31 (2009), 299–309; I. F. Lyle, 'John Hunter, Gilbert White, and the Migration of Swallows', *Annals of the Royal College of Surgeons in England* 60 (1978), 487–491; Robert Hunt, *Popular Romances of the West of England* (London, 1865), p. 423.
13 N. B. Davies and J. A. Welbergen, 'Cuckoo–Hawk Mimicry? An Experimental Test', *Proceedings of the Royal Society* 275 (2008), 1817–1822.
14 Owen, *Welsh Folk-Lore*, p. 317; Harry Speight, *Chronicles and Stories of Old Bingley* (London, 1898), p. 41.
15 *Bath Chronicle*, 10 September 1863; *Hartland and West Country Chronicle*, 25 July 1933.
16 Francis Grose, *Provincial Glossary* (London, 1787); 'Among the Cider-Makers', *Cornhill Magazine* 13, N.S. (1889), p. 483; Udal, 'Dorsetshire Folk-speech', 35.
17 John M. Wilson, *The Rural Cyclopedia* (Edinburgh, 1847–1849), p. 129.
18 *Kelso Chronicle*, 16 May 1862.
19 *Nottingham Evening Post*, 7 March 1931.
20 Douglas Anderson, 'Noyfull Fowles and Vermyn: Parish Payments for Killing Wildlife in Hampshire 1533–1863', *Proceedings of Hampshire Field Club and Archaeological Society* 60 (2005), 23.
21 J. Van Voorst, *A History of British Quadrupeds, Including the Cetacea* (London, 1874), p. 139; Georgina F. Jackson, *Shropshire Word-Book* (1879), p. 311.
22 Gervase Markham, *Markham's Master-piece: Containing All Knowledge Belonging to the Smith, Farrier, or Horse-leach* (London, 1703), p. 149.
23 Augustus Jessopp, 'Moles', *The Nineteenth Century* 42 (1897), 276; Wayland D. Hand, 'The Mole in Folk Medicine: A Survey from Indic Antiquity to Modern America II', in Hand (ed.), *American Folk Medicine*, pp. 37–48.
24 Ella Mary Leather, *Folk-Lore of Herefordshire* (Hereford, 1912), p. 24.
25 Edward Jesse, *Gleanings in Natural History, with Local Recollections* (London, 1835), p. 219.
26 *Notes & Queries*, 5 June 1852, 534. See also Robert Hawker, 'The First Mole in Cornwall; a Morality from the Stowe of Morwenna, in the Rocky Land', *Notes & Queries*, 7 September (1850), 225.
27 William Delisle Hay, *An Elementary Text-Book of British Fungi* (London, 1887), p. 227.
28 James Britten, *Popular British Fungi* (London, 1878), pp. 4, 19.

29 A. B. Steele, 'Fungus Folk-Lore', *Transactions of the Edinburgh Field Naturalist's and Microscopical Society* 2 (1891), 176–177.
30 M. C. Cooke, *Our Reptiles* (London, 1865), p. 130.
31 Stephen Glover, *The History and Gazetteer of the County of Derby* (Derby, 1831), Vol. 1, p. 153.
32 David Badham, *A Treatise on the Esculent Funguses of England* (London, 1847), p. 37.
33 John Bell, 'Mushrooms', *Journal of the Society of Arts* 29 (1868), 517.
34 William Shakespeare, *Love's Labour's Lost* (London, 1788), p. 102.
35 John Jamieson, *An Etymological Dictionary of the Scottish Language* (Edinburgh, 1808), Vol. 1.
36 Llewellynn Jewitt, 'Notes on the Folk-Lore of Fungi', *The Reliquary* 1 (1860–1861), 117.
37 John Trotter Brockett, *Glossary of North Country Words* (Newcastle, 1846), p. 67.
38 Kelly Brenner, 'Folklore and Nature: Fairy Butter' (2020), www.metrofieldguide.com/folklore-nature-fairy-butter/
39 *Knaresborough Post*, 22 May 1875.
40 Anderson, 'Noyfull Fowles', 220.
41 William Ellis, *The Modern Husbandman* (London, 1750), Vol. 3, p. 107.
42 John Leonard Knapp, *The Journal of a Naturalist* (London, 1829), p. 135.
43 John George Wood, *The Illustrated Natural History* (London, 1865), Vol. 2, p. 448.
44 *Lake's Falmouth Packet*, 19 April 1884.
45 *Bicester Herald*, 27 November 1908.
46 *Derby Daily Telegraph*, 11 September 1922.
47 *Derbyshire Times*, 4 August 1928.
48 Davide Ermacora, 'The Comparative Milk-suckling Reptile', in F. Arena, Y. Foehr-Janssens, I. Papaikonomou, and F. Prescendi (eds), *Allaitement entre humains et animaux: représentations et pratiques de l'Antiquité à aujourd'hui*, Anthropozoologica 52 (2017), 59–81.
49 *Gloucestershire Echo*, 19 August 1910.
50 *West Sussex Gazette*, 4 July 1957.
51 Thomas Elworthy, *The Dialect of West Somerset* (London, 1875), p. 250; William Barnes, *Glossary of the Dorset Dialect* (Dorchester and London, 1886), p. 65; William Carr, *The Dialect of Craven* (London, 1828), p. 9. For its folk names on the Continent see Anita Albus, *On Rare Birds*, trans. Gerald Chapple (London, 2011), pp. 125–151.
52 Henry Innes, *Goldsmith's Natural History* (London, 1853), p. 343.
53 Owen Davies, *Witchcraft, Magic and Culture* (Manchester, 1999), pp. 189–190; Bodil Nildin-Wall and Jan Wall, 'The Witch as Hare or the Witch's Hare: Popular Legends and Beliefs in Nordic Tradition', *Folklore* 104 (1993), pp. 67–76; Thomas Waters, *Cursed Britain* (New Haven, CT, 2019), pp. 80–85.
54 *John O'Groat Journal*, 5 September 1856.
55 John Atkinson, *Forty Years in a Moorland Parish* (London, 1891), p. 89.
56 Michael Sauter, 'Finding "The Babes in the Wood" in the Religious World of English Culture', *Logos* 24 (2021), 27–55.
57 *Westmorland Gazette*, 27 December 1862.
58 Hunt, *Popular Romances* (1865), p. 235.
59 Hutton, *Stations*, pp. 97–99.
60 George Smith, *Six Pastorals* (London, 1770), p. 30.
61 Simon Young, 'The "Black Gentry": The Rookery and the Folklore of Desertion', *Folklore* 134 (2023), 530–555.

Notes and references

62 Edward Lisle, *Observations in Husbandry* (London, 1757), p. 397; Charles Swainson, *Provincial Names and Folk Lore of British Birds* (London, 1885), pp. 87–88.
63 Owen, *Welsh Folk-Lore*, p. 316.
64 Charlotte Burne, *Shropshire Folk-Lore* (London, 1883), p. 218.
65 *Broughty Ferry Guide and Advertiser*, 16 April 1915.
66 Sabine Baring-Gould, *The Vicar of Morwenstow: A Life of Robert Stephen Hawker* (London, 1876), p. 101.
67 *Monmouthshire Merlin*, 8 June 1877; *Newbury Weekly News and General Advertiser*, 11 October 1888.
68 *Wetherby News*, 31 July 1879.
69 *Driffield Times*, 31 August 1895; K. G. Spencer, 'Birds in Lancashire Folk-Lore', *Journal of the Lancashire Dialect Society* 12 (1963), 19.
70 Jacqueline Simpson and Steve Roud, *Oxford Dictionary of English Folklore* (Oxford, 2000), p. 222.
71 *Notes & Queries*, 20 January (1866), 59.
72 *Notes & Queries*, 3 February (1866), 109.
73 *The Scotsman*, 23 September 1925.
74 *Blyth News*, 4 June 1931; *Derbyshire Times*, 3 February 1934.
75 Jackson, *Shropshire Word-Book*, p. 179.
76 Frank Cowan, *Curious Facts in the History of Insects* (Philadelphia, PA, 1865), pp. 17–23.
77 W. W. Spicer, 'Ladybirds', *Hardwicke's Science-Gossip* (London, 1874), p. 131.
78 Forby, *The Vocabulary of East Anglia* (London, 1830), Vol. 1, p. 25.
79 Helen Frisby, '"Them Owls Know": Portending Death in Later Nineteenth- and Early Twentieth-century England', *Folklore* 126 (2015), 201–202.
80 Roud, *Superstitions*, p. 26.
81 Roy Vickery, 'Mother-Die: Plant Names and Folk Beliefs', *Folklore* 130 (2019), 89–96.
82 Roud, *Superstitions*, pp. 144–145.
83 Thomas Browne, *Pseudodoxia epidemica* (London, 1672), p. 109.
84 Latham, 'West Sussex Superstitions', p. 57.
85 *Eastern Evening News*, 2 March 1907.
86 Roud, *Superstitions*, pp. 350–351; Brand, *Observations* (1900), pp. 693–695.
87 Samuel Rowland, *More Knaves Yet* (c. 1613), p. C3r.
88 William Ellis, *Agriculture Improv'd* (London, 1745), p. 100.
89 *Daily Mirror*, 27 April 1944.
90 Roy Vickery, *Garlands, Conkers and Mother-Die: British and Irish Plant-lore* (London, 2010); Vickery, *Dictionary of Plant-lore* (Oxford, 1997); www.plant-lore.com
91 *Lincolnshire Echo*, 9 June 1923.
92 *Sydenham, Forest Hill & Penge Gazette*, 6 June 1874.

Chapter 6: Folk medicine

1 William George Black, 'Folk Medicine', *Journal of the British Archaeological Association* 34 (1878), 327.
2 Cited in Glyn Penrhyn Jones, 'Folk Medicine in Eighteenth-Century Wales', *Folk Life* 7 (1969), 69.
3 Simon Young, 'What's Up Doc? Seventh Sons in Victorian and Edwardian Lancashire', *Folklore* 130 (2019), 395–414.

4 Cecil G. Helman, '"Feed a Cold, Starve a Fever": Folk Models of Infection in an English Suburban Community, and Their Relation to Medical Treatment', *Culture, Medicine and Psychiatry* 2 (1978), 115.
5 John Sinclair (ed.), *The Statistical Account of Scotland* (London, 1792), Vol. 2, p. 496; John Crichton, 'Case of the Leaping Ague of Angus-shire', *Edinburgh Medical and Surgical Journal* 31 (1829), 299–301.
6 John Thomson, *An Account of the Life, Lectures, and Writings of William Cullen* (London, 1859), Vol. 2, p. 707.
7 Owen Davies, 'Hag-riding in Nineteenth-Century West Country England and Modern Newfoundland: An Examination of an Experience-centred Witchcraft Tradition', *Folk Life* 35 (1996), 36–53.
8 John Ewart Simpkins, Robert Craig Maclagan, and David Rorie (eds), *Examples of Printed Folk-lore Concerning Fife with Some Notes on Clackmannan And Kinross-shires* (London, 1914), p. 405; David Buchan (ed.), *Folk Tradition and Folk Medicine in Scotland: The Writings of David Rorie* (Edinburgh, 1994).
9 *St. Andrews Gazette*, 26 February 1876.
10 John Coakley Lettsom, *History of the Origin of Medicine* (London, 1778), p. 150.
11 John C. Knowlson, *The Yorkshire Cattle-Doctor and Farrier*, 2nd edn (London, 1834), pp. 103–104.
12 Edward Peacock, *A Glossary of Words used in the Wapentakes of Manley and Corringham, Lincolnshire* (London, 1889), Vol. 2, p. 548.
13 *Peterborough Advertiser*, 19 March 1902.
14 *Crewe Chronicle*, 9 April 1938.
15 Mark R. Taylor, 'Norfolk Folklore', *Folklore* 40 (1929), 120.
16 *The North Wales Chronicle*, 12 November 1829.
17 *Bucks Gazette*, 29 May 1830; Robert Philip, *The Housewife's Reason Why* (London, 1857), p. 321.
18 *Newmarket Journal*, 20 September 1913.
19 *Staffordshire Advertiser*, 6 December 1919.
20 Gillian Bennett, *Bodies: Sex, Violence, Disease, and Death in Contemporary Legend* (Jackson, MS, 2005), pp. 3–60; Wayland Hand, *Magical Medicine* (Berkeley, CA, 1980), pp. 251–261.
21 Napier, *Folk Lore* (1879), p. 104.
22 *Belfast Weekly News*, 14 September 1889.
23 *Essex Newsman*, 30 April 1904.
24 *Oxford Times*, 20 February 1892.
25 *South Wales Echo*, 13 August 1895.
26 *Nottingham Evening Post*, 7 March 1931; *Ripon Observer*, 7 August 1902.
27 Helman, '"Feed a Cold"', 118–119.
28 Davies, *Troubled by Faith*, pp. 134–135.
29 *The Lancet*, 1 June 1895, 1416.
30 Black, *Folk Medicine*, p. 35.
31 *Northampton Chronicle and Echo*, 4 July 1925.
32 Owen Davies and Francesca Matteoni, '"A Virtue beyond All Medicine": The Hanged Man's Hand, Gallows Tradition and Healing in Eighteenth- and Nineteenth-century England', *Social History of Medicine* 28 (2015), 686–705.
33 Rachael Pymm, 'Snakestone Bead Folklore', *Folklore* 129 (2018), 397–419.
34 Hannah Bower, 'An Overlooked Eighteenth-Century Scrofula Pamphlet: Changing Forms and Changing Readers, 1760–1824', *Science Museum Group Journal* 12 (2019), 191–210.

Notes and references

35 Morley, *An Essay on the Nature and Cure of the King's Evil*, 3rd edn (London, 1766), pp. 15, 16.
36 George Tucker, 'Employment of Sulphur in Rheumatism', *The Lancet*, 7 March (1835), 810–811.
37 Edward Lovett, *Magic of Modern Loncno* (Croydon, 1925), pp. 22–24.
38 *Gentleman's Magazine*, August (1826), 127.
39 Roud, *Superstitions*, p. 243. On the rabbit's foot see Owen Davies, *A Supernatural War* (Oxford, 2018), pp. 145–146.
40 Edward T. Blake, 'The Medical Basis of Charms', *Dublin University Magazine* 90 (1877), 505.
41 *Illustrated Sporting and Dramatic News*, 25 August 1894.
42 Christopher J. Duffin, 'The Mole: An Unusual Item of Materia Medica', *Acta Historiae Medicinae* 41 (2022), 7–23; *Exeter and Plymouth Gazette*, 4 January 1840; W. Hy. Jones, 'Lincolnshire Folk Lore', *Lincolnshire Notes & Queries* 2 (1891), p. 43.
43 Henry Mayew, *London Labour and the London Poor* (London, 1861–1862), Vol. 2, p. 93.
44 John Pechey, *A Plain Introduction to the Art of Physick* (London, 1697), p. 204.
45 William Ellis, *The Country Housewife's Family Companion* (London, 1750), p. 291.
46 *Warwick and Warwickshire Advertiser*, 2 January 1937.
47 F. H. Marsden, 'Some Notes on the Folklore of Upper Calderdale', *Folklore* 43 (1932), 256.
48 Lovett, *Magic*, pp. 81–85.
49 Opie and Tatem, *Dictionary of Superstitions*; Roud, *Superstitions*, p. 43.
50 E. Wright, 'Scraps of English Folklore, XV', *Folklore* 37 (1926), 366.
51 *Daily Mirror*, 11 July 1955.
52 *Civil & Military Gazette* (Lahore), 13 May 1913.
53 *The People*, 10 September 1961.
54 *Wolverton Express*, 30 June 1961.
55 *Liverpool Daily Post*, 8 March 1978.
56 Richard Blakeborough, *Wit, Character, Folklore and Customs of the North Riding of Yorkshire* (Saltburn, 1911), p. 138; William Henderson, *Notes on the Folk Lore of the Northern Counties of England and the Borders* (London, 1879), p. 155.
57 William Ellis, *The Country Gentleman* (Dublin, 1780), p. 350; Blakeborough, *North Riding of Yorkshire*, p. 145.
58 Simpkins, Maclagan, and Rorie, *Fife*, p. 411.
59 Gideon Harvey, *The Family-Physician, and the House-Apothecary* (London, 1678), pp. 29–30; Sarah Harrison's *The House-keeper's Pocket-book* (London, 1755), p. 10.
60 *Henley Advertiser*, 20 June 1874; M. E. White, 'Faith in Snails as Curative Agents', *Folklore* 72 (1961), 353–354.
61 John R. Wise, *The New Forest: Its History and its Scenery* (London, [1863] 1880), p. 176.
62 Gabrielle Hatfield, *Warts: Summary of Wart-cure Survey for the Folklore Society* (London, 1998).
63 See David Elliston Allen and Gabrielle Hatfield, *Medicinal Plants in Folk Tradition: An Ethnobotany of Britain and Ireland* (Portland, 2004); Roy Vickery, *Vickery's Folk Flora* (London, 2019).
64 M. J. Berkeley, *Outlines of British Fungology* (London, 1860), p. 66.
65 John Hill, *The Family Herbal, or, An Account of all those English Plants, which Are Remarkable for Their Virtues* (Bungay, 1812), p. 181.
66 *Runcorn Guardian*, 2 April 1902.

Notes and references

67 Simpkins, Maclagan, and Rorie, *Fife*, p. 409.
68 *Exeter and Plymouth Gazette*, 11 February 1902.
69 *Birmingham Daily Gazette*, 4 January 1939; *Holloway Press*, 15 July 1949.
70 See Davies, *Troubled by Faith*.
71 Richard Mabey, *Flora Britannica* (London, 1996), p. 380; Roy Vickery, www.plant-lore.com
72 Nina Nissen, 'Practitioners of Western Herbal Medicine and Their Practice in the UK: Beginning to Sketch the Profession', *Complementary Therapies in Clinical Practice* 16 (2010), 181–186; Ayo Wahlberg, 'Rescuing Folk Remedies: Ethnoknowledge and the Reinvention of Indigenous Herbal Medicine in Britain', in Ronnie Moore and Stuart McClean (eds), *Folk Healing and Health Care Practices in Britain and Ireland* (New York, 2010), pp. 130–156.
73 Rumana Zahna et al., 'Use of Herbal Medicines: Pilot Survey of UK Users' Views', *Complementary Therapies in Medicine* 44 (2019), 83–90.
74 Geraldine Lee-Treweek, 'Born to It and then Pushed Out of It: Folk Healing in the New Complementary and Alternative Medicine Marketplace', in Moore and McClean (eds), *Folk Healing*, pp. 201–226; Katherine Hunt and Edzard Ernst, 'Patients' use of CAM: Results from the Health Survey for England 2005', *Focus on Alternative and Complementary Therapies* 15 (2010), 101–103.
75 Suzanne Newcombe, 'Ayurvedic Medicine in Britain and the Epistemology of Practicing Medicine in "Good Faith"', in Dagmar Wujastyk and Frederick M. Smith (eds), *Modern and Global Ayurveda: Pluralism and Paradigms* (Albany, NY, 2008), pp. 257–285.
76 Gill Green et al., '"We Are Not completely Westernised": Dual Medical Systems and Pathways to Health Care among Chinese Migrant Women in England', *Social Science & Medicine* 62 (2006), 1498–1509.

Chapter 7: Living in a supernatural world

1 Odic or Od power was a variation on the idea of a life force, which only a few sensitive people could see. The term was coined in 1845 by Carl von Reichenbach.
2 See, for example, Richard Noakes, 'Spiritualism, Science and the Supernatural in mid-Victorian Britain', in Nicola Bown, Carolyn Burdett, and Pamela Thurschwell (eds), *The Victorian Supernatural* (Cambridge, 2004), pp. 23–44.
3 Kristof Smeyers, 'Supernaturals: Qualifying the Supernatural', *Magic, Ritual, and Witchcraft* 16 (2021), 386.
4 Marjaana Lindeman and Annika M. Svedholm, 'What's in a Term? Paranormal, Superstitious, Magical and Supernatural: Beliefs by Any other Name Would Mean the Same', *Review of General Psychology* 16 (2012), 241–255.
5 Leigh T. I. Penman, 'The History of the Word "Paranormal"', *Notes & Queries* 62 (2015), 33; Olu Jenzen and Sally R. Munt (eds), *The Ashgate Research Companion to Paranormal Cultures* (Aldershot, 2013). Quote from Bill Ellis, *Aliens, Ghosts, and Cults: Legends We Live* (Jackson, MS, 2003), p. 157. See also Bob Trubshaw, *Creating the Paranormal* (Orston, [2012] 2023).
6 Margaret Bennett, 'Stories of the Supernatural: From Local Memorate to Scottish Legend', in Lizanne Henderson (ed.), *Fantastical Imaginations: The Supernatural in Scottish History and Culture* (Edinburgh, 2009), pp. 167–184.
7 For example, Jason Semmens, *The Witch of the West: Or, the Strange and Wonderful History of Thomasine Blight* (Privately published, 2004); Edmund Standing, 'The Life and

Crimes of James Tuckett', https://edmundstanding.wordpress.com/jamestuckett/; Owen Davies, *A People Bewitched: Witchcraft and Magic in Nineteenth-century Somerset* (Bruton, 1999).

8 Ronald Hutton, *The Witch* (New Haven, CT, 2018), p. xi; Tabitha Stanmore, *Love Spells and Lost Treasure* (Cambridge, 2022).

9 Owen Davies, *Cunning-Folk: Popular Magic in English History* (London, 2003); Tabitha Stanmore, *Cunning Folk: Life in the Era of Practical Magic* (London, 2024); Waters, *Cursed Britain*.

10 Stephanie Elizabeth Churms, *Romanticism and Popular Magic: Poetry and Cultures of the Occult in the 1790s* (London, 2019); Ronald Hutton, 'Witches and Cunning Folk in British Literature 1800–1940', *Preternature* 7 (2018), 27–49.

11 Dirk Johannsen, 'The Prophet and the Sorcerer: Becoming a Cunning-Man in Nineteenth-century Norway', *Folklore* 129 (2018), 39–57; Timothy Tangherlini, '"How Do You Know She's a Witch?": Witches, Cunning Folk, and Competition in Denmark', *Western Folklore* 59 (2000), 289–290.

12 Leather, *Folk-Lore of Herefordshire*, p. 59.

13 Lisa Tallis, 'The "Doctor Faustus" of Cwrt-y-Cadno: A New Perspective on John Harries and Popular Medicine in Wales', *Welsh History Review* 24 (2009), 1–28; Richard C. Allen, 'Wizards or Charlatans – Doctors or Herbalists? An Appraisal of the "Cunning Men" of Cwrt y Cadno, Carmarthenshire', *The North American Journal of Welsh Studies* 1 (2001), 68–85.

14 Davies, *Folk-Lore of West and Mid-Wales*, pp. 263, 255; Marie Trevelyan, *Folk-Lore and Folk-Stories of Wales* (London, 1909), pp. 217–218.

15 Blakeborough, *Yorkshire Wit*, p. 187; Atkinson, *Forty Years*, p. 110; Waters, *Cursed Britain*, pp. 24–25.

16 Atkinson, *Forty Years*, p. 119.

17 Davies, *A People Bewitched*.

18 James Sharpe, *Witchcraft in Early Modern England* (London, 2001), p. 26; Davies, *Witchcraft, Magic and Culture*, p. 193; Davies, *People Bewitched*, p. 116; Waters, *Cursed Britain*, p. 99.

19 See Hutton, *The Witch*, pp. 244–252; Ronald Hutton, 'Witch-Hunting in Celtic Societies', *Past & Present* 212 (2011), 43–71; Andrew Sneddon, *Witchcraft and Magic in Ireland* (London, 2015), pp. 53–56.

20 *Transactions of the Devonshire Association* lxvii (1935), 136–137; Davies, *A People Bewitched*, p. 149.

21 Owen Davies, 'The Witch of Endor in History and Folklore', *Folklore* 134 (2023), 1–22.

22 See, Mirjam Mencej, *Styrian Witches in European Perspective: Ethnographic Fieldwork* (London, 2017), pp. 313–322, 347; Willem de Blécourt, 'The Witch, her Victim, the Unwitcher and the Researcher: The Continued Existence of Traditional Witchcraft', in Willem de Blécourt, Ronald Hutton, and Jean La Fontaine (eds), *Witchcraft and Magic in Europe: The Twentieth Century* (London, 1999), 141–220.

23 Davies, *Witchcraft, Magic and Culture*, p. 170.

24 Amy Boucher, 'Reclaiming Nanny Morgan', https://nearlyknowledgeablehistory.blogspot.com/2022/08/nanny-morgan-and-shropshire-witch.html; Burne, *Shropshire Folk-Lore*, p. 160.

25 Atkinson, *Forty Years*, p. 81.

26 Davies, *Witchcraft, Magic and Culture*, pp. 189–191; Paweł Rutkowski, 'Animal Transformation in Early Modern English Witchcraft Pamphlets', *Anglica* 28 (2019), 21–34.

27 William Ross, *Aberdour and Inchcolme* (Edinburgh, 1885), p. 327.

28 Edward Hamer, 'Parochial Account of Llandloes', *Montgomeryshire Collections* 10 (1877), 243–244.
29 Owen, *Welsh Folk-Lore*, p. 236.
30 MacDonald, 'Migratory Legends of the Supernatural', 37.
31 Davies, *Witchcraft, Magic and Culture*, p. 188.
32 Sarah Bartels, *The Devil and the Victorians: Supernatural Evil in Nineteenth-Century English Culture* (New York, 2021); Jeremy Harte, *Cloven Country: The Devil and the English Landscape* (London, 2022); Karl Bell, 'Humanising the Devil, 1850–2000', in Michelle Brock, Richard Raiswell, and David Winter (eds), *The Routledge History of the Devil in the Western Tradition* (London, 2025).
33 See, for example, Leather, *Folk-Lore of Herefordshire*, p. 40.
34 Ülo Valk, *The Black Gentleman* (Helsinki, 2001); Darren Oldridge, *The Devil in Early Modern England* (Stroud, 2000), pp. 59–61; Davies, *Troubled by Faith*, p. 209. See also, Bob Trubshaw (ed.), *Explore Phantom Black Dogs* (Loughborough, 2005); Mark Norman, *Black Dog Folklore* (London, 2015).
35 J. A. Penny, *More Folklore Round Horncastle* (Horncastle, 1922), pp. 64–65; James Obelkevitch, *Religion and Rural Society* (Oxford, 1976), pp. 277–278.
36 Owen, *Welsh Folk-Lore*, pp. 147–150; Harte, *Cloven Country*, pp. 215–219; Katharine Briggs, *A Dictionary of British Folk-Tales in the English Language* (London, 1970–1971).
37 *Merry Drollery Compleat* (London, 1691), pp. 17–21.
38 Ian Spring, 'The Devil and the Feathery Wife', *Folklore* 99 (1988), 139–145.
39 Wirt Sikes, *British Goblins*, pp. 207–208.
40 Adam N. Coward, 'Edmund Jones and the Pwcca'r Trwyn', *Folklore* 126 (2015), 177–295.
41 Edmund Jones, *Relation of Apparitions of Spirits in the Principality of Wales* (1780), p. 71, Preface, p. 29.
42 Davies, *Troubled by Faith*, p. 204.
43 Davies, *Supernatural War*, p. 60; David Clarke, *The Angel of Mons: Phantom Soldiers and Ghostly Guardians* (Chichester, 2004).
44 Theo Brown, *The Fate of the Dead* (Ipswich, 1979), p. 1.
45 Gillian Bennett, *Alas, Poor Ghost! Traditions of Belief in Story and Discourse* (Logan, 1999); Paul Cowdell, 'Belief in Ghosts in Post-war England', PhD thesis, University of Hertfordshire, 2011. Martha McGill, *Ghosts in Enlightenment Scotland* (Martlesham, 2018); Davies, *The Haunted*; Sasha Handley, *Visions of an Unseen World: Ghost Beliefs and Ghost Stories in Eighteenth Century England* (London, 2007); Delyth Badder and Mark Norman, *The Folklore of Wales: Ghosts* (Cardiff, 2023).
46 Davies, *The Haunted*, p. 76; Brendan C. Walsh, '"He Could Raise and Lay Ghosts at His Will": Victorian Folklorists and the Creation of Early Modern Clerical Ghost-laying', *Folklore* 134 (2023), 281–303.
47 A. L. Clark, 'Some Wiltshire Folk-Lore', *Wiltshire Notes and Queries* 1 (1896), 59.
48 Burne, *Shropshire Folk-Lore*, p. 138.
49 J. Noake, 'Superstitions of Worcestershire', *Gentleman's Magazine* July (1855), 58.
50 *The Star*, 16 January 1894.
51 See Katharine Briggs, *A Dictionary of Fairies* (London, 1976); Lizanne Henderson and Edward J. Cowan, *Scottish Fairy Belief* (East Linton, 2001); Jeremy Harte, *Explore Fairy Traditions* (Loughborough, 2004); Simon Young and Ceri Houlbrook (eds), *Magical Folk: British and Irish Fairies, 500 AD to the Present* (London, 2018); Julian Goodare, 'The Cult of the Seely Wights in Scotland', *Folklore* 123 (2012), 198–219.

52 Henderson and Cowan, *Scottish Fairy Belief*, pp. 46–47.
53 Simon Young, 'Public Bogies and Supernatural Landscapes in North-Western England in the 1800s', *Time and Mind* 13 (2020), 399–424.
54 Simon Young and Davide Ermacora, 'Introducing the Social Supernatural', in Simon Young and Davide Ermacora (eds), *The Exeter Companion to Fairies, Nereids, Trolls and other Social Supernatural Beings: European Traditions* (Exeter, 2024), pp. 1–11.
55 Francis Young, *Twilight of the Godlings: The Shadowy Beginnings of Britain's Supernatural Beings* (Cambridge, 2023), pp. 250–305; Ronald Hutton, 'The Making of the Early Modern British Fairy Tradition', *Historical Journal* 57 (2014), 1157–1175; Richard Sugg, *Fairies: A Dangerous History* (London, 2018); Diane Purkiss, *Troublesome Things* (London, 2000); Henderson and Cowan, *Scottish Fairy Belief*.
56 Hutton, *The Witch*; Henderson and Cowan, *Scottish Fairy Belief*; Julian Goodare, 'Boundaries of the Fairy Realm in Scotland', in Karen E. Olsen and Jan Veenstra (eds), *Airy Nothings*, pp. 139–169 (Leiden, 2014); Emma Wilby, *Cunning Folk and Familiar Spirits* (Brighton, 2005).
57 Henderson and Cowan, *Scottish Fairy Belief*, pp. 172–176.
58 Robert Kirk, *The Secret Commonwealth*, ed. Andrew Lang (London, 1893), pp. 7, 11, 12.
59 See Karl Bell, *The Magical Imagination: Magic and Modernity in Urban England, 1780–1914* (Cambridge, 2012).
60 James, *Folklore of Cornwall*, pp. 136–147.
61 *A Selection of Curious Articles from the Gentleman's Magazine* (London, 1811), Vol. 3, pp. 216–217.
62 Owen, *Welsh Folk-Lore*, pp. 115, 120; *Wrexham and Denbighshire Advertiser*, 16 April 1890.
63 James M. Mackinlay, *Folklore of Scottish Lochs and Springs* (Glasgow, 1893), p. 180.
64 Roy Vickery, 'Lemna Minor and Jenny Greenteeth', *Folklore* 94 (1983), 247–250.
65 Davies, *Folk-Lore of West and Mid-Wales*, p. 148; Davies, *Troubled by Faith*, pp. 241–245.
66 Margaret Bennett, 'Balquhidder Revisited: Fairylore in the Scottish Highlands, 1690–1990', in Peter Narváez (ed.), *The Good People* (New York, 1991), pp. 94–116.
67 Janet Bord, *Fairies: Real Encounters with Little People* (London, 1997); Andy Letcher, 'The Scouring of the Shires: Fairies, Trolls and Pixies in Eco-Protest Culture', *Folklore* 112 (2001), 147–161; Simon Young, *Fairy Census 2* (2023), pp. 17–113.
68 David Clarke and Andy Roberts, *Flying Saucerers: A Social History of UFOlogy* (Loughborough, 2007).
69 Jacques Vallée, *Passport to Magonia, From Folklore to Flying Saucers* (Brisbane, [1969] 2014), p. 8.
70 See Thomas E. Bullard, 'UFO Abduction Reports: The Supernatural Narrative Returns in Technological Guise', *Journal of American Folklore* 102 (1989), 47–170; Thomas E. Bullard, *The Myth and Mystery of UFOs* (Lawrence, KS, 2010); Peter M. Rojcewicz, 'Between One Eye Blink and the Next: Fairies, UFOs, and Problems of Knowledge', in Narváez (ed.), *The Good People*, pp. 479–514.
71 Linda Dégh, 'UFOs and How Folklorists Should Look at Them', *Fabula* 18 (1977), 242–248; Ellis, *Aliens, Ghosts*, pp. 142–161; William J. Dewan, '"A Saucerful of Secrets": An Interdisciplinary Analysis of UFO Experiences', *Journal of American Folklore* 119 (2006), 184–202; Erik A. W. Östling, '"I Figured that in My Dreams, I Remembered What Actually Happened": On Abduction Narratives as Emergent Folklore', in Benjamin E. Zeller (ed.), *Handbook of UFO Religions* (Leiden, 2021), pp. 197–232.
72 Dégh, 'UFOS', 243.

73 David Clarke, 'Extraordinary Experiences with UFOs', in Jenzen and Munt (eds), *The Ashgate Research Companion*, pp. 79–93; David Clarke, *Britain's X-Traordinary Files* (London, 2014).
74 Robin Gwyndaf, 'The Past in the Present: Folk Beliefs in Welsh Oral Tradition', *Fabula* 35 (1994), 240.
75 Rob Irving, 'Legend Landscapes: Sacred Mobilities in the "Legend Trip" Tradition', in Avril Maddrell, Alan Terry, and Tim Gale (eds), *Sacred Mobilities: Journeys of Belief and Belonging* (London, 2016), pp. 95–115; Theo Meder, 'Crop Circle Tales: Narrative Testimonies from the Dutch Frontier Science Movement', in P. Margry and H. Roodenburg (eds), *Reframing Dutch Culture. Between Otherness and Authenticity* (Aldershot, 2007), pp. 135–157.
76 See Barbara Walker, 'Introduction', in Barbara Walker (ed.), *Folklore and the Supernatural* (Logan, 1995), p. 7.

Chapter 8: Ritual in the landscape

1 https://nrfa.ceh.ac.uk/uk-river-flow-regimes; www.ons.gov.uk/economy/environmentalaccounts/bulletins/uknaturalcapitalforpeatlands/naturalcapitalaccounts
2 Mayhew, *London Labour*, p. 155.
3 www.nationaltrustcollections.org.uk/object/1140390; Thomas Ackroyd, *Thames: Sacred River* (London, 2008), p. 87.
4 Lara Maiklem, *Mudlarking: Lost and Found on the River Thames* (London, 2020), p. 154; Jennifer Lee, 'Medieval Pilgrims' Badges in Rivers: The Curious History of a Non-theory', *Journal of Art Historiography* 11 (December 2014) 1–11.
5 Maiklem, *Mudlarking*, p. 157.
6 www.museumoflondon.org.uk/discover/sorcery-display-witch-bottles
7 Joseph Glanvill, *Saducismus Triumphatus, or, a Full and Plain Evidence Concerning Witches and Apparitions* (London, 1681), p. 206.
8 Museum of London, 18013.
9 Lucy Hornberger, '"The Thames is the New Ganges": Visarjan Immersion Rituals, the Adoption and Sanctification of Britain's Rivers, and Issues of Identity and Belonging among British Hindus' (unpublished research).
10 www.baps.org/News/2017/HH-Pramukh-Swami-Maharajs-Asthipushpa-Visarjan-11648.aspx
11 *The Telegraph*, 10 October 2004; *Hindustan Times*, 4 February 2014.
12 Vicky Munro, 'Hindu god Ganesh paraded through Hounslow streets and immersed in the Thames for festival', *MyLondon*, 21 September 2018, www.mylondon.news/news/west-london-news/hindu-god-ganesh-paraded-through-15180184; 'Thames Immersion for Hindu Idols, *BBC News*, 2 October 2006, http://news.bbc.co.uk/1/hi/england/london/5401122.stm; BBC NEWS | England | Merseyside | 'River marks religious ceremony', BBC News at Ten, 14 September 2008, http://news.bbc.co.uk/1/hi/england/merseyside/7615595.stm; *Berkshire Live*, 9 September 2022.
13 Maiklem, *Mudlarking*, p. 158.
14 Kate Sumnall and Thomas Ardill, 'Mudlarks: Rescuing Relics from the River Thames', Museum of London, 17 September 2019, www.londonmuseum.org.uk/blog/mudlarks-rescuing-relics-from-the-river-thames/; www.londonmuseum.org.uk/collections/about/what-we-collect/archaeological-collections/ (accessed 14 March 2025); Museum of London, 2004.73/10.

15 Record ID: LIN-E7E358 – MODERN votive model (finds.org.uk); Record ID: LIN-A784E5 – MODERN votive model (finds.org.uk). See also Record ID: LIN-E884E8 – MODERN bowl (finds.org.uk); Sumnall and Ardill, 'Mudlarks'.
16 James Thurgill, 'Enchanted Geographies: Experiences of Place in Contemporary British Landscape Mysticism', PhD thesis, Royal Holloway, University of London, 2014, pp. 181–182; Ethan Doyle White, 'Around the Witches' Circle: Exploring Wicca's Usage of Archaeological Sites', in Jutta Leskovar and Raimund Karl (eds), *Archaeological Sites as Space for Modern Spiritual Practice* (Newcastle upon Tyne, 2018), p. 182.
17 See Claire Slack, 'Sharing Sacred Spaces: Exploring British Pagan Sacred Sites as Space of Contemporary Ritual and Belief', PhD thesis, University of Hertfordshire, forthcoming.
18 Debora Moretti and Sheriden Toso, 'Ritual Litter: Pagan Votive Offerings at Historic and Nature Sites in the UK', in Genevieve Godin, Þóra Pétursdóttir, Estelle Praet, and John Schofield (eds), *The Routledge Handbook of Archaeology and Plastics* (London, 2024), pp. 405–421; Jenny Blain and Robert J. Wallis, *Sacred Sites, Contested Rites/Rights* (Brighton, 2007), p. 140; Jutta Leskovar, 'Neo-Paganism and Sacred Places: A Survey in Austria and Beyond', in Leskovar and Karl, *Archaeological Sites*, p.134; Ethan Doyle White, 'Old Stones, New Rites: Contemporary Interactions with the Medway Megaliths', *Material Religion* 12 (2016), 362.
19 Kathryn Rountree, 'Performing the Divine: Neo-Pagan Pilgrimages and Embodiment at Sacred Sites', *Body & Society* 12 (2006), 100.
20 www.cbcew.org.uk/short-plenary-resolutions-autumn-2023/
21 Carolus de Smedt, 'Documenta de S. Wenefreda', *Analecta Bollandiana* 6 (1887), 307–308; Colleen M. Seguin, 'Cures and Controversy in Early Modern Wales: The Struggle to Control St. Winifred's Well', *North American Journal of Welsh Studies* 3 (2003), 1–17.
22 BL, MS Cotton Vitellius C. I, fols 81v–82r. Cited in Seguin, 'Cures and Controversy', p. 9; David Thomas, 'Saint Winifred's Well and Chapel, Holywell', *Journal of the Historical Society of the Church in Wales* 8 (1958), 15–31.
23 de Smedt, 'Documenta', 318, 325, 310.
24 de Smedt, 'Documenta', 329, 351.
25 Janet Bord, 'St Winefride's Well, Holywell, Clwyd', *Folklore* 105 (1994), 99.
26 Bord, 'St Winefride's Well', pp. 99–100.
27 de Smedt, 'Documenta', 329–330, 341–342, 348.
28 Joseph Addison, 'The Adventures of a Shilling', in John Richard Green (ed.), *Essays of Joseph Addison* (London, 1710), p. 323.
29 Robert Charles Hope, *The Legends and Lore of Holy Wells in England; Including Rivers, Lakes, Fountains and Springs* (London, 1893), p. 14.
30 Edwin Sidney Hartland, 'Pin-Wells and Rag-Bushes', *Folklore* 4(4) (1893), 451–470, at p. 460.
31 A. T. Lucas, 'Sacred Trees of Ireland', *Journal of the Cork Historical and Archaeological Society* 68 (1963), 16–54, at p. 40.
32 Hartland, 'Pin-Wells', p. 463.
33 Thomas Pennant, *A Tour in Scotland and Voyage to the Hebrides* (Dublin, 1775), p. 330.
34 Ceri Houlbrook, *The Magic of Coin-trees from Religion to Recreation* (London, 2018).
35 David Duff (ed.) *Victoria in the Highlands: The Personal Journal of Her Majesty Queen Victoria* (London, 1968), pp. 332–333.
36 Houlbrook, *Magic of Coin-trees*.
37 *Shields Daily Gazette*, 5 January 1955.

38 *Dundee Courier*, 29 December 1954; *Lincolnshire Standard and Boston Guardian*, 16 April 1955.
39 *Kinematograph Weekly*, 13 January 1955; 23 September 1954; 2 December 1954.
40 *Lincolnshire Standard and Boston Guardian*, 16 April 1955; *Shields Daily Gazette*, 29 December 1954; *Kinematograph Weekly*, 2 December 1954.
41 *Kinematograph Weekly*, 13 January 1955.
42 *Kinematograph Weekly*, 13 January 1955; *Weekly Dispatch (London)*, 25 August 1957.
43 *Winsford Chronicle*, 1 September 1962.
44 *Kensington Post*, 26 October 1956.
45 *Belfast News-Letter*, 19 December 1962; *Birmingham Daily Post*, 21 May 1963; *Biggleswade Chronicle*, 21 December 1962.
46 https://youtu.be/7UfiCa244XE
47 www.dailymail.co.uk/news/article-11217801/Moment-Princess-Wales-takes-little-girl-lay-corgi-teddy-flower-tribute.html
48 www.dailyrecord.co.uk/news/uk-world-news/sweet-sketch-queen-paddington-bear-27162968
49 Sylvia Grider, 'Spontaneous Shrines: A Modern Response to Tragedy and Disaster', *New Directions in Folklore* 5 (2001), 2.
50 www.iwm.org.uk/memorials; Jane Furlong, Lorraine Knight and Simon Slocombe, '"They Shall Grow Not Old": An Analysis of Trends in Memorialisation Based on Information Held by the UK National Inventory of War Memorials', *Cultural Trends* 12 (2002), 9.
51 Furlong et al., '"They Shall Grow Not Old"', 32.
52 *Hartlepool Northern Daily Mail*, 24 August 1921.
53 *Eastbourne Chronicle*, 17 November 1928.
54 www.britishlegion.org.uk/evolution-of-the-poppy
55 *Eastbourne Chronicle*, 17 November 1928.
56 Caroline Winter, 'Pilgrims and Votives at War Memorials: A Vow to Remember', *Annals of Tourism Research Volume* 76 (2019), 117–128.
57 Note Jack Santino's dismissal of the term 'makeshift memorial' as 'condescending and inaccurate': Jack Santino, 'Performative Commemoratives, the Personal, and the Public: Spontaneous Shrines, Emergent Ritual, and the Field of Folklore', *Journal of American Folklore* 117 (2004), 369.
58 Jennifer Clark and Majella Franzmann, 'Authority from Grief, Presence and Place in the Making of Roadside Memorials', *Death Studies* 30 (2006), 580; Helen Frisby, *Traditions of Death and Burial* (Oxford, 2019), p. 84.
59 Paul Graves-Brown and Hilary Orange, '"The Stars Look Very Different Today": Celebrity Veneration, Grassroot Memorials and the Apotheosis of David Bowie', *Material Religion* 13 (2017), 121–122; Hilary Orange and Paul Graves-Brown, '"My Death Waits There among the Flowers": Popular Music Shrines in London as Memory and Remembrance', in Sarah De Nardi, Hilary Orange, Steven High, and Eerika Koskinen-Koivisto (eds), *The Routledge Handbook of Memory and Place* (Abingdon, 2019), p. 352; www.northumberlandgazette.co.uk/sport/football/tributes-after-ashington-born-england-and-man-utd-legend-sir-bobby-charlton-dies-aged-86-4382302
60 Melissa Beattie, 'A Most Peculiar Memorial: Cultural Heritage and Fiction', in John Schofield (ed.), *Who Needs Experts? Counter-mapping Cultural Heritage* (Farnham, 2014), pp. 215–224.

61 Greenhalgh, S. 'Our Lady of Flowers: The Ambiguous Politics of Diana's Floral Revolution', in A. Kear and D. L. Steinberg (eds), (1999) *Mourning Diana: Nation, Culture and the Performance of Grief* (London, 1999), pp. 40–59; George Monger and Jennifer Chandler, 'Pilgrimage to Kensington Palace', *Folklore* 109 (1998), 107.
62 www.bbc.co.uk/news/uk-england-manchester-67742568; www.thenationalnews.com/arts-culture/art-design/2024/05/02/gaza-murals/
63 Ceri Houlbrook, *Unlocking the Love-Lock: The History and Heritage of a Contemporary Custom* (Oxford, 2021).
64 www.chroniclelive.co.uk/news/north-east-news/womans-heartache-after-love-lock-16051715; www.chroniclelive.co.uk/news/north-east-news/love-locks-removed-high-level-16042122

Chapter 9: Childlore

1 www.theguardian.com/commentisfree/2024/feb/14/brexit-tackle-politics-children-football
2 Nicholas Orme, 'The Culture of Children in Medieval England', *Past & Present* 148 (1995), 48–88, at 63–64; Richard Carew, *The Survey of Cornwall* (London, 1602 [1769]), p. 125.
3 *London Daily Chronicle*, 28 March 1924; *Worthing Gazette*, 10 November 1943.
4 *Yorkshire Evening Post*, 21 April 1913.
5 Julia Bishop, '"Tag, You've Got Coronavirus!" Chase Games in a Covid Frame', in Anna Beresin and Julia Bishops (eds), *Play in a Covid Frame: Everyday Pandemic Creativity in a Time of Isolation* (London, 2023), pp. 3–32.
6 Georgina Boyes, 'Alice Bertha Gomme (1852–1938): A Reassessment of the Work of a Folklorist', *Folklore* 101 (1990), 199, 203; Edward W. B. Nicholson, *Golspie: Contributions to Its Folklore* (London, 1897).
7 Iona Opie and Peter Opie, *The Lore and Language of Schoolchildren* (Oxford, 1959 [1987]); Julia C. Bishop, 'From "Breathless Catalogue" to "Beyond Text": A Hundred Years of Children's Folklore Collecting', *Folklore* 127 (2016), 134.
8 Boyes, 'Alice Bertha Gomme', 203.
9 Mark Holloway, *Norman Douglas: A Biography* (London, 1976), p. 225; Bishop, 'From "Breathless Catalogue"', 125.
10 https://movingimage.nls.uk/film/0799
11 https://boltonworktown.co.uk/photograph/boys-peing-on-wasteland; Mathew Thomson, *Lost Freedom: The Landscape of the Child and the British Post-war Settlement* (Oxford, 2013), p. 32.
12 Gary Cross, 'Play, Games, and Toys', in Paula Fass (ed.), *The Routledge History of Childhood in the Western World* (Abingdon, 2012), pp. 267–282, at p. 269.
13 Simon Bronner, 'Material Folk Culture of children', in B. Sutton-Smith, J. Mechling, T. W. Johnson, and F. R. McMahon (eds), *Children's Folklore: A Source Book* (Logan, 1999), pp. 251–271.
14 Personal communication from Lyn Stevens, curator, Museum of Childhood, Edinburgh, 15 February 2024. See also Steve Roud, *The Lore of the Playground: One Hundred Years of Children's Games, Rhymes and Traditions* (London, 2010), p. xii.
15 http://irisharchaeology.ie/2013/02/a-hoard-of-16th-and-17th-century-childrens-toys/; www.harboroughmuseum.org.uk/displays/growing-up/#highlight-modal

16 Orme, 'Culture of Children'.
17 Sidney Painter, *William Marshal, Knight-Errant, Baron, and Regent of England* (Toronto, 1982), p. 15.
18 *Daily News*, 3 June 1915; *West London Observer*, 27 September 1940; *Birmingham Daily Post*, 7 April 1970; *Sheerness Guardian*, 4 March 1939; *Daily Mirror*, 26 March 1953.
19 www.capitalcollections.org.uk/view-item?i=17236&fullPage=1&WINID=1733392792913; www.capitalcollections.org.uk/view-item?i=17233&fullPage=1&WINID=1733392815921
20 Cited in *Durham County Advertiser*, 9 May 1884.
21 M. Tindal, 'Gutter Games', *Pearson's Magazine*, September 1904, cited in *Dublin Evening Telegraph*, 5 September 1904.
22 Cf. *Yorkshire Post*, 9 January 1932; *Hendon Times*, 23 March 1934.
23 *Kenilworth Advertiser*, 12 May 1923; *Belfast Telegraph*, 2 January 1937; *Walsall Observer*, 24 June 1933; *Liverpool Echo*, 18 January 1969.
24 Roud, *Lore of the Playground*, p. 394.
25 Iona Opie and Peter Opie, *Children's Games in Street and Playground* (Oxford, 1969), p. 226.
26 Roald Dahl, *My Year* (London, 1993), pp. 45–46.
27 Edmund Routledge, *Every Boy's Book: A Complete Encyclopædia of Sports and Amusements*, (London, 1856 [1869]).
28 R. Tucker, 'The Game of Conquerors', *The Athenaeum*, 28 January 1899, 113; Charles Higham, 'The Game of Conquerors', *The Athenaeum*, 21 January 1899, 83.
29 *Bedfordshire Times*, 13 September 1957; *Cheltenham Chronicle*, 23 September 1944.
30 *Manchester Evening News*, 12 May 1936; *Scunthorpe Evening Telegraph*, 3 October 1984; *Maidstone Telegraph*, 16 October 1987; *Manchester Evening News*, 25 October 1997; *Shropshire Star*, 9 October 1993; *Wolverhampton Express and Star*, 11 October 1995; *Northampton Chronicle*, 12 December 2000.
31 Opie and Opie, *Children's Games*, p. 230.
32 *Scunthorpe Evening Telegraph*, 3 October 1984.
33 www.worldconkerchampionships.com/rules.php
34 www.theguardian.com/commentisfree/2013/oct/21/conkers-cracked-headmaster-playground-nostalgia
35 George Monger, 'The Seamier Side of Childlore', *FLS Children's Folklore Newsletter* 3 (1989), 1–7, at 5.
36 Bishop, '"Tag, You've Got Coronavirus!"', p. 21.
37 Monger, 'The Seamier Side of Childlore', 1.
38 Opie and Opie, *Lore and Language*, pp. 95–96; Boyes, 'Alice Bertha Gomme', 203.
39 Patricia M. Meley, 'Paper Power: A Search for Meaning in the Folded Paper Toys of Pre-adolescents', *Children's Folklore Review* 11(2) (1989), 3–5; Bronner, 'Material Folk Culture of Children', pp. 259–260; https://collections.museumsvictoria.com.au/items/254059
40 *Cambridge Daily News*, 16 October 1985.
41 Charles Mathews, *The Life and Correspondence of Charles Mathews, the Elder, Comedian* (London, 1860), p. 19.
42 *Dover Express*, 26 August 1910; *Sunday Illustrated*, 4 February 1923. See also www.dailymail.co.uk/news/article-2111963/Schoolboys-100-year-old-paper-planes-pre-date-manned-flight-eaves-chapel.html
43 Katherine V. Huntley, 'Children's Graffiti in Roman Pompeii and Herculaneum', in Sally Crawford, Dawn Hadley, and Gillian Shepherd (eds), *The Oxford Handbook of the Archaeology of Childhood* (Oxford, 2018), pp. 376–386, at pp. 380–381.

44 *Globe*, 19 April 1892.
45 Cited in Orme, 'The Culture of Children', p. 79.
46 https://canmore.org.uk/site/22552/luing-kilchattan-old-parish-church
47 www.bbc.co.uk/news/uk-england-nottinghamshire-34112451
48 www.cranbrookschool.co.uk/200-year-old-graffiti-found-in-school/ (accessed 10 July 2024).
49 Aaron Sheon, 'The Discovery of Graffiti', *Art Journal* 36 (1976), 16–22.
50 Kate Giles and Mel Giles, 'Signs of the Times: Nineteenth–twentieth-century graffiti in the farms of the Yorkshire Wolds', in J. Oliver and T. Neal (eds), *Wild Signs: Graffiti in Archaeology and History* (Oxford, 2010), pp. 47–59, at p. 57.
51 www.lincolnshire.gov.uk/news/article/91/historic-graffiti-discovered-marking-the-start-of-world-war-one
52 https://boltonworktown.co.uk/themes/graffiti
53 Thomson, *Lost Freedom*, p. 32.
54 See, for example, the leaver's shirt archived by the Museum of Youth Culture, OL_School leaver shirt_3170041 and OL_school leaver shirt back_3170038 (images not accessible online).
55 www.mumsnet.com/talk/education/570104-when-did-the-shirt-signing-thing-start
56 www.bbc.co.uk/news/education-10697022
57 www.bbc.co.uk/news/education-10697022
58 www.fredperry.com/leavers-fred-perry-shirt-sm7182-n11.html. We thank Jaymie Tapsell for bringing this to our attention.
59 Keith Thomas, *Rule and Misrule in the Schools of Early Modern England* (Reading, 1976), p. 32.
60 Thomas, *Rule and Misrule*, p. 29.
61 William Steven, *The History of the High School of Edinburgh* (Edinburgh, 1849), p. 18.
62 *Neighbours*, Episodes 2970, 2971, 2974, 2975, 2978 (1997); Episode 3027 (1998); Episodes 3440, 3441 (1999); Episode 3863 (2001); Episode 4625 (2004); Episodes 4827, 4831, 4832 (2005); Episode 5148 (2007); Episode 5598 (2008); Episode 5620 (2009); Episode 6281 (2011); Episode 7243 (2015); Episodes 7719, 7720, 7721, 7726, 7730 (2017).
63 www.yourlocalguardian.co.uk/news/2253100.schoolboys-threatened-with-expulsion-for-last-day-pranks/; www.scotsman.com/news/scottish-news/entire-scottish-school-class-excluded-after-muck-up-day-pranks-go-too-far-547658
64 www.thescottishsun.co.uk/news/12528424/teacher-in-hospital-and-locusts-released-elgin/
65 Bodleian Libraries, University of Oxford, MS. Opie 9 fol. 330r. OP/A/1/9/6/30/3.
66 Opie and Opie, *Lore and Language*, p. 377.
67 Opie and Opie, *Lore and Language*, p. 382.
68 Roald Dahl, *More About Boy* (London, 1984 [2008]), 'The Great Mouse Plot'.
69 Cath Bannister, *Scouting and Guiding in Britain: The Ritual Socialisation of Young People* (Cham, 2022), p. 156.

Chapter 10: Domestic life

1 Shelley Mallett, 'Understanding Home: A Critical Review of the Literature', *The Sociological Review* 52 (2004), 62–89.
2 Carole Després, 'The Meaning of Home: Literature Review and Directions for Future Research and Theoretical Development', *The Journal of Architectural and Planning Research* 8(2) (1991), 96–115.

3. www.gov.uk/government/statistics/end-of-life-care-profiles-february-2018-update/statistical-commentary-end-of-life-care-profiles-february-2018-update
4. Barbara Newman and Leslie Newman, 'Some Birth Customs in East Anglia', *Folklore* 50 (1938), 187; Margaret Bennett, *Scottish Customs from the Cradle to the Grave* (Edinburgh, 2012).
5. *Cheshire Observer*, 6 May 1882.
6. Anne Cameron, 'Female Birthing Customs and Beliefs', in Katie Barclay and Deborah Simonton (eds), *Women in Eighteenth-century Scotland* (London, 2013); Davies, *Supernatural War*, pp. 147–148.
7. Leather, *Folk-Lore of Herefordshire*, p. 111.
8. Newman and Newman, 'Some Birth Customs', 180.
9. Carly Gieseler, *Gender-reveal Parties as Mediated Events: Celebrating Identity in Pink and Blue* (Lanham, MD, 2020).
10. Udal, *Dorsetshire Folk-Lore*, p. 184.
11. John Rhys, *Celtic Folklore* (Oxford, 1901), Vol. 2, p. 601.
12. *Newbury Weekly News*, 11 October 1888.
13. Opie and Tatem, *Dictionary of Superstitions*, pp. 42–45, 238–240.
14. George Monger, '"To Marry in May": An Investigation of a Superstition', *Folklore* 105 (1994), 104–108.
15. Brian Dempsey, 'Making the Gretna Blacksmith Redundant: Who Worried, Who Spoke, Who Was Heard on the Abolition of Irregular Marriage in Scotland?', *Journal of Legal History* 30 (2009), 23–52; Leah Leneman, '"A Natural Foundation in Equity": Marriage and Divorce in Eighteenth and Nineteenth-century Scotland', *Scottish Economic and Social History* 20 (2000), 207.
16. Samuel Pyeatt Menefee, *Wives for Sale* (Oxford, 1981), pp. 9–12.
17. *Bell's Life*, 30 March 1823; *Hereford Times*, 9 March 1850.
18. T. W. Thompson, 'Gypsy Marriage in England', *Journal of the Gypsy Lore Society* 3rd S. 6 (1927), 171–179.
19. *South Wales Daily News*, 27 November 1900.
20. Menefee, *Wives for Sale*; E. P. Thompson, *Customs in Common* (London, 1991); Stéphanie Prevost, 'For a Bunch of Blue Ribbons: Taking a Look at Wife-selling in the Black Country and the West Midlands', *The Blackcountryman Magazine* (2016), 51–57.
21. *Falkirk Herald*, 18 December 1862.
22. Christopher J. Duffin, 'Herbert Toms (1874–1940), Witch Stones, and *Porosphaera* Beads', *Folklore* 122 (2011), 84–101; Owen Davies, 'Urbanisation and the Decline of Witchcraft: An Examination of London', *Journal of Social History* 30(3) (1997), 597–617, at 611.
23. Davies and Houlbrook, *Building Magic*, pp. 131–138.
24. E. J. Rudsdale, 'Thunderbolts', *Folklore* 49(1) (1938) 48–50, at 49.
25. *Pearson's Weekly*, 4 October 1906.
26. Hermann Muthesius, *The English House*, ed. by Dennis Sharp, trans. by Janet Seligman (London, 1979), p. 181.
27. Hutton, *Stations*, pp. 38–40; Davies, *Supernatural War*, p. 143.
28. Duffin, 'Herbert Toms', p. 91.
29. See Davies and Houlbrook, *Building Magic*, pp. 136–138; Deborah Sugg Ryan, *Ideal Homes, 1918–39: Domestic Design and Suburban Modernism* (Manchester, 2018).
30. Day Survey Respondent 007, June 1937–August 1938; Day Survey Respondent 195, June 1937– August 1938; Day Survey Respondent 495, June 1937–November 1937, Mass Observation Archive, University of Sussex Special Collections.

Notes and references

31 *Edinburgh Evening News*, 17 June 1944.
32 *Ripon Gazette*, 18 November 1899; *Newcastle Journal*, 3 November 1986.
33 Natália Ramos and Ivete Monteiro, 'Health Beliefs and Protection Practices in the Hindu Community in Portugal', *EC Psychology and Psychiatry* 9 (2020), 78.
34 www.livemint.com/Opinion/FdZnsX29qCcIBrPSv3BRBP/Old-beliefs-new-cars-and-a-lemon.html; www.spotboye.com/bollywood/news/amitabh-bachchan-hopes-2021-is-better-hangs-lemon-and-green-chillies-his-brahmastra-co-star-mouni-roy-has-something-to-say/5fd8592c751d1e12dbfdfb34
35 *Times of India*, 23 April 2022; personal communication from Kavi Pujara, 10 July 2024. See Kavi Pujara, *The Golden Mile* (Richmond, 2022).
36 Annabelle Wilkins, *Migration, Work and Home-making in the City: Dwelling and Belonging among Vietnamese Communities in London* (Abingdon, 2019), pp. 105, 109, 110.
37 Venetia J. Newall, 'Two English Fire Festivals in Relation to Their Contemporary Social Setting', *Western Folklore* 31 (1972), 253–254; M. E. Ringwood, 'New Year Customs in Co. Durham', *Folklore* 71 (1960), 254–255.
38 A. R. Wright, *British Calendar Customs: England*. Vol. 2, *Fixed Festivals* (London, 1938), pp. 2–11; *Pinner Observer*, 24 December 1987.
39 Hunt, *Popular Romances*, p. 382; Wright, *Calendar Customs*, p. 4.
40 *Rugby Advertiser*, 23 December 1960; *Newcastle Daily Chronicle*, 2 January 1907; *Newcastle Chronicle*, 29 December 1900.
41 *Northern Weekly Gazette*, 4 January 1913.
42 Wright, *Calendar Customs*, p. 11; *Rugby Advertiser*, 23 December 1960; *Sunday Post*, 26 December 1948.
43 *Edinburgh Evening News*, 29 December 1962.
44 J. Charles Cox (ed.), *Memorials of Old Derbyshire* (London, 1907), p. 365.
45 *Dundee Evening Telegraph*, 5 January 1897; W. H. Pool, 'Court Sequel to "First-Footing"', *Hartlepool Northern Daily Mail*, 19 January 1959, p. 7.
46 *Newcastle Daily Chronicle*, 2 January 1907.
47 *Shields Daily Gazette*, 1 January 1997.
48 Richard Bradley, 'What Is the New Year Derbyshire Tradition of First Footing?' *Derbyshire Life* (2023), www.greatbritishlife.co.uk/magazines/derbyshire/23994473.new-year-derbyshire-tradition-first-footing/
49 *Dover Express*, 12 May 1899; *Hereford Journal*, 17 November 1847.
50 'The Majority of J. H. Greville Smyth, Esq.', *Illustrated London News*, 10 January 1857, 10.
51 Cf. Vyta Baselice, Dante Burrichter, and Peter N. Stearns, 'Debating the Birthday: Innovation and Resistance in Celebrating Children', *The Journal of the History of Childhood and Youth* 12 (2019), 262–284; Hizky Shoham, 'It Is about Time: Birthdays as Modern Rites of Temporality', *Time & Society* 30 (2021), 78–99.
52 *St. Pancras Gazette*, 27 November 1869; *Perthshire Constitutional & Journal*, 5 January 1874.
53 Edith Nesbit, *The Railway Children* (London, 1906), chapter 4.
54 'Continental Folk-Lore Notes', *The Folk-lore Journal* 1 (1883), 381–382.
55 *Wallington and Carshalton Herald*, 18 February 1891.
56 A. A. Milne, *Winnie the Pooh* (London, 1926), chapter 6.
57 Enid Blyton, *The Exciting Birthday* (London, 1931), pp. 13–14.
58 *South London Press*, Friday 14 May 1909.
59 *Long Eaton Advertiser*, 25 April 1942; *Surrey Advertiser*, 24 October 1942; *Bradford Observer*, 3 August 1942; *Derbyshire Times*, 11 December 1942; *Wiltshire Times and Trowbridge Advertiser*, 13 March 1943.

Notes and references

60 https://hgsheritage.org.uk/Detail/objects/WW2-6-6
61 Anne Rosa Coward, 'My Birthday Party, 1944', *BBC: WW2 People's War* (2004), www.bbc.co.uk/history/ww2peopleswar/stories/38/a2301238.shtml
62 Diarist 5311, 1943, Sutton Coldfield, Warwickshire, Mass Observation Archive, University of Sussex Special Collections.
63 *Holyhead Mail and Anglesey Herald*, 30 July 1943.
64 Gerd Baumann, 'Ritual Implicates "Others": Rereading Durkheim in a Plural Society', in Daniel de Coppet (ed.), *Understanding Rituals* (London, 1992), p. 106.
65 Baumann, 'Ritual Implicates "Others"', pp. 106–107.
66 Marc Kosciejew, 'Documenting Queen Victoria's Christmas Tree: A Conceptual Analysis of Newspapers, Communities, and Holiday Traditions', *Media History* 27 (2021), 462.
67 *Fife Herald*, 26 December 1844.
68 *Illustrated London News*, 23 December 1848.
69 Kosciejew, 'Documenting Queen Victoria's Christmas Tree'.
70 *Dundee Evening Telegraph*, 17 December 1926; *Somerset Guardian and Radstock Observer*, 29 December 1933; *Cannock Chase Courier*, 25 December 1897,
71 *Detroit Post and Tribune*, 23 December 1882.
72 See for example *Uxbridge & West Drayton Gazette*, 23 November 1907; *Hunts County News*, 25 December 1909.
73 *Montrose Standard*, 29 December 1949.
74 *Southall Gazette*, 8 November 1985; *Middlesex Chronicle*, 19 October 1995.
75 *Liverpool Daily Post*, 17 October 1963.
76 *Leicester Daily Mercury*, 28 January 1994.
77 www.vam.ac.uk/articles/the-first-christmas-card
78 György Buday, *The History of the Christmas Card* (London, 1954).
79 www.kamalkoria.com/post/diwali-card-collection; personal communication from Kranti Koria, 10 June 2024.
80 https://afrotouch.design/pages/georginas-story; www.postalmuseum.org/blog/meet-the-maker-georgina-fihosy/; https://afrotouch.design/collections/christmas-cards?page=1
81 Helena Margaret Tuomainen, 'Ethnic Identity, (Post)Colonialism and Foodways: Ghanaians in London', *Food, Culture & Society* 12 (2009), 535–536.
82 Tuomainen, 'Ethnic Identity', p. 541.
83 Tuomainen, 'Ethnic Identity', p. 543.
84 Marta Rabikowaska and Kathy Burrell, 'The Material Worlds of Recent Polish Migrants: Transnationalism, Food, Shops and Home', in Kathy Burrell and Anne J. Kershen (eds), *Polish Migration to the UK in the 'New' European Union: After 2004* (Abingdon, 2009), p. 416; www.theguardian.com/uk/2007/nov/26/immigration.lifeandhealth
85 www.independent.co.uk/life-style/food-and-drink/polish-chrismas-dinner-carp-wigilia-borscht-barszcz-kompot-pierogi-ruskie-eastern-europe-a8118281.html
86 www.bbc.co.uk/religion/religions/christianity/christmas/nonchristian.shtml
87 Amna Khana, Andrew Lindridgeb, and Theeranuch Pusaksrikit, 'Why Some South Asian Muslims Celebrate Christmas: Introducing "Acculturation Trade-offs"', *Journal of Business Research* 82 (2018), 296–297.
88 Thomas Tusser, *Fiue Hundred Pointes of Good Husbandrie* (London, 1557 [1878]), 31.29.3.
89 Isabella Beeton, *The Book of Household Management* (London, 1859–1861), p. 1005; Andrew F. Smith, *The Turkey: An American Story* (Champaign, 2009), p. 38.
90 'Folk Lore', *Notes & Queries* 312 (1861), 491.

91 *Mid Sussex Times*, 26 November 1982; *Suffolk and Essex Free Press*, 17 November 1988.
92 www.bbc.co.uk/news/uk-51991887
93 Shirin Hirsch and Andrew Smith, 'A View through a Window: Social Relations, Material Objects and Locality', *The Sociological Review* 66 (2018), 225.
94 Amanda Vickery, 'An Englishman's Home is His Castle? Thresholds, Boundaries and Privacies in the Eighteenth-century London House', *Past & Present* 199 (2008), 147–173.
95 Hirsch and Smith, 'A View', p. 226.
96 Sophie Parkes-Nield, 'Five COVID Customs which Emerged during Lockdown', *The Conversation*, 30 September 2020, https://theconversation.com/five-covid-customs-which-emerged-during-lockdown-146130. Examples were collected by the Lockdown Lore Project run by the Elphinstone Institute, Aberdeen University, www.abdn.ac.uk/elphinstone/public-engagement/LockdownLore.php#Handcrafted%20Responses
97 www.vam.ac.uk/archives/unit/ARC197233
98 www.ctvnews.ca/health/coronavirus/teddy-bears-in-london-u-k-windows-spread-cheer-amid-coronavirus-1.4863499 (accessed 1 May 2024); www.plymouthherald.co.uk/news/teddy-bears-started-appearing-windows-3987780.
99 Nicolas Le Bigre, 'Play and Vulnerability in Scotland during the Covid-19 Pandemic', in Anna Beresin and Julia Bishop (eds), *Play in a Covid Frame: Everyday Pandemic Creativity in a Time of Isolation* (Cambridge, 2023), pp. 239–364.
100 *The Guardian*, 26 March 2020.
101 https://metro.co.uk/2021/07/02/mums-wish-cake-hack-lets-daughter-blow-out-candles-hygienically-14865110/; https://metro.co.uk/2019/03/13/blowing-candles-birthday-cake-actually-really-unhygienic-8895622/; https://www.foodrepublic.com/1564654/the-blowzee-shark-tank-now/; www.adweek.com/creativity/general-mills-solves-birthday-cake-conundrum-with-covid-19-safe-candle/

Chapter 11: Broadcasting folklore

1 www.cambridge-news.co.uk/news/local-news/peculiar-history-ely-eel-festival-12961935
2 Vanessa Toulmin, Patrick Russell and Simon Popple (eds), *The Lost World of Mitchell and Kenyon: Edwardian Britain on Film* (London, 2004).
3 Vanessa Toulmin, '"Local Films for Local People": Travelling Showmen and the Commissioning of Local Films in Great Britain, 1900–1902', *Film History* 13 (2001), 125.
4 Martin L. Johnson, '"Did the Cameraman Film You?" Finding the Folk in H. Lee Waters's Movies of Local People', *Western Folklore* 64 (2005), 231–242.
5 https://player.bfi.org.uk/free/film/watch-knutsford-royal-may-day-carnival-1904-1904-online; https://player.bfi.org.uk/free/film/watch-buxton-well-dressing-1904-1904-online
6 John Widdowson, 'Mitchell and Kenyon: Ceremonial Processions and Folk Traditions', in Toulmin, Russell, and Popple (eds), *Lost World*, pp. 137–150.
7 Emily Rutherford, 'Researching and Teaching with British Newsreels', *Twentieth Century British History* 32 (2021), 441–461.
8 Thomas Hajkowski, *The BBC and National Identity in Britain, 1922–1953* (Manchester, 2010). For *Radio Times* listings see https://genome.ch.bbc.co.uk/genome

9 Andrew Walker, 'Reporting the Haxey Hood, c. 1840–1959', *Tradition Today* 11 (2022), 8, 9.
10 *Radio Times*, 14 October (1932), 134.
11 *Radio Times*, 15 May (1936), 3.
12 www.macearchive.org/search?for=pancake%20racing&from=&to=
13 www.macearchive.org/search?for=cheese+rolling&from=&to=
14 https://player.bfi.org.uk/free/film/watch-hindu-festival-1969-online
15 *Aberdeen Press and Journal*, 31 December 1932.
16 Margaret Patricia Duesenberry, 'Fiddle Tunes on Air: A Study of Gatekeeping and Traditional Music at the BBC in Scotland, 1923–1957', PhD thesis, University of California (Berkeley), 2000.
17 Derek Johnston, 'Tradition, Nation and the Power of the Schedule', conference paper 2019. See also Derek Johnston, *Haunted Seasons: Television Ghost Stories for Christmas and Horror for Halloween* (Basingstoke, 2015).
18 *Dundee Evening Telegraph*, 16 January 1934.
19 Marie Slocombe, 'The BBC Folk Music Collection', *Folklore and Folk Music Archivist* 7 (1964), 3–13.
20 *Sherborne Mercury*, 2 April 1850.
21 For example, *Stratford-upon-Avon Herald*, 29 March 1929.
22 *Dundee Courier*, 1 April 1914.
23 *Daily Herald*, 2 April 1957; *Daily Record*, 1 April 1965.
24 *Daily Mirror*, 2 April 1970; *Daily Herald*, 2 April 1962; Moira Smith, 'Arbiters of Truth at Play: Media April Fools' Day Hoaxes', *Folklore* 120 (2009), 274–290; www.theguardian.com/news/datablog/2012/apr/01/guardian-april-fools-list
25 Tom Burns, 'Folklore in the Mass Media: Television', *Folklore Forum* 2(4) (1969), 90–106.
26 https://publications.parliament.uk/pa/ld200910/ldselect/ldcomuni/37/3707.htm; www.statista.com/statistics/269969/number-of-tv-households-in-the-uk/
27 Priscilla Denby, 'Folklore in Mass Media', *Folklore Forum* 4 (1971), 113–125.
28 *Coronation Street*, Episode 26 (13 March 1961).
29 Alexander Esway, *The Wizard in The Wall* (film) (London, 1934).
30 Linda Dégh and Andrew Vázsonyi, 'Magic for Sale: Marchen and Legend in TV Advertising', *Fabula* 20(1–3) (1979), 47–68; Preston Wittwer, 'Don Draper Thinks Your Ad Is Cliché: Fairy Tale Iconography in TV Commercials', *Humanities* 2016, 5(2) (2016), 1.
31 www.moreaboutadvertising.com/2024/08/neverland-turns-to-fiction-for-new-rightmove-ooh-campaign/
32 Dégh and Vázsonyi, 'Does the Word "Dog" Bite?', 7–8.
33 Stith Thompson, *The Folktale* (Berkeley, 1946 [1977]), p. 461.
34 Laraine Porter, '"Temporary American citizens": British Cinema in the 1920s', in I. Q. Hunter, Laraine Porter, and Justin Smith (eds), *The Routledge Companion to British Cinema History* (Abingdon, 2017), pp. 34–46, at p. 42; www.screenonline.org.uk/film/cinemas/sect3.html
35 *Brechin Advertiser*, 8 April 1952; *Streatham News*, 31 August 1951; *Gloucester Citizen*, 20 October 1951; *Worthing Herald*, 10 August 1951.
36 Davies, *The Haunted*, p. 212; www.screenonline.org.uk/film/id/1018662/index.html
37 *Wales on Sunday*, 27 February 1994.
38 John Aberth, *A Knight at the Movies: Medieval History on Film* (Abingdon, 2003), p. 2.
39 Aberth, *Knight at the Movies*, p. 21.

40 Aberth, *Knight at the Movies*, p. 23.
41 Christopher A. Snyder, '"Who Are the Britons?": Questions of Ethnic and National Identity in Arthurian Films', *Arthuriana* 29 (2019), 6–23, at 18.
42 Snyder, '"Who Are the Britons?"', 14.
43 Christopher Jensen, 'An Arthur for the Brexit Era: Joe Cornish's *The Kid Who Would Be King*', in Karl Fugelso (ed.), *Studies in Medievalism XXIX: Politics and Medievalism* (Cambridge, 2020), pp. 39–46.
44 Diana Ortega Martín, 'Nationhood, the Arthurian Myth, and the (De)Construction of Mythical England in Ben Wheatley's Kill List', *Amaltea* 15 (2023), 1–8.
45 Dennis Tredy, '"The forme to the fynisment foldes ful selden" (l.499): A Comparison of David Lowery's Screenplay and His 2021 Film Adaptation *The Green Knight*', *Arthuriana* 34 (2024), 21–42.
46 Robinson Murphy, 'The Death-driven Eco-ethics of David Lowery's *The Green Knight* (2021) and Darren Aronofsky's *mother!* (2017)', *Quarterly Review of Film and Video* (2023), 1–19.
47 Michael Dylan Foster, 'Introduction: The Challenge of the Folkloresque', in Michael Dylan Foster and Jeffrey A. Tolbert (eds), *The Folkloresque: Reframing Folklore in a Popular Culture World* (Logan, 2015), p. 5.
48 *The Scotsman*, 20 July 2002; *Aberdeen Press and Journal*, 30 October 2000; *Aberdeen Press and Journal*, 27 October 2003.
49 Mikel J. Koven, 'The Folklore Fallacy: A Folkloristic/Filmic Perspective on "The Wicker Man"', *Fabula* 48 (2007), 270–280.
50 Bruce Jackson, 'A Film Note', *Journal of American Folklore* 102 (1989), 388–389, at 389.
51 Ashley Orr, 'Plotting Jane Austen: Heritage Sites as Fictional Worlds in the Literary Tourist's Imagination', *International Journal of Heritage Studies* 24(3) (2018), 243–255.
52 Contessa Small, 'Children's Fan-play, Folklore and Participatory Culture: Harry Potter Costumes, Role-play and Spells', *Ethnologies*, 38 (2016), 255–289.
53 Small, 'Children's Fan-play', 275.
54 https://player.bfi.org.uk/free/film/watch-kidnapping-by-indians-1899-1899-online; www.bbc.co.uk/news/uk-england-lancashire-50211023. Sadly, references to children playing cowboys tend to appear in newspapers only following an accident. Cf. *Sheffield Daily Telegraph*, 9 July 1913; *Halifax Evening Courier*, 25 August 1955.
55 *Mirror*, 26 March 1953.
56 https://collections-search.bfi.org.uk/web/Details/ChoiceFilmWorks/150046762
57 Rebekah Willett, 'Remixing Children's Cultures: Media-referenced Play on the Playground', in Chris Richards and Andrew Burn (eds), *Children's Games in the New Media Age* (Abingdon, 2014), pp. 133–151.
58 *Birmingham Daily Post*, 24 May 1968; *Wolverhampton Express and Star*, 17 July 1969.
59 *Daily Mirror*, 22 March 1966; https://poohsticks.uk/should-i-bring-my-own-stick-to-the-championships/; http://news.bbc.co.uk/1/hi/england/2853091.stm
60 www.theguardian.com/technology/2015/aug/26/revealed-how-to-pick-perfect-poohstick

Chapter 12: Digital folklore

1 Barbara Kirshenblatt-Gimblett, 'The Electronic Vernacular', in George E. Marcus (ed.), *Connected: Engagements with Media* (Chicago, 1996), pp. 21–65; Alan Dundes, 'Folkloristics in the Twenty-first Century (AGS Invited Presidential Plenary Address,

2004)', *The Journal of American Folklore* 118(470) (2005), 406; Tok Thompson, 'Netizens, Revolutionaries, and the Inalienable Right to the Internet', in Trevor Blank (ed.), *Folk Culture in the Digital Age* (Logan, 2012), p. 53; Trevor Blank and Lynne S. McNeill (eds), *Slender Man Is Coming: Creepypasta and Contemporary Legends on the Internet* (Logan, 2018).
2. Trevor Blank, 'Examining the Transmission of Urban Legends: Making the Case for Folklore Fieldwork on the Internet', *Folklore Forum* 37 (2007), 15–26.
3. www.statista.com/statistics/468663/uk-internet-penetration/; www.ofcom.org.uk/media-use-and-attitudes/online-habits/uk-internet-use-surges/
4. Mariann Domokos, 'Towards Methodological Issues in Electronic Folklore', *Slovak Ethnology* 2 (2014), 284.
5. www.thefolklorepodcast.com/; https://folklorethursday.com/; Brittany Warman, 'Fairy Tales and Digital Culture', in Andrew Teverson (ed.), *The Fairy Tale World* (Abingdon, 2019), pp. 273–283, at p. 274.
6. www.thirskmuseum.org/displays.html
7. Dawn M. Walls-Thumma, 'Affirmational and Transformational Values and Practices in the Tolkien Fanfiction Community', *Journal of Tolkien Research* 8(1) (2019) Article 6.
8. Anne Kustritz, 'Fairy Tale, Fan Fiction, and Popular Media', in Teverson (ed.), *The Fairy Tale World*, p. 284; Sarah Emily Jones, 'From Folklore to Fanfic: An Examination of Transformative Texts through Subversion, Sexuality, and Social Commentary', PhD thesis, University of Canterbury, 2022, pp. 19–20.
9. Walls-Thumma, 'Affirmational and Transformational Values', 2.
10. https://archiveofourown.org/
11. Kustritz, 'Fairy Tale, Fan Fiction', p. 284.
12. Kainosite, 'Cysylltiad', *Archive of Our Own* (2016), https://archiveofourown.org/works/8889643
13. Plato_rocks, 'Full Circle', *Archive of Our Own* (2022), https://archiveofourown.org/works/41670471
14. Kustritz, 'Fairy Tale, Fan Fiction', p. 292; Jones, *From Folklore to Fanfic*.
15. Bacchilega, *Fairy Tales Transformed?*
16. Jones, *From Folklore to Fanfic*, p. 1.
17. https://fanlore.org/wiki/Fanlore:About
18. Kellye Ann Guinan, 'Culture and Community Online How Fanfiction Creates a Sense of Social Identity by Reshaping Popular Media', thesis, Middle Tennessee State University, 2017.
19. Una McCormack, 'Finding Ourselves in the (Un)Mapped Lands: Women's Reparative Readings of The Lord of the Rings', in Janet Brennan Croft and Leslie A. Donovan (eds), *Perilous and Fair: Women in the Works and Life of J. R. R. Tolkien* (Altadena, 2015), pp. 309–326, at p. 310.
20. Walls-Thumma, 'Affirmational and Transformational Values', p. 29.
21. www.vanderwal.net/folksonomy.html
22. Guilherme Giolo and Michaël Berghman, 'The Aesthetics of the Self: The Meaning-making of Internet Aesthetics', *First Monday*, 28(3) (2013).
23. Emelie Larsson and Jenny Ingridsdotter, 'The Enchanted North Nature, Place and Gender in "Off the Grid" Social Media Representations', *Anthropological Journal of European Cultures* 32 (2023), 45–67. For example, www.pinterest.com/scullyno/fairycore/ and https://fr.pinterest.com/aestheludo/fairycore-fairy-grunge-pixiecore/

24 www.vam.ac.uk/mused/fashion/how-fairycore-are-you/?srsltid=AfmBOorJQee5clC L6FXoFR61pAGBZRHcHPH9wudCqn18D0CrFGqo_6EC
25 https://aesthetics.fandom.com/wiki/Spriggancore. For example, www.pinterest.com/pin/dark-fairycore-578079302173988047/
26 https://aesthetics.fandom.com/wiki/Selkiecore
27 www.theguardian.com/fashion/2021/jul/30/goblincore-fashion-trend-embraces-chaos-dirt-mud; for example, www.pinterest.com/vesania94/goblincore/
28 Chris Miller, 'How Modern Witches Enchant TikTok: Intersections of Digital, Consumer, and Material Culture(s) on #WitchTok', *Religions* 13(2) (2022); Ceri Houlbrook and Julia Phillips, '"For All of Your Protection Needs": Tracing the "Witch Bottle" from the Early Modern Period to TikTok', *Magic, Ritual, and Witchcraft* 18(1) (2023), 1–31.
29 www.tiktok.com/@thecitywitchuk/video/7028138542735871238
30 www.tiktok.com/@thecitywitchuk/video/7031937560251223301 (accessed 3 November 2024).
31 Richard Dawkins, *The Selfish Gene* (Oxford, 1976), p. 206.
32 Limor Shifman, 'The Cultural Logic of Photo-Based Meme Genres', *Journal of Visual Culture* 13 (2014), 342.
33 Rayane Boumakh and Sarra Hadjailla, 'Teaching Aspects of British Culture Using Memes', Masters thesis, Guelma University, 2023.
34 www.tiktok.com/@michaelmcdon_backup8/video/7411991710084910369 (accessed 12 October 2024).
35 www.youtube.com/watch?v=gpSIzxoTaoY; Ian Kinane, 'For Your Eyes Only? Brexit, Bond, and British Meme Culture', in Ian Kinane (ed.), *Isn't It Ironic? Irony in Contemporary Popular Culture* (London, 2021), pp. 39–61.
36 Liam McLoughlin and Rosalynd Southern, 'By Any Memes Necessary? Small Political Acts, Incidental Exposure and Memes during the 2017 UK General Election', *The British Journal of Politics and International Relations* 23 (2021), 60–84, Figure 3; Jonathan Dean, 'Sorted for Memes and Gifs: Visual Media and Everyday Digital Politics', *Political Studies Review* 17 (2019), 255–266, Figure 1.
37 https://imgflip.com/meme/176779849/James-Bond-and-The-Queen
38 Andrea Fazio, Tommaso Reggiani, and Francesco Scervini. 'Social Media Charity Campaigns and Pro-social Behaviour: Evidence from the Ice Bucket Challenge', *Journal of Economic Psychology* 96 (2023), 1–19.
39 George Rossolatos, 'The Ice-bucket Challenge: The Legitimacy of the Memetic Mode of Cultural Reproduction Is the Message', *Signs and Society* 3 (2015), 139–143.
40 For an in-depth investigation into the history and contemporary adaptations of these 'ritual games', see Lucy Mc Granaghan, '"Do Not Play the Midnight Game": The Folklore of Ritual Games and Those Who Play Them', PhD thesis, University of Hertfordshire, forthcoming.
41 www.tiktok.com/@syl_k_smooth/video/7103565048806640901
42 www.theguardian.com/uk/2005/apr/26/ukcrime.mobilephones
43 www.vice.com/en/article/a-complete-history-of-happy-slapping/
44 Linda M. Scott, 'Classic Campaigns – "You Know When You've Been Tango'd": The Orange Man Commercial', *Advertising & Society Review* 14 (2013), 1–5.
45 *Manchester Metro News*, 12 February 1993; *Aberdare Leader*, 25 March 1993.
46 Marek Palasinski, 'Turning Assault into a "Harmless Prank": Teenage Perspectives on Happy Slapping', *Journal of Interpersonal Violence* 28 (2013), 1909–1923.

47 http://news.bbc.co.uk/1/hi/7244782.stm?lsm; www.mirror.co.uk/news/uk-news/happy-slapping-pair-jailed-for-street-attack-237950; www.dailymail.co.uk/news/article-1297742/Happy-slapper-grandfather-killers-sent-total-8-years.html
48 https://saferinternet.org.uk/online-issue/online-challenges
49 Richard Lawrence, 'The Old English Village', *Creepypasta Wiki* (2013), https://creepypasta.fandom.com/wiki/The_Old_English_Village
50 Inaaace, 'The Queen's Guard', *Creepypasta Wiki* (2015), https://creepypasta.fandom.com/wiki/The_Queen%27s_Guard
51 www.youtube.com/watch?v=hTCy7RAPOfU
52 www.youtube.com/watch?v=2vqIyJR9ckc
53 Chiara Zuanni and Campbell Price, 'The Mystery of the "Spinning Statue" at Manchester Museum', *Material Religion* 14 (2018), 235–251.
54 www.youtube.com/watch?v=AbXEHu27qUI
55 See, for example, www.smithsonianmag.com/smart-news/museums-ancient-egyptian-statue-mysteriously-rotates-3012854/; https://edition.cnn.com/2013/06/25/world/europe/uk-spinning-statue-mystery/index.html; https://cairoscene.com/buzz/egyptian-curse-hits-manchester
56 https://x.com/hauntedscouse
57 www.youtube.com/@HauntedScouse
58 https://scarfolk.blogspot.com/
59 Bob Fischer, 'The Haunted Generation', *Fortean Times* 354 (June 2017) 30–37; see also Diane A. Rodgers, 'Something "Wyrd" This Way Comes: Folklore and British Television', *Folklore* 130 (2019), 133–152.
60 Quoted in Fiona Maher, 'Visit Hookland', *Fortean Times* 354 (June 2017) 38–39, at 38.
61 https://x.com/HooklandGuide
62 David R. Sutton, Bob Richard, and Paul Sieveking, 'Editorial', *Fortean Times* 354 (June 2017) 2.

Chapter 13: *The folklore of nations*

1 Jodie Matthews, 'Where Are the Romanies? An Absent Presence in Narratives of Britishness', *Identity Papers: A Journal of British and Irish Studies* 1 (2015), 79–90.
2 Prys Morgan, 'From a Death to a View: The Hunt for the Welsh Past in the Romantic Period', in Hobsbawm and Ranger (eds), *Invention of Tradition*, pp. 43–101; Roslyn Blyn-Ladrew, 'Welsh Gipsies, and Celtic Folklore in the Cauldron of Regeneration', *Western Folklore*, 57 (1998), 231–232.
3 Celyn Gurden-Williams, 'Lady Llanover and the Creation of a Welsh Cultural Utopia', PhD thesis, Cardiff University, 2008; Michael Freeman, 'Perceptions of Welshness: Tourists' Impressions of the Material and Traditional Culture of Wales, 1770–1840', *Folk Life* 53 (2015), 57–71; Juliette Wood, 'Perceptions of the Past in Welsh Folklore Studies', *Folklore* 108 (1997), 93–102.
4 Marion Löffler, 'A Century of Change: The Eisteddfod and Welsh Cultural Nationalism', in Krisztina Lajosi and Andreas Stynen (eds), *The Matica and Beyond: Cultural Associations and Nationalism in Europe* (Leiden, 2020), pp. 233–255.
5 Ronald L. Lewis, *Iron Artisans: Welsh Immigrants and the American Age of Steel* (Pittsburgh, PA, 2023).

6. Bill Jones, 'Welsh Identities in Ballarat, Australia, during the Late Nineteenth Century', *Welsh History Review* 20 (2000), 284, 285.
7. *Western Mail*, 8 February 1934.
8. Adam Coward, 'Rejecting Mother's Blessing: The Absence of the Fairy in the Welsh Search for Identity', *Proceedings of the Harvard Celtic Colloquium* 29 (2009), 57–69.
9. *Monmouthshire Merlin*, 15 May 1830; W. Howells, *Cambrian Superstitions, Comprising Ghosts, Omens, Witchcraft, Traditions, &c* (Tipton, 1831), pp. 7–8.
10. *Transactions of the National Eisteddfod of Wales, Aberdare, 1885* (Cardiff, 1887), p. 184; Trefor M. Owen, 'West Glamorgan Customs', *Folk Life* 3 (1965), 46–54.
11. Davies, *Folk-Lore*, p. vii.
12. David R. Howell, 'It's Mari Lwyd Season – but Who Owns the Tradition?' *Nation Cymru*, 6 January 2022; *Nation Cymru*, 22 December 2023.
13. Michael Newton, 'The Gaelic Diaspora in North America', in Murray Stewart Leith and Duncan Sim (eds), *The Modern Scottish Diaspora: Contemporary Debates and Perspectives* (Edinburgh, 2014), pp. 136–152; Margaret Bennett, *The Last Stronghold: Scottish Gaelic Traditions of Newfoundland* (Edinburgh, 1989).
14. David Hesse, *Warrior Dreams: Playing Scotsmen in Mainland Europe* (Manchester, 2014). See also, Ian Brown, *Performing Scottishness: Enactment and National Identities* (London, 2020).
15. Grant Jarvie, *Highland Games: The Making of the Myth* (Edinburgh, 1991).
16. *Inverness Courier*, 12 October 1842.
17. Courtney W. Mason, 'The Glengarry Highland Games, 1948–2003: Problematizing the Role of Tourism, Scottish Cultural Institutions, and the Cultivation of Nostalgia in the Construction of Identities', *International Journal of Canadian Studies* 35 (2007), 13–38.
18. Elspeth A. Frew and Judith Mair, 'Hogmanay Rituals: Scotland's New Year's Eve Celebrations', in Jennifer Laing and Warwick Frost (eds), *Rituals and Traditional Events in the Modern World* (Abingdon, 2015), pp. 159–171.
19. Paul Malgrati, 'Geography and Typology of Contemporary Burns Suppers', *Burns Chronicle* 130 (2021), 127–148.
20. *Aberdeen Evening Express*, 2 December 1879; *Stirling Observer*, 10 January 1867.
21. Tanja Bueltmann, *Clubbing Together: Ethnicity, Civility and Formal Sociability in the Scottish Diaspora to 1930* (Liverpool, 2014), p. 190.
22. Alex Salmond 'Preface', in D. McCrone and G. McPherson (eds), *National Days* (London, 2009), p. xiv.
23. Katherine Haldane Grenier, *Tourism and Identity in Scotland, 1770–1914* (London, 2017); Rachael Ironside and Stewart Massie, 'The Folklore-centric Gaze: A Relational Approach to Landscape, Folklore and Tourism', *Time and Mind* 13 (2020), 227–244; Lorna J. Philip, 'Selling the Nation: The Commodification of Monstrous, Mythical and Fantastical Creatures', *Scottish Geographical Journal* (2024), 1–16; Rebecca Finkel, 'Event Tourism and Social Responsibility: Tensions between Global and Local', *Transforming Tourism: Regional Perspectives on a Global Phenomenon* (Brussels, 2020), pp. 60–67.
24. Marion Gibson, Shelley Trower, and Garry Tregidga (eds), *Mysticism, Myth and Celtic Identity* (Abingdon, 2013).
25. Ronald Hutton, 'Celtic New Year and Feast of the Dead', *Folklore* 135 (2024), 69–86; Juliette Wood, 'Folklore Studies at the Celtic Dawn: The Role of Alfred Nutt as Publisher and Scholar', *Folklore* 110 (1999), 3–12.
26. Ronald Hutton, *The Pagan Religions of the Ancient British Isles* (Oxford, 1991).

27 Adriene Baron Tacla and Elva Johnston, 'New perspectives in Celtic Studies: Where Shall We Go from Now On?', *Tempo* 24 (2018), 613–630.
28 Marion Bowman, 'Reinventing the Celts', *Religion* 23 (1993), 152; David C. Harvey, Rhys Jones, Neil McInroy, and Cristine Milligan (eds), *Celtic Geographies: Old Cultures, New Times* (London, 2002); Amy Hale, 'Whose Celtic Cornwall? The Ethnic Cornish meet Celtic Spirituality', in Harvey et al. (eds), *Celtic Geographies*, pp. 157–173; Jason Semmens, 'Bucca Redivivus: History, Folklore and the Construction of Ethnic Identity within Modern Pagan Witchcraft in Cornwall', *Cornish Studies* 18 (2010), 141–161.
29 Jonathan Roper, 'England: The Land Without Folklore?' in Baycroft and Hopkin (eds), *Folklore and Nationalism*, pp. 227–253.
30 Tanja Bueltmann, David T. Gleeson, and Donald M. MacRaild (eds), *Locating the English Diaspora, 1500–2010* (Liverpool, 2012), p. 13.
31 Derek Schofield, 'Visions of English Identity: The Country Dance and Shakespeareland', in Matthew Cheeseman and Carina Hart (eds), *Folklore and Nation in Britain and Ireland* (New York, 2022), pp. 114–132.
32 Tanja Bueltmann, David T. Gleeson and Donald M. MacRaild, 'Invisible Diaspora? English Ethnicity in the United States before 1920', *Journal of American Ethnic History* 33 (2014), 5–30; Allison Thompson, *May Day Festivals in America, 1830 to the Present* (Jefferson, 2009).
33 *Middlebury Register*, 13 May 1904; *University Missourian*, 7 May 1916.
34 Gerald M. Sider, 'Christmas Mumming and the New Year in Outport Newfoundland', *Past & Present* 71 (1976), 102–125; Joy Fraser, 'Mumming, Violence and the Law in Conception Bay and St. John's, Newfoundland, 1831–1863', *Shima: The International Journal of Research into Island Cultures* 3 (2009), 70–88.
35 Rhett Krause, 'Morris Dance and America Prior to 1913', *American Morris Newsletter* 17 (1993), 12–27; https://morrisdancing.fandom.com/wiki/Pre-1980s_morris_in_North_America
36 Daniel J. Walkowitz, *City Folk: English Country Dance and the Politics of the Folk in Modern America* (New York, 2010).
37 Jennifer Nalewicki, 'New York's Cideries Bring the Tradition of Wassailing to the Finger Lakes', *Smithsonian Magazine*, 26 December 2019.
38 Cater and Cater, *Wassailing: Reawakening*, pp. 234–240.
39 Alicia Marchant, '"Three Cheers to the Old Apple Tree!": Wassailing and the Affective Performances of Heritage', *Parergon* 36 (2019), 141–162.
40 Nalewicki, 'New York's Cideries'.
41 Simpson and Roud, *Dictionary*, p. v.
42 See David Matless, *Landscape and Englishness*, 2nd edn (London, 2016), pp. 176–181, 203–207; Georgina Boyes, '"Potencies of the Earth": Rolf Gardiner and the English Folk Dance Revival', in Matthew Jefferies and Mike Tyldesley (eds), *Rolf Gardiner: Folk, Nature and Culture in Interwar Britain* (London, 2011), pp. 65–95; Matt Simons, 'Embodied Englishness in the Inter-war Morris Revival', in Cheeseman and Hart (eds), *Folklore and Nation*, pp. 132–146.
43 Andrew Robinson, 'Photographic Surveys of Calendar Customs: Preserving Identity in Times of Change', in Cheeseman and Hart (eds), *Folklore and Nation*, pp. 177–186.
44 David McCrone, 'The Rise and Rise of English Nationalism?', *Political Quarterly* 94 (2023), 604–612; Ross Bond and Michael Rosie, 'Routes into Scottishness', in Catherine Bromley, John Curtice, David McCrone, and Alison Park (eds), *Has Devolution Delivered?* (Edinburgh, 2006), p. 144.

45 https://johnmajorarchive.org.uk/1993/04/22/mr-majors-speech-to-conservative-group-for-europe-22-april-1993/
46 Caroline Lucas, 'The Imagined Folk of England: Whiteness, Folk Music and Fascism', *Critical Race and Whiteness Studies* 9 (2013), 1–19.
47 On landscape and Englishness, see David Matless, *About England* (London, 2023); Paul Readman, *Storied Ground: Landscape and the Shaping of English National Identity* (Cambridge, 2018); Christopher Shaw and Malcolm Chase (eds), *The Imagined Past: History and Nostalgia* (Manchester, 1989), pp. 12–14.
48 Matthew Cheeseman, 'English Nationalism, Folklore, and Indigeneity', in Robert Edgar and Wayne Johnson (eds), *The Routledge Companion to Folk Horror* (London, 2024), pp. 404–418; Donna Weston and Andy Bennett (eds), *Paganism and Popular Music* (London, 2013).
49 www.cpre.org.uk/discover/folklore-of-the-land/
50 www.english-heritage.org.uk/tellingtales/
51 Robinson, 'Photographic Surveys', pp. 177–186; T. Winter and S. Keegan-Phipps, *Performing Englishness. Identity and politics in a Contemporary Folk Resurgence* (Manchester, 2013); Desdemona McCannon, 'From Folk Culture to Modern British', *VAROOM* 11 (2009), 28–34.
52 James Tapper, 'Maypole Sales Are Up as May Day Celebrations Come Back into Style', *The Guardian*, 29 April 2018.
53 *Independent*, 6 June 2007.
54 David McCrone, 'Scotland Days: Evolving Nation and Icons', in D. McCrone and G. McPherson (eds), *National Days* (London, 2009), pp. 26–40.
55 See, for example, Paul Ward, *Britishness since 1870* (London, 2004); Anne Spry Rush, *Bonds of Empire: West Indians and Britishness from Victoria to Decolonization* (Oxford, 2011); Brad Beaven and John Griffiths, 'The City and Imperial Propaganda: A Comparative Study of Empire Day in England, Australia and New Zealand, c. 1903–1914', *Journal of Urban History* 42 (2016), 377–395; Benedict Anderson, *Imagined Communities* (London, 1983).
56 John Vincenta, John Harris, Edward (Ted) Kianc and Andrew Billings, 'The Isles of Wonder: A New Jerusalem? British Newspaper Narratives about the Opening Ceremony of the XXXth Olympiad', *Sport in Society* 22 (2019), 1275–1296; Michael Silk, '"Isles of Wonder": Performing the Mythopoeia of Utopic Multi-ethnic Britain', *Media, Culture & Society* 37 (2015), 68–84; Benedict Anderson, *Imagined Communities* (London, 1983).
57 *A Community of Communities and Citizens: Cohesion and Justice in the Future of Britain* (London, 2000).
58 Gibson, Trower, and Tregidga (eds), *Mysticism, Myth*, p. 9.
59 Dan Ben-Amos, 'Between Intangible Cultural Heritage and Folklore', *folklor/edebiyat yıl* 29 (2023), 347–386; Natsuko Akagawa and Laurajane Smith (eds), *Safeguarding Intangible Heritage: Practices and Politics* (London, 2019).
60 www.gov.uk/government/news/oh-no-it-isnt-panto-set-to-be-formally-recognised-as-uk-joins-unesco-convention

Index

Page numbers in *italics* refer to figures

Abbots Bromley, Staffordshire 44, 220
Aberaman, Wales 247
Aberdeen, Scotland 50, 177, 191
Aberdeenshire 120
Addison, Joseph 162
Addy, Sidney Oldall 4
advertising 37, 129, 204, 226–227, 246
agriculture 7, 12, 19, 24–28, 29, 30, 38, 102, 106, 127, 151
Ainstable, Cumbria 115
Ainsworth, William Harrison 58
Aira Force, Cumbria 164
Alderley Edge, Cheshire 73, 74
Alford, Lincolnshire 127
Alford, Violet 39
All Hallows *see* Halloween
All Souls' Day 22
almanacs 13, 98, 274
amulets 8, 9, 126–129
Andersen, Hans Christian 229
angels 145–146, 148, 150
Anglicanism 53, 111
April Fools' Day 223–224
Aristotle 98, 108
Armada Day 34–35
Armistice Day ('Poppy Day') 35–36
Arthuriana 51, 66, 67–68, 72, 73, 76, 92, 229–232, 262
Ash, Surrey 107
Ash Wednesday 20
Ashburton, Devon 59
astrology 117, 158

Atkinson, John 109, 140, 142
Aubrey, John 3
authenticity, concept of 14–16, 41, 61, 69, 70, 271
autoethnography 180

Bacon, Francis 2
Badham, David 104–105
Bakewell, Derbyshire 173
ballads 2, 8, 15, 41, 70, 77, 82, 85, 109, 145, 199, 223
Ballarat, Australia 258
Ballinascarthy, Ireland 82
Balquhidder, Scotland 149, 151
Banks, Joseph 69
Baring-Gould, Sabine 10
Bath, Somerset 155
Becket, Thomas 157
bees 99, 105, 114, 196
Beeton, Isabella 211
begging 21, 25, 26, 27, 28, 37, 46, 47, 48, 52, 128, 222
Bell, John 105
bell ringing 34, 60
Beoley, Worcestershire 148
Beowulf 65, 66, 75, 238
Berkeley, Miles Joseph 132
Berkshire 75, 104, 111, 131, 196
bestiaries 88–89
Bible, the 117, 142, 195, 200–201
Biddenden, Kent *32*
Bideford, Devon 59

Index

big cats, alien 87–88
Bigfoot 15, 87
Biggleswade, Bedfordshire 166
birds 97, 101, 106, 109, 110, 112–113, 192
Birinus, St 157
Birmingham, West Midlands 165, 195, 222, 247
birthdays 173, 203–206, 214
Black, William George 116, 133
Blackburn, Lancashire 184, 234
blackface 45, 61, 218
Blackley, Lancashire 81, 82
blood sports 20, 22, 46–47, 54
Blyton, Enid 205
Bodmin, Cornwall 86, 88, 177
Boer War 167, 168
boggarts 81, 82, 147, 148, 237
Bombay (Mumbai), India 261
Bonfire Night 23, 40, 48
bonfires 3, 24, 33, 34, 35
Bootle, Lancashire 218
Borders, Scottish 130
Boscobel House, Shropshire 33
Bottrell, William 78, 80
bounds, beating the 21, 59–60, 219
Bourne, Henry 3
Bradford, Yorkshire 210
Bradford-on-Avon, Wiltshire 61
Brand, John 2–3, 4–5
Brexit 85, 177, 193, 210, 242, 266
Bridgwater, Somerset 51, 103
Briggs, Katharine 71, 81–82, 148
Bristol 86, 165
British Broadcasting Corporation (BBC) 60, 92, 167, 170, 210, 220–223, 231
Britten, James 104
Brockett, John Trotter 106
Bromley and Hayes, London 56
Bromyard, Herefordshire 103
Brookes, William Penny 54
Broughty Ferry, Scotland 111
Browne, Thomas 114
Brunvand, Jan Harold 84, 85
Brutus the Trojan 66
Buckland, Oxfordshire 75
Buddhism 201–202
Burgess, John Haldane 52
Burne, Charlotte 6, 111, 132, 142, 147
Burns Night 40, 260, 261
Burry Man, Queensferry 42–43

Burton, Robert 101
butterflies 97
Buxton, Derbyshire 218, 219

Calderdale 129
Cambridge, Cambridgeshire 12, 47
Cambridgeshire 185
Candlemas 27
Campbell, John Francis 79
Canada 212, 264
Carbondale, Pennsylvania 258
Cardiff, Wales 121, 170
Caribbean community 8, 81, 256
carnivals 50–51, 52, 60, 62, *270*, 271
Carroll, Lewis 74, 228
Carter, Angela 73
Catholicism 2, 3, 9, 19, 20, 146, 160, 200, 201, 274
Celliwig, Cornwall 67
Celticism 233–234, 262–263, 271
Ceylon (Sri Lanka) 10
Chambers, Robert 4, 91
chapbooks 13, 145
charities 19, 22, 31–33, 39, 42, 50, 51, 162, 164–166, 167, 202, 244, 247, 268
Charles I, king of England 33
Charles II, king of England 33
Charlotte, queen of the United Kingdom 206
Charlton, Bobby 169
charmers 117–118
Cheddar Gorge 75
cheese rolling 22, 222, 271
Cheshire 75, 103
Chester, Cheshire 166
Chester-le-Street, Co. Durham 49
Chicago, Illinois 259
childbirth 126, 195–196
childlore 177–193
Chinese New Year 8, 40, *62*
Chingford, Essex 23
Christmas 20, 24, 27, 28, 31, 32, 37, 39, 40, 44, 45, 46, 93, 191, 200, 209–211, 213, 258, 264
Christmas trees 20, 206–209
clapping, pandemic 1, 214
class 1, 15, 112, 129, 200
clubs 33, 53–54
Clun, Shropshire 125
Cobbett, William 87

coins, ritual bending of 161–162
Colchester, Essex 123
commercialisation 37–40, 85
Commondale, Yorkshire 109
comparativism 10, 11, 262
conkers 181, 184–186, 187, 192
Conwy, Wales 57
Cooper, Susan 73, 75
Corby, Northamptonshire 29
Cornwall 25, 78, 86, 101, 110, 149, 152, 262
Cottingley fairies 249
Covid-19 178, 186, 212, 241
creativity 62, 243, 252, 258, 269
creepypasta 248–249, 252
Creswell Crags, Nottinghamshire 65, 155
cricket 7, 50, 54–55, 267, 269
Croker, Thomas Crofton 82–83
crop circles 153–154
cross-dressing 45, 264
Crowle, Yorkshire 197
'Crownation Day' 33–34
cryptids 86–90, 249
cunning-folk 115, 117–118, 139, 141, 144, 147, 158, 251
cures, traditional 103, 116, 119, 123, 124, 131, 132, 134, 161
Cury, Cornwall 80–81
Cwrt-y-Cadno, Wales 140

Dacre, Cumbria 33
Dahl, Roald 184, 192–193
Danby, Yorkshire 142
dance, folk 9, 23, 41, 52, 56, 60, 206, 219–220, 224, 260, 264–265, 266 *see also* Molly dancing; Morris dancing
Davies, Jonathan Caredig 13, 151, 259
death 103, 104, 110, 146, 194, 196
  portents of 113–115
deathwatch beetle 114
Dee, River 156
Dégh, Linda 152
Derbyshire 65, 104, 105, 112, 155, 159, 203, 221
Devil, the 105, 137, 139, 144–148, 154
devil's coach horse beetle 100
Devil's Dyke, the 268
Devon 10, 25, 88, 102, 111, 187
dialect 5, 25, 65, 103, 104, 105, 108, 130, 148, 150, 223, 251, 260
Diana, princess of Wales 170–171

Dickens, Charles 51, 85, 200, 207
digital folklore 1, 236–252
Disney, Walt 188, 228, 235
Disraeli, Benjamin 36–37
Ditchfield, Peter Hampson 7
divination 2, 22, 98, 115, 141, 195
divorce 197–198
Diwali 22–23, 40, 159, 207–208
doles 31–33, 58
Dolfawr, Wales 143
domestic spirits 81–83
Dorset 100, 102, 104, 108, 196, 266
dragonflies 100, 249
dragons 11, 65, 74, 75, 87, 89, 102, 226, 231, 232
dressing-up 41–46
Dundee, Scotland 119, 146, 203
Dundes, Alan 8
Dunfermline, Scotland 35
Dunmow Flitch 58–60, 219–221
Durham, Co. Durham 186, 202

earthworms 102, 130
East Anglia 12, 60, 108, 113, 148, 196
Easter 20–21, 31, 33, 39, 40, 49, 274–275
Eastern Europe 6
'economy, makeshift' 25, 31
Edinburgh, Scotland 36, 68, 91, 179, 180, 182, *183*, 191, 197, 201, 203
Edmonton, Canada 258
Edwinstowe, Nottinghamshire 93
Eid 23–24, 40, 207
eisteddfodau 257–260, 271
Elizabeth I, queen of England 33, 34, 160
Elizabeth II, queen of the United Kingdom 166–168, 242, 244
Ellis, Henry 3
Ellis, William 106, 115, 128, 130
Ely, Cambridgeshire 217
Emerson, Peter Henry 101
Empire, British 9, 10, 36, 230, 261, 266, 267
Empire Day 34, 269
Epiphany 20, 26
ethnography 12, 133, 142, 201, 209, 224
Evans, George Ewart 12
Evans-Wentz, Walter 151
evolution, cultural 8–11
extraterrestrials 151–154

Index

fairies 8, 56, 70, 71, 79, 81–82, 83, 105–106, 126, 141, 147, 148–152, *153*, 226, 249
fairs 21, 22, 28–31, 46, 49, 52, 218, 219, 274
fairytales 1, 9, 10, 70–71, 73–74, 77, 80, 142, 178, 226–229, 238–239, 240
'fakelore' 15–16
Falmouth, Cornwall 107
fan fiction 238–239, 248
fantasy fiction 72–76, 234, 237
Farnham, Essex 26
Father Christmas 178, 208
Father's Day 40
feasting 20, 25, 33, 52, 209–212
Felstead, Essex 58
fertility 9, 24, 42, 56, 156, 268
fêtes 49–50
film 164–166, 179, 218, 219, 221, 225, 226, 228–234, 238, 240, 244, 252
Fingal's Cave 69
First World War 5, 35, 38, 168, 188, 195, 219, 269
first-footing 202–203, 222, 261
Fittleworth, Sussex 6
folk horror 232–233, 267
'folkcore' 239–242
'folklife', concept of 12
Folklore Society 4–5, 6, 10–11, 79, 87, 116, 178, 211, 262
folkloresque 232–234
folklorism 15, 16
'folklure', folklore as 224–227
'folksonomy' 240
football, 'folk' 20, 48–49, 54–55
Forest of Dean 217
Forfar, Scotland 192
France 6, 10, 35, 56, 169, 268
Frazer, James 11, 44
Freemasonry 257, 261
fungi 104–106

Galen 119
Galloway 5
games, traditional 5, 21, 22, 41, 50, 53, 54, 178–179, 180, 181, 186, 188, 223, 245, 260–261
Gardiner, Rolf 266
Gardner, Gerald 241
Garner, Alan 72–73, 75, 238
Gaza war 171
gender 1, 60, 73, 74, 178, 217, 239

Geoffrey of Monmouth 66
ghost-laying 147
ghost tours 1, 91
ghosts 8, 71–72, 91, 146–148, 151, 153, 229, 233, 237, 250, 251
giants 66, 67, 74, 78, 79, 227
Glasgow, Scotland 36, 213
gleaning 14, 25–26
Glentham, Lincolnshire 31
Gloucestershire 105
Golspie, Scotland 179
Gomme, George Laurence 4, 9, 79
Good Friday 21, 31, 274
graffiti 156, 187–188
Grant, Isabel 12
Gravesend, Kent 48
Gregor, Walter 5
Grimm, Brothers 70, 77, 229, 263
Guest, Charlotte 67
Guildford, Surrey 48
Gutch, Eliza 6
Guy Fawkes, *see* Bonfire Night

hag-riding 120
Hall, Augusta 256
Hallaton, Leicestershire 49, 155
Halloween 22, 40, 86, 149, 221
Halstead, Essex 126
Hamer, Edward 143
Hanway, Jonas 53
hares 98, 99, 107, 127, 143
Harpenden, Hertfordshire 59
Harries, John 140
Harrowden, Northamptonshire 50
Hartlepool, Co. Durham 203
Hartland, Edwin Sidney 163, 196
harvest 24–26, 50, 52–53, 55, 60, 111
Hastings, Sussex 53
hauntology 251, 252
Hawker, Robert 111
Haxey, Lincolnshire 49, 220, 224, *225*
Hazlitt, William Carew 3
hedgehogs 97, 106–108
Helston, Cornwall 219, 221
Henderson, William 5, 130
Henry IV, king of England 177
Heptonstall Pace-Egging 60
herbalism 117, 127–128, 132, 133–134, 139
Hereford, Herefordshire 140, 219
Herefordshire 103, 140

323

Index

Highland Games 260–261
Highlands, Scottish 67, 79, 109, 163, 260
Hill, John 132
Hinckley Bullockers 60
Hinduism 22–23, 158–159, 201, 207–208, 210, 222
hobbyhorses 28, 44, 265
Hogmanay 27, 222–223, 260, 261, 271, 275
Holy Week 21
Holywell, Wales 160–162
Hone, William 4, 26, 43
Hope, Robert Charles 163
Howells, William 259
Howitt, William 54
Hoy, isle of 79
Hunstanton, Norfolk 158
Hunt, Robert 101, 110, 139, 202
Hurstpierpoint, Sussex 129

Ilford, Greater London 51, 219
Ilminster, Somerset 54
inclusivity 60–62, 209
Ingleton, Yorkshire 164
invaders, animal 120–124
Ipswich, Suffolk 192
Ireland 12, 22, 83, 110, 152, 179, 197, 223, 258, 262
Irving, Washington 77, 92–93
Islam 23, 120, 201, 210, 257
Italy 35, 66, 172, 213, 256

Jack-in-the-Green 42–43, 53, 56, 61, 264, 265
Jacobs, Joseph 10
James, Robert 117
Jamieson, John 119
Japan 6
Jarvis, Anna 38–39
Jefferies, Richard 49
Jenner, Edward 115
Jenny Greenteenth 150
Jesse, Edward 103
Jessopp, Augustus 103
Jewitt, Llewellyn 105
John, king of England 77
Jones, Edmund 148
Judaism 171–172, 201, 210

Keats, John 69
Keighley, Yorkshire 247

kelpies 150, 262
Kenilworth, Warwickshire 182
King's Evil (scrofula) 126, 128
Kingsley, Charles 229
Kingston, Jamaica 261
Kirk, Robert 149, 151
'kitchen-sink' approach to folklore 10
Knapp, John Leonard 106
knockers 149–150, 221
Knutsford, Cheshire 57, 218
Korean War 168
Krampus 15, 260

Lady Day 19–20
Lambeth, London 126
landscape 48, 68, 69, 75, 81, 90, 144, 145, 147, 151, 153, 155–173, 240, 248, 252, 262, 265, 267, 268
Lang, Andrew 55, 71
last-day rituals 188–192
Latham, Charlotte 6, 100, 114
Lawson, Joseph 20, 55
Leather, Ella 103, 195
Leeds, Yorkshire 165–166, *270*
legend-tripping 90–91, 93, 153, 172, 250
Leicester, Leicestershire 23, 42, 158, 201, 208
Lent 20, 38
Lettsom, John Coakley 121
Lewes, Sussex 48
Lewis, C. S. 74
Leyland, Lancashire 218
life cycles 2, 194
Lincolnshire 10, 34, 84, 145, 155, 159, 164, 185, 188, 220
Linnaeus, Carl 108
Lisle, Edward 110–111
Little Gaddesden, Hertfordshire 106, 128
Littler, Richard 251–252
Liverpool, Merseyside 146, 150, 158, 173, 207, 251
Llandaff, Wales 192
Llandudno, Wales 219
Llanfyllin, Wales 184
Llangollen, Wales 258
Llanidloes, Wales 143
Llwyn Llywyd, Wales 150
Llyn y Fan Fach, Wales 80
Loch Ness Monster 15, 86, 89–90, 237, 262

Index

Lochabar, Scotland 83
London 8, 21, 23, 28, 33, 42, 50, 51, 53, 55, 56, 59, 88, 89, 91, 119, 121, 123, 126, 127–128, 129, 132, 155, 157, 158, 166, 167, 168, 169, 171, 173, 181, 182, 185, 187, 197, 198, 201–202, 206, 209, 210, 219, 222, 231, 234, 235, 238, 244, 246, 247, 248, 256, 257, 259, 269
Long Marston, Warwickshire 130
Lönnrot, Elias 76
Loughborough, Leicestershire 35, 184
love-locks 1, 156, 171–173
Lovett, Edward 8, 126, 129
Loxley Chase 77
luck 13, 97, 110–113, 115, 127, 156, 164, 166, 180, 189, 199–200, 202, 211
Luing, isle of 187
Lunar New Year 40
Lytham, Lancashire 57

Mabinogion 66–67, *68*, 72
MacCaig, Norman 179
McCrae, John 169
MacDonald, George 73, 76, 229
Mackay, John and Aldie 89
Mackenzie, George 91
MacPherson, James ('Ossian') 67–70
Madagascar 6
magic, popular 2, 8, 9–10, 11, 80, 117, 124, 139, 163, 195, 226
magicians, *see* cunning-folk
Maidenhead, Berkshire 210
Malory, Thomas 76
Man, Isle of 100, 110, 141, 262
Manchester 30, 169, 170, *171*, 206, 210, 211, 218, 247, 250
Manchester, New Hampshire 264
Marazion, Cornwall 123
Maree, Isle 163–164
Mari Lwyd 28, 58, 259–260
Market Harborough, Leicestershire 181–182
markets 24, 28, 30, 132
Marett, Robert Ranulph 11
marriage 196–198
Marshal, William, earl of Pembroke 181
Martinmas 31, 44
Marykirk, Scotland 207

Mass Observation Project 179, 188, 200, 205
'Matter of Britain' 66
Maundy Thursday 33
May Day 35, 37, 42, *43*, 50, 53, 55–58, 218, 224, 264, 266, 268
May Kings 42, 57–58
May Queens 42, 50, 55–58, 60, 218, 219, 264
Mayhew, Henry 127
maypoles 7, 37, 52, 56, 58, 59, 218, 233, 264, 268, 269
medicine, folk 2, 116–134
Melrose, Scotland 49
memes, online 1, 167, 242–244, 245, 248, 252
memorates 86, 88, 91–92, 107, 140, 141, 145, 147
Mendips 148
mermaids 79, 80–81, 240
Mersey, River 158
Michael, Moina 169
Michaelmas 29
Middlebury, Vermont 264
Middleton, Greater Manchester 57
Midsummer 3
Milburn, Westmorland 14
milk-stealers 106–109, 141, 143
Milton Keynes, Buckinghamshire 210
Minehead, Somerset 127
mines 75, 132, 149–150, 181, 258
mischief night 22
moles 97, 102–104, 106, 127
Molly dancing 45, 60, 61
Monmouth, Wales 30
More, Thomas 75
Moreton-in-Marsh, Gloucestershire 75
Morgan, Ann 'Nanny' 142
Morganwg, Iolo (Edward Williams) 257
Morley, John 126
Morris, Lewis 149–150
Morris dancing 1, 14, 22, 41, 50, 52, 56, 60–61, 218, 264, 265, 266
Moser, Hans 15
Mother's Day 37–39
motifs, folktale 67, 71, 72, 73–75, 78, 80, 81, 83, 140, 143, 152, 225, 229, 233, 263
Much Wenlock, Shropshire 54
Muck-up Day 191

mudlarking 156–158
Müller, Catherine-Elise (Hélène Smith) 151
multiculturalism 1, 8, 60, 230, 270–271
'multifolkloric', Britain as 268–271
mumming 3, 20, 21, 26, 44, 45, 60, 61, 264
Murray, Margaret 241
museums 9–10, 11–12, 199, 213, 237, 250, 271
Myddfai, Physicians of 80, 117
Mynyddislwyn, Wales 146

Napier, James 97, 122
National Health Service (NHS) 213–214, 269
Nazism 266
New Forest 131
New Year's Day 3, 19, 27, 40, 202–203, 222, 261
Newark, Nottinghamshire 188
Newbury, Berkshire 75, 181
Newcastle-under-Lyme, Staffordshire 48
Newcastle-upon-Tyne, Northumberland 3, 82, 101, 165, 173, 201
Newell, Venetia 8
Newfoundland 260, 264
Newland, Yorkshire 198
Newport, Wales 122
newspapers 8, 13, 22, 23–24, 30, 34, 36, 37, 48, 53, 57, 59, 84–85, 86, 88, 89, 104, 107, 111, 112, 113, 114, 115, 122, 123, 125, 126, 129, 131, 132, 139, 146, 148, 165–166, 173, 178, 181, 184, 185, 187, 195, 199, 202, 204, 205, 206, 214, 222, 223, 224, 226, 228, 235, 246, 259, 260
Newton Abbot, Devon 50
Nobottle, Northamptonshire 75
Northamptonshire 57–58, 104, 125
Northumberland 82, 87
Norwich, Norfolk 34, 38, 121
Notting Hill Carnival 51, 62, 271
Nottingham, Nottinghamshire 39, 77, 187
Nottinghamshire 54, 65, 102, 155
Nova Scotia 260
Nugee, George 56–57
Nutt, Alfred Trubner 262

Oak Apple Day 33
Oddington, Oxfordshire 107
Okehampton, Devon 219
Olney, Buckinghamshire 222
Ombersley, Worcestershire 45
omens 2, 3, 13–14, 103, 113–115, 195, 202
Opie, Iona 13, 179, 185, 186, 192, 211
orality 84
ostension 90, 93, 228, 234, 238, 248, 252
Oundle, Northamptonshire 46
Owen, Elias 100, 101, 111, 150, 259
Oxford, Oxfordshire 48, 75

Paddington Bear 166–167, *168*
Padstow, Cornwall 61, 62, 220, 221, 224
paganism 3, 9, 26, 44, 61, 210, 230, 233–234, 262–263
    contemporary 157, 159–160, 241
pageants 51–52, 56, 59, 60, 264, 269
Paracelsus 119, 124, 126
Peate, Iorwerth 12
Pechey, John 128
Penistone, Yorkshire 32
Pennant, Thomas 163
Penton Mewsey, Hampshire 103
performance 41–62
Perth, Scotland 165
Piddle Hinton, Dorset 31
pilgrimage 153, 157, 159–161, 163, 200, 234
Pitt Rivers, Augustus 9–10
play, embodied 234
Pliny the Elder 98, 108
Plough Monday 26–27, 41–42, 43–44, 45, 47, 49, 60, 219, 264, 266
Polish community 210
Poltergeists 82, 91
Poohsticks 235
Poor Laws 25, 26, 47
Porter, Enid 12
Porthcawl, Wales 121
Portsmouth, Hampshire 35, 205
Portugal 6
Pratchett, Terry 74
Preston, Lancashire 218
Pride Month 40
Protest 156, 170, 178, 191
Protestantism 2, 3, 19, 20, 22, 38, 137, 146, 160, 200
Pullman, Phillip 75, 234
Punjabi community 206
Puritanism 55

Index

Quakers 54

radio 92, 220–224, 228
Ramadhan 23
Ramsey, Cambridgeshire 43, 44, 114
Rashford, Marcus 170, 171
Raunds, Northamptonshire 42
Reading, Berkshire 112
Rebecca Riots 45
Redditch, Worcestershire 181
Redruth, Cornwall 50, 110
Reformation, the 2, 19, 22, 58, 146, 160
Remembrance Sunday 36
Restoration of the Monarchy 33
revivals 11, 15, 16, 41, 58–60, 61, 185, 219, 222, 233, 255, 257, 261, 264, 265–266, 268
Rhyl, Wales 56
Rhys, John 196, 259, 263
Ribble, River 150
Richard II, king of England 177
ritual year, the 19–40
Robin Hood 7, 56, 77, 92–93, 181, 229, 235, 243, 264
Robins, Danny 92
Roby, John 81, 82, 83
Rogationtide 21
Romani community 8, 31, 108, 118, 197, 255
Rome, Italy 22, 38, 49–54
    Milvio Bridge 172
    Trevi Fountain 165–166
Rorie, David 120, 132
Roud, Steve 13, 184
rough music 45
Rowling, J. K. 74, 234, 238, 239

St Albans, Hertfordshire 59, 219
St Andrew's Day 260, 261–262, 275
St Clement's Day 27
St Fagans, Wales 12
St George's Day 263–264
St Mark's Eve 22, 149
St Stephen's Day 110
St Thomas's Day 27, 31
St Valentine's Day 22, 37, 38, 40
Saviour's Letters 195, 201
Scotland 5, 12, 22, 24, 27, 28, 31, 37, 48, 49, 67, 68, 69–70, 78, 79, 80, 83, 86, 89–90, 97–98, 104, 105, 109, 110, 113, 119, 120, 122, 126, 131, 141, 145, 148, 149, 150, 151, 152, 163–164, 179, 182, 191, 195, 197, 202, 207, 221, 233, 234, 237, 258, 260–261, 266, 267, 275
Scott, Walter 262
Second World War 34, 119, 133, 168, 178, 205, 269
Selby, Yorkshire 198
selkies 79–80, 240
Shakespeare, William 7, 71–72, 105, 219, 264, 267, 269
shapeshifting 142, 144, 148, 150
Sheerness, Kent 181
Sherwood Forest 77, 92–93, 235
Shetland 44, 52, 150, 262
Shipton, Mother 139
Shrewsbury, Shropshire 161
Shropshire 103, 125, 142
Shrovetide 20, 47, 48–49, 50, 191, 222
Sikes, Wirt 145
Sikhism 206, 207
Silvertown, London 123
Slough, Berkshire 158
Smith, George 110
snakes 97, 98, 102, 107–108, 122–123, 126, 127
Soar, River 158
song, folk 24, 25, 27, 28, 41, 56, 60, 100, 145, 179, 223, 224, 266
South Africa 7
South Shields, Co. Durham 23, 165
Southwell, David 251–252
Spicer, George 89
sport 2, 20, 22, 41, 46–47, 53, 54–55, 58, 245, 261
Staffa, isle of 69
Stamford, Lincolnshire 46
Stanford, Kent 123
Star Carr, Yorkshire 155
Stephen, king of England 181
Sternberg, Thomas 5
Stillingfleet, Benjamin 98
Stockport, Cheshire 247
Stockton-on-the-Forest, Yorkshire 31
Stonehaven, Scotland 173
storytelling 65–76, 78, 85, 155, 238, 252, 256, 260
Stratford-on-Avon, Warwickshire 219
straw bears 43–44

Index

supernatural, definition of 137–38
superstition 2, 3, 5, 6, 9, 100, 103, 104, 108, 111–112, 113, 116, 121, 146, 196, 204, 258, 259
suppression of folk customs 46–49
'survivals', folklore as 3, 8–11, 14, 43, 88, 262, 268
Sussex 6, 87, 100, 108, 110, 114
Sydow, Carl Wilhelm von 78

tar barrels, rolling 14, 48, 52, 264
Tasmania 265
Taunton, Somerset 51
television 91, 167, 170, 199, 218, 221–226, 228, 229, 230, 231, 232–233, 238, 251, 252, 266
Tennyson, Alfred 69
Thames, River 66, 157–159
Thompson, Stith 74, 81, 83, 228
Thoms, William John 2, 4, 5–6
Thirsk, Yorkshire 237
Tingewick, Buckinghamshire 14
Tintagel, Cornwall 92
tipcat (game) 182, 184, 187
Tissington, Derbyshire 219
toads 98, 104, 127–128
Tolkien, J. R. R. 65, 75–76, 237–239, 242
Tooth Fairy, the 178
Torquay, Devon 6
toys 179, 180–184
Trafalgar Day 37, 268
transference, magical 124–125, 127
Trinidad 81
Twelfth Night 27, 110
Tylor, Edward Burnett 10

United States, the 6, 38, 83, 90, 151, 169, 196, 212, 214, 245
Up-helly-aa festival 52, 262
urban legends 83–85, 118, 248
urbanisation 7, 52, 98, 198
Uther Pendragon 66
Uxbridge, Middlesex 26

Vagrancy Act 26, 47, 139
Vallée, Jacques 151–152

VE Day 35
Victoria, queen of the United Kingdom 34, 36, 51, 69, 164, 204, 206, 261
Vietnamese community 201–202

'wake' days 22, 28, 31, 49
Wales 12, 13, 21, 27, 28, 67, 70, 72, 73, 78, 88, 100, 101, 110, 121, 126, 139, 141, 149–150, 152, 153, 156, 221, 229, 232, 256, 258–260, 262, 266
Walsall, Staffordshire 166
Waltham Abbey, Essex 146
Walton-on-Trent, Derbyshire 185
Warwickshire 129, 161
wassailing 24, 27, 58, 61, 265
Waterloo Day 35
Wath, Yorkshire 32
wells 160, 162–163, 164
well-dressing 218, 219
West Haddon, Northamptonshire 125
Wharfe, River 156
Whittlesey, Cambridgeshire 43–44
Whitsun (Pentecost) 20, 21–22, 31, 50, 54, 60, 218, 219
wife selling 198
Wight, Isle of 184
Wigton, Cumbria 30
Wilson, John Marius 102
witch-bottles 157–158
witchcraft 8, 71, 80–81, 109, 117, 120, 125, 133, 138–144, 148, 149, 150, 161, 195, 199, 226, 241–242, 251
Witham, River 155
Woking, Surrey 23
Wolverhampton, Staffordshire 122
Wood, John George 107
Worcester, battle of 33
Worcestershire 221
Wordsworth, William 69
Worthing, Sussex 48
Wrexham, Wales 149
Wright, Arthur 10
Wyatt's Rebellion 177

Ystrad Meurig, Wales 143, 196
Yule logs 200, 202